CouchDB 2.0 Reference Manual

A catalogue record for this book is available from the Hong Kong Public Libraries.

Published in Hong Kong by Samurai Media Limited.

Email: info@samuraimedia.org

ISBN 978-988-8381-65-4

## CHAPTER 1

Introduction

CouchDB is a database that completely embraces the web. Store your data with JSON documents. Access your documents with your web browser, *via HTTP*. *Query*, *combine*, and *transform* your documents with *JavaScript*. CouchDB works well with modern web and mobile apps. You can even serve web apps directly out of CouchDB. And you can distribute your data, or your apps, efficiently using CouchDB's *incremental replication*. CouchDB supports master-master setups with *automatic conflict* detection.

CouchDB comes with a suite of features, such as on-the-fly document transformation and real-time *change notifications*, that makes *web app* development a breeze. It even comes with an easy to use *web administration console*. You guessed it, served up directly out of CouchDB! We care a lot about distributed scaling. CouchDB is highly available and partition tolerant, but is also *eventually consistent*. And we care *a lot* about your data. CouchDB has a fault-tolerant storage engine that puts the safety of your data first.

In this section you'll learn about every basic bit of CouchDB, see upon what conceptions and technologies it built and walk through short tutorial that teach how to use CouchDB.

1.1 Technical Overview

1.1.1 Document Storage

A CouchDB server hosts named databases, which store **documents**. Each document is uniquely named in the database, and CouchDB provides a RESTful *HTTP API* for reading and updating (add, edit, delete) database documents.

Documents are the primary unit of data in CouchDB and consist of any number of fields and attachments. Documents also include metadata that's maintained by the database system. Document fields are uniquely named and contain values of *varying types* (text, number, boolean, lists, etc), and there is no set limit to text size or element count.

The CouchDB document update model is lockless and optimistic. Document edits are made by client applications loading documents, applying changes, and saving them back to the database. If another client editing the same document saves their changes first, the client gets an edit conflict error on save. To resolve the update conflict, the latest document version can be opened, the edits reapplied and the update tried again.

Document updates (add, edit, delete) are all or nothing, either succeeding entirely or failing completely. The database never contains partially saved or edited documents.

1.1.2 ACID Properties

The CouchDB file layout and commitment system features all *Atomic Consistent Isolated Durable* (ACID) properties. On-disk, CouchDB never overwrites committed data or associated structures, ensuring the database file is always in a consistent state. This is a "crash-only" design where the CouchDB server does not go through a shut down process, it's simply terminated.

Document updates (add, edit, delete) are serialized, except for binary blobs which are written concurrently. Database readers are never locked out and never have to wait on writers or other readers. Any number of clients can be reading documents without being locked out or interrupted by concurrent updates, even on the same document. CouchDB read operations use a *Multi-Version Concurrency Control* (MVCC) model where each client sees a consistent snapshot of the database from the beginning to the end of the read operation.

Documents are indexed in B-trees by their name (DocID) and a Sequence ID. Each update to a database instance generates a new sequential number. Sequence IDs are used later for incrementally finding changes in a database. These B-tree indexes are updated simultaneously when documents are saved or deleted. The index updates always occur at the end of the file (append-only updates).

Documents have the advantage of data being already conveniently packaged for storage rather than split out across numerous tables and rows in most database systems. When documents are committed to disk, the document fields and metadata are packed into buffers, sequentially one document after another (helpful later for efficient building of views).

When CouchDB documents are updated, all data and associated indexes are flushed to disk and the transactional commit always leaves the database in a completely consistent state. Commits occur in two steps:

1. All document data and associated index updates are synchronously flushed to disk.

2. The updated database header is written in two consecutive, identical chunks to make up the first 4k of the file, and then synchronously flushed to disk.

In the event of an OS crash or power failure during step 1, the partially flushed updates are simply forgotten on restart. If such a crash happens during step 2 (committing the header), a surviving copy of the previous identical headers will remain, ensuring coherency of all previously committed data. Excepting the header area, consistency checks or fix-ups after a crash or a power failure are never necessary.

1.1.3 Compaction

Wasted space is recovered by occasional compaction. On schedule, or when the database file exceeds a certain amount of wasted space, the compaction process clones all the active data to a new file and then discards the old file. The database remains completely online the entire time and all updates and reads are allowed to complete successfully. The old database file is deleted only when all the data has been copied and all users transitioned to the new file.

1.1.4 Views

ACID properties only deal with storage and updates, but we also need the ability to show our data in interesting and useful ways. Unlike SQL databases where data must be carefully decomposed into tables, data in CouchDB is stored in semi-structured documents. CouchDB documents are flexible and each has its own implicit structure, which alleviates the most difficult problems and pitfalls of bi-directionally replicating table schemas and their contained data.

But beyond acting as a fancy file server, a simple document model for data storage and sharing is too simple to build real applications on – it simply doesn't do enough of the things we want and expect. We want to slice and dice and see our data in many different ways. What is needed is a way to filter, organize and report on data that hasn't been decomposed into tables.

See also:

Guide to Views

View Model

To address this problem of adding structure back to unstructured and semi-structured data, CouchDB integrates a view model. Views are the method of aggregating and reporting on the documents in a database, and are built on-demand to aggregate, join and report on database documents. Because views are built dynamically and don't affect the underlying document, you can have as many different view representations of the same data as you like.

View definitions are strictly virtual and only display the documents from the current database instance, making them separate from the data they display and compatible with replication. CouchDB views are defined inside special **design documents** and can replicate across database instances like regular documents, so that not only data replicates in CouchDB, but entire application designs replicate too.

JavaScript View Functions

Views are defined using JavaScript functions acting as the map part in a map-reduce system. A *view function* takes a CouchDB document as an argument and then does whatever computation it needs to do to determine the data that is to be made available through the view, if any. It can add multiple rows to the view based on a single document, or it can add no rows at all.

See also:

View functions

View Indexes

Views are a dynamic representation of the actual document contents of a database, and CouchDB makes it easy to create useful views of data. But generating a view of a database with hundreds of thousands or millions of documents is time and resource consuming, it's not something the system should do from scratch each time.

To keep view querying fast, the view engine maintains indexes of its views, and incrementally updates them to reflect changes in the database. CouchDB's core design is largely optimized around the need for efficient, incremental creation of views and their indexes.

Views and their functions are defined inside special "design" documents, and a design document may contain any number of uniquely named view functions. When a user opens a view and its index is automatically updated, all the views in the same design document are indexed as a single group.

The view builder uses the database sequence ID to determine if the view group is fully up-to-date with the database. If not, the view engine examines the all database documents (in packed sequential order) changed since the last refresh. Documents are read in the order they occur in the disk file, reducing the frequency and cost of disk head seeks.

The views can be read and queried simultaneously while also being refreshed. If a client is slowly streaming out the contents of a large view, the same view can be concurrently opened and refreshed for another client without blocking the first client. This is true for any number of simultaneous client readers, who can read and query the view while the index is concurrently being refreshed for other clients without causing problems for the readers.

As documents are processed by the view engine through your 'map' and 'reduce' functions, their previous row values are removed from the view indexes, if they exist. If the document is selected by a view function, the function results are inserted into the view as a new row.

When view index changes are written to disk, the updates are always appended at the end of the file, serving to both reduce disk head seek times during disk commits and to ensure crashes and power failures can not cause corruption of indexes. If a crash occurs while updating a view index, the incomplete index updates are simply lost and rebuilt incrementally from its previously committed state.

1.1.5 Security and Validation

To protect who can read and update documents, CouchDB has a simple reader access and update validation model that can be extended to implement custom security models.

See also:

/db/_security

Administrator Access

CouchDB database instances have administrator accounts. Administrator accounts can create other administrator accounts and update design documents. Design documents are special documents containing view definitions and other special formulas, as well as regular fields and blobs.

Update Validation

As documents are written to disk, they can be validated dynamically by JavaScript functions for both security and data validation. When the document passes all the formula validation criteria, the update is allowed to continue. If the validation fails, the update is aborted and the user client gets an error response.

Both the user's credentials and the updated document are given as inputs to the validation formula, and can be used to implement custom security models by validating a user's permissions to update a document.

A basic "author only" update document model is trivial to implement, where document updates are validated to check if the user is listed in an "author" field in the existing document. More dynamic models are also possible, like checking a separate user account profile for permission settings.

The update validations are enforced for both live usage and replicated updates, ensuring security and data validation in a shared, distributed system.

See also:

Validate document update functions

1.1.6 Distributed Updates and Replication

CouchDB is a peer-based distributed database system. It allows users and servers to access and update the same shared data while disconnected. Those changes can then be replicated bi-directionally later.

The CouchDB document storage, view and security models are designed to work together to make true bi-directional replication efficient and reliable. Both documents and designs can replicate, allowing full database applications (including application design, logic and data) to be replicated to laptops for offline use, or replicated to servers in remote offices where slow or unreliable connections make sharing data difficult.

The replication process is incremental. At the database level, replication only examines documents updated since the last replication. Then for each updated document, only fields and blobs that have changed are replicated across the network. If replication fails at any step, due to network problems or crash for example, the next replication restarts at the same document where it left off.

Partial replicas can be created and maintained. Replication can be filtered by a JavaScript function, so that only particular documents or those meeting specific criteria are replicated. This can allow users to take subsets of a large shared database application offline for their own use, while maintaining normal interaction with the application and that subset of data.

Conflicts

Conflict detection and management are key issues for any distributed edit system. The CouchDB storage system treats edit conflicts as a common state, not an exceptional one. The conflict handling model is simple and "non-destructive" while preserving single document semantics and allowing for decentralized conflict resolution.

CouchDB allows for any number of conflicting documents to exist simultaneously in the database, with each database instance deterministically deciding which document is the "winner" and which are conflicts. Only the winning document can appear in views, while "losing" conflicts are still accessible and remain in the database until deleted or purged during database compaction. Because conflict documents are still regular documents, they replicate just like regular documents and are subject to the same security and validation rules.

When distributed edit conflicts occur, every database replica sees the same winning revision and each has the opportunity to resolve the conflict. Resolving conflicts can be done manually or, depending on the nature of the data and the conflict, by automated agents. The system makes decentralized conflict resolution possible while maintaining single document database semantics.

Conflict management continues to work even if multiple disconnected users or agents attempt to resolve the same conflicts. If resolved conflicts result in more conflicts, the system accommodates them in the same manner, determining the same winner on each machine and maintaining single document semantics.

See also:

Replication and conflict model

Applications

Using just the basic replication model, many traditionally single server database applications can be made distributed with almost no extra work. CouchDB replication is designed to be immediately useful for basic database applications, while also being extendable for more elaborate and full-featured uses.

With very little database work, it is possible to build a distributed document management application with granular security and full revision histories. Updates to documents can be implemented to exploit incremental field and blob replication, where replicated updates are nearly as efficient and incremental as the actual edit differences ("diffs").

The CouchDB replication model can be modified for other distributed update models. If the storage engine is enhanced to allow multi-document update transactions, it is possible to perform Subversion-like "all or nothing" atomic commits when replicating with an upstream server, such that any single document conflict or validation failure will cause the entire update to fail. Like Subversion, conflicts would be resolved by doing a "pull" replication to force the conflicts locally, then merging and re-replicating to the upstream server.

1.1.7 Implementation

CouchDB is built on the Erlang OTP platform, a functional, concurrent programming language and development platform. Erlang was developed for real-time telecom applications with an extreme emphasis on reliability and availability.

Both in syntax and semantics, Erlang is very different from conventional programming languages like C or Java. Erlang uses lightweight "processes" and message passing for concurrency, it has no shared state threading and all data is immutable. The robust, concurrent nature of Erlang is ideal for a database server.

CouchDB is designed for lock-free concurrency, in the conceptual model and the actual Erlang implementation. Reducing bottlenecks and avoiding locks keeps the entire system working predictably under heavy loads. CouchDB can accommodate many clients replicating changes, opening and updating documents, and querying views whose indexes are simultaneously being refreshed for other clients, without needing locks.

For higher availability and more concurrent users, CouchDB is designed for "shared nothing" clustering. In a "shared nothing" cluster, each machine is independent and replicates data with its cluster mates, allowing individual server failures with zero downtime. And because consistency scans and fix-ups aren't needed on restart, if the entire cluster fails – due to a power outage in a datacenter, for example – the entire CouchDB distributed system becomes immediately available after a restart.

CouchDB is built from the start with a consistent vision of a distributed document database system. Unlike cumbersome attempts to bolt distributed features on top of the same legacy models and databases, it is the result of careful ground-up design, engineering and integration. The document, view, security and replication models, the special purpose query language, the efficient and robust disk layout and the concurrent and reliable nature of the Erlang platform are all carefully integrated for a reliable and efficient system.

1.2 Why CouchDB?

Apache CouchDB is one of a new breed of database management systems. This topic explains why there's a need for new systems as well as the motivations behind building CouchDB.

As CouchDB developers, we're naturally very excited to be using CouchDB. In this topic we'll share with you the reasons for our enthusiasm. We'll show you how CouchDB's schema-free document model is a better fit for common applications, how the built-in query engine is a powerful way to use and process your data, and how CouchDB's design lends itself to modularization and scalability.

1.2.1 Relax

If there's one word to describe CouchDB, it is *relax*. It is the byline to CouchDB's official logo and when you start CouchDB, you see:

```
Apache CouchDB has started. Time to relax.
```

Why is relaxation important? Developer productivity roughly doubled in the last five years. The chief reason for the boost is more powerful tools that are easier to use. Take Ruby on Rails as an example. It is an infinitely complex framework, but it's easy to get started with. Rails is a success story because of the core design focus on ease of use. This is one reason why CouchDB is relaxing: learning CouchDB and understanding its core concepts should feel natural to most everybody who has been doing any work on the Web. And it is still pretty easy to explain to non-technical people.

Getting out of the way when creative people try to build specialized solutions is in itself a core feature and one thing that CouchDB aims to get right. We found existing tools too cumbersome to work with during development or in production, and decided to focus on making CouchDB easy, even a pleasure, to use.

Another area of relaxation for CouchDB users is the production setting. If you have a live running application, CouchDB again goes out of its way to avoid troubling you. Its internal architecture is fault-tolerant, and failures occur in a controlled environment and are dealt with gracefully. Single problems do not cascade through an entire server system but stay isolated in single requests.

CouchDB's core concepts are simple (yet powerful) and well understood. Operations teams (if you have a team; otherwise, that's you) do not have to fear random behavior and untraceable errors. If anything should go wrong, you can easily find out what the problem is, but these situations are rare.

CouchDB is also designed to handle varying traffic gracefully. For instance, if a website is experiencing a sudden spike in traffic, CouchDB will generally absorb a lot of concurrent requests without falling over. It may take a little more time for each request, but they all get answered. When the spike is over, CouchDB will work with regular speed again.

The third area of relaxation is growing and shrinking the underlying hardware of your application. This is commonly referred to as scaling. CouchDB enforces a set of limits on the programmer. On first look, CouchDB might seem inflexible, but some features are left out by design for the simple reason that if CouchDB supported them, it would allow a programmer to create applications that couldn't deal with scaling up or down.

Note: CouchDB doesn't let you do things that would get you in trouble later on. This sometimes means you'll have to unlearn best practices you might have picked up in your current or past work.

1.2.2 A Different Way to Model Your Data

We believe that CouchDB will drastically change the way you build document-based applications. CouchDB combines an intuitive document storage model with a powerful query engine in a way that's so simple you'll probably be tempted to ask, "Why has no one built something like this before?"

> Django may be built for the Web, but CouchDB is built of the Web. I've never seen software that so completely embraces the philosophies behind HTTP. CouchDB makes Django look old-school in the same way that Django makes ASP look outdated.
>
> —Jacob Kaplan-Moss, Django developer

CouchDB's design borrows heavily from web architecture and the concepts of resources, methods, and representations. It augments this with powerful ways to query, map, combine, and filter your data. Add fault tolerance, extreme scalability, and incremental replication, and CouchDB defines a sweet spot for document databases.

1.2.3 A Better Fit for Common Applications

We write software to improve our lives and the lives of others. Usually this involves taking some mundane information such as contacts, invoices, or receipts and manipulating it using a computer application. CouchDB is a great fit for common applications like this because it embraces the natural idea of evolving, self-contained documents as the very core of its data model.

Self-Contained Data

An invoice contains all the pertinent information about a single transaction the seller, the buyer, the date, and a list of the items or services sold. As shown in *Figure 1. Self-contained documents*, there's no abstract reference on this piece of paper that points to some other piece of paper with the seller's name and address. Accountants appreciate the simplicity of having everything in one place. And given the choice, programmers appreciate that, too.

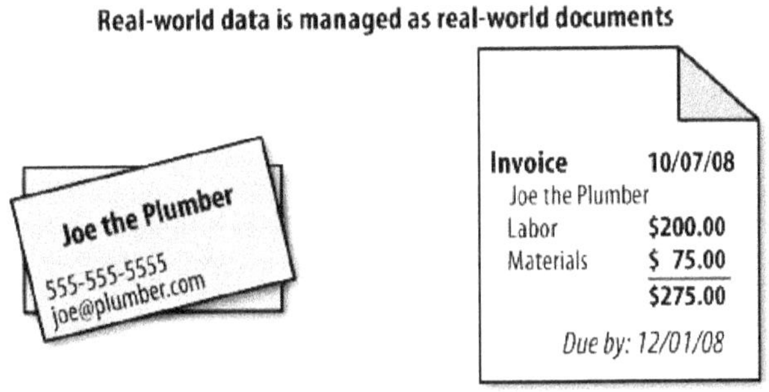

Fig. 1.1: Figure 1. Self-contained documents

Yet using references is exactly how we model our data in a relational database! Each invoice is stored in a table as a row that refers to other rows in other tables one row for seller information, one for the buyer, one row for each item billed, and more rows still to describe the item details, manufacturer details, and so on and so forth.

This isn't meant as a detraction of the relational model, which is widely applicable and extremely useful for a number of reasons. Hopefully, though, it illustrates the point that sometimes your model may not "fit" your data in the way it occurs in the real world.

Let's take a look at the humble contact database to illustrate a different way of modeling data, one that more closely "fits" its real-world counterpart – a pile of business cards. Much like our invoice example, a business card contains all the important information, right there on the cardstock. We call this "self-contained" data, and it's an important concept in understanding document databases like CouchDB.

Syntax and Semantics

Most business cards contain roughly the same information – someone's identity, an affiliation, and some contact information. While the exact form of this information can vary between business cards, the general information being conveyed remains the same, and we're easily able to recognize it as a business card. In this sense, we can describe a business card as a *real-world document*.

Jan's business card might contain a phone number but no fax number, whereas J. Chris's business card contains both a phone and a fax number. Jan does not have to make his lack of a fax machine explicit by writing something as ridiculous as "Fax: None" on the business card. Instead, simply omitting a fax number implies that he doesn't have one.

We can see that real-world documents of the same type, such as business cards, tend to be very similar in *semantics* – the sort of information they carry, but can vary hugely in *syntax*, or how that information is structured. As human beings, we're naturally comfortable dealing with this kind of variation.

While a traditional relational database requires you to model your data *up front*, CouchDB's schema-free design unburdens you with a powerful way to aggregate your data *after the fact*, just like we do with real-world documents. We'll look in depth at how to design applications with this underlying storage paradigm.

1.2.4 Building Blocks for Larger Systems

CouchDB is a storage system useful on its own. You can build many applications with the tools CouchDB gives you. But CouchDB is designed with a bigger picture in mind. Its components can be used as building blocks that solve storage problems in slightly different ways for larger and more complex systems.

Whether you need a system that's crazy fast but isn't too concerned with reliability (think logging), or one that guarantees storage in two or more physically separated locations for reliability, but you're willing to take a performance hit, CouchDB lets you build these systems.

There are a multitude of knobs you could turn to make a system work better in one area, but you'll affect another area when doing so. One example would be the CAP theorem discussed in *Eventual Consistency*. To give you an idea of other things that affect storage systems, see *Figure 2* and *Figure 3*.

By reducing latency for a given system (and that is true not only for storage systems), you affect concurrency and throughput capabilities.

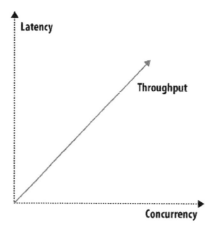

Fig. 1.2: Figure 2. Throughput, latency, or concurrency

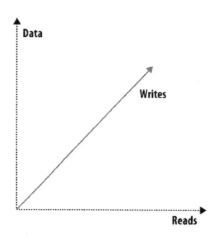

Fig. 1.3: Figure 3. Scaling: read requests, write requests, or data

When you want to scale out, there are three distinct issues to deal with: scaling read requests, write requests, and data. Orthogonal to all three and to the items shown in *Figure 2* and *Figure 3* are many more attributes like reliability or simplicity. You can draw many of these graphs that show how different features or attributes pull into different directions and thus shape the system they describe.

CouchDB is very flexible and gives you enough building blocks to create a system shaped to suit your exact problem. That's not saying that CouchDB can be bent to solve any problem – CouchDB is no silver bullet – but in the area of data storage, it can get you a long way.

1.2.5 CouchDB Replication

CouchDB replication is one of these building blocks. Its fundamental function is to synchronize two or more CouchDB databases. This may sound simple, but the simplicity is key to allowing replication to solve a number of problems: reliably synchronize databases between multiple machines for redundant data storage; distribute data to a cluster of CouchDB instances that share a subset of the total number of requests that hit the cluster (load balancing); and distribute data between physically distant locations, such as one office in New York and another in Tokyo.

CouchDB replication uses the same REST API all clients use. HTTP is ubiquitous and well understood. Replication works incrementally; that is, if during replication anything goes wrong, like dropping your network connection, it will pick up where it left off the next time it runs. It also only transfers data that is needed to synchronize databases.

A core assumption CouchDB makes is that things can go wrong, like network connection troubles, and it is designed for graceful error recovery instead of assuming all will be well. The replication system's incremental design shows that best. The ideas behind "things that can go wrong" are embodied in the Fallacies of Distributed Computing:

- The network is reliable.
- Latency is zero.
- Bandwidth is infinite.
- The network is secure.
- Topology doesn't change.
- There is one administrator.
- Transport cost is zero.
- The network is homogeneous.

Existing tools often try to hide the fact that there is a network and that any or all of the previous conditions don't exist for a particular system. This usually results in fatal error scenarios when something finally goes wrong. In contrast, CouchDB doesn't try to hide the network; it just handles errors gracefully and lets you know when actions on your end are required.

1.2.6 Local Data Is King

CouchDB takes quite a few lessons learned from the Web, but there is one thing that could be improved about the Web: latency. Whenever you have to wait for an application to respond or a website to render, you almost always wait for a network connection that isn't as fast as you want it at that point. Waiting a few seconds instead of milliseconds greatly affects user experience and thus user satisfaction.

What do you do when you are offline? This happens all the time – your DSL or cable provider has issues, or your iPhone, G1, or Blackberry has no bars, and no connectivity means no way to get to your data.

CouchDB can solve this scenario as well, and this is where scaling is important again. This time it is scaling down. Imagine CouchDB installed on phones and other mobile devices that can synchronize data with centrally hosted CouchDBs when they are on a network. The synchronization is not bound by user interface constraints like subsecond response times. It is easier to tune for high bandwidth and higher latency than for low bandwidth and very low latency. Mobile applications can then use the local CouchDB to fetch data, and since no remote networking is required for that, latency is low by default.

Can you really use CouchDB on a phone? Erlang, CouchDB's implementation language has been designed to run on embedded devices magnitudes smaller and less powerful than today's phones.

1.2.7 Wrapping Up

The next document *Eventual Consistency* further explores the distributed nature of CouchDB. We should have given you enough bites to whet your interest. Let's go!

1.3 Eventual Consistency

In the previous document *Why CouchDB?*, we saw that CouchDB's flexibility allows us to evolve our data as our applications grow and change. In this topic, we'll explore how working "with the grain" of CouchDB promotes simplicity in our applications and helps us naturally build scalable, distributed systems.

1.3.1 Working with the Grain

A *distributed system* is a system that operates robustly over a wide network. A particular feature of network computing is that network links can potentially disappear, and there are plenty of strategies for managing this type of network segmentation. CouchDB differs from others by accepting eventual consistency, as opposed to putting absolute consistency ahead of raw availability, like RDBMS or Paxos. What these systems have in common is an awareness that data acts differently when many people are accessing it simultaneously. Their approaches differ when it comes to which aspects of *consistency*, *availability*, or *partition* tolerance they prioritize.

Engineering distributed systems is tricky. Many of the caveats and "gotchas" you will face over time aren't immediately obvious. We don't have all the solutions, and CouchDB isn't a panacea, but when you work with CouchDB's grain rather than against it, the path of least resistance leads you to naturally scalable applications.

Of course, building a distributed system is only the beginning. A website with a database that is available only half the time is next to worthless. Unfortunately, the traditional relational database approach to consistency makes it very easy for application programmers to rely on global state, global clocks, and other high availability no-nos, without even realizing that they're doing so. Before examining how CouchDB promotes scalability, we'll look at the constraints faced by a distributed system. After we've seen the problems that arise when parts of your application can't rely on being in constant contact with each other, we'll see that CouchDB provides an intuitive and useful way for modeling applications around high availability.

1.3.2 The CAP Theorem

The CAP theorem describes a few different strategies for distributing application logic across networks. CouchDB's solution uses replication to propagate application changes across participating nodes. This is a fundamentally different approach from consensus algorithms and relational databases, which operate at different intersections of consistency, availability, and partition tolerance.

The CAP theorem, shown in *Figure 1. The CAP theorem*, identifies three distinct concerns:

- **Consistency**: All database clients see the same data, even with concurrent updates.
- **Availability**: All database clients are able to access some version of the data.
- **Partition tolerance**: The database can be split over multiple servers.

Pick two.

When a system grows large enough that a single database node is unable to handle the load placed on it, a sensible solution is to add more servers. When we add nodes, we have to start thinking about how to partition data between them. Do we have a few databases that share exactly the same data? Do we put different sets of data on different database servers? Do we let only certain database servers write data and let others handle the reads?

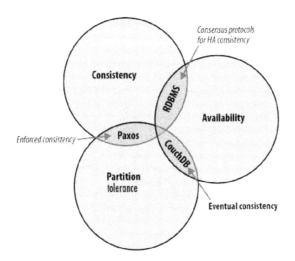

Fig. 1.4: Figure 1. The CAP theorem

Regardless of which approach we take, the one problem we'll keep bumping into is that of keeping all these database servers in sync. If you write some information to one node, how are you going to make sure that a read request to another database server reflects this newest information? These events might be milliseconds apart. Even with a modest collection of database servers, this problem can become extremely complex.

When it's absolutely critical that all clients see a consistent view of the database, the users of one node will have to wait for any other nodes to come into agreement before being able to read or write to the database. In this instance, we see that availability takes a backseat to consistency. However, there are situations where availability trumps consistency:

> Each node in a system should be able to make decisions purely based on local state. If you need to do something under high load with failures occurring and you need to reach agreement, you're lost. If you're concerned about scalability, any algorithm that forces you to run agreement will eventually become your bottleneck. Take that as a given.

> —Werner Vogels, Amazon CTO and Vice President

If availability is a priority, we can let clients write data to one node of the database without waiting for other nodes to come into agreement. If the database knows how to take care of reconciling these operations between nodes, we achieve a sort of "eventual consistency" in exchange for high availability. This is a surprisingly applicable trade-off for many applications.

Unlike traditional relational databases, where each action performed is necessarily subject to database-wide consistency checks, CouchDB makes it really simple to build applications that sacrifice immediate consistency for the huge performance improvements that come with simple distribution.

1.3.3 Local Consistency

Before we attempt to understand how CouchDB operates in a cluster, it's important that we understand the inner workings of a single CouchDB node. The CouchDB API is designed to provide a convenient but thin wrapper around the database core. By taking a closer look at the structure of the database core, we'll have a better understanding of the API that surrounds it.

The Key to Your Data

At the heart of CouchDB is a powerful *B-tree* storage engine. A B-tree is a sorted data structure that allows for searches, insertions, and deletions in logarithmic time. As *Figure 2. Anatomy of a view request* illustrates, CouchDB uses this B-tree storage engine for all internal data, documents, and views. If we understand one, we will understand them all.

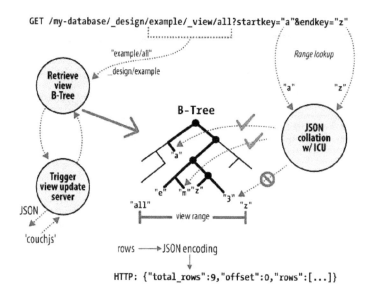

Fig. 1.5: Figure 2. Anatomy of a view request

CouchDB uses MapReduce to compute the results of a view. MapReduce makes use of two functions, "map" and "reduce", which are applied to each document in isolation. Being able to isolate these operations means that view computation lends itself to parallel and incremental computation. More important, because these functions produce key/value pairs, CouchDB is able to insert them into the B-tree storage engine, sorted by key. Lookups by key, or key range, are extremely efficient operations with a B-tree, described in *big O* notation as O(log N) and O(log N + K), respectively.

In CouchDB, we access documents and view results by key or key range. This is a direct mapping to the underlying operations performed on CouchDB's B-tree storage engine. Along with document inserts and updates, this direct mapping is the reason we describe CouchDB's API as being a thin wrapper around the database core.

Being able to access results by key alone is a very important restriction because it allows us to make huge performance gains. As well as the massive speed improvements, we can partition our data over multiple nodes, without affecting our ability to query each node in isolation. BigTable, Hadoop, SimpleDB, and memcached restrict object lookups by key for exactly these reasons.

No Locking

A table in a relational database is a single data structure. If you want to modify a table – say, update a row – the database system must ensure that nobody else is trying to update that row and that nobody can read from that row while it is being updated. The common way to handle this uses what's known as a lock. If multiple clients want to access a table, the first client gets the lock, making everybody else wait. When the first client's request is processed, the next client is given access while everybody else waits, and so on. This serial execution of requests, even when they arrived in parallel, wastes a significant amount of your server's processing power. Under high load, a relational database can spend more time figuring out who is allowed to do what, and in which order, than it does doing any actual work.

Note: Modern relational databases avoid locks by implementing MVCC under the hood, but hide it from the end user, requiring them to coordinate concurrent changes of single rows or fields.

Instead of locks, CouchDB uses *Multi-Version Concurrency Control* (MVCC) to manage concurrent access to the database. *Figure 3. MVCC means no locking* illustrates the differences between MVCC and traditional locking mechanisms. MVCC means that CouchDB can run at full speed, all the time, even under high load. Requests are run in parallel, making excellent use of every last drop of processing power your server has to offer.

Documents in CouchDB are versioned, much like they would be in a regular version control system such as Subversion. If you want to change a value in a document, you create an entire new version of that document and

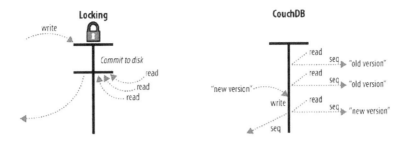

Fig. 1.6: Figure 3. MVCC means no locking

save it over the old one. After doing this, you end up with two versions of the same document, one old and one new.

How does this offer an improvement over locks? Consider a set of requests wanting to access a document. The first request reads the document. While this is being processed, a second request changes the document. Since the second request includes a completely new version of the document, CouchDB can simply append it to the database without having to wait for the read request to finish.

When a third request wants to read the same document, CouchDB will point it to the new version that has just been written. During this whole process, the first request could still be reading the original version.

A read request will always see the most recent snapshot of your database at the time of the beginning of the request.

1.3.4 Validation

As application developers, we have to think about what sort of input we should accept and what we should reject. The expressive power to do this type of validation over complex data within a traditional relational database leaves a lot to be desired. Fortunately, CouchDB provides a powerful way to perform per-document validation from within the database.

CouchDB can validate documents using JavaScript functions similar to those used for MapReduce. Each time you try to modify a document, CouchDB will pass the validation function a copy of the existing document, a copy of the new document, and a collection of additional information, such as user authentication details. The validation function now has the opportunity to approve or deny the update.

By working with the grain and letting CouchDB do this for us, we save ourselves a tremendous amount of CPU cycles that would otherwise have been spent serializing object graphs from SQL, converting them into domain objects, and using those objects to do application-level validation.

1.3.5 Distributed Consistency

Maintaining consistency within a single database node is relatively easy for most databases. The real problems start to surface when you try to maintain consistency between multiple database servers. If a client makes a write operation on server A, how do we make sure that this is consistent with server B, or C, or D? For relational databases, this is a very complex problem with entire books devoted to its solution. You could use multi-master, single-master, partitioning, sharding, write-through caches, and all sorts of other complex techniques.

1.3.6 Incremental Replication

CouchDB's operations take place within the context of a single document. As CouchDB achieves eventual consistency between multiple databases by using incremental replication you no longer have to worry about your database servers being able to stay in constant communication. Incremental replication is a process where document changes are periodically copied between servers. We are able to build what's known as a *shared nothing* cluster of databases where each node is independent and self-sufficient, leaving no single point of contention across the system.

Need to scale out your CouchDB database cluster? Just throw in another server.

As illustrated in *Figure 4. Incremental replication between CouchDB nodes*, with CouchDB's incremental replication, you can synchronize your data between any two databases however you like and whenever you like. After replication, each database is able to work independently.

You could use this feature to synchronize database servers within a cluster or between data centers using a job scheduler such as cron, or you could use it to synchronize data with your laptop for offline work as you travel. Each database can be used in the usual fashion, and changes between databases can be synchronized later in both directions.

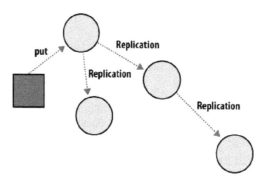

Fig. 1.7: Figure 4. Incremental replication between CouchDB nodes

What happens when you change the same document in two different databases and want to synchronize these with each other? CouchDB's replication system comes with automatic conflict detection and resolution. When CouchDB detects that a document has been changed in both databases, it flags this document as being in conflict, much like they would be in a regular version control system.

This isn't as troublesome as it might first sound. When two versions of a document conflict during replication, the winning version is saved as the most recent version in the document's history. Instead of throwing the losing version away, as you might expect, CouchDB saves this as a previous version in the document's history, so that you can access it if you need to. This happens automatically and consistently, so both databases will make exactly the same choice.

It is up to you to handle conflicts in a way that makes sense for your application. You can leave the chosen document versions in place, revert to the older version, or try to merge the two versions and save the result.

1.3.7 Case Study

Greg Borenstein, a friend and coworker, built a small library for converting Songbird playlists to JSON objects and decided to store these in CouchDB as part of a backup application. The completed software uses CouchDB's MVCC and document revisions to ensure that Songbird playlists are backed up robustly between nodes.

Note: Songbird is a free software media player with an integrated web browser, based on the Mozilla XULRunner platform. Songbird is available for Microsoft Windows, Apple Mac OS X, Solaris, and Linux.

Let's examine the workflow of the Songbird backup application, first as a user backing up from a single computer, and then using Songbird to synchronize playlists between multiple computers. We'll see how document revisions turn what could have been a hairy problem into something that *just works*.

The first time we use this backup application, we feed our playlists to the application and initiate a backup. Each playlist is converted to a JSON object and handed to a CouchDB database. As illustrated in *Figure 5. Backing up to a single database*, CouchDB hands back the document ID and revision of each playlist as it's saved to the database.

After a few days, we find that our playlists have been updated and we want to back up our changes. After we have fed our playlists to the backup application, it fetches the latest versions from CouchDB, along with

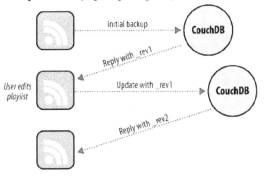

Fig. 1.8: Figure 5. Backing up to a single database

the corresponding document revisions. When the application hands back the new playlist document, CouchDB requires that the document revision is included in the request.

CouchDB then makes sure that the document revision handed to it in the request matches the current revision held in the database. Because CouchDB updates the revision with every modification, if these two are out of sync it suggests that someone else has made changes to the document between the time we requested it from the database and the time we sent our updates. Making changes to a document after someone else has modified it without first inspecting those changes is usually a bad idea.

Forcing clients to hand back the correct document revision is the heart of CouchDB's optimistic concurrency.

We have a laptop we want to keep synchronized with our desktop computer. With all our playlists on our desktop, the first step is to "restore from backup" onto our laptop. This is the first time we've done this, so afterward our laptop should hold an exact replica of our desktop playlist collection.

After editing our Argentine Tango playlist on our laptop to add a few new songs we've purchased, we want to save our changes. The backup application replaces the playlist document in our laptop CouchDB database and a new document revision is generated. A few days later, we remember our new songs and want to copy the playlist across to our desktop computer. As illustrated in *Figure 6. Synchronizing between two databases*, the backup application copies the new document and the new revision to the desktop CouchDB database. Both CouchDB databases now have the same document revision.

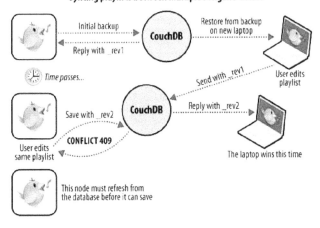

Fig. 1.9: Figure 6. Synchronizing between two databases

Because CouchDB tracks document revisions, it ensures that updates like these will work only if they are based on current information. If we had made modifications to the playlist backups between synchronization, things wouldn't go as smoothly.

We back up some changes on our laptop and forget to synchronize. A few days later, we're editing playlists on our desktop computer, make a backup, and want to synchronize this to our laptop. As illustrated in *Figure 7.* *Synchronization conflicts between two databases*, when our backup application tries to replicate between the two databases, CouchDB sees that the changes being sent from our desktop computer are modifications of out-of-date documents and helpfully informs us that there has been a conflict.

Recovering from this error is easy to accomplish from an application perspective. Just download CouchDB's version of the playlist and provide an opportunity to merge the changes or save local modifications into a new playlist.

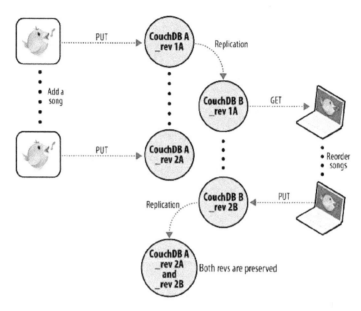

Fig. 1.10: Figure 7. Synchronization conflicts between two databases

1.3.8 Wrapping Up

CouchDB's design borrows heavily from web architecture and the lessons learned deploying massively distributed systems on that architecture. By understanding why this architecture works the way it does, and by learning to spot which parts of your application can be easily distributed and which parts cannot, you'll enhance your ability to design distributed and scalable applications, with CouchDB or without it.

We've covered the main issues surrounding CouchDB's consistency model and hinted at some of the benefits to be had when you work *with* CouchDB and not against it. But enough theory – let's get up and running and see what all the fuss is about!

1.4 Getting Started

In this document, we'll take a quick tour of CouchDB's features, familiarizing ourselves with Futon, the built-in administration interface. We'll create our first document and experiment with CouchDB views.

1.4.1 All Systems Are Go!

We'll have a very quick look at CouchDB's bare-bones Application Programming Interface (API) by using the command-line utility curl. Please note that this is not the only way of talking to CouchDB. We will show you plenty more throughout the rest of the documents. What's interesting about curl is that it gives you control over raw HTTP requests, and you can see exactly what is going on "underneath the hood" of your database.

Make sure CouchDB is still running, and then do:

```
curl http://127.0.0.1:5984/
```

This issues a GET request to your newly installed CouchDB instance.

The reply should look something like:

```
{
    "couchdb": "Welcome",
    "uuid": "85fb71bf700c17267fef77535820e371",
    "version": "1.4.0",
    "vendor": {
        "version": "1.4.0",
        "name": "The Apache Software Foundation"
    }
}
```

Not all that spectacular. CouchDB is saying "hello" with the running version number.

Next, we can get a list of databases:

```
curl -X GET http://127.0.0.1:5984/_all_dbs
```

All we added to the previous request is the _all_dbs string.

The response should look like:

```
["_replicator","_users"]
```

Oh, that's right, we didn't create any databases yet! All we see is an empty list.

Note: The curl command issues GET requests by default. You can issue POST requests using `curl -X POST`. To make it easy to work with our terminal history, we usually use the `-X` option even when issuing GET requests. If we want to send a POST next time, all we have to change is the method.

HTTP does a bit more under the hood than you can see in the examples here. If you're interested in every last detail that goes over the wire, pass in the `-v` option (e.g., `curl -vX GET`), which will show you the server curl tries to connect to, the request headers it sends, and response headers it receives back. Great for debugging!

Let's create a database:

```
curl -X PUT http://127.0.0.1:5984/baseball
```

CouchDB will reply with:

```
{"ok":true}
```

Retrieving the list of databases again shows some useful results this time:

```
curl -X GET http://127.0.0.1:5984/_all_dbs
```

```
["baseball"]
```

Note: We should mention JavaScript Object Notation (JSON) here, the data format CouchDB speaks. JSON is a lightweight data interchange format based on JavaScript syntax. Because JSON is natively compatible with JavaScript, your web browser is an ideal client for CouchDB.

Brackets ([ ]) represent ordered lists, and curly braces ({ }) represent key/value dictionaries. Keys must be strings, delimited by quotes ("), and values can be strings, numbers, booleans, lists, or key/value dictionaries. For a more detailed description of JSON, see Appendix E, JSON Primer.

Let's create another database:

```
curl -X PUT http://127.0.0.1:5984/baseball
```

CouchDB will reply with:

```
{"error":"file_exists","reason":"The database could not be created,
the file already exists."}
```

We already have a database with that name, so CouchDB will respond with an error. Let's try again with a different database name:

```
curl -X PUT http://127.0.0.1:5984/plankton
```

CouchDB will reply with:

```
{"ok":true}
```

Retrieving the list of databases yet again shows some useful results:

```
curl -X GET http://127.0.0.1:5984/_all_dbs
```

CouchDB will respond with:

```
["baseball", "plankton"]
```

To round things off, let's delete the second database:

```
curl -X DELETE http://127.0.0.1:5984/plankton
```

CouchDB will reply with:

```
{"ok":true}
```

The list of databases is now the same as it was before:

```
curl -X GET http://127.0.0.1:5984/_all_dbs
```

CouchDB will respond with:

```
["baseball"]
```

For brevity, we'll skip working with documents, as the next section covers a different and potentially easier way of working with CouchDB that should provide experience with this. As we work through the example, keep in mind that "under the hood" everything is being done by the application exactly as you have been doing here manually. Everything is done using GET, PUT, POST, and DELETE with a URI.

1.4.2 Welcome to Futon

After having seen CouchDB's raw API, let's get our feet wet by playing with Futon, the built-in administration interface. Futon provides full access to all of CouchDB's features and makes it easy to work with some of the more complex ideas involved. With Futon we can create and destroy databases; view and edit documents; compose and run MapReduce views; and trigger replication between databases.

To load Futon in your browser, visit:

```
http://127.0.0.1:5984/_utils/
```

If you're running version 0.9 or later, you should see something similar to *Figure 1. The Futon welcome screen*. In later documents, we'll focus on using CouchDB from server-side languages such as Ruby and Python. As such, this document is a great opportunity to showcase an example of natively serving up a dynamic web application using nothing more than CouchDB's integrated web server, something you may wish to do with your own applications.

The first thing we should do with a fresh installation of CouchDB is run the test suite to verify that everything is working properly. This assures us that any problems we may run into aren't due to bothersome issues with our setup. By the same token, failures in the Futon test suite are a red flag, telling us to double-check our installation before attempting to use a potentially broken database server, saving us the confusion when nothing seems to be working quite like we expect!

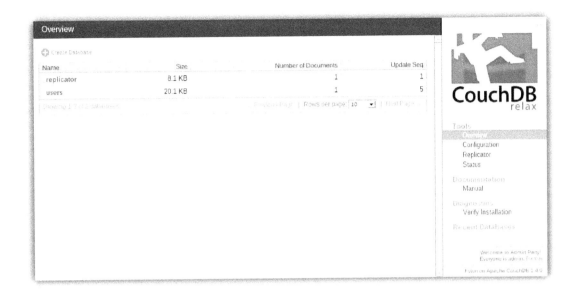

Fig. 1.11: Figure 1. The Futon welcome screen

Some common network configurations cause the replication test to fail when accessed via the localhost address. You can fix this by accessing CouchDB via 127.0.0.1, e.g. http://127.0.0.1:5984/_utils/.

1.4.3 Your First Database and Document

Creating a database in Futon is simple. From the overview page, click "Create Database." When asked for a name, enter hello-world and click the Create button.

After your database has been created, Futon will display a list of all its documents. This list will start out empty (*Figure 3. An empty database in Futon*), so let's create our first document. Click the "New Document" link and then the Create button in the pop up. Make sure to leave the document ID blank, and CouchDB will generate a UUID for you.

For demoing purposes, having CouchDB assign a UUID is fine. When you write your first programs, we recommend assigning your own UUIDs. If you rely on the server to generate the UUID and you end up making two POST requests because the first POST request bombed out, you might generate two docs and never find out about the first one because only the second one will be reported back. Generating your own UUIDs makes sure that you'll never end up with duplicate documents.

Futon will display the newly created document, with its _id and _rev as the only fields. To create a new field, click the "Add Field" button. We'll call the new field hello. Click the green check icon (or hit the Enter key) to finalize creating the hello field. Double-click the hello field's value (default null) to edit it.

You can experiment with other JSON values; e.g., [1, 2, "c"] or {"foo": "bar"}. Once you've entered your values into the document, make a note of its _rev attribute and click "Save Document." The result should look like *Figure 4. A "hello world" document in Futon*.

You'll notice that the document's _rev has changed. We'll go into more detail about this in later documents, but for now, the important thing to note is that _rev acts like a safety feature when saving a document. As long as you and CouchDB agree on the most recent _rev of a document, you can successfully save your changes.

Futon also provides a way to display the underlying JSON data, which can be more compact and easier to read, depending on what sort of data you are dealing with. To see the JSON version of our "hello world" document, click the Source tab. The result should look like *Figure 5. The JSON source of a "hello world" document in Futon*.

Fig. 1.12: Figure 3. An empty database in Futon

Fig. 1.13: Figure 4. A "hello world" document in Futon

Fig. 1.14: Figure 5. The JSON source of a "hello world" document in Futon

1.4.4 Running a Query Using MapReduce

Traditional relational databases allow you to run any queries you like as long as your data is structured correctly. In contrast, CouchDB uses predefined map and reduce functions in a style known as MapReduce. These functions provide great flexibility because they can adapt to variations in document structure, and indexes for each document can be computed independently and in parallel. The combination of a map and a reduce function is called a view in CouchDB terminology.

For experienced relational database programmers, MapReduce can take some getting used to. Rather than declaring which rows from which tables to include in a result set and depending on the database to determine the most efficient way to run the query, reduce queries are based on simple range requests against the indexes generated by your map functions.

Map functions are called once with each document as the argument. The function can choose to skip the document altogether or emit one or more view rows as key/value pairs. Map functions may not depend on any information outside of the document. This independence is what allows CouchDB views to be generated incrementally and in parallel.

CouchDB views are stored as rows that are kept sorted by key. This makes retrieving data from a range of keys efficient even when there are thousands or millions of rows. When writing CouchDB map functions, your primary goal is to build an index that stores related data under nearby keys.

Before we can run an example MapReduce view, we'll need some data to run it on. We'll create documents carrying the price of various supermarket items as found at different shops. Let's create documents for apples, oranges, and bananas. (Allow CouchDB to generate the _id and _rev fields.) Use Futon to create documents that have a final JSON structure that looks like this:

```
{
    "_id": "00a271787f89c0ef2e10e88a0c0001f4",
    "_rev": "1-2628a75ac8c3abfffc8f6e30c9949fd6",
    "item": "apple",
    "prices": {
        "Fresh Mart": 1.59,
        "Price Max": 5.99,
        "Apples Express": 0.79
    }
}
```

This document should look like *Figure 6. An example document with apple prices in Futon* when entered into Futon.

Fig. 1.15: Figure 6. An example document with apple prices in Futon

OK, now that that's done, let's create the document for oranges:

```
{
    "_id": "00a271787f89c0ef2e10e88a0c0003f0",
    "_rev": "1-e9680c5d9a688b4ff8dd68549e8e072c",
    "item": "orange",
    "prices": {
        "Fresh Mart": 1.99,
        "Price Max": 3.19,
        "Citrus Circus": 1.09
    }
}
```

And finally, the document for bananas:

```
{
    "_id": "00a271787f89c0ef2e10e88a0c00048b",
    "_rev": "1-60e25d93dc12884676d037400a6fa189",
    "item": "banana",
    "prices": {
        "Fresh Mart": 1.99,
        "Price Max": 0.79,
        "Banana Montana": 4.22
    }
}
```

Imagine we're catering a big luncheon, but the client is very price-sensitive. To find the lowest prices, we're going to create our first view, which shows each fruit sorted by price. Click "hello-world" to return to the hello-world overview, and then from the "View" select field choose "Temporary view..." to create a new view.

Edit the map function, on the left, so that it looks like the following:

```
function(doc) {
    var shop, price, value;
    if (doc.item && doc.prices) {
        for (shop in doc.prices) {
```

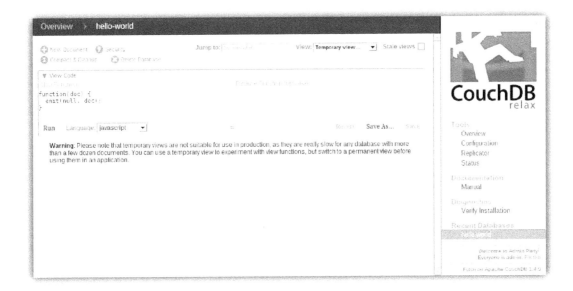

Fig. 1.16: Figure 7. A temporary view in Futon

```
            price = doc.prices[shop];
            value = [doc.item, shop];
            emit(price, value);
        }
    }
}
```

This is a JavaScript function that CouchDB runs for each of our documents as it computes the view. We'll leave the reduce function blank for the time being.

Click "Run" and you should see result rows like in *Figure 8. The results of running a view in Futon*, with the various items sorted by price. This map function could be even more useful if it grouped the items by type so that all the prices for bananas were next to each other in the result set. CouchDB's key sorting system allows any valid JSON object as a key. In this case, we'll emit an array of [item, price] so that CouchDB groups by item type and price.

Let's modify the view function so that it looks like this:

```
function(doc) {
    var shop, price, key;
    if (doc.item && doc.prices) {
        for (shop in doc.prices) {
            price = doc.prices[shop];
            key = [doc.item, price];
            emit(key, shop);
        }
    }
}
```

Here, we first check that the document has the fields we want to use. CouchDB recovers gracefully from a few isolated map function failures, but when a map function fails regularly (due to a missing required field or other JavaScript exception), CouchDB shuts off its indexing to prevent any further resource usage. For this reason, it's important to check for the existence of any fields before you use them. In this case, our map function will skip the first "hello world" document we created without emitting any rows or encountering any errors. The result of this query should look like *Figure 9. The results of running a view after grouping by item type and price*.

Once we know we've got a document with an item type and some prices, we iterate over the item's prices and emit key/values pairs. The key is an array of the item and the price, and forms the basis for CouchDB's sorted index.

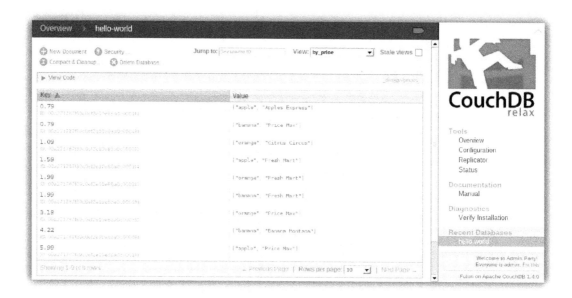

Fig. 1.17: Figure 8. The results of running a view in Futon

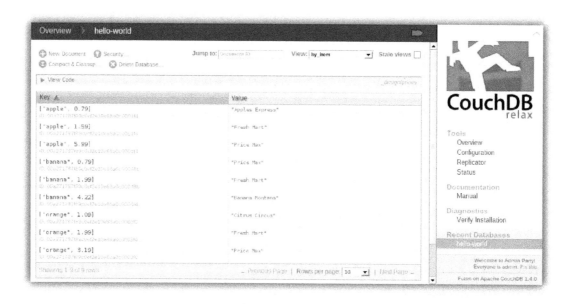

Fig. 1.18: Figure 9. The results of running a view after grouping by item type and price

In this case, the value is the name of the shop where the item can be found for the listed price.

View rows are sorted by their keys – in this example, first by item, then by price. This method of complex sorting is at the heart of creating useful indexes with CouchDB.

MapReduce can be challenging, especially if you've spent years working with relational databases. The important things to keep in mind are that map functions give you an opportunity to sort your data using any key you choose, and that CouchDB's design is focused on providing fast, efficient access to data within a range of keys.

1.4.5 Triggering Replication

Futon can trigger replication between two local databases, between a local and remote database, or even between two remote databases. We'll show you how to replicate data from one local database to another, which is a simple way of making backups of your databases as we're working through the examples.

First we'll need to create an empty database to be the target of replication. Return to the overview and create a database called hello-replication. Now click "Replicator" in the sidebar and choose hello-world as the source and hello-replication as the target. Click "Replicate" to replicate your database. The result should look something like *Figure 10. Running database replication in Futon*.

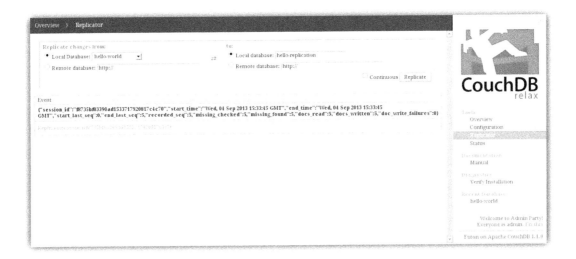

Fig. 1.19: Figure 10. Running database replication in Futon

Note: For larger databases, replication can take much longer. It is important to leave the browser window open while replication is taking place. As an alternative, you can trigger replication via curl or some other HTTP client that can handle long-running connections. If your client closes the connection before replication finishes, you'll have to retrigger it. Luckily, CouchDB's replication can take over from where it left off instead of starting from scratch.

1.4.6 Wrapping Up

Now that you've seen most of Futon's features, you'll be prepared to dive in and inspect your data as we build our example application in the next few documents. Futon's pure JavaScript approach to managing CouchDB shows how it's possible to build a fully featured web application using only CouchDB's HTTP API and integrated web server.

But before we get there, we'll have another look at CouchDB's HTTP API – now with a magnifying glass. Let's curl up on the couch and relax.

1.5 The Core API

This document explores the CouchDB in minute detail. It shows all the nitty-gritty and clever bits. We show you best practices and guide you around common pitfalls.

We start out by revisiting the basic operations we ran in the previous document *Getting Started*, looking behind the scenes. We also show what Futon needs to do behind its user interface to give us the nice features we saw earlier.

This document is both an introduction to the core CouchDB API as well as a reference. If you can't remember how to run a particular request or why some parameters are needed, you can always come back here and look things up (we are probably the heaviest users of this document).

While explaining the API bits and pieces, we sometimes need to take a larger detour to explain the reasoning for a particular request. This is a good opportunity for us to tell you why CouchDB works the way it does.

The API can be subdivided into the following sections. We'll explore them individually:

- *Server*
- *Databases*
- *Documents*
- *Replication*
- *Wrapping Up*

1.5.1 Server

This one is basic and simple. It can serve as a sanity check to see if CouchDB is running at all. It can also act as a safety guard for libraries that require a certain version of CouchDB. We're using the curl utility again:

```
curl http://127.0.0.1:5984/
```

CouchDB replies, all excited to get going:

```
{
    "couchdb": "Welcome",
    "uuid": "85fb71bf700c17267fef77535820e371",
    "vendor": {
        "name": "The Apache Software Foundation",
        "version": "1.5.0"
    },
    "version": "1.5.0"
}
```

You get back a JSON string, that, if parsed into a native object or data structure of your programming language, gives you access to the welcome string and version information.

This is not terribly useful, but it illustrates nicely the way CouchDB behaves. You send an HTTP request and you receive a JSON string in the HTTP response as a result.

1.5.2 Databases

Now let's do something a little more useful: *create databases*. For the strict, CouchDB is a *database management system* (DMS). That means it can hold multiple databases. A database is a bucket that holds "related data". We'll explore later what that means exactly. In practice, the terminology is overlapping – often people refer to a DMS as "a database" and also a database within the DMS as "a database." We might follow that slight oddity, so don't get confused by it. In general, it should be clear from the context if we are talking about the whole of CouchDB or a single database within CouchDB.

Now let's make one! We want to store our favorite music albums, and we creatively give our database the name albums. Note that we're now using the -X option again to tell curl to send a PUT request instead of the default GET request:

```
curl -X PUT http://127.0.0.1:5984/albums
```

CouchDB replies:

```
{"ok":true}
```

That's it. You created a database and CouchDB told you that all went well. What happens if you try to create a database that already exists? Let's try to create that database again:

```
curl -X PUT http://127.0.0.1:5984/albums
```

CouchDB replies:

```
{"error":"file_exists","reason":"The database could not be created, the file already exis
```

We get back an error. This is pretty convenient. We also learn a little bit about how CouchDB works. CouchDB stores each database in a single file. Very simple.

Let's create another database, this time with curl's -v (for "verbose") option. The verbose option tells curl to show us not only the essentials – the HTTP response body – but all the underlying request and response details:

```
curl -vX PUT http://127.0.0.1:5984/albums-backup
```

curl elaborates:

```
* About to connect() to 127.0.0.1 port 5984 (#0)
*   Trying 127.0.0.1... connected
* Connected to 127.0.0.1 (127.0.0.1) port 5984 (#0)
> PUT /albums-backup HTTP/1.1
> User-Agent: curl/7.16.3 (powerpc-apple-darwin9.0) libcurl/7.16.3 OpenSSL/0.9.71 zlib/1.
> Host: 127.0.0.1:5984
> Accept: */*
>
< HTTP/1.1 201 Created
< Server: CouchDB (Erlang/OTP)
< Date: Sun, 05 Jul 2009 22:48:28 GMT
< Content-Type: text/plain;charset=utf-8
< Content-Length: 12
< Cache-Control: must-revalidate
<
{"ok":true}
* Connection #0 to host 127.0.0.1 left intact
* Closing connection #0
```

What a mouthful. Let's step through this line by line to understand what's going on and find out what's important. Once you've seen this output a few times, you'll be able to spot the important bits more easily.

```
* About to connect() to 127.0.0.1 port 5984 (#0)
```

This is curl telling us that it is going to establish a TCP connection to the CouchDB server we specified in our request URI. Not at all important, except when debugging networking issues.

```
*   Trying 127.0.0.1... connected
* Connected to 127.0.0.1 (127.0.0.1) port 5984 (#0)
```

curl tells us it successfully connected to CouchDB. Again, not important if you aren't trying to find problems with your network.

The following lines are prefixed with > and < characters. The > means the line was sent to CouchDB verbatim (without the actual >). The < means the line was sent back to curl by CouchDB.

```
> PUT /albums-backup HTTP/1.1
```

This initiates an HTTP request. Its *method* is PUT, the *URI* is /albums-backup, and the HTTP version is HTTP/1.1. There is also HTTP/1.0, which is simpler in some cases, but for all practical reasons you should be using HTTP/1.1.

Next, we see a number of *request headers*. These are used to provide additional details about the request to CouchDB.

```
> User-Agent: curl/7.16.3 (powerpc-apple-darwin9.0) libcurl/7.16.3 OpenSSL/0.9.71 zlib/1.
```

The User-Agent header tells CouchDB which piece of client software is doing the HTTP request. We don't learn anything new: it's curl. This header is often useful in web development when there are known errors in client implementations that a server might want to prepare the response for. It also helps to determine which platform a user is on. This information can be used for technical and statistical reasons. For CouchDB, the User-Agent header is irrelevant.

```
> Host: 127.0.0.1:5984
```

The Host header is required by HTTP 1.1. It tells the server the hostname that came with the request.

```
> Accept: */*
```

The Accept header tells CouchDB that curl accepts any media type. We'll look into why this is useful a little later.

```
>
```

An empty line denotes that the request headers are now finished and the rest of the request contains data we're sending to the server. In this case, we're not sending any data, so the rest of the curl output is dedicated to the HTTP response.

```
< HTTP/1.1 201 Created
```

The first line of CouchDB's HTTP response includes the HTTP version information (again, to acknowledge that the requested version could be processed), an HTTP *status code*, and a *status code message*. Different requests trigger different response codes. There's a whole range of them telling the client (curl in our case) what effect the request had on the server. Or, if an error occurred, what kind of error. RFC 2616 (the HTTP 1.1 specification) defines clear behavior for response codes. CouchDB fully follows the RFC.

The 201 Created status code tells the client that the resource the request was made against was successfully created. No surprise here, but if you remember that we got an error message when we tried to create this database twice, you now know that this response could include a different response code. Acting upon responses based on response codes is a common practice. For example, all response codes of 400 Bad Request or larger tell you that some error occurred. If you want to shortcut your logic and immediately deal with the error, you could just check a >= 400 response code.

```
< Server: CouchDB (Erlang/OTP)
```

The Server header is good for diagnostics. It tells us which CouchDB version and which underlying Erlang version we are talking to. In general, you can ignore this header, but it is good to know it's there if you need it.

```
< Date: Sun, 05 Jul 2009 22:48:28 GMT
```

The Date header tells you the time of the server. Since client and server time are not necessarily synchronized, this header is purely informational. You shouldn't build any critical application logic on top of this!

```
< Content-Type: text/plain;charset=utf-8
```

The Content-Type header tells you which MIME type the HTTP response body is and its encoding. We already know CouchDB returns JSON strings. The appropriate Content-Type header is *application/json*. Why do we see *text/plain*? This is where pragmatism wins over purity. Sending an *application/json* Content-Type header will make a browser offer you the returned JSON for download instead of just displaying it. Since it is extremely useful to be able to test CouchDB from a browser, CouchDB sends a *text/plain* content type, so all browsers will display the JSON as text.

Note: There are some extensions that make your browser JSON-aware, but they are not installed by default. For more information, look at the popular JSONView extension, available for both Firefox and Chrome.

Do you remember the Accept request header and how it is set to */* to express interest in any MIME type? If you send Accept: application/json in your request, CouchDB knows that you can deal with a pure JSON response with the proper Content-Type header and will use it instead of text/plain.

```
< Content-Length: 12
```

The Content-Length header simply tells us how many bytes the response body has.

```
< Cache-Control: must-revalidate
```

This Cache-Control header tells you, or any proxy server between CouchDB and you, not to cache this response.

```
<
```

This empty line tells us we're done with the response headers and what follows now is the response body.

```
{"ok":true}
```

We've seen this before.

```
* Connection #0 to host 127.0.0.1 left intact
* Closing connection #0
```

The last two lines are curl telling us that it kept the TCP connection it opened in the beginning open for a moment, but then closed it after it received the entire response.

Throughout the documents, we'll show more requests with the -v option, but we'll omit some of the headers we've seen here and include only those that are important for the particular request.

Creating databases is all fine, but how do we get rid of one? Easy – just change the HTTP method:

```
> curl -vX DELETE http://127.0.0.1:5984/albums-backup
```

This deletes a CouchDB database. The request will remove the file that the database contents are stored in. There is no *"Are you sure?"* safety net or any *"Empty the trash"* magic you've got to do to delete a database. Use this command with care. Your data will be deleted without a chance to bring it back easily if you don't have a backup copy.

This section went knee-deep into HTTP and set the stage for discussing the rest of the core CouchDB API. Next stop: documents.

1.5.3 Documents

Documents are CouchDB's central data structure. The idea behind a document is, unsurprisingly, that of a real-world document – a sheet of paper such as an invoice, a recipe, or a business card. We already learned that CouchDB uses the JSON format to store documents. Let's see how this storing works at the lowest level.

Each document in CouchDB has an *ID*. This ID is unique per database. You are free to choose any string to be the ID, but for best results we recommend a UUID (or GUID), i.e., a Universally (or Globally) Unique IDentifier. UUIDs are random numbers that have such a low collision probability that everybody can make thousands of UUIDs a minute for millions of years without ever creating a duplicate. This is a great way to ensure two independent people cannot create two different documents with the same ID. Why should you care what somebody else is doing? For one, that somebody else could be you at a later time or on a different computer; secondly, CouchDB replication lets you share documents with others and using UUIDs ensures that it all works. But more on that later; let's make some documents:

```
curl -X PUT http://127.0.0.1:5984/albums/6e1295ed6c29495e54cc05947f18c8af -d '{"title":"T
```

CouchDB replies:

```
{"ok":true,"id":"6e1295ed6c29495e54cc05947f18c8af","rev":"1-2902191555"}
```

The curl command appears complex, but let's break it down. First, -X PUT tells curl to make a PUT request. It is followed by the URL that specifies your CouchDB IP address and port. The resource part of the URL /albums/6e1295ed6c29495e54cc05947f18c8af specifies the location of a document inside our albums database. The wild collection of numbers and characters is a UUID. This UUID is your document's ID. Finally, the -d flag tells curl to use the following string as the body for the PUT request. The string is a simple JSON structure including title and artist attributes with their respective values.

Note: If you don't have a UUID handy, you can ask CouchDB to give you one (in fact, that is what we did just now without showing you). Simply send a *GET /_uuids* request:

```
curl -X GET http://127.0.0.1:5984/_uuids
```

CouchDB replies:

```
{"uuids":["6e1295ed6c29495e54cc05947f18c8af"]}
```

Voilà, a UUID. If you need more than one, you can pass in the ?count=10 HTTP parameter to request 10 UUIDs, or really, any number you need.

To double-check that CouchDB isn't lying about having saved your document (it usually doesn't), try to retrieve it by sending a GET request:

```
curl -X GET http://127.0.0.1:5984/albums/6e1295ed6c29495e54cc05947f18c8af
```

We hope you see a pattern here. Everything in CouchDB has an address, a URI, and you use the different HTTP methods to operate on these URIs.

CouchDB replies:

```
{"_id":"6e1295ed6c29495e54cc05947f18c8af","_rev":"1-2902191555","title":"There is Nothing
```

This looks a lot like the document you asked CouchDB to save, which is good. But you should notice that CouchDB added two fields to your JSON structure. The first is _id, which holds the UUID we asked CouchDB to save our document under. We always know the ID of a document if it is included, which is very convenient.

The second field is _rev. It stands for *revision*.

Revisions

If you want to change a document in CouchDB, you don't tell it to go and find a field in a specific document and insert a new value. Instead, you load the full document out of CouchDB, make your changes in the JSON structure (or object, when you are doing actual programming), and save the entire new revision (or version) of that document back into CouchDB. Each revision is identified by a new _rev value.

If you want to update or delete a document, CouchDB expects you to include the _rev field of the revision you wish to change. When CouchDB accepts the change, it will generate a new revision number. This mechanism ensures that, in case somebody else made a change without you knowing before you got to request the document update, CouchDB will not accept your update because you are likely to overwrite data you didn't know existed. Or simplified: whoever saves a change to a document first, wins. Let's see what happens if we don't provide a _rev field (which is equivalent to providing a outdated value):

```
curl -X PUT http://127.0.0.1:5984/albums/6e1295ed6c29495e54cc05947f18c8af \
    -d '{"title":"There is Nothing Left to Lose","artist":"Foo Fighters","year":"1997"}'
```

CouchDB replies:

```
{"error":"conflict","reason":"Document update conflict."}
```

If you see this, add the latest revision number of your document to the JSON structure:

```
curl -X PUT http://127.0.0.1:5984/albums/6e1295ed6c29495e54cc05947f18c8af \
    -d '{"_rev":"1-2902191555","title":"There is Nothing Left to Lose","artist":"Foo Fig
```

Now you see why it was handy that CouchDB returned that _rev when we made the initial request. CouchDB replies:

```
{"ok":true,"id":"6e1295ed6c29495e54cc05947f18c8af","rev":"2-8aff9ee9d06671fa89c99d20a4b3a
```

CouchDB accepted your write and also generated a new revision number. The revision number is the *MD5 hash* of the transport representation of a document with an N- prefix denoting the number of times a document got updated. This is useful for replication. See *Replication and conflict model* for more information.

There are multiple reasons why CouchDB uses this revision system, which is also called Multi-Version Concurrency Control (MVCC). They all work hand-in-hand, and this is a good opportunity to explain some of them.

One of the aspects of the HTTP protocol that CouchDB uses is that it is stateless. What does that mean? When talking to CouchDB you need to make requests. Making a request includes opening a network connection to CouchDB, exchanging bytes, and closing the connection. This is done every time you make a request. Other protocols allow you to open a connection, exchange bytes, keep the connection open, exchange more bytes later – maybe depending on the bytes you exchanged at the beginning – and eventually close the connection. Holding a connection open for later use requires the server to do extra work. One common pattern is that for the lifetime of a connection, the client has a consistent and static view of the data on the server. Managing huge amounts of parallel connections is a significant amount of work. HTTP connections are usually short-lived, and making the same guarantees is a lot easier. As a result, CouchDB can handle many more concurrent connections.

Another reason CouchDB uses MVCC is that this model is simpler conceptually and, as a consequence, easier to program. CouchDB uses less code to make this work, and less code is always good because the ratio of defects per lines of code is static.

The revision system also has positive effects on replication and storage mechanisms, but we'll explore these later in the documents.

> **Warning:** The terms *version* and *revision* might sound familiar (if you are programming without version control, stop reading this guide right now and start learning one of the popular systems). Using new versions for document changes works a lot like version control, but there's an important difference: **CouchDB does not guarantee that older versions are kept around**.

Documents in Detail

Now let's have a closer look at our document creation requests with the curl -v flag that was helpful when we explored the database API earlier. This is also a good opportunity to create more documents that we can use in later examples.

We'll add some more of our favorite music albums. Get a fresh UUID from the /_uuids resource. If you don't remember how that works, you can look it up a few pages back.

```
curl -vX PUT http://127.0.0.1:5984/albums/70b50bfa0a4b3aed1f8aff9e92dc16a0 \
    -d '{"title":"Blackened Sky","artist":"Biffy Clyro","year":2002}'
```

> **Note:** By the way, if you happen to know more information about your favorite albums, don't hesitate to add more properties. And don't worry about not knowing all the information for all the albums. CouchDB's schema-less documents can contain whatever you know. After all, you should relax and not worry about data.

Now with the -v option, CouchDB's reply (with only the important bits shown) looks like this:

```
> PUT /albums/70b50bfa0a4b3aed1f8aff9e92dc16a0 HTTP/1.1
>
< HTTP/1.1 201 Created
< Location: http://127.0.0.1:5984/albums/70b50bfa0a4b3aed1f8aff9e92dc16a0
< ETag: "1-e89c99d29d06671fa0a4b3ae8aff9e"
```

```
<
{"ok":true,"id":"70b50bfa0a4b3aed1f8aff9e92dc16a0","rev":"1-e89c99d29d06671fa0a4b3ae8aff9
```

We're getting back the 201 Created HTTP status code in the response headers, as we saw earlier when we created a database. The Location header gives us a full URL to our newly created document. And there's a new header. An ETag in HTTP-speak identifies a specific version of a resource. In this case, it identifies a specific version (the first one) of our new document. Sound familiar? Yes, conceptually, an ETag is the same as a CouchDB document revision number, and it shouldn't come as a surprise that CouchDB uses revision numbers for ETags. ETags are useful for caching infrastructures.

Attachments

CouchDB documents can have attachments just like an email message can have attachments. An attachment is identified by a name and includes its MIME type (or Content-Type) and the number of bytes the attachment contains. Attachments can be any data. It is easiest to think about attachments as files attached to a document. These files can be text, images, Word documents, music, or movie files. Let's make one.

Attachments get their own URL where you can upload data. Say we want to add the album artwork to the 6e1295ed6c29495e54cc05947f18c8af document (*"There is Nothing Left to Lose"*), and let's also say the artwork is in a file *artwork.jpg* in the current directory:

```
curl -vX PUT http://127.0.0.1:5984/albums/6e1295ed6c29495e54cc05947f18c8af/artwork.jpg?re
    --data-binary @artwork.jpg -H "Content-Type:image/jpg"
```

Note: The --data-binary @ option tells curl to read a file's contents into the HTTP request body. We're using the -H option to tell CouchDB that we're uploading a JPEG file. CouchDB will keep this information around and will send the appropriate header when requesting this attachment; in case of an image like this, a browser will render the image instead of offering you the data for download. This will come in handy later. Note that you need to provide the current revision number of the document you're attaching the artwork to, just as if you would update the document. Because, after all, attaching some data is changing the document.

You should now see your artwork image if you point your browser to http://127.0.0.1:5984/albums/6e1295ed6c29495e54cc05947f18c8af/artwork.jpg

If you request the document again, you'll see a new member:

```
curl http://127.0.0.1:5984/albums/6e1295ed6c29495e54cc05947f18c8af
```

CouchDB replies:

```
{
    "_id": "6e1295ed6c29495e54cc05947f18c8af",
    "_rev": "3-131533518",
    "title": "There is Nothing Left to Lose",
    "artist": "Foo Fighters",
    "year": "1997",
    "_attachments": {
        "artwork.jpg": {
            "stub": true,
            "content_type": "image/jpg",
            "length": 52450
        }
    }
}
```

_attachments is a list of keys and values where the values are JSON objects containing the attachment metadata. stub=true tells us that this entry is just the metadata. If we use the ?attachments=true HTTP option when requesting this document, we'd get a Base64 encoded string containing the attachment data.

We'll have a look at more document request options later as we explore more features of CouchDB, such as replication, which is the next topic.

1.5.4 Replication

CouchDB replication is a mechanism to synchronize databases. Much like rsync synchronizes two directories locally or over a network, replication synchronizes two databases locally or remotely.

In a simple POST request, you tell CouchDB the *source* and the *target* of a replication and CouchDB will figure out which documents and new document revisions are on *source* that are not yet on *target*, and will proceed to move the missing documents and revisions over.

We'll take an in-depth look at replication in the document *Introduction to Replication*; in this document, we'll just show you how to use it.

First, we'll create a target database. Note that CouchDB won't automatically create a target database for you, and will return a replication failure if the target doesn't exist (likewise for the source, but that mistake isn't as easy to make):

```
curl -X PUT http://127.0.0.1:5984/albums-replica
```

Now we can use the database *albums-replica* as a replication target:

```
curl -vX POST http://127.0.0.1:5984/_replicate \
    -d '{"source":"albums","target":"albums-replica"}' \
    -H "Content-Type: application/json"
```

Note: CouchDB supports the option "create_target":true placed in the JSON POSTed to the *_replicate* URL. It implicitly creates the target database if it doesn't exist.

CouchDB replies (this time we formatted the output so you can read it more easily):

```
{
    "history": [
        {
            "start_last_seq": 0,
            "missing_found": 2,
            "docs_read": 2,
            "end_last_seq": 5,
            "missing_checked": 2,
            "docs_written": 2,
            "doc_write_failures": 0,
            "end_time": "Sat, 11 Jul 2009 17:36:21 GMT",
            "start_time": "Sat, 11 Jul 2009 17:36:20 GMT"
        }
    ],
    "source_last_seq": 5,
    "session_id": "924e75e914392343de89c99d29d06671",
    "ok": true
}
```

CouchDB maintains a *session history* of replications. The response for a replication request contains the history entry for this *replication session*. It is also worth noting that the request for replication will stay open until replication closes. If you have a lot of documents, it'll take a while until they are all replicated and you won't get back the replication response until all documents are replicated. It is important to note that replication replicates the database only as it was at the point in time when replication was started. So, any additions, modifications, or deletions subsequent to the start of replication will not be replicated.

We'll punt on the details again – the "ok": true at the end tells us all went well. If you now have a look at the albums-replica database, you should see all the documents that you created in the albums database. Neat, eh?

What you just did is called local replication in CouchDB terms. You created a local copy of a database. This is useful for backups or to keep snapshots of a specific state of your data around for later. You might want to do this if you are developing your applications but want to be able to roll back to a stable version of your code and data.

There are more types of replication useful in other situations. The source and target members of our replication request are actually links (like in HTML) and so far we've seen links relative to the server we're working on (hence

---

local). You can also specify a remote database as the target:

```
curl -vX POST http://127.0.0.1:5984/_replicate \
    -d '{"source":"albums","target":"http://example.org:5984/albums-replica"}' \
    -H "Content-Type:application/json"
```

Using a *local source* and a *remote target* database is called *push replication*. We're pushing changes to a remote server.

Note: Since we don't have a second CouchDB server around just yet, we'll just use the absolute address of our single server, but you should be able to infer from this that you can put any remote server in there.

This is great for sharing local changes with remote servers or buddies next door.

You can also use a *remote source* and a *local target* to do a *pull replication*. This is great for getting the latest changes from a server that is used by others:

```
curl -vX POST http://127.0.0.1:5984/_replicate \
    -d '{"source":"http://example.org:5984/albums-replica","target":"albums"}' \
    -H "Content-Type:application/json"
```

Finally, you can run remote replication, which is mostly useful for management operations:

```
curl -vX POST http://127.0.0.1:5984/_replicate \
    -d '{"source":"http://example.org:5984/albums","target":"http://example.org:5984/alb
    -H"Content-Type: application/json"
```

Note: CouchDB and REST

CouchDB prides itself on having a RESTful API, but these replication requests don't look very RESTy to the trained eye. What's up with that? While CouchDB's core database, document, and attachment API are RESTful, not all of CouchDB's API is. The replication API is one example. There are more, as we'll see later in the documents.

Why are there RESTful and non-RESTful APIs mixed up here? Have the developers been too lazy to go REST all the way? Remember, REST is an architectural style that lends itself to certain architectures (such as the CouchDB document API). But it is not a one-size-fits-all. Triggering an event like replication does not make a whole lot of sense in the REST world. It is more like a traditional remote procedure call. And there is nothing wrong with this.

We very much believe in the "use the right tool for the job" philosophy, and REST does not fit every job. For support, we refer to Leonard Richardson and Sam Ruby who wrote RESTful Web Services (O'Reilly), as they share our view.

1.5.5 Wrapping Up

This is still not the full CouchDB API, but we discussed the essentials in great detail. We're going to fill in the blanks as we go. For now, we believe you're ready to start building CouchDB applications.

See also:

Complete HTTP API Reference:

- *Server API Reference*
- *Database API Reference*
- *Document API Reference*
- *Replication API*

1.6 Security

In this document, we'll look at the basic security mechanisms in CouchDB: the *Admin Party*, *Basic Authentication*, *Cookie Authentication*; how CouchDB handles users and protects their credentials.

1.6.1 Authentication

The Admin Party

When you start out fresh, CouchDB allows any request to be made by anyone. Create a database? No problem, here you go. Delete some documents? Same deal. CouchDB calls this the *Admin Party*. Everybody has privileges to do anything. Neat.

While it is incredibly easy to get started with CouchDB that way, it should be obvious that putting a default installation into the wild is adventurous. Any rogue client could come along and delete a database.

A note of relief: by default, CouchDB will listen only on your loopback network interface (`127.0.0.1` or `localhost`) and thus only you will be able to make requests to CouchDB, nobody else. But when you start to open up your CouchDB to the public (that is, by telling it to bind to your machine's public IP address), you will want to think about restricting access so that the next bad guy doesn't ruin your admin party.

In our previous discussions, we dropped some keywords about how things without the *Admin Party* work. First, there's *admin* itself, which implies some sort of super user. Then there are *privileges*. Let's explore these terms a little more.

CouchDB has the idea of an *admin user* (e.g. an administrator, a super user, or root) that is allowed to do anything to a CouchDB installation. By default, everybody is an admin. If you don't like that, you can create specific admin users with a username and password as their credentials.

CouchDB also defines a set of requests that only admin users are allowed to do. If you have defined one or more specific admin users, CouchDB will ask for identification for certain requests:

- Creating a database (`PUT /database`)
- Deleting a database (`DELETE /database`)
- Setup a database security (`PUT /database/_security`)
- Creating a design document (`PUT /database/_design/app`)
- Updating a design document (`PUT /database/_design/app?rev=1-4E2`)
- Deleting a design document (`DELETE /database/_design/app?rev=2-6A7`)
- Execute a temporary view (`POST /database/_temp_view`)
- Triggering compaction (`POST /database/_compact`)
- Reading the task status list (`GET /_active_tasks`)
- Restarting the server (`POST /_restart`)
- Reading the active configuration (`GET /_config`)
- Updating the active configuration (`PUT /_config/section/key`)

Creating New Admin User

Let's do another walk through the API using *curl* to see how CouchDB behaves when you add admin users.

```
> HOST="http://127.0.0.1:5984"
> curl -X PUT $HOST/database
{"ok":true}
```

When starting out fresh, we can add a database. Nothing unexpected. Now let's create an admin user. We'll call her `anna`, and her password is `secret`. Note the double quotes in the following code; they are needed to denote a string value for the *configuration API*:

```
> curl -X PUT $HOST/_config/admins/anna -d '"secret"'
""
```

As per the *_config* API's behavior, we're getting the previous value for the config item we just wrote. Since our admin user didn't exist, we get an empty string.

Hashing Passwords

Seeing the plain-text password is scary, isn't it? No worries, CouchDB doesn't show the plain-text password anywhere. It gets hashed right away. The hash is that big, ugly, long string that starts out with `-hashed-`. How does that work?

1. Creates a new 128-bit UUID. This is our *salt*.

2. Creates a sha1 hash of the concatenation of the bytes of the plain-text password and the salt (`sha1(password + salt)`).

3. Prefixes the result with `-hashed-` and appends `,salt`.

To compare a plain-text password during authentication with the stored hash, the same procedure is run and the resulting hash is compared to the stored hash. The probability of two identical hashes for different passwords is too insignificant to mention (c.f. Bruce Schneier). Should the stored hash fall into the hands of an attacker, it is, by current standards, way too inconvenient (i.e., it'd take a lot of money and time) to find the plain-text password from the hash.

But what's with the `-hashed-` prefix? When CouchDB starts up, it reads a set of *.ini* files with config settings. It loads these settings into an internal data store (not a database). The config API lets you read the current configuration as well as change it and create new entries. CouchDB is writing any changes back to the *.ini* files.

The *.ini* files can also be edited by hand when CouchDB is not running. Instead of creating the admin user as we showed previously, you could have stopped CouchDB, opened your *local.ini*, added `anna = secret` to the `admins`, and restarted CouchDB. Upon reading the new line from *local.ini*, CouchDB would run the hashing algorithm and write back the hash to *local.ini*, replacing the plain-text password. To make sure CouchDB only hashes plain-text passwords and not an existing hash a second time, it prefixes the hash with `-hashed-`, to distinguish between plain-text passwords and hashed passwords. This means your plain-text password can't start with the characters `-hashed-`, but that's pretty unlikely to begin with.

Note: Since *1.3.0 release* CouchDB uses `-pbkdf2-` prefix by default to sign about using PBKDF2 hashing algorithm instead of *SHA1*.

Basic Authentication

Now that we have defined an admin, CouchDB will not allow us to create new databases unless we give the correct admin user credentials. Let's verify:

```
> curl -X PUT $HOST/somedatabase
{"error":"unauthorized","reason":"You are not a server admin."}
```

That looks about right. Now we try again with the correct credentials:

```
> HOST="http://anna:secret@127.0.0.1:5984"
> curl -X PUT $HOST/somedatabase
{"ok":true}
```

If you have ever accessed a website or FTP server that was password-protected, the `username:password@` URL variant should look familiar.

If you are security conscious, the missing s in `http://` will make you nervous. We're sending our password to CouchDB in plain text. This is a bad thing, right? Yes, but consider our scenario: CouchDB listens on `127.0.0.1` on a development box that we're the sole user of. Who could possibly sniff our password?

If you are in a production environment, however, you need to reconsider. Will your CouchDB instance communicate over a public network? Even a LAN shared with other collocation customers is public. There are multiple ways to secure communication between you or your application and CouchDB that exceed the scope of this documentation. CouchDB as of version *1.1.0* comes with *SSL built in*.

See also:

Basic Authentication API Reference

Cookie Authentication

Basic authentication that uses plain-text passwords is nice and convenient, but not very secure if no extra measures are taken. It is also a very poor user experience. If you use basic authentication to identify admins, your application's users need to deal with an ugly, unstylable browser modal dialog that says non-professional at work more than anything else.

To remedy some of these concerns, CouchDB supports cookie authentication. With cookie authentication your application doesn't have to include the ugly login dialog that the users' browsers come with. You can use a regular HTML form to submit logins to CouchDB. Upon receipt, CouchDB will generate a one-time token that the client can use in its next request to CouchDB. When CouchDB sees the token in a subsequent request, it will authenticate the user based on the token without the need to see the password again. By default, a token is valid for 10 minutes.

To obtain the first token and thus authenticate a user for the first time, the username and password must be sent to the *_session* API. The API is smart enough to decode HTML form submissions, so you don't have to resort to any smarts in your application.

If you are not using HTML forms to log in, you need to send an HTTP request that looks as if an HTML form generated it. Luckily, this is super simple:

```
> HOST="http://127.0.0.1:5984"
> curl -vX POST $HOST/_session \
        -H 'Content-Type:application/x-www-form-urlencoded' \
        -d 'name=anna&password=secret'
```

CouchDB replies, and we'll give you some more detail:

```
< HTTP/1.1 200 OK
< Set-Cookie: AuthSession=YW5uYTo0QUIzOTdFQjrC4ipN-D-53hw1sJepVzcVxnriEw;
< Version=1; Path=/; HttpOnly
> ...
<
{"ok":true}
```

A 200 OK response code tells us all is well, a Set-Cookie header includes the token we can use for the next request, and the standard JSON response tells us again that the request was successful.

Now we can use this token to make another request as the same user without sending the username and password again:

```
> curl -vX PUT $HOST/mydatabase \
        --cookie AuthSession=YW5uYTo0QUIzOTdFQjrC4ipN-D-53hw1sJepVzcVxnriEw \
        -H "X-CouchDB-WWW-Authenticate: Cookie" \
        -H "Content-Type:application/x-www-form-urlencoded"
{"ok":true}
```

You can keep using this token for 10 minutes by default. After 10 minutes you need to authenticate your user again. The token lifetime can be configured with the timeout (in seconds) setting in the *couch_httpd_auth* configuration section.

See also:

Cookie Authentication API Reference

1.6.2 Authentication Database

You may already note that CouchDB administrators are defined within the config file and are wondering if regular users are also stored there. No, they are not. CouchDB has a special *authentication database*, named _users by default, that stores all registered users as JSON documents.

This special database is a *system database*. This means that while it shares the common *database API*, there are some special security-related constraints applied. Below is a list of how the *authentication database* is different from the other databases.

- Only administrators may browse list of all documents (*GET /_users/_all_docs*)
- Only administrators may listen to *changes feed* (*GET /_users/_changes*)
- Only administrators may execute design functions like *views*, *shows* and *others*
- There is a special design document _auth that cannot be modified
- Every document except the *design documents* represent registered CouchDB users and belong to them
- Users may only access (*GET /_users/org.couchdb.user:Jan*) or modify (*PUT /_users/org.couchdb.user:Jan*) documents that they own

These draconian rules are necessary since CouchDB cares about its users' personal information and will not disclose it to just anyone. Often, user documents contain system information like *login*, *password hash* and *roles*, apart from sensitive personal information like real name, email, phone, special internal identifications and more. This is not information that you want to share with the World.

Users Documents

Each CouchDB user is stored in document format. These documents contain several *mandatory* fields, that CouchDB needs for authentication:

- **_id** (*string*): Document ID. Contains user's login with special prefix *Why the org.couchdb.user: prefix?*
- **derived_key** (*string*): PBKDF2 key
- **name** (*string*): User's name aka login. **Immutable** e.g. you cannot rename an existing user - you have to create new one
- **roles** (*array* of *string*): List of user roles. CouchDB doesn't provide any builtin roles, so you're free to define your own depending on your needs. However, you cannot set system roles like _admin there. Also, only administrators may assign roles to users - by default all users have no roles
- **password_sha** (*string*): Hashed password with salt. Used for simple *password_scheme*
- **password_scheme** (*string*): Password hashing scheme. May be simple or pbkdf2
- **salt** (*string*): Hash salt. Used for simple *password_scheme*
- **type** (*string*): Document type. Constantly has the value user

Additionally, you may specify any custom fields that relate to the target user. This is a good place to store user's private information because only the target user and CouchDB administrators may browse it.

Why the org.couchdb.user: prefix?

The reason there is a special prefix before a user's login name is to have namespaces that users belong to. This prefix is designed to prevent replication conflicts when you try merging two or more *_user* databases.

For current CouchDB releases, all users belong to the same org.couchdb.user namespace and this cannot be changed. This may be changed in future releases.

Creating a New User

Creating a new user is a very trivial operation. You just need to do a PUT request with the user's data to CouchDB. Let's create a user with login *jan* and password *apple*:

```
curl -X PUT http://localhost:5984/_users/org.couchdb.user:jan \
    -H "Accept: application/json" \
    -H "Content-Type: application/json" \
    -d '{"name": "jan", "password": "apple", "roles": [], "type": "user"}'
```

This *curl* command will produce the following HTTP request:

```
PUT /_users/org.couchdb.user:jan HTTP/1.1
Accept: application/json
Content-Length: 62
Content-Type: application/json
Host: localhost:5984
User-Agent: curl/7.31.0
```

And CouchDB responds with:

```
HTTP/1.1 201 Created
Cache-Control: must-revalidate
Content-Length: 83
Content-Type: application/json
Date: Fri, 27 Sep 2013 07:33:28 GMT
ETag: "1-e0ebfb84005b920488fc7a8cc5470cc0"
Location: http://localhost:5984/_users/org.couchdb.user:jan
Server: CouchDB (Erlang OTP)

{"ok":true,"id":"org.couchdb.user:jan","rev":"1-e0ebfb84005b920488fc7a8cc5470cc0"}
```

The document was successfully created! The user *jan* should now exist in our database. Let's check if this is true:

```
curl -X POST http://localhost:5984/_session -d 'name=jan&password=apple'
```

CouchDB should respond with:

```
{"ok":true,"name":"jan","roles":[]}
```

This means that the username was recognized and the password's hash matches with the stored one. If we specify an incorrect login and/or password, CouchDB will notify us with the following error message:

```
{"error":"unauthorized","reason":"Name or password is incorrect."}
```

Password Changing

Let's define what is password changing from the point of view of CouchDB and the authentication database. Since "users" are "documents", this operation is just updating the document with a special field `password` which contains the *plain text password*. Scared? No need to be. The authentication database has a special internal hook on document update which looks for this field and replaces it with the *secured hash* depending on the chosen `password_scheme`.

Summarizing the above process - we need to get the document's content, add the `password` field with the new password in plain text and then store the JSON result to the authentication database.

```
curl -X GET http://localhost:5984/_users/org.couchdb.user:jan
```

```
{
    "_id": "org.couchdb.user:jan",
    "_rev": "1-e0ebfb84005b920488fc7a8cc5470cc0",
    "derived_key": "e579375db0e0c6a6fc79cd9e36a36859f71575c3",
    "iterations": 10,
```

```
    "name": "jan",
    "password_scheme": "pbkdf2",
    "roles": [],
    "salt": "1112283cf988a34f124200a050d308a1",
    "type": "user"
}
```

Here is our user's document. We may strip hashes from the stored document to reduce the amount of posted data:

```
curl -X PUT http://localhost:5984/_users/org.couchdb.user:jan \
    -H "Accept: application/json" \
    -H "Content-Type: application/json" \
    -H "If-Match: 1-e0ebfb84005b920488fc7a8cc5470cc0" \
    -d '{"name":"jan", "roles":[], "type":"user", "password":"orange"}'
```

```
{"ok":true,"id":"org.couchdb.user:jan","rev":"2-ed293d3a0ae09f0c624f10538ef33c6f"}
```

Updated! Now let's check that the password was really changed:

```
curl -X POST http://localhost:5984/_session -d 'name=jan&password=apple'
```

CouchDB should respond with:

```
{"error":"unauthorized","reason":"Name or password is incorrect."}
```

Looks like the password `apple` is wrong, what about `orange`?

```
curl -X POST http://localhost:5984/_session -d 'name=jan&password=orange'
```

CouchDB should respond with:

```
{"ok":true,"name":"jan","roles":[]}
```

Hooray! You may wonder why this was so complex - we need to retrieve user's document, add a special field to it, and post it back. Where is that one big button that changes the password without worrying about the document's content? Actually, *Futon* has one such thing at the bottom right corner if you are logged in. Using that will hide all the implementation details described above and keep it really simple for you.

Note: There is no password confirmation for API request: you should implement it on your application layer like Futon does.

Users Public Information

New in version 1.4.

Sometimes users *want* to share some information with the world. For instance, their contact email to let other users get in touch with them. To solve this problem, but still keep sensitive and private information secured, there is a special *configuration* option `public_fields`. In this option you may define a comma-separated list of users document fields that will be publicly available.

Normally, if you request a user document and you're not an administrator or the document's owner, CouchDB will respond with 404 Not Found:

```
curl http://localhost:5984/_users/org.couchdb.user:robert
```

```
{"error":"not_found","reason":"missing"}
```

This response is constant for both cases when user exists or doesn't exist for security reasons.

Now let's share the field `name`. First, set up the `public_fields` configuration option. Remember, that this action requires administrator privileges. The next command will prompt you for user *admin*'s password:

curl -X PUT http://localhost:5984/_config/couch_http_auth/public_fields -H   "Content-Type: application/json" -d '"name"' -u admin

What has changed? Let's check Robert's document once again:

```
curl http://localhost:5984/_users/org.couchdb.user:robert
```

```
{"_id":"org.couchdb.user:robert","_rev":"6-869e2d3cbd8b081f9419f190438ecbe7","name":"robe
```

Good news! Now we may read the field name in *every user document without needing to be an administrator.*
Keep in mind, though, not to publish sensitive information, especially without user's consent!

1.6.3 Authorization

Now that you have a few users who can log in, you probably want to set up some restrictions on what actions they
can perform based on their identity and their roles. Each database on a CouchDB server can contain its own set
of authorization rules that specify which users are allowed to read and write documents, create design documents,
and change certain database configuration parameters. The authorization rules are set up by a server admin and
can be modified at any time.

Database authorization rules assign a user into one of two classes:

- *members*, who are allowed to read all documents and create and modify any document except for design
  documents.

- *admins*, who can read and write all types of documents, modify which users are members or admins, and
  set certain per-database configuration options.

Note that a database admin is not the same as a server admin – the actions of a database admin are restricted to a
specific database.

When a database is first created, there are no members or admins. HTTP requests that have no authentication
credentials or have credentials for a normal user are treated as members, and those with server admin credentials
are treated as database admins. To change the default permissions, you must create a *_security* document in the
database:

```
> curl -X PUT http://localhost:5984/mydatabase/_security \
    -u anna:secret \
    -H "Content-Type: application/json" \
    -d '{"admins": { "names": [], "roles": [] }, "members": { "names": ["jan"], "roles":
```

The HTTP request to create the *_security* document must contain the credentials of a server admin. CouchDB will
respond with:

```
{"ok":true}
```

The database is now secured against anonymous reads and writes:

```
> curl http://localhost:5984/mydatabase/
```

```
{"error":"unauthorized","reason":"You are not authorized to access this db."}
```

You declared user "jan" as a member in this database, so he is able to read and write normal documents:

```
> curl -u jan:apple http://localhost:5984/mydatabase/
```

```
{"db_name":"mydatabase","doc_count":1,"doc_del_count":0,"update_seq":3,"purge_seq":0,
"compact_running":false,"disk_size":12376,"data_size":272,"instance_start_time":"13976728
"disk_format_version":6,"committed_update_seq":3}
```

If Jan attempted to create a design doc, however, CouchDB would return a 401 Unauthorized error because the
username "jan" is not in the list of admin names and the *_users/org.couchdb.user:jan* document doesn't contain
a role that matches any of the declared admin roles. If you want to promote Jan to an admin, you can update
the security document to add *"jan"* to the *names* array under *admin*. Keeping track of individual database admin
usernames is tedious, though, so you would likely prefer to create a database admin role and assign that role to the
org.couchdb.user:jan user document:

```
> curl -X PUT http://localhost:5984/mydatabase/_security \
    -u anna:secret \
    -H "Content-Type: application/json" \
    -d '{"admins": { "names": [], "roles": ["mydatabase_admin"] }, "members": { "names":
```

See the _security document reference page_ for additional details about specifying database members and admins.

1.7 Futon: Web GUI Administration Panel

Futon is a native web-based interface built into CouchDB. It provides a basic interface to the majority of the functionality, including the ability to create, update, delete and view documents and views, provides access to the configuration parameters, and an interface for initiating replication.

The default view is the Overview page which provides you with a list of the databases. The basic structure of the page is consistent regardless of the section you are in. The main panel on the left provides the main interface to the databases, configuration or replication systems. The side panel on the right provides navigation to the main areas of Futon interface:

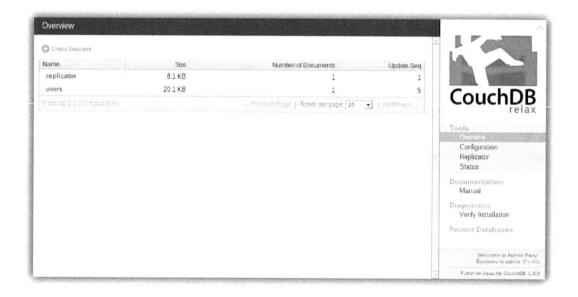

Fig. 1.20: Futon Overview

The main sections are:

- Overview

  The main overview page, which provides a list of the databases and provides the interface for querying the database and creating and updating documents. See _Managing Databases and Documents_.

- Configuration

  An interface into the configuration of your CouchDB installation. The interface allows you to edit the different configurable parameters. For more details on configuration, see _Configuring CouchDB_ section.

- Replicator

  An interface to the replication system, enabling you to initiate replication between local and remote databases. See _Configuring Replication_.

- Status

Displays a list of the running background tasks on the server. Background tasks include view index building, compaction and replication. The Status page is an interface to the *Active Tasks* API call.

- Verify Installation

  The Verify Installation allows you to check whether all of the components of your CouchDB installation are correctly installed.

- Test Suite

  The Test Suite section allows you to run the built-in test suite. This executes a number of test routines entirely within your browser to test the API and functionality of your CouchDB installation. If you select this page, you can run the tests by using the Run All button. This will execute all the tests, which may take some time.

1.7.1 Managing Databases and Documents

You can manage databases and documents within Futon using the main Overview section of the Futon interface.

To create a new database, click the Create Database ELLIPSIS button. You will be prompted for the database name, as shown in the figure below.

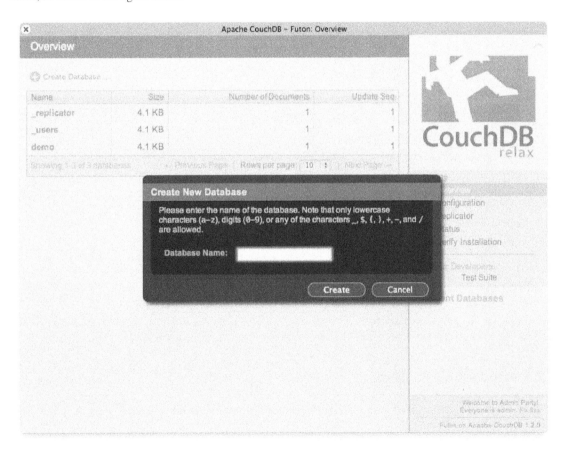

Fig. 1.21: Creating a Database

Once you have created the database (or selected an existing one), you will be shown a list of the current documents. If you create a new document, or select an existing document, you will be presented with the edit document display.

Editing documents within Futon requires selecting the document and then editing (and setting) the fields for the document individually before saving the document back into the database.

For example, the figure below shows the editor for a single document, a newly created document with a single ID, the document `_id` field.

Fig. 1.22: Editing a Document

To add a field to the document:

1. Click Add Field.

2. In the fieldname box, enter the name of the field you want to create. For example, "company".

3. Click the green tick next to the field name to confirm the field name change.

4. Double-click the corresponding Value cell.

5. Enter a company name, for example "Example".

6. Click the green tick next to the field value to confirm the field value.

7. The document is still not saved as this point. You must explicitly save the document by clicking the Save Document button at the top of the page. This will save the document, and then display the new document with the saved revision information (the `_rev` field).

The same basic interface is used for all editing operations within Futon. You *must* remember to save the individual element (fieldname, value) using the green tick button, before then saving the document.

1.7.2 Configuring Replication

When you click the Replicator option within the Tools menu you are presented with the Replicator screen. This allows you to start replication between two databases by filling in or selecting the appropriate options within the form provided.

To start a replication process, either the select the local database or enter a remote database name into the corresponding areas of the form. Replication occurs from the database on the left to the database on the right.

If you are specifying a remote database name, you must specify the full URL of the remote database (including the host, port number and database name). If the remote instance requires authentication, you can specify the username and password as part of the URL, for example `http://username:pass@remotehost:5984/demo`.

To enable continuous replication, click the Continuous checkbox.

Fig. 1.23: Edited Document

Fig. 1.24: Replication Form

To start the replication process, click the Replicate button. The replication process should start and will continue in the background. If the replication process will take a long time, you can monitor the status of the replication using the Status option under the Tools menu.

Once replication has been completed, the page will show the information returned when the replication process completes by the API.

The Replicator tool is an interface to the underlying replication API. For more information, see */_replicate*. For more information on replication, see *Replication*.

1.8 cURL: Your Command Line Friend

The `curl` utility is a command line tool available on Unix, Linux, Mac OS X and Windows and many other platforms. `curl` provides easy access to the HTTP protocol (among others) directly from the command-line and is therefore an ideal way of interacting with CouchDB over the HTTP REST API.

For simple `GET` requests you can supply the URL of the request. For example, to get the database information:

```
shell> curl http://127.0.0.1:5984
```

This returns the database information (formatted in the output below for clarity):

```
{
    "couchdb": "Welcome",
    "uuid": "85fb71bf700c17267fef77535820e371",
    "vendor": {
        "name": "The Apache Software Foundation",
        "version": "1.4.0"
    },
    "version": "1.4.0"
}
```

Note: For some URLs, especially those that include special characters such as ampersand, exclamation mark, or question mark, you should quote the URL you are specifying on the command line. For example:

```
shell> curl 'http://couchdb:5984/_uuids?count=5'
```

You can explicitly set the HTTP command using the `-X` command line option. For example, when creating a database, you set the name of the database in the URL you send using a PUT request:

```
shell> curl -X PUT http://127.0.0.1:5984/demo
{"ok":true}
```

But to obtain the database information you use a `GET` request (with the return information formatted for clarity):

```
shell> curl -X GET http://127.0.0.1:5984/demo
{
    "compact_running" : false,
    "doc_count" : 0,
    "db_name" : "demo",
    "purge_seq" : 0,
    "committed_update_seq" : 0,
    "doc_del_count" : 0,
    "disk_format_version" : 5,
    "update_seq" : 0,
    "instance_start_time" : "1306421773496000",
    "disk_size" : 79
}
```

For certain operations, you must specify the content type of request, which you do by specifying the `Content-Type` header using the `-H` command-line option:

```
shell> curl -H 'Content-Type: application/json' http://127.0.0.1:5984/_uuids
```

You can also submit 'payload' data, that is, data in the body of the HTTP request using the -d option. This is useful if you need to submit JSON structures, for example document data, as part of the request. For example, to submit a simple document to the demo database:

```
shell> curl -H 'Content-Type: application/json' \
            -X POST http://127.0.0.1:5984/demo \
            -d '{"company": "Example, Inc."}'
{"ok":true,"id":"8843faaf0b831d364278331bc3001bd8",
 "rev":"1-33b9fbce46930280dab37d672bbc8bb9"}
```

In the above example, the argument after the -d option is the JSON of the document we want to submit.

The document can be accessed by using the automatically generated document ID that was returned:

```
shell> curl -X GET http://127.0.0.1:5984/demo/8843faaf0b831d364278331bc3001bd8
{"_id":"8843faaf0b831d364278331bc3001bd8",
 "_rev":"1-33b9fbce46930280dab37d672bbc8bb9",
 "company":"Example, Inc."}
```

The API samples in the *API Basics* show the HTTP command, URL and any payload information that needs to be submitted (and the expected return value). All of these examples can be reproduced using curl with the command-line examples shown above.

## CHAPTER 2

Installation

2.1 Installation on Unix-like systems

A high-level guide to Unix-like systems, inc. Mac OS X and Ubuntu.

This document is the canonical source of installation information. However, many systems have gotchas that you need to be aware of. In addition, dependencies frequently change as distributions update their archives. If you're running into trouble, be sure to check out the wiki. If you have any tips to share, please also update the wiki so that others can benefit from your experience.

See also:

Community installation guides

2.1.1 Troubleshooting

- There is a troubleshooting guide.
- There is a wiki for general documentation.
- There are collection of friendly mailing lists.

Please work through these in order if you experience any problems.

2.1.2 Dependencies

You should have the following installed:

- Erlang OTP (>=R14B01, =<R17)
- ICU
- OpenSSL
- Mozilla SpiderMonkey (1.8.5)
- GNU Make
- GNU Compiler Collection
- libcurl
- help2man
- Python (>=2.7) for docs
- Python Sphinx (>=1.1.3)

It is recommended that you install Erlang OTP R13B-4 or above where possible. You will only need libcurl if you plan to run the JavaScript test suite. And help2man is only need if you plan on installing the CouchDB man pages. Python and Sphinx are only required for building the online documentation.

Debian-based Systems

You can install the dependencies by running:

```
sudo apt-get install build-essential
sudo apt-get install erlang-base-hipe
sudo apt-get install erlang-dev
sudo apt-get install erlang-manpages
sudo apt-get install erlang-eunit
sudo apt-get install erlang-nox
sudo apt-get install libicu-dev
sudo apt-get install libmozjs-dev
sudo apt-get install libcurl4-openssl-dev
```

There are lots of Erlang packages. If there is a problem with your install, try a different mix. There is more information on the wiki. Additionally, you might want to install some of the optional Erlang tools which may also be useful.

Be sure to update the version numbers to match your system's available packages.

Unfortunately, it seems that installing dependencies on Ubuntu is troublesome.

See also:

- Installing on Debian
- Installing on Ubuntu

RedHat-based (Fedora, Centos, RHEL) Systems

You can install the dependencies by running:

```
sudo yum install autoconf
sudo yum install autoconf-archive
sudo yum install automake
sudo yum install curl-devel
sudo yum install erlang-asn1
sudo yum install erlang-erts
sudo yum install erlang-eunit
sudo yum install erlang-os_mon
sudo yum install erlang-xmerl
sudo yum install help2man
sudo yum install js-devel
sudo yum install libicu-devel
sudo yum install libtool
sudo yum install perl-Test-Harness
```

While CouchDB builds against the default js-devel-1.7.0 included in some distributions, it's recommended to use a more recent js-devel-1.8.5.

Mac OS X

Follow *Installation with HomeBrew* reference till *brew install couchdb* step.

2.1.3 Installing

Once you have satisfied the dependencies you should run:

```
./configure
```

This script will configure CouchDB to be installed into */usr/local* by default.

If you wish to customise the installation, pass *–help* to this script.

If everything was successful you should see the following message:

```
You have configured Apache CouchDB, time to relax.
```

Relax.

To install CouchDB you should run:

```
make && sudo make install
```

You only need to use *sudo* if you're installing into a system directory.

Try *gmake* if *make* is giving you any problems.

If everything was successful you should see the following message:

```
You have installed Apache CouchDB, time to relax.
```

Relax.

2.1.4 First Run

You can start the CouchDB server by running:

```
sudo -i -u couchdb couchdb
```

This uses the *sudo* command to run the *couchdb* command as the *couchdb* user.

When CouchDB starts it should eventually display the following message:

```
Apache CouchDB has started, time to relax.
```

Relax.

To check that everything has worked, point your web browser to:

```
http://127.0.0.1:5984/_utils/index.html
```

From here you should verify your installation by pointing your web browser to:

```
http://localhost:5984/_utils/verify_install.html
```

2.1.5 Security Considerations

You should create a special *couchdb* user for CouchDB.

On many Unix-like systems you can run:

```
adduser --system \
        --home /usr/local/var/lib/couchdb \
        --no-create-home \
        --shell /bin/bash \
        --group --gecos \
        "CouchDB Administrator" couchdb
```

On Mac OS X you can use the Workgroup Manager to create users.

You must make sure that:

- The user has a working POSIX shell
- The user's home directory is */usr/local/var/lib/couchdb*

You can test this by:

- Trying to log in as the *couchdb* user
- Running *pwd* and checking the present working directory

Change the ownership of the CouchDB directories by running:

```
chown -R couchdb:couchdb /usr/local/etc/couchdb
chown -R couchdb:couchdb /usr/local/var/lib/couchdb
chown -R couchdb:couchdb /usr/local/var/log/couchdb
chown -R couchdb:couchdb /usr/local/var/run/couchdb
```

Change the permission of the CouchDB directories by running:

```
chmod 0770 /usr/local/etc/couchdb
chmod 0770 /usr/local/var/lib/couchdb
chmod 0770 /usr/local/var/log/couchdb
chmod 0770 /usr/local/var/run/couchdb
```

2.1.6 Running as a Daemon

SysV/BSD-style Systems

You can use the *couchdb* init script to control the CouchDB daemon.

On SysV-style systems, the init script will be installed into:

```
/usr/local/etc/init.d
```

On BSD-style systems, the init script will be installed into:

```
/usr/local/etc/rc.d
```

We use the *[init.d|rc.d]* notation to refer to both of these directories.

You can control the CouchDB daemon by running:

```
/usr/local/etc/[init.d|rc.d]/couchdb [start|stop|restart|status]
```

If you wish to configure how the init script works, you can edit:

```
/usr/local/etc/default/couchdb
```

Comment out the *COUCHDB_USER* setting if you're running as a non-superuser.

To start the daemon on boot, copy the init script to:

```
/etc/[init.d|rc.d]
```

You should then configure your system to run the init script automatically.

You may be able to run:

```
sudo update-rc.d couchdb defaults
```

If this fails, consult your system documentation for more information.

A *logrotate* configuration is installed into:

```
/usr/local/etc/logrotate.d/couchdb
```

Consult your *logrotate* documentation for more information.

It is critical that the CouchDB logs are rotated so as not to fill your disk.

2.2 Installation on Windows

There are two ways to install CouchDB on Windows.

2.2.1 Installation from binaries

This is the simplest way to go.

1. Get the latest Windows binaries from CouchDB web site. Old releases are available at archive.

2. Follow the installation wizard steps:

    • Next on "Welcome" screen

    • Accept the License agreement

    • Select the installation directory

    • Specify "Start Menu" group name

    • Approve that you'd like to install CouchDB as service and let it be started automatically after installation (probably, you'd like so)

    • Verify installation settings

    • Install CouchDB

3. Open up Futon (if you hadn't selected autostart CouchDB after installation, you have to start it first manually)

4. It's time to Relax!

Note: In some cases you might been asked to reboot Windows to complete installation process, because of using on different Microsoft Visual C++ runtimes by CouchDB.

Note: Upgrading note

It's recommended to uninstall previous CouchDB version before upgrading, especially if the new one is built against different Erlang release. The reason is simple: there may be leftover libraries with alternative or incompatible versions from old Erlang release that may create conflicts, errors and weird crashes.

In this case, make sure you backup of your *local.ini* config and CouchDB database/index files.

2.2.2 Installation from sources

If you're Windows geek, this section is for you!

Troubleshooting

    • There is a troubleshooting guide.

    • There is a wiki for general documentation.

    • And some Windows-specific tips.

- There are collection of friendly mailing lists.

Please work through these in order if you experience any problems.

Dependencies

You should have the following installed:

- Erlang OTP (>=14B01, <R17)
- ICU (>=4.*)
- OpenSSL (>0.9.8r)
- Mozilla SpiderMonkey (=1.8.5)
- Cygwin
- Microsoft SDK 7.0 or 7.1
- libcurl (>=7.20)
- help2man
- Python (>=2.7) for docs
- Python Sphinx (>=1.1.3)

You will only need libcurl if you plan to run the JavaScript test suite. And help2man is only need if you plan on installing the CouchDB man pages. Python and Sphinx are only required for building the online documentation.

General Notes

- When installing Cygwin, be sure to select all the *development* tools.
- When installing Erlang, you must build it from source.
- The CouchDB build requires a number of the Erlang build scripts.
- All dependent libraries should be built with the same version of Microsoft SDK.
- Do not try to link against libraries built with, or included in, Cygwin or MingW. They are not compatible with the Erlang/OTP or CouchDB build scripts.
- ICU version 4.6 and later will build cleanly using MSBuild.
- Python and Sphinx are optional for building the online documentation. Use cygwin-provided Python and install Sphinx via easy_install or pip. Further information is here http://pypi.python.org/pypi/setuptools#id4

Setting Up Cygwin

Before starting any Cygwin terminals, run:

```
set CYGWIN=nontsec
```

To set up your environment, run:

```
[VS_BIN]/vcvars32.bat
```

Replace [VS_BIN] with the path to your Visual Studio *bin* directory.

You must check that:

- The which link command points to the Microsoft linker.
- The which cl command points to the Microsoft compiler.
- The which mc command points to the Microsoft message compiler.

- The `which mt` command points to the Microsoft manifest tool.
- The `which nmake` command points to the Microsoft make tool.

If you do not do this, the build may fail due to Cygwin ones found in */usr/bin* being used instead.

Building Erlang

You must include Win32 OpenSSL, built statically from source. Use exactly the same version as required by the Erlang/OTP build process.

However, you can skip the GUI tools by running:

```
echo "skipping gs" > lib/gs/SKIP

echo "skipping ic" > lib/ic/SKIP

echo "skipping jinterface" > lib/jinterface/SKIP
```

Follow the rest of the Erlang instructions as described.

After running:

```
./otp_build release -a
```

You should run:

```
./release/win32/Install.exe -s
```

This will set up the release/win32/bin directory correctly. The CouchDB installation scripts currently write their data directly into this location.

To set up your environment for building CouchDB, run:

```
eval `./otp_build env_win32`
```

To set up the *ERL_TOP* environment variable, run:

```
export ERL_TOP=[ERL_TOP]
```

Replace `[ERL_TOP]` with the Erlang source directory name.

Remember to use */cygdrive/c/* instead of *c:/* as the directory prefix.

To set up your path, run:

```
export PATH=$ERL_TOP/release/win32/erts-5.8.5/bin:$PATH
```

If everything was successful, you should be ready to build CouchDB.

Relax.

Building CouchDB

Note that *win32-curl* is only required if you wish to run the developer tests.

The documentation step may be skipped using `--disable-docs` if you wish.

Once you have satisfied the dependencies you should run:

```
./configure \
    --with-js-include=/cygdrive/c/path_to_spidermonkey_include \
    --with-js-lib=/cygdrive/c/path_to_spidermonkey_lib \
    --with-win32-icu-binaries=/cygdrive/c/path_to_icu_binaries_root \
    --with-erlang=$ERL_TOP/release/win32/usr/include \
    --with-win32-curl=/cygdrive/c/path/to/curl/root/directory \
```

```
--with-openssl-bin-dir=/cygdrive/c/openssl/bin \
--with-msvc-redist-dir=/cygdrive/c/dir/with/vcredist_platform_executable \
--disable-init \
--disable-launchd \
--prefix=$ERL_TOP/release/win32
```

This command could take a while to complete.

If everything was successful you should see the following message:

```
You have configured Apache CouchDB, time to relax.
```

Relax.

To install CouchDB you should run:

```
make install
```

If everything was successful you should see the following message:

```
You have installed Apache CouchDB, time to relax.
```

Relax.

To build the .exe installer package, you should run:

```
make dist
```

Alternatively, you may run CouchDB directly from the build tree, but to avoid any contamination do not run *make dist* after this.

First Run

You can start the CouchDB server by running:

```
$ERL_TOP/release/win32/bin/couchdb.bat
```

When CouchDB starts it should eventually display the following message:

```
Apache CouchDB has started, time to relax.
```

Relax.

To check that everything has worked, point your web browser to:

```
http://127.0.0.1:5984/_utils/index.html
```

From here you should run the verification tests in Firefox.

See also:

Glazier: Automate building of CouchDB from source on Windows

2.3 Installation on Mac OS X

2.3.1 Installation using the Apache CouchDB native application

The easiest way to run CouchDB on Mac OS X is through the native Mac OS X application. Just follow the below instructions:

1. Download Apache CouchDB for Mac OS X. Old releases are available at archive.

2. Double click on the Zip file

3. Drag and drop the Apache CouchDB.app into Applications folder

That's all, now CouchDB is installed on your Mac:

1. Run Apache CouchDB application

2. Open up Futon, the CouchDB admin interface

3. Time to Relax!

2.3.2 Installation with HomeBrew

You can install the build tools by running:

```
open /Applications/Installers/Xcode\ Tools/XcodeTools.mpkg
```

You will need Homebrew installed to use the *brew* command. To install the other *dependencies* run next commands:

```
brew install autoconf
brew install autoconf-archive
brew install automake
brew install libtool
brew install erlang
brew install icu4c
brew install spidermonkey
brew install curl
```

You may want to link ICU so that CouchDB can find the header files automatically:

```
brew link icu4c
```

The same is true for recent versions of Erlang:

```
brew link erlang
```

Now it's time to brew CouchDB:

```
brew install couchdb
```

The above Erlang install will use the bottled (pre-compiled) version if you are: using */usr/local* for *homebrew*, and on 10.6 or 10.7. If you're not on one of these, *homebrew* will build from source, so consider doing:

```
brew install erlang --no-docs
```

to trim down compilation time.

If you're hacking on CouchDB, and we hope you will, you may try the current git-based master (head) branch, or the next development release using this `couchdb` recipe, using either `--head` or `--devel` options respectively. This will allow quick installation of the future release branch when it becomes active. If you're not sure if you need this, then you probably don't. In both cases we assume you are comfortable identifying bugs, and handling any potential upgrades between commits to the codebase.

```
brew install [--devel|--head] couchdb
```

Note: OS X Lion might hang on the final brew. See the thread at https://github.com/mxcl/homebrew/issues/7024 it seems in most cases to be resolved by breaking out with CTRL-C and then repeating with `brew install -v couchdb`.

If you wish to have CouchDB run as a daemon then, set up the account, using the "User & Groups" preference pane:

- Create a standard user *couchdb* with home directory as */usr/local/var/lib/couchdb*

- Create a group called *couchdb* and add yourself, the *couchdb* user, and any others you want to be able to edit config or db files directly to it. Use the *advanced* group options to ensure the internal name is also correctly called *couchdb*.

Some versions of Mac OS X ship a problematic OpenSSL library. If you're experiencing troubles with CouchDB crashing intermittently with a segmentation fault or a bus error, you will need to install your own version of OpenSSL.

Running as a Daemon

You can use the *launchctl* command to control the CouchDB daemon.

You can load the configuration by running:

```
sudo launchctl load \
    /usr/local/Library/LaunchDaemons/org.apache.couchdb.plist
```

You can stop the CouchDB daemon by running:

```
sudo launchctl unload \
    /usr/local/Library/LaunchDaemons/org.apache.couchdb.plist
```

You can start CouchDB by running:

```
sudo launchctl start org.apache.couchdb
```

You can restart CouchDB by running:

```
sudo launchctl stop org.apache.couchdb
```

You can edit the launchd configuration by running:

```
open /usr/local/Library/LaunchDaemons/org.apache.couchdb.plist
```

To start the daemon on boot, copy the configuration file to:

```
/Library/LaunchDaemons
```

Consult your system documentation for more information.

2.3.3 Installation from MacPorts

To install CouchDB using MacPorts you have 2 package choices:

- couchdb - the latest release version
- couchdb-devel - updated every few weeks with the latest from the master branch

```
$ sudo port install couchdb
```

should be enough. MacPorts takes care of installing all necessary dependencies. If you have already installed some of the CouchDB dependencies via MacPorts, run this command to check and upgrade any outdated ones, after installing CouchDB:

```
$ sudo port upgrade couchdb
```

This will upgrade dependencies recursively, if there are more recent versions available. If you want to run CouchDB as a service controlled by the OS, load the launchd configuration which comes with the project, with this command:

```
$ sudo port load couchdb
```

and it should be up and accessible via Futon at http://127.0.0.1:5984/_utils. It should also be restarted automatically after reboot.

Updating the ports collection. The collection of port files has to be updated to reflect the latest versions of available packages. In order to do that run:

```
$ sudo port selfupdate
```

to update the port tree, and then install just as explained.

2.4 Installation on FreeBSD

2.4.1 Installation from ports

```
cd /usr/ports/databases/couchdb
make install clean
```

This will install CouchDB from the ports collection.

Start script

The following options for /etc/rc.conf or /etc/rc.conf.local are supported by the start script (defaults shown):

```
couchdb_enable="NO"
couchdb_enablelogs="YES"
couchdb_user="couchdb"
```

After enabling the couchdb rc service use the following command to start CouchDB:

```
/usr/local/etc/rc.d/couchdb start
```

This script responds to the arguments *start*, *stop*, *status*, *rcvar* etc..

The start script will also use settings from the following config files:

* /usr/local/etc/couchdb/default.ini
* /usr/local/etc/couchdb/local.ini

Administrators should use default.ini as reference and only modify the local.ini file.

Post install

In case the install script fails to install a noninteractive user "couchdb" to be used for the database, the user needs to be created manually:

I used the pw command to add a user "couchdb" in group "couchdb":

```
pw user add couchdb
pw user mod couchdb -c 'CouchDB, time to relax' -s /usr/sbin/nologin -d /var/lib/couchdb
pw group add couchdb
```

The user is added to /etc/passwd and should look similar to the following:

```
shell#  grep couchdb /etc/passwd
couchdb:*:1013:1013:Couchdb, time to relax:/var/lib/couchdb/:/usr/sbin/nologin
```

To change any of these settings, please refrain from editing */etc/passwd* and instead use pw user mod ... or vipw. Make sure that the user has no shell, but instead uses /usr/sbin/nologin. The '*' in the second field means that this user can not login via password authorization. For details use man 5 passwd.

Configuring CouchDB

3.1 Introduction Into Configuring

3.1.1 Configuration files

> **Warning:** The following section covering load order of config files applies only to UNIX-ish systems. For Windows, only the provided `default.ini` and `local.ini` files are relevant. These can of course have content appended, which achieves the same type of functionality as outlined for UNIX-ish systems below.

By default, CouchDB reads configuration files from the following locations, in the following order:

1. LOCALCONFDIR/default.ini

2. LOCALCONFDIR/default.d/*.ini

3. PLUGINS_DIR/*/priv/default.d/*.ini

4. LOCALCONFDIR/local.ini

5. LOCALCONFDIR/local.d/*.ini

The LOCALCONFDIR points to the directory that contains configuration files (`/usr/local/etc/couchdb` by default). This variable may vary from the target operation system and may be changed during building from the source code. For binary distributions, it mostly points to the installation path (e.g. `C:\Program Files\CouchDB\etc\couchdb` for Windows).

To see the actual configuration files chain run in shell:

```
couchdb -c
```

This will print out all *actual* configuration files that will form the result CouchDB configuration:

```
/etc/couchdb/default.ini
/etc/couchdb/default.d/geocouch.ini
/etc/couchdb/local.ini
/etc/couchdb/local.d/geocouch.ini
/etc/couchdb/local.d/vendor.ini
```

Settings in successive documents override the settings in earlier entries. For example, setting the `httpd/bind_address` parameter in `local.ini` would override any setting in `default.ini`.

> **Warning:** The `default.ini` file may be overwritten during an upgrade or re-installation, so localised changes should be made to the `local.ini` file or files within the `local.d` directory.

The configuration files chain may be changed by specifying additional sources by using next command line options:

- `-a`: adds configuration file to the chain

- `-A`: adds configuration directory to the chain

Let's add these options and see how the configuration chain changes:

```
shell> couchdb -c -a /home/couchdb/custom.ini
/etc/couchdb/default.ini
/etc/couchdb/default.d/geocouch.ini
/etc/couchdb/local.ini
/etc/couchdb/local.d/geocouch.ini
/etc/couchdb/local.d/vendor.ini
/home/couchdb/custom.ini
```

In case when */home/couchdb/custom.ini* exists it will be added to the configuration chain.

3.1.2 Parameter names and values

All parameter names are *case-sensitive*. Every parameter takes a value of one of five types: *boolean*, *integer*, *string*, tuple and proplist. Boolean values can be written as `true` or `false`.

Parameters with value type of *tuple* or *proplist* are following the Erlang requirement for style and naming.

3.1.3 Setting parameters via the configuration file

The common way to set some parameters is to edit the *local.ini* file which is mostly located in the *etc/couchdb* directory relative your installation path root.

For example:

```
; This is a comment
[section]
param = value ; inline comments are allowed
```

Each configuration file line may contains *section* definition, *parameter* specification, empty (space and newline characters only) or *commented* line. You can set up *inline* commentaries for *sections* or *parameters*.

The *section* defines group of parameters that are belongs to some specific CouchDB subsystem. For instance, `httpd` section holds not only HTTP server parameters, but also others that directly interacts with it.

The *parameter* specification contains two parts divided by the *equal* sign (=): the parameter name on the left side and the parameter value on the right one. The leading and following whitespace for = is an optional to improve configuration readability.

Note: In case when you'd like to remove some parameter from the *default.ini* without modifying that file, you may override in *local.ini*, but without any value:

```
[httpd_global_handlers]
_all_dbs =
```

This could be read as: "remove the *_all_dbs* parameter from the *httpd_global_handlers* section if it was ever set before".

The semicolon (`;`) signs about *commentary* start: everything after this character is counted as commentary and doesn't process by CouchDB.

After editing of configuration file CouchDB server instance should be restarted to apply these changes.

3.1.4 Setting parameters via the HTTP API

Alternatively, configuration parameters could be set via the *HTTP API*. This API allows to change CouchDB configuration on-the-fly without requiring a server restart:

```
curl -X PUT http://localhost:5984/_config/uuids/algorithm -d '"random"'
```

In the response the old parameter's value returns:

```
"sequential"
```

You should be careful with changing configuration via the HTTP API since it's easy to make CouchDB unavailable. For instance, if you'd like to change the *httpd/bind_address* for a new one:

```
curl -X PUT http://localhost:5984/_config/httpd/bind_address -d '"10.10.0.128"'
```

However, if you make a typo, or the specified IP address is not available from your network, CouchDB will be unavailable for you in both cases and the only way to resolve this will be by remoting into the server, correcting the errant file, and restarting CouchDB. To protect yourself against such accidents you may set the *httpd/config_whitelist* of permitted configuration parameters for updates via the HTTP API. Once this option is set, further changes to non-whitelisted parameters must take place via the configuration file, and in most cases, also requires a server restart before hand-edited options take effect.

3.2 Base Configuration

3.2.1 Base CouchDB Options

`[couchdb]`

attachment_stream_buffer_size

Higher values may result in better read performance due to fewer read operations and/or more OS page cache hits. However, they can also increase overall response time for writes when there are many attachment write requests in parallel.

```
[couchdb]
attachment_stream_buffer_size = 4096
```

database_dir

Specifies location of CouchDB database files (`*.couch` named). This location should be writable and readable for the user the CouchDB service runs as (`couchdb` by default).

```
[couchdb]
database_dir = /var/lib/couchdb
```

delayed_commits

When this config value as `false` the CouchDB provides guaranty of *fsync* call before return 201 Created response on each document saving. Setting this config value as `true` may raise some overall performance with cost of losing durability - it's strongly not recommended to do such in production:

```
[couchdb]
delayed_commits = false
```

> **Warning:** Delayed commits are a feature of CouchDB that allows it to achieve better write performance for some workloads while sacrificing a small amount of durability. The setting causes CouchDB to wait up to a full second before committing new data after an update. If the server crashes before the header is written then any writes since the last commit are lost.

file_compression

Changed in version 1.2: Added Google Snappy compression algorithm.

Method used to compress everything that is appended to database and view index files, except for attachments (see the *attachments* section). Available methods are:

- none: no compression

- snappy: use Google Snappy, a very fast compressor/decompressor

- deflate_N: use zlib's deflate; N is the compression level which ranges from 1 (fastest, lowest compression ratio) to 9 (slowest, highest compression ratio)

```
[couchdb]
file_compression = snappy
```

fsync_options

Specifies when to make *fsync* calls. *fsync* makes sure that the contents of any file system buffers kept by the operating system are flushed to disk. There is generally no need to modify this parameter.

```
[couchdb]
fsync_options = [before_header, after_header, on_file_open]
```

max_dbs_open

This option places an upper bound on the number of databases that can be open at once. CouchDB reference counts database accesses internally and will close idle databases as needed. Sometimes it is necessary to keep more than the default open at once, such as in deployments where many databases will be replicating continuously.

```
[couchdb]
max_dbs_open = 100
```

max_document_size

Changed in version 1.3: This option now actually works.

Defines a maximum size for JSON documents, in bytes. This limit does not apply to attachments, since they are transferred as a stream of chunks. If you set this to a small value, you might be unable to modify configuration options, database security and other larger documents until a larger value is restored by editing the configuration file.

```
[couchdb]
max_document_size = 4294967296 ; 4 GB
```

os_process_timeout

If an external process, such as a query server or external process, runs for this amount of milliseconds without returning any results, it will be terminated. Keeping this value smaller ensures you get expedient errors, but you may want to tweak it for your specific needs.

```
[couchdb]
os_process_timeout = 5000 ; 5 sec
```

uri_file

This file contains the full URI that can be used to access this instance of CouchDB. It is used to help discover the port CouchDB is running on (if it was set to 0 (e.g. automatically assigned any free one). This file should be writable and readable for the user that runs the CouchDB service (couchdb by default).

```
[couchdb]
uri_file = /var/run/couchdb/couchdb.uri
```

util_driver_dir

Specifies location of binary drivers (*icu*, *ejson*, etc.). This location and its contents should be readable for the user that runs the CouchDB service.

```
[couchdb]
util_driver_dir = /usr/lib/couchdb/erlang/lib/couch-1.5.0/priv/lib
```

uuid

New in version 1.3.

Unique identifier for this CouchDB server instance.

```
[couchdb]
uuid = 0a959b9b8227188afc2ac26ccdf345a6
```

view_index_dir

Specifies location of CouchDB view index files. This location should be writable and readable for the user that runs the CouchDB service (couchdb by default).

```
[couchdb]
view_index_dir = /var/lib/couchdb
```

3.3 couch_peruser

3.3.1 couch_peruser Options

`[couch_peruser]`

enable

If set to true, couch_peruser ensures that a private per-user database exists for each document in _users. These databases are writable only by the corresponding user. Databases are in the following form: userdb-{hex encoded username}.

```
[couch_peruser]
enable = false
```

delete_dbs

If set to true and a user is deleted, the respective database gets deleted as well.

```
[couch_peruser]
delete_dbs = false
```

3.4 CouchDB HTTP Server

3.4.1 HTTP Server Options

`[httpd]`

allow_jsonp

The true value of this option enables JSONP support (it's false by default):

```
[httpd]
allow_jsonp = false
```

authentication_handlers

List of used authentication handlers that used by CouchDB. You may extend them via third-party plugins or remove some of them if you won't let users to use one of provided methods:

```
[httpd]
authentication_handlers = {couch_httpd_oauth, oauth_authentication_handler}, {cou
```

- {couch_httpd_oauth, oauth_authentication_handler}: handles OAuth;

- {couch_httpd_auth, cookie_authentication_handler}: used for Cookie auth;

- {couch_httpd_auth, proxy_authentication_handler}: used for Proxy auth;

- {couch_httpd_auth, default_authentication_handler}: used for Basic auth;

• `{couch_httpd_auth, null_authentication_handler}`: disables auth. Everlasting *Admin Party*!

bind_address

Defines the IP address by which CouchDB will be accessible:

```
[httpd]
bind_address = 127.0.0.1
```

To let CouchDB listen any available IP address, just set up `0.0.0.0` value:

```
[httpd]
bind_address = 0.0.0.0
```

For IPv6 support you need to set `::1` if you want to let CouchDB listen local address:

```
[httpd]
bind_address = ::1
```

or `::` for any available:

```
[httpd]
bind_address = ::
```

changes_timeout

Specifies default *timeout* value for *Changes Feed* in milliseconds (60000 by default):

```
[httpd]
changes_feed = 60000 ; 60 seconds
```

config_whitelist

Sets the configuration modification whitelist. Only whitelisted values may be changed via the *config API*. To allow the admin to change this value over HTTP, remember to include `{httpd, config_whitelist}` itself. Excluding it from the list would require editing this file to update the whitelist:

```
[httpd]
config_whitelist = [{httpd,config_whitelist}, {log,level}, {etc,etc}]
```

default_handler

Specifies default HTTP requests handler:

```
[httpd]
default_handler = {couch_httpd_db, handle_request}
```

enable_cors

New in version 1.3.

Controls *CORS* feature:

```
[httpd]
enable_cors = false
```

log_max_chunk_size

Defines maximum chunk size in bytes for *_log* resource:

```
[httpd]
log_max_chunk_size = 1000000
```

port

Defined the port number to listen:

```
[httpd]
port = 5984
```

To let CouchDB handle any free port, set this option to 0:

```
[httpd]
port = 0
```

After that, CouchDB URI could be located within the URI file.

redirect_vhost_handler
This option customizes the default function that handles requests to *virtual hosts*:

```
[httpd]
redirect_vhost_handler = {Module, Fun}
```

The specified function take 2 arguments: the Mochiweb request object and the target path.

server_options
Server options for the MochiWeb component of CouchDB can be added to the configuration files:

```
[httpd]
server_options = [{backlog, 128}, {acceptor_pool_size, 16}]
```

secure_rewrites
This option allow to isolate databases via subdomains:

```
[httpd]
secure_rewrites = true
```

socket_options
The socket options for the listening socket in CouchDB can be specified as a list of tuples. For example:

```
[httpd]
socket_options = [{recbuf, 262144}, {sndbuf, 262144}, {nodelay, true}]
```

The options supported are a subset of full options supported by the TCP/IP stack. A list of the supported options are provided in the Erlang inet documentation.

vhost_global_handlers
List of global handlers that are available for *virtual hosts*:

```
[httpd]
vhost_global_handlers = _utils, _uuids, _session, _oauth, _users
```

x_forwarded_host
The *x_forwarded_host* header (X-Forwarded-Host by default) is used to forward the original value of the Host header field in case, for example, if a reverse proxy is rewriting the "Host" header field to some internal host name before forward the request to CouchDB:

```
[httpd]
x_forwarded_host = X-Forwarded-Host
```

This header has higher priority above Host one, if only it exists in the request.

x_forwarded_proto
x_forwarded_proto header (X-Forwarder-Proto by default) is used for identifying the originating protocol of an HTTP request, since a reverse proxy may communicate with CouchDB instance using HTTP even if the request to the reverse proxy is HTTPS:

```
[httpd]
x_forwarded_proto = X-Forwarded-Proto
```

x_forwarded_ssl
The *x_forwarded_ssl* header (X-Forwarded-Ssl by default) tells CouchDB that it should use the *https* scheme instead of the *http*. Actually, it's a synonym for X-Forwarded-Proto: https header, but used by some reverse proxies:

```
[httpd]
x_forwarded_ssl = X-Forwarded-Ssl
```

WWW-Authenticate

Set this option to trigger basic-auth popup on unauthorized requests:

```
[httpd]
WWW-Authenticate = Basic realm="Welcome to the Couch!"
```

3.4.2 Secure Socket Level Options

[ssl]

CouchDB supports SSL natively. All your secure connection needs can now be served without needing to set up and maintain a separate proxy server that handles SSL.

SSL setup can be tricky, but the configuration in CouchDB was designed to be as easy as possible. All you need is two files; a certificate and a private key. If you bought an official SSL certificate from a certificate authority, both should be in your possession already.

If you just want to try this out and don't want to pay anything upfront, you can create a self-signed certificate. Everything will work the same, but clients will get a warning about an insecure certificate.

You will need the OpenSSL command line tool installed. It probably already is.

```
shell> mkdir /etc/couchdb/cert
shell> cd /etc/couchdb/cert
shell> openssl genrsa > privkey.pem
shell> openssl req -new -x509 -key privkey.pem -out couchdb.pem -days 1095
shell> chmod 600 privkey.pem couchdb.pem
shell> chown couchdb privkey.pem couchdb.pem
```

Now, you need to edit CouchDB's configuration, either by editing your local.ini file or using the /_config API calls or the configuration screen in Futon. Here is what you need to do in local.ini, you can infer what needs doing in the other places.

At first, *enable the HTTPS daemon*:

```
[daemons]
httpsd = {couch_httpd, start_link, [https]}
```

Next, under the [ssl] section set up the newly generated certificates:

```
[ssl]
cert_file = /etc/couchdb/cert/couchdb.pem
key_file = /etc/couchdb/cert/privkey.pem
```

For more information please read certificates HOWTO.

Now start (or restart) CouchDB. You should be able to connect to it using HTTPS on port 6984:

```
shell> curl https://127.0.0.1:6984/
curl: (60) SSL certificate problem, verify that the CA cert is OK. Details:
error:14090086:SSL routines:SSL3_GET_SERVER_CERTIFICATE:certificate verify failed
More details here: http://curl.haxx.se/docs/sslcerts.html

curl performs SSL certificate verification by default, using a "bundle"
of Certificate Authority (CA) public keys (CA certs). If the default
bundle file isn't adequate, you can specify an alternate file
using the --cacert option.
If this HTTPS server uses a certificate signed by a CA represented in
the bundle, the certificate verification probably failed due to a
problem with the certificate (it might be expired, or the name might
not match the domain name in the URL).
```

```
If you'd like to turn off curl's verification of the certificate, use
the -k (or --insecure) option.
```

Oh no! What happened?! Remember, clients will notify their users that your certificate is self signed. `curl` is the client in this case and it notifies you. Luckily you trust yourself (don't you?) and you can specify the `-k` option as the message reads:

```
shell> curl -k https://127.0.0.1:6984/
{"couchdb":"Welcome","version":"1.5.0"}
```

All done.

cacert_file
> The path to a file containing PEM encoded CA certificates. The CA certificates are used to build the server certificate chain, and for client authentication. Also the CAs are used in the list of acceptable client CAs passed to the client when a certificate is requested. May be omitted if there is no need to verify the client and if there are not any intermediate CAs for the server certificate:

```
[ssl]
cacert_file = /etc/ssl/certs/ca-certificates.crt
```

cert_file
> Path to a file containing the user's certificate:

```
[ssl]
cert_file = /etc/couchdb/cert/couchdb.pem
```

key_file
> Path to file containing user's private PEM encoded key:

```
[ssl]
key_file = /etc/couchdb/cert/privkey.pem
```

password
> String containing the user's password. Only used if the private keyfile is password protected:

```
[ssl]
password = somepassword
```

ssl_certificate_max_depth
> Maximum peer certificate depth (must be set even if certificate validation is off):

```
[ssl]
ssl_certificate_max_depth = 1
```

verify_fun
> The verification fun (optional) if not specified, the default verification fun will be used:

```
[ssl]
verify_fun = {Module, VerifyFun}
```

verify_ssl_certificates
> Set to *true* to validate peer certificates:

```
[ssl]
verify_ssl_certificates = false
```

fail_if_no_peer_cert
> Set to *true* to terminate the TLS/SSL handshake with a *handshake_failure* alert message if the client does not send a certificate. Only used if *verify_ssl_certificates* is *true*. If set to *false* it will only fail if the client sends an invalid certificate (an empty certificate is considered valid):

```
[ssl]
fail_if_no_peer_cert = false
```

secure_renegotiate

Set to *true* to reject renegotiation attempt that does not live up to RFC 5746:

```
[ssl]
secure_renegotiate = true
```

ciphers

Set to the cipher suites that should be supported which can be specified in erlang format "{ecdhe_ecdsa,aes_128_cbc,sha256}" or in OpenSSL format "ECDHE-ECDSA-AES128-SHA256".

```
[ssl]
ciphers = ["ECDHE-ECDSA-AES128-SHA256", "ECDHE-ECDSA-AES128-SHA"]
```

tls_versions

Set to a list of permitted SSL/TLS protocol versions:

```
[ssl]
tls_versions = [tlsv1 | 'tlsv1.1' | 'tlsv1.2']
```

3.4.3 Cross-Origin Resource Sharing

[cors]

New in version 1.3: added CORS support, see JIRA COUCHDB-431

CORS, or "Cross-Origin Resource Sharing", allows a resource such as a web page running JavaScript inside a browser, to make AJAX requests (XMLHttpRequests) to a different domain, without compromising the security of either party.

A typical use case is to have a static website hosted on a CDN make requests to another resource, such as a hosted CouchDB instance. This avoids needing an intermediary proxy, using *JSONP* or similar workarounds to retrieve and host content.

While CouchDB's integrated HTTP server has support for document attachments makes this less of a constraint for pure CouchDB projects, there are many cases where separating the static content from the database access is desirable, and CORS makes this very straightforward.

By supporting CORS functionality, a CouchDB instance can accept direct connections to protected databases and instances, without the browser functionality being blocked due to same-origin constraints. CORS is supported today on over 90% of recent browsers.

CORS support is provided as experimental functionality in 1.3, and as such will need to be enabled specifically in CouchDB's configuration. While all origins are forbidden from making requests by default, support is available for simple requests, preflight requests and per-vhost configuration.

This section requires *httpd/enable_cors* option have true value:

```
[httpd]
enable_cors = true
```

credentials

By default, neither authentication headers nor cookies are included in requests and responses. To do so requires both setting XmlHttpRequest.withCredentials = true on the request object in the browser and enabling credentials support in CouchDB.

```
[cors]
credentials = true
```

CouchDB will respond to a credentials-enabled CORS request with an additional header, Access-Control-Allow-Credentials=true.

origins

List of origins separated by a comma, * means accept all. You can't set origins = * and credentials = true option at the same time:

```
[cors]
origins = *
```

Access can be restricted by protocol, host and optionally by port. Origins must follow the scheme:
http://example.com:80:

```
[cors]
origins = http://localhost, https://localhost, http://couch.mydev.name:8080
```

Note that by default, no origins are accepted. You must define them explicitly.

headers
List of accepted headers separated by a comma:

```
[cors]
headers = X-Couch-Id, X-Couch-Rev
```

methods
List of accepted methods:

```
[cors]
methods = GET,POST
```

See also:

Original JIRA implementation ticket

Standards and References:

- IETF RFCs relating to methods: **RFC 2618, RFC 2817, RFC 5789**

- IETF RFC for Web Origins: **RFC 6454**

- W3C CORS standard

Mozilla Developer Network Resources:

- Same origin policy for URIs

- HTTP Access Control

- Server-side Access Control

- JavaScript same origin policy

Client-side CORS support and usage:

- CORS browser support matrix

- COS tutorial

- XHR with CORS

Per Virtual Host Configuration

To set the options for a *vhosts*, you will need to create a section with the vhost name prefixed by `cors:`.
Example case for the vhost *example.com*:

```
[cors:example.com]
credentials = false
; List of origins separated by a comma
origins = *
; List of accepted headers separated by a comma
headers = X-CouchDB-Header
; List of accepted methods
methods = HEAD, GET
```

3.4.4 Virtual Hosts

[vhosts]

CouchDB can map requests to different locations based on the `Host` header, even if they arrive on the same inbound IP address.

This allows different virtual hosts on the same machine to map to different databases or design documents, etc. The most common use case is to map a virtual host to a *Rewrite Handler*, to provide full control over the application's URIs.

To add a virtual host, add a *CNAME* pointer to the DNS for your domain name. For development and testing, it is sufficient to add an entry in the hosts file, typically */etc/hosts'* on Unix-like operating systems:

```
# CouchDB vhost definitions, refer to local.ini for further details
127.0.0.1        couchdb.local
```

Test that this is working:

```
$ ping -n 2 couchdb.local
PING couchdb.local (127.0.0.1) 56(84) bytes of data.
64 bytes from localhost (127.0.0.1): icmp_req=1 ttl=64 time=0.025 ms
64 bytes from localhost (127.0.0.1): icmp_req=2 ttl=64 time=0.051 ms
```

Finally, add an entry to your *configuration file* in the `[vhosts]` section:

```
[vhosts]
couchdb.local:5984 = /example
*.couchdb.local:5984 = /example
```

If your CouchDB is listening on the the default HTTP port (80), or is sitting behind a proxy, then you don't need to specify a port number in the *vhost* key.

The first line will rewrite the request to display the content of the *example* database. This rule works only if the `Host` header is `couchdb.local` and won't work for *CNAMEs*. The second rule, on the other hand, matches all *CNAMEs* to *example* db, so that both *www.couchdb.local* and *db.couchdb.local* will work.

Rewriting Hosts to a Path

Like in the *_rewrite* handler you can match some variable and use them to create the target path. Some examples:

```
[vhosts]
*.couchdb.local = /*
:dbname. = /:dbname
:ddocname.:dbname.example.com = /:dbname/_design/:ddocname/_rewrite
```

The first rule passes the wildcard as *dbname*. The second one does the same, but uses a variable name. And the third one allows you to use any URL with *ddocname* in any database with *dbname*.

You could also change the default function to handle request by changing the setting `httpd/redirect_vhost_handler`.

3.5 Authentication and Authorization

3.5.1 Server Administrators

[admins]

A default CouchDB install provides admin-level access to all connecting users. This configuration is known as *Admin Party*, and is not recommended for in-production usage. You can crash the party simply by creating the first admin account. CouchDB server administrators and passwords are not stored in the _users database, but in the `local.ini` file, which should be appropriately secured and readable only by system administrators:

```
[admins]
;admin = mysecretpassword
admin = -hashed-6d3c30241ba0aaa4e16c6ea99224f915687ed8cd,7f4a3e05e0cbc6f48a0035e3508e
architect = -pbkdf2-43ecbd256a70a3a2f7de40d2374b6c3002918834,921a12f74df0c1052b3e562a
```

Administrators can be added directly to the [admins] section, and when CouchDB is restarted, the passwords will be salted and encrypted. You may also use the HTTP interface to create administrator accounts; this way, you don't need to restart CouchDB, and there's no need to temporarily store or transmit passwords in plaintext. The HTTP _config/admins endpoint supports querying, deleting or creating new admin accounts:

```
GET /_config/admins HTTP/1.1
Accept: application/json
Host: localhost:5984
```

```
HTTP/1.1 200 OK
Cache-Control: must-revalidate
Content-Length: 196
Content-Type: application/json
Date: Fri, 30 Nov 2012 11:37:18 GMT
Server: CouchDB (Erlang/OTP)
```

```
{
    "admin": "-hashed-6d3c30241ba0aaa4e16c6ea99224f915687ed8cd,7f4a3e05e0cbc6f48a0035
    "architect": "-pbkdf2-43ecbd256a70a3a2f7de40d2374b6c3002918834,921a12f74df0c1052b
}
```

If you already have a salted, encrypted password string (for example, from an old local.ini file, or from a different CouchDB server), then you can store the "raw" encrypted string, without having CouchDB doubly encrypt it.

```
PUT /_config/admins/architect?raw=true HTTP/1.1
Accept: application/json
Content-Type: application/json
Content-Length: 89
Host: localhost:5984

"-pbkdf2-43ecbd256a70a3a2f7de40d2374b6c3002918834,921a12f74df0c1052b3e562a23cd227f,1(
```

```
HTTP/1.1 200 OK
Cache-Control: must-revalidate
Content-Length: 89
Content-Type: application/json
Date: Fri, 30 Nov 2012 11:39:18 GMT
Server: CouchDB (Erlang/OTP)

"-pbkdf2-43ecbd256a70a3a2f7de40d2374b6c3002918834,921a12f74df0c1052b3e562a23cd227f,1(
```

Further details are available in *security*, including configuring the work factor for PBKDF2, and the algorithm itself at PBKDF2 (RFC-2898).

Changed in version 1.4: *PBKDF2* server-side hashed salted password support added, now as a synchronous call for the _config/admins API.

3.5.2 Authentication Configuration

[couch_httpd_auth]

allow_persistent_cookies
    Makes cookies persistent if true.

```
[couch_httpd_auth]
allow_persistent_cookies = false
```

auth_cache_size

Number of *User Context Object* to cache in memory, to reduce disk lookups.

```
[couch_httpd_auth]
auth_cache_size = 50
```

authentication_db

Specifies the name of the system database for storing CouchDB users.

```
[couch_httpd_auth]
authentication_db = _users
```

> **Warning:** If you change the database name, do not forget to remove or clean up the old database, since it will no longer be protected by CouchDB.

authentication_redirect

Specifies the location for redirection on successful authentication if a `text/html` response is accepted by the client (via an `Accept` header).

```
[couch_httpd_auth]
authentication_redirect = /_utils/session.html
```

iterations

New in version 1.3.

The number of iterations for password hashing by the PBKDF2 algorithm. A higher number provides better hash durability, but comes at a cost in performance for each request that requires authentication.

```
[couch_httpd_auth]
iterations = 10000
```

min_iterations

New in version 1.6.

The minimum number of iterations allowed for passwords hashed by the PBKDF2 algorithm. Any user with fewer iterations is forbidden.

```
[couch_httpd_auth]
min_iterations = 100
```

max_iterations

New in version 1.6.

The maximum number of iterations allowed for passwords hashed by the PBKDF2 algorithm. Any user with greater iterations is forbidden.

```
[couch_httpd_auth]
max_iterations = 100000
```

proxy_use_secret

When this option is set to `true`, the `couch_httpd_auth/secret` option is required for *Proxy Authentication*.

```
[couch_httpd_auth]
proxy_use_secret = false
```

public_fields

New in version 1.4.

A comma-separated list of field names in user documents (in `couch_httpd_auth/authentication_db`) that can be read by any user. If unset or not specified, authenticated users can only retrieve their own document.

```
[couch_httpd_auth]
public_fields = first_name, last_name, contacts, url
```

Note: Using the `public_fields` whitelist for user document properties requires setting the `couch_httpd_auth/users_db_public` option to `true` (the latter option has no other purpose):

```
[couch_httpd_auth]
users_db_public = true
```

require_valid_user

When this option is set to `true`, no requests are allowed from anonymous users. Everyone must be authenticated.

```
[couch_httpd_auth]
require_valid_user = false
```

secret

The secret token is used for *Proxy Authentication* and for *Cookie Authentication*.

```
[couch_httpd_auth]
secret = 92de07df7e7a3fe14808cef90a7cc0d91
```

timeout

Number of seconds since the last request before sessions will be expired.

```
[couch_httpd_auth]
timeout = 600
```

users_db_public

New in version 1.4.

Allow all users to view user documents. By default, only admins may browse all users documents, while users may browse only their own document.

```
[couch_httpd_auth]
users_db_public = false
```

x_auth_roles

The HTTP header name (X-Auth-CouchDB-Roles by default) that contains the list of a user's roles, separated by a comma. Used for *Proxy Authentication*.

```
[couch_httpd_auth]
x_auth_roles = X-Auth-CouchDB-Roles
```

x_auth_token

The HTTP header name (X-Auth-CouchDB-Token by default) containing the token used to authenticate the authorization. This token is an *HMAC-SHA1* created from the `couch_httpd_auth/secret` and `couch_httpd_auth/x_auth_username`. The secret key should be the same on the client and the CouchDB node. This token is optional if the value of the `couch_httpd_auth/proxy_use_secret` option is not `true`. Used for *Proxy Authentication*.

```
[couch_httpd_auth]
x_auth_roles = X-Auth-CouchDB-Token
```

x_auth_username

The HTTP header name (X-Auth-CouchDB-UserName by default) containing the username. Used for *Proxy Authentication*.

```
[couch_httpd_auth]
x_auth_username = X-Auth-CouchDB-UserName
```

3.5.3 HTTP OAuth Configuration

[couch_httpd_oauth]

New in version 1.2.

use_users_db

CouchDB is able to store OAuth credentials within user documents instead of config file by using this option:

```
[couch_httpd_oauth]
use_users_db = true
```

If set to `true`, OAuth token and consumer secrets will be looked up in the *authentication database*. These secrets are stored in a top level field named `"oauth"` in user documents, as below.

```
{
    "_id": "org.couchdb.user:joe",
    "type": "user",
    "name": "joe",
    "password_sha": "fe95df1ca59a9b567bdca5cbaf8412abd6e06121",
    "salt": "4e170ffeb6f34daecfd814dfb4001a73"
    "roles": ["foo", "bar"],
    "oauth": {
        "consumer_keys": {
            "consumerKey1": "key1Secret",
            "consumerKey2": "key2Secret"
        },
        "tokens": {
            "token1": "token1Secret",
            "token2": "token2Secret"
        }
    }
}
```

3.5.4 OAuth Configuration

[oauth_*]

To let users be authenticated by *OAuth Authentication* (**RFC 5849**), three special sections must be set up in the *configuration* file:

1. The Consumer secret:

```
[oauth_consumer_secrets]
consumer1 = sekr1t
```

2. Token secrets:

```
[oauth_token_secrets]
token1 = tokensekr1t
```

3. A mapping from tokens to users:

```
[oauth_token_users]
token1 = couchdb_username
```

3.6 Compaction Configuration

3.6.1 Database Compaction Options

`[database_compaction]`

doc_buffer_size
Specifies the copy buffer's maximum size in bytes:

```
[database_compaction]
doc_buffer_size = 524288
```

checkpoint_after
Triggers a checkpoint after the specified amount of bytes were successfully copied to the compacted database:

```
[database_compaction]
checkpoint_after = 5242880
```

3.6.2 Compaction Daemon Rules

`[compactions]`
A list of rules to determine when to run automatic compaction. The *daemons/compaction_daemon* compacts databases and their respective view groups when all the condition parameters are satisfied. Configuration can be per-database or global, and it has the following format:

```
[compactions]
database_name = [ {ParamName, ParamValue}, {ParamName, ParamValue}, ... ]
_default = [ {ParamName, ParamValue}, {ParamName, ParamValue}, ... ]
```

For example:

```
[compactions]
_default = [{db_fragmentation, "70%"}, {view_fragmentation, "60%"}, {from, "23:00"},
```

- **db_fragmentation**: If the ratio of legacy data, including metadata, to current data in the database file size is equal to or greater than this value, this condition is satisfied. The percentage is expressed as an integer percentage. This value is computed as:

```
(file_size - data_size) / file_size * 100
```

The data_size and file_size values can be obtained when querying *GET /{db}*.

- **view_fragmentation**: If the ratio of legacy data, including metadata, to current data in a view index file size is equal to or greater then this value, this database compaction condition is satisfied. The percentage is expressed as an integer percentage. This value is computed as:

```
(file_size - data_size) / file_size * 100
```

The data_size and file_size values can be obtained when querying a *view group's information URI*.

- **from** and **to**: The period for which a database (and its view group) compaction is allowed. The value for these parameters must obey the format:

```
HH:MM - HH:MM  (HH in [0..23], MM in [0..59])
```

- **strict_window**: If a compaction is still running after the end of the allowed period, it will be canceled if this parameter is set to *true*. It defaults to *false* and is meaningful only if the *period* parameter is also specified.

•parallel_view_compaction: If set to *true*, the database and its views are compacted in parallel. This is only useful on certain setups, like for example when the database and view index directories point to different disks. It defaults to *false*.

Before a compaction is triggered, an estimation of how much free disk space is needed is computed. This estimation corresponds to two times the data size of the database or view index. When there's not enough free disk space to compact a particular database or view index, a warning message is logged.

Examples:

1. [{db_fragmentation, "70%"}, {view_fragmentation, "60%"}]

   The *foo* database is compacted if its fragmentation is 70% or more. Any view index of this database is compacted only if its fragmentation is 60% or more.

2. [{db_fragmentation, "70%"}, {view_fragmentation, "60%"}, {from, "00:00"}, {to, "04:00"}]

   Similar to the preceding example but a compaction (database or view index) is only triggered if the current time is between midnight and 4 AM.

3. [{db_fragmentation, "70%"}, {view_fragmentation, "60%"}, {from, "00:00"}, {to, "04:00"}, {strict_window, true}]

   Similar to the preceding example - a compaction (database or view index) is only triggered if the current time is between midnight and 4 AM. If at 4 AM the database or one of its views is still compacting, the compaction process will be canceled.

4. [{db_fragmentation, "70%"}, {view_fragmentation, "60%"}, {from, "00:00"}, {to, "04:00"}, {strict_window, true}, {parallel_view_compaction, true}]

   Similar to the preceding example, but a database and its views can be compacted in parallel.

3.6.3 Configuration of Compaction Daemon

[compaction_daemon]

check_interval
   The delay, in seconds, between each check for which database and view indexes need to be compacted:

```
[compaction_daemon]
check_interval = 300
```

min_file_size
   If a database or view index file is smaller than this value (in bytes), compaction will not happen. Very small files always have high fragmentation, so compacting them is inefficient.

```
[compaction_daemon]
min_file_size = 131072
```

3.6.4 Views Compaction Options

[view_compaction]

keyvalue_buffer_size
   Specifies maximum copy buffer size in bytes used during compaction:

```
[view_compaction]
keyvalue_buffer_size = 2097152
```

3.7 Logging

3.7.1 Logging options

`[log]`
> CouchDB logging configuration.

> **`file`**
>> Specifies the location of file for logging output:

```
[log]
file = /var/log/couchdb/couch.log
```

>> This path should be readable and writable for user that runs CouchDB service (*couchdb* by default).

> **`level`**
>> Changed in version 1.3:: Added `warning` level.

>> Logging level defines how verbose and detailed logging will be:

```
[log]
level = info
```

>> Available levels:

>>> •`debug`: Very informative and detailed debug logging. Includes HTTP headers, external processes communications, authorization information and more;

>>> •`info`: Informative logging. Includes HTTP requests headlines, startup of an external processes etc.

>>> •`warning`: Warning messages are alerts about edge situations that may lead to errors. For instance, compaction daemon alerts about low or insufficient disk space at this level.

>>> •`error`: Error level includes only things that going wrong, crush reports and HTTP error responses (5xx codes).

>>> •`none`: Disables logging any messages.

> **`include_sasl`**
>> Includes SASL information in logs:

```
[log]
include_sasl = true
```

3.7.2 Per module logging

`[log_level_by_module]`
> New in version 1.3.

> In this section you can specify *log level* on a per-module basis:

```
[log_level_by_module]
couch_httpd = debug
couch_replicator = info
couch_query_servers = error
```

See src/*/*.erl for available modules.

3.8 Replicator

3.8.1 Replicator Database Configuration

[replicator]
New in version 1.2.

db

Specifies replicator database name:

```
[replicator]
db = _replicator
```

max_replication_retry_count

Maximum replication retry count can be a non-negative integer or "infinity":

```
[replicator]
max_replication_retry_count = 10
```

worker_batch_size

With lower batch sizes checkpoints are done more frequently. Lower batch sizes also reduce the total amount of used RAM memory:

```
[replicator]
worker_batch_size = 500
```

worker_processes

More worker processes can give higher network throughput but can also imply more disk and network IO:

```
[replicator]
worker_processes = 4
```

http_connections

Maximum number of HTTP connections per replication:

```
[replicator]
http_connections = 20
```

connection_timeout

HTTP connection timeout per replication. Even for very fast/reliable networks it might need to be increased if a remote database is too busy:

```
[replicator]
connection_timeout = 30000
```

retries_per_request

If a request fails, the replicator will retry it up to N times:

```
[replicator]
retries_per_request = 10
```

socket_options

Some socket options that might boost performance in some scenarios:

- {nodelay, boolean()}

- {sndbuf, integer()}

- {recbuf, integer()}

- {priority, integer()}

See the inet Erlang module's man page for the full list of options:

         Chapter 3. Configuring CouchDB

```
[replicator]
socket_options = [{keepalive, true}, {nodelay, false}]
```

checkpoint_interval
New in version 1.6.

Defines replication checkpoint interval in milliseconds. *Replicator* will `requests` from the Source database at the specified interval:

```
[replicator]
checkpoint_interval = 5000
```

Lower intervals may be useful for frequently changing data, while higher values will lower bandwidth and make fewer requests for infrequently updated databases.

use_checkpoints
New in version 1.6.

If `use_checkpoints` is set to `true`, CouchDB will make checkpoints during replication and at the completion of replication. CouchDB can efficiently resume replication from any of these checkpoints:

```
[replicator]
use_checkpoints = true
```

Note: Checkpoints are stored in *local documents* on both the source and target databases (which requires write access).

Warning: Disabling checkpoints is **not recommended** as CouchDB will scan the Source database's changes feed from the beginning.

cert_file
Path to a file containing the user's certificate:

```
[replicator]
cert_file = /full/path/to/server_cert.pem
```

key_file
Path to file containing user's private PEM encoded key:

```
[replicator]
key_file = /full/path/to/server_key.pem
```

password
String containing the user's password. Only used if the private keyfile is password protected:

```
[replicator]
password = somepassword
```

verify_ssl_certificates
Set to true to validate peer certificates:

```
[replicator]
verify_ssl_certificates = false
```

ssl_trusted_certificates_file
File containing a list of peer trusted certificates (in the PEM format):

```
[replicator]
ssl_trusted_certificates_file = /etc/ssl/certs/ca-certificates.crt
```

ssl_certificate_max_depth
Maximum peer certificate depth (must be set even if certificate validation is off):

```
[replicator]
ssl_certificate_max_depth = 3
```

3.9 Query Servers

3.9.1 Query Servers Definition

[query_servers]

Changed in version 1.2:: Added CoffeeScript query server

CouchDB delegates computation of *design documents* functions to external query servers. The external query server is a special OS process which communicates with CouchDB over standard input/output using a very simple line-based protocol with JSON messages.

The external query server may be defined in configuration file following next pattern:

```
[query_servers]
LANGUAGE = PATH ARGS
```

Where:

- •LANGUAGE: is a programming language which code this query server may execute. For instance, there are *python*, *ruby*, *clojure* and other query servers in wild. This value is also used for *ddoc* field language to determine which query server processes the functions.

  Note, that you may set up multiple query servers for the same programming language, but you have to name them different (like *python-dev* etc.).

- •PATH: is a system path to the executable binary program that runs the query server.

- •ARGS: optionally, you may specify additional command line arguments for the executable PATH.

The default query server is written in *JavaScript*, running via Mozilla SpiderMonkey:

```
[query_servers]
javascript = /usr/bin/couchjs /usr/share/couchdb/server/main.js
coffeescript = /usr/bin/couchjs /usr/share/couchdb/server/main-coffee.js
```

See also:

Native Erlang Query Server that allows to process Erlang *ddocs* and runs within CouchDB bypassing stdio communication and JSON serialization/deserialization round trip overhead.

3.9.2 Query Servers Configuration

[query_server_config]

commit_freq

Specifies the delay in seconds before view index changes are committed to disk. The default value is 5:

```
[query_server_config]
commit_freq = 5
```

os_process_limit

Amount of time in seconds that the Query Server may process CouchDB command:

```
[query_server_config]
os_process_limit = 10
```

CouchDB will raise *os_process_timeout* error and kill the process in case the Query Server doesn't return any result within this limit.

reduce_limit

Controls *Reduce overflow* error that raises when output of *reduce functions* is too big:

```
[query_server_config]
reduce_limit = true
```

Normally, you don't have to disable (by setting `false` value) this option since main propose of *reduce* functions is to *reduce* the input.

3.9.3 Native Erlang Query Server

[native_query_servers]

> **Warning:** Due to security restrictions, the Erlang query server is disabled by default.
> Unlike the JavaScript query server, the Erlang one does not runs in a sandbox mode. This means that
> Erlang code has full access to your OS, filesystem and network, which may lead to security issues. While
> Erlang functions are faster than JavaScript ones, you need to be careful about running them, especially
> if they were written by someone else.

CouchDB has a native Erlang query server, allowing you to write your map/reduce functions in Erlang.

First, you'll need to edit your *local.ini* to include a `[native_query_servers]` section:

```
[native_query_servers]
erlang = {couch_native_process, start_link, []}
```

To see these changes you will also need to restart the server. To test out using *Erlang views*, visit the *Futon* admin interface, create a new database and open a temporary view. You should now be able to select `erlang` from the language drop-down.

Let's try an example of map/reduce functions which count the total documents at each number of revisions (there are x many documents at version "1", and y documents at "2"... etc). Add a few documents to the database, then enter the following functions as a temporary view:

```
%% Map Function
fun({Doc}) ->
    <<K,_/binary>> = proplists:get_value(<<"_rev">>, Doc, null),
    V = proplists:get_value(<<"_id">>, Doc, null),
    Emit(<<K>>, V)
end.

%% Reduce Function
fun(Keys, Values, ReReduce) -> length(Values) end.
```

If all has gone well, after running the view you should see a list of the total number of documents at each revision number.

3.10 External Processes

3.10.1 OS Daemons

[os_daemons]

This is a simple feature that allows users to configure CouchDB so that it maintains a given OS level process alive. If the process dies for any reason, CouchDB will restart it. If the process restarts too often, then CouchDB will mark it has halted and not attempt to restart it. The default max restart rate is 3 times in the last 5 seconds. These parameters are *adjustable*.

Commands that are started in this manner will have access to a simple API over stdio to request configuration parameters or to add log statements to CouchDB's logs.

To configure an OS process as a CouchDB os_daemon, create a section in your *local.ini* like such:

```
[os_daemons]
daemon_name = /path/to/command -with args
```

This will make CouchDB bring up the command and attempt to keep it alive. To request a configuration parameter, an *os_daemon* can write a simple JSON message to stdout like such:

```
["get", "os_daemons"]\n
```

which would return:

```
{"daemon_name": "/path/to/command -with args"}\n
```

Or:

```
["get", "os_daemons", "daemon_name"]\n
```

which would return:

```
"/path/to/command -with args"\n
```

There's no restriction on what configuration variables are visible. There's also no method for altering the configuration.

If you would like your OS daemon to be restarted in the event that the configuration changes, you can send the following messages:

```
["register", $(SECTION)]\n
```

When anything in that section changes, your OS process will be rebooted so it can pick up the new configuration settings. If you want to listen for changes on a specific key, you can send something like:

```
["register", $(SECTION), $(KEY)]\n
```

In this case, CouchDB will only restart your daemon if that exact section/key pair changes, instead of anything in that entire section.

Logging commands look like:

```
["log", $(JSON_MESSAGE)]\n
```

Where $(JSON_MESSAGE) is arbitrary JSON data. These messages are logged at the 'info' level. If you want to log at a different level you can pass messages like such:

```
["log", $(JSON_MESSAGE), {"level": $(LEVEL)}]\n
```

Where $(LEVEL) is one of "debug", "info", or "error".

When implementing a daemon process to be managed by CouchDB you should remember to use a method like checking the parent process id or if stdin has been closed. These flags can tell you if your daemon process has been orphaned so you can exit cleanly.

There is no interactivity between CouchDB and the running process, but you can use the OS Daemons service to create new HTTP servers and responders and then use the new proxy service to redirect requests and output to the CouchDB managed service. For more information on proxying, see *CouchDB As Proxy*. For further background on the OS Daemon service, see *CouchDB Externals API*.

3.10.2 OS Daemons settings

`[os_daemon_settings]`

max retries
Specifies maximum attempts to run `os_daemons` before mark them halted:

```
[os_daemon_settings]
max_retries = 3
```

retry_time
Delay in seconds between `os_daemons` restarts:

```
[os_daemon_settings]
retry_time = 5
```

3.10.3 Update notifications

[update_notification]
CouchDB is able to spawn OS processes to notify them about recent databases updates. The notifications are in form of JSON messages sent as a line of text, terminated by CR (\n) character, to the OS processes through *stdout*:

```
[update_notification]
;unique notifier name=/full/path/to/exe -with "cmd line arg"
index_updater = ruby /usr/local/bin/index_updater.rb
```

The update notification messages are depend upon of event type:

•**Database created**:

```
{"type":"created","db":"dbname"}
```

•**Database updated**: this event raises when any document gets updated for specified database:

```
{"type":"updated","db":"dbname"}
```

•**Design document updated**: for design document updates there is special event raised in additional to regular db update one:

```
{"type":"ddoc_updated","db":"dbname","id":"_design/ddoc_name"}
```

•**Database deleted**:

```
{"type":"deleted","db":"dbname"}
```

Note: New line (\n) trailing character was removed from examples.

3.11 HTTP Resource Handlers

3.11.1 Global HTTP Handlers

[httpd_global_handlers]
These HTTP resources are provided for CouchDB server root level.

/

```
[httpd_global_handlers]
/ = {couch_httpd_misc_handlers, handle_welcome_req, <<"Welcome">>}
```

favicon.ico
The favicon handler looks for *favicon.ico* file within specified directory:

```
[httpd_global_handlers]
favicon.ico = {couch_httpd_misc_handlers, handle_favicon_req, "/usr/share/couchd
```

_active_tasks

```
[httpd_global_handlers]
_active_tasks = {couch_httpd_misc_handlers, handle_task_status_req}
```

_all_dbs
Provides a list of all server's databases:

```
[httpd_global_handlers]
_all_dbs = {couch_httpd_misc_handlers, handle_all_dbs_req}
```

Note: Sometimes you don't want to disclose database names for everyone, but you also don't like/want/able to set up any proxies in front of CouchDB. Removing this handler disables _all_dbs resource and there will be no way to get list of available databases.

The same also is true for other resource handlers.

_config
Provides resource to work with CouchDB config *remotely*. Any config changes that was made via HTTP API are applied automatically on fly and doesn't requires server instance to be restarted:

```
[httpd_global_handlers]
_config = {couch_httpd_misc_handlers, handle_config_req}
```

_log

```
[httpd_global_handlers]
_log = {couch_httpd_misc_handlers, handle_log_req}
```

_oauth

```
[httpd_global_handlers]
_oauth = {couch_httpd_oauth, handle_oauth_req}
```

_replicate
Provides an API to run *temporary replications*:

```
[httpd_global_handlers]
_replicate = {couch_replicator_httpd, handle_req}
```

_restart

```
[httpd_global_handlers]
_restart = {couch_httpd_misc_handlers, handle_restart_req}
```

_session
Provides a resource with information about the current user's session:

```
[httpd_global_handlers]
_session = {couch_httpd_auth, handle_session_req}
```

_stats

```
[httpd_global_handlers]
_stats = {couch_httpd_stats_handlers, handle_stats_req}
```

_utils
> The _utils_ handler serves _Futon's_ web administration page.

```
[httpd_global_handlers]
_utils = {couch_httpd_misc_handlers, handle_utils_dir_req, "/usr/share/couchdb/w:
```

> In similar way, you may set up custom handler to let CouchDB serve any static files.

_uuids
> Provides a resource to get UUIDs generated by CouchDB:

```
[httpd_global_handlers]
_uuids = {couch_httpd_misc_handlers, handle_uuids_req}
```

> This is useful when your client environment isn't capable of providing truly random IDs (web browsers e.g.).

3.11.2 Database HTTP Handlers

[httpd_db_handlers]
> These HTTP resources are available on every CouchDB database.

_all_docs

```
[httpd_db_handlers]
_all_docs = {couch_mrview_http, handle_all_docs_req}
```

_local_docs

```
[httpd_db_handlers]
_local_docs = {couch_mrview_http, handle_local_docs_req}
```

_design_docs

```
[httpd_db_handlers]
_design_docs = {couch_mrview_http, handle_design_docs_req}
```

_changes

```
[httpd_db_handlers]
_changes = {couch_httpd_db, handle_changes_req}
```

_compact

```
[httpd_db_handlers]
_compact = {couch_httpd_db, handle_compact_req}
```

_design

```
[httpd_db_handlers]
_design = {couch_httpd_db, handle_design_req}
```

_temp_view

```
[httpd_db_handlers]
_temp_view = {couch_mrview_http, handle_temp_view_req}
```

```
_view_cleanup
```

```
[httpd_db_handlers]
_view_cleanup = {couch_mrview_http, handle_cleanup_req}
```

3.11.3 Design Documents HTTP Handlers

`[httpd_design_handlers]`

These HTTP resources are provided for design documents.

_compact

```
[httpd_design_handlers]
_compact = {couch_mrview_http, handle_compact_req}
```

_info

```
[httpd_design_handlers]
_info = {couch_mrview_http, handle_info_req}
```

_list

```
[httpd_design_handlers]
_list = {couch_mrview_show, handle_view_list_req}
```

_rewrite

```
[httpd_design_handlers]
_rewrite = {couch_httpd_rewrite, handle_rewrite_req}
```

_show

```
[httpd_design_handlers]
_show = {couch_mrview_show, handle_doc_show_req}
```

_update

```
[httpd_design_handlers]
_update = {couch_mrview_show, handle_doc_update_req}
```

_view

```
[httpd_design_handlers]
_view = {couch_mrview_http, handle_view_req}
```

3.12 CouchDB Internal Services

3.12.1 CouchDB Daemonized Mini Apps

`[daemons]`

auth_cache

This daemon provides authentication caching to avoid repeated opening and closing of the _users database for each request requiring authentication:

```
[daemons]
auth_cache={couch_auth_cache, start_link, []}
```

compaction_daemon

Automatic compaction daemon:

```
[daemons]
compaction_daemon={couch_compaction_daemon, start_link, []}
```

external_manager

External processes manager:

```
[daemons]
external_manager={couch_external_manager, start_link, []}
```

httpd

HTTP server daemon:

```
[daemons]
httpd={couch_httpd, start_link, []}
```

httpsd

Provides *SSL support*. The default ssl port CouchDB listens on is *6984*:

```
[daemons]
httpsd = {couch_httpd, start_link, [https]}
```

index_server

The *couch_index* application is responsible for managing all of the different types of indexers. This manages the process handling for keeping track of the index state as well as managing the updater and compactor handling:

```
[daemons]
index_server={couch_index_server, start_link, []}
```

os_daemons

OS Daemons manager:

```
[daemons]
os_daemons={couch_os_daemons, start_link, []}
```

query_servers

Query servers manager:

```
[daemons]
query_servers={couch_query_servers, start_link, []}
```

replicator_manager

Replications manager:

```
[daemons]
replicator_manager={couch_replicator_manager, start_link, []}
```

stats_aggregator

Runtime statistics aggregator:

```
[daemons]
stats_aggregator={couch_stats_aggregator, start, []}
```

stats_collector

Runtime statistics collector:

3.12. CouchDB Internal Services

```
[daemons]
stats_collector={couch_stats_collector, start, []}
```

uuids

UUIDs generator daemon:

```
[daemons]
uuids={couch_uuids, start, []}
```

vhosts

Virtual hosts manager. Provides dynamic add of vhosts without restart, wildcards support and dynamic routing via pattern matching

```
[daemons]
vhosts={couch_httpd_vhost, start_link, []}
```

3.13 Miscellaneous Parameters

3.13.1 Configuration of Attachment Storage

[attachments]

compression_level

Defines zlib compression level for the attachments from 1 (lowest, fastest) to 9 (highest, slowest). A value of 0 disables compression:

```
[attachments]
compression_level = 8
```

compressible_types

Since compression is ineffective for some types of files, it is possible to let CouchDB compress only some types of attachments, specified by their MIME type:

```
[attachments]
compressible_types = text/*, application/javascript, application/json, applicatic
```

3.13.2 Statistic Calculation

[stats]

rate

Rate of statistics gathering in milliseconds:

```
[stats]
rate = 1000
```

samples

Samples are used to track the mean and standard value deviation within specified intervals (in seconds):

```
[stats]
samples = [0, 60, 300, 900]
```

3.13.3 UUIDs Configuration

[uuids]

algorithm

Changed in version 1.3: Added utc_id algorithm.

CouchDB provides various algorithms to generate the UUID values that are used for document _id‘s by default:

```
[uuids]
algorithm = sequential
```

Available algorithms:

• random: 128 bits of random awesome. All awesome, all the time:

```
{
    "uuids": [
        "5fcbbf2cb171b1d5c3bc6df3d4affb32",
        "9115e0942372a87a977f1caf30b2ac29",
        "3840b51b0b81b46cab99384d5cd106e3",
        "b848dbdeb422164babf2705ac18173e1",
        "b7a8566af7e0fc02404bb676b47c3bf7",
        "a006879afdcae324d70e925c420c860d",
        "5f7716ee487cc4083545d4ca02cd45d4",
        "35fdd1c8346c22ccc43cc45cd632e6d6",
        "97bbdb4a1c7166682dc026e1ac97a64c",
        "eb242b506a6ae330bda6969bb2677079"
    ]
}
```

• sequential: Monotonically increasing ids with random increments. The first 26 hex characters are random, the last 6 increment in random amounts until an overflow occurs. On overflow, the random prefix is regenerated and the process starts over.

```
{
    "uuids": [
        "4e17c12963f4bee0e6ec90da54804894",
        "4e17c12963f4bee0e6ec90da5480512f",
        "4e17c12963f4bee0e6ec90da54805c25",
        "4e17c12963f4bee0e6ec90da54806ba1",
        "4e17c12963f4bee0e6ec90da548072b3",
        "4e17c12963f4bee0e6ec90da54807609",
        "4e17c12963f4bee0e6ec90da54807718",
        "4e17c12963f4bee0e6ec90da54807754",
        "4e17c12963f4bee0e6ec90da54807e5d",
        "4e17c12963f4bee0e6ec90da54808d28"
    ]
}
```

• utc_random: The time since Jan 1, 1970 UTC, in microseconds. The first 14 characters are the time in hex. The last 18 are random.

```
{
    "uuids": [
        "04dd32b3af699659b6db9486a9c58c62",
        "04dd32b3af69bb1c2ac7ebfee0a50d88",
        "04dd32b3af69d8591b99a8e86a76e0fb",
        "04dd32b3af69f4a18a76efd89867f4f4",
        "04dd32b3af6a1f7925001274bbfde952",
        "04dd32b3af6a3fe8ea9b120ed906a57f",
        "04dd32b3af6a5b5c518809d3d4b76654",
        "04dd32b3af6a78f6ab32f1e928593c73",
        "04dd32b3af6a99916c665d6bbf857475",
        "04dd32b3af6ab558dd3f2c0afacb7d66"
```

```
        ]
    }
```

• utc_id: The time since Jan 1, 1970 UTC, in microseconds, plus the utc_id_suffix string. The first 14 characters are the time in hex. The *uuids/utc_id_suffix* string value is appended to these.

```
{
    "uuids": [
        "04dd32bd5eabcc@mycouch",
        "04dd32bd5eabee@mycouch",
        "04dd32bd5eac05@mycouch",
        "04dd32bd5eac28@mycouch",
        "04dd32bd5eac43@mycouch",
        "04dd32bd5eac58@mycouch",
        "04dd32bd5eac6e@mycouch",
        "04dd32bd5eac84@mycouch",
        "04dd32bd5eac98@mycouch",
        "04dd32bd5eacad@mycouch"
    ]
}
```

Note: Impact of UUID choices: the choice of UUID has a significant impact on the layout of the B-tree, prior to compaction.

For example, using a sequential UUID algorithm while uploading a large batch of documents will avoid the need to rewrite many intermediate B-tree nodes. A random UUID algorithm may require rewriting intermediate nodes on a regular basis, resulting in significantly decreased throughput and wasted disk space space due to the append-only B-tree design.

It is generally recommended to set your own UUIDs, or use the sequential algorithm unless you have a specific need and take into account the likely need for compaction to re-balance the B-tree and reclaim wasted space.

utc_id_suffix
New in version 1.3.

The utc_id_suffix value will be appended to UUIDs generated by the utc_id algorithm. Replicating instances should have unique utc_id_suffix values to ensure uniqueness of utc_id ids.

```
[uuid]
utc_id_suffix = my-awesome-suffix
```

max_count
New in version 1.5.1.

No more than this number of UUIDs will be sent in a single request. If more UUIDs are requested, an HTTP error response will be thrown.

```
[uuid]
max_count = 1000
```

3.13.4 Vendor information

[vendor]
New in version 1.3.

CouchDB distributors have the option of customizing CouchDB's welcome message. This is returned when requesting GET /.

```
[vendor]
name = The Apache Software Foundation
version = 1.5.0
```

3.13.5 Content-Security-Policy

[csp]
> Experimental support of CSP Headers for /_utils (Fauxton).

> **enable**
> > Enable the sending of the Header Content-Security-Policy:

```
[csp]
enable = true
```

> **header_value**
> > You can change the default value for the Header which is sent:

```
[csp]
header_value = default-src 'self'; img-src *; font-src *;
```

3.14 Proxying Configuration

3.14.1 CouchDB As Proxy

The HTTP proxy feature makes it easy to map and redirect different content through your CouchDB URL. The proxy works by mapping a pathname and passing all content after that prefix through to the configured proxy address.

Configuration of the proxy redirect is handled through the [httpd_global_handlers] section of the CouchDB configuration file (typically local.ini). The format is:

```
[httpd_global_handlers]
PREFIX = {couch_httpd_proxy, handle_proxy_req, <<"DESTINATION">>}
```

Where:

- PREFIX

  Is the string that will be matched. The string can be any valid qualifier, although to ensure that existing database names are not overridden by a proxy configuration, you can use an underscore prefix.

- DESTINATION

  The fully-qualified URL to which the request should be sent. The destination must include the http prefix. The content is used verbatim in the original request, so you can also forward to servers on different ports and to specific paths on the target host.

The proxy process then translates requests of the form:

```
http://couchdb:5984/PREFIX/path
```

To:

```
DESTINATION/path
```

Note: Everything after PREFIX including the required forward slash will be appended to the DESTINATION.

The response is then communicated back to the original client.

For example, the following configuration:

```
[httpd_global_handlers]
_google = {couch_httpd_proxy, handle_proxy_req, <<"http://www.google.com">>}
```

Would forward all requests for `http://couchdb:5984/_google` to the Google website.

The service can also be used to forward to related CouchDB services, such as *Lucene*:

```
[httpd_global_handlers]
_fti = {couch_httpd_proxy, handle_proxy_req, <<"http://127.0.0.1:5985">>}
```

Note: The proxy service is basic. If the request is not identified by the DESTINATION, or the remainder of the PATH specification is incomplete, the original request URL is interpreted as if the PREFIX component of that URL does not exist.

For example, requesting `http://couchdb:5984/_intranet/media` when `/media` on the proxy destination does not exist, will cause the request URL to be interpreted as `http://couchdb:5984/media`. Care should be taken to ensure that both requested URLs and destination URLs are able to cope.

## CHAPTER 4

Replication

The replication is an incremental one way process involving two databases (a source and a destination).

The aim of the replication is that at the end of the process, all active documents on the source database are also in the destination database and all documents that were deleted in the source databases are also deleted (if exists) on the destination database.

The replication process only copies the last revision of a document, so all previous revisions that were only on the source database are not copied to the destination database.

4.1 Introduction to Replication

One of CouchDB's strengths is the ability to synchronize two copies of the same database. This enables users to distribute data across several nodes or datacenters, but also to move data more closely to clients.

Replication involves a source and a destination database, which can be on the same or on different CouchDB instances. The aim of the replication is that at the end of the process, all active documents on the source database are also in the destination database and all documents that were deleted in the source databases are also deleted on the destination database (if they even existed).

4.1.1 Triggering Replication

Replication is controlled through documents in the _replicator_ database, where each document describes one replication process (see *Replication Settings*).

A replication is triggered by storing a replication document in the replicator database. Its status can be inspected through the active tasks API (see */_active_tasks* and *Replication Status*). A replication can be stopped by deleting the document, or by updating it with its *cancel* property set to *true*.

4.1.2 Replication Procedure

During replication, CouchDB will compare the source and the destination database to determine which documents differ between the source and the destination database. It does so by following the *Changes Feeds* on the source and comparing the documents to the destination. Changes are submitted to the destination in batches where they can introduce conflicts. Documents that already exist on the destination in the same revision are not transferred. As the deletion of documents is represented by a new revision, a document deleted on the source will also be deleted on the target.

A replication task will finish once it reaches the end of the changes feed. If its *continuous* property is set to true, it will wait for new changes to appear until the task is cancelled. Replication tasks also create checkpoint documents on the destination to ensure that a restarted task can continue from where it stopped, for example after it has crashed.

When a replication task is initiated on the sending node, it is called *push* replication, if it is initiated by the receiving node, it is called *pull* replication.

4.1.3 Master - Master replication

One replication task will only transfer changes in one direction. To achieve master-master replication, it is possible to set up two replication tasks in opposite direction. When a change is replicated from database A to B by the first task, the second task from B to A will discover that the new change on B already exists in A and will wait for further changes.

4.1.4 Controlling which Documents to Replicate

There are two ways for controlling which documents are replicated, and which are skipped. *Local* documents are never replicated (see *Local (non-replicating) Documents*).

Additionally, *Filter functions* can be used in a replication (see *Replication Settings*). The replication task will then evaluate the filter function for each document in the changes feed. The document will only be replicated if the filter returns *true*.

4.1.5 Migrating Data to Clients

Replication can be especially useful for bringing data closer to clients. PouchDB implements the replication algorithm of CouchDB in JavaScript, making it possible to make data from a CouchDB database available in an offline browser application, and synchronize changes back to CouchDB.

4.2 CouchDB Replication Protocol

Version 3

The *CouchDB Replication Protocol* is a protocol for synchronising JSON documents between 2 peers over HTTP/1.1 by using the public *CouchDB REST API* and is based on the Apache CouchDB MVCC Data model.

4.2.1 Preface

Language

The key words "MUST", "MUST NOT", "REQUIRED", "SHALL", "SHALL NOT", "SHOULD", "SHOULD NOT", "RECOMMENDED", "MAY", and "OPTIONAL" in this document are to be interpreted as described in RFC 2119.

Goals

The primary goal of this specification is to describe the *CouchDB Replication Protocol* under the hood.

The secondary goal is to provide enough detailed information about the protocol to make it easy to build tools on any language and platform that can synchronize data with CouchDB.

Definitions

JSON: JSON (JavaScript Object Notation) is a text format for the serialization of structured data. It is described in ECMA-262 and RFC 4627.

URI: A URI is defined by RFC 3986. It can be a URL as defined in RFC 1738.

ID: An identifier (could be a UUID) as described in RFC 4122.

Revision: A MVCC token value of following pattern: N-sig where N is ALWAYS a positive integer and sig is the Document signature (custom). Don't mix it up with the revision in version control systems!

Leaf Revision: The last Document Revision in a series of changes. Documents may have multiple Leaf Revisions (aka Conflict Revisions) due to concurrent updates.

Document: A document is a JSON object with an ID and Revision defined in _id and _rev fields respectively. A Document's ID MUST be unique within the Database where it is stored.

Database: A collection of Documents with a unique URI.

Changes Feed: A stream of Document-changing events (create, update, delete) for the specified Database.

Sequence ID: An ID provided by the Changes Feed. It MUST be incremental, but MAY NOT always be an integer.

Source: Database from where the Documents are replicated.

Target: Database where the Documents are replicated to.

Replication: The one-way directed synchronization process of Source and Target endpoints.

Checkpoint: Intermediate Recorded Sequence ID used for Replication recovery.

Replicator: A service or an application which initiates and runs Replication.

Filter Function: A special function of any programming language that is used to filter Documents during Replication (see *Filter functions*)

Filter Function Name: An ID of a Filter Function that may be used as a symbolic reference (aka callback function) to apply the related Filter Function to Replication.

Filtered Replication: Replication of Documents from Source to Target using a Filter Function.

Full Replication: Replication of all Documents from Source to Target.

Push Replication: Replication process where Source is a local endpoint and Target is remote.

Pull Replication: Replication process where Source is a remote endpoint and Target is local.

Continuous Replication: Replication that "never stops": after processing all events from the Changes Feed, the Replicator doesn't close the connection, but awaits new change events from the Source. The connection is kept alive by periodic heartbeats.

Replication Log: A special Document that holds Replication history (recorded Checkpoints and a few more statistics) between Source and Target.

Replication ID: A unique value that unambiguously identifies the Replication Log.

4.2.2 Replication Protocol Algorithm

The *CouchDB Replication Protocol* is not *magical*, but an agreement on usage of the public *CouchDB HTTP REST API* to enable Documents to be replicated from Source to Target.

The reference implementation, written in Erlang, is provided by the couch_replicator module in Apache CouchDB.

It is RECOMMENDED that one follow this algorithm specification, use the same HTTP endpoints, and run requests with the same parameters to provide a completely compatible implementation. Custom Replicator implementations MAY use different HTTP API endpoints and request parameters depending on their local specifics and they MAY implement only part of the Replication Protocol to run only Push or Pull Replication. However, while such solutions could also run the Replication process, they loose compatibility with the CouchDB Replicator.

Verify Peers

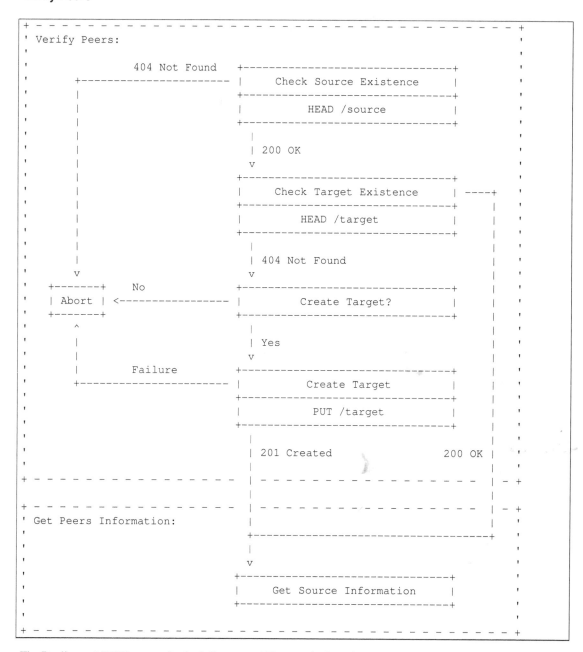

The Replicator MUST ensure that both Source and Target exist by using *HEAD /{db}* requests.

Check Source Existence

Request:

```
HEAD /source HTTP/1.1
Host: localhost:5984
User-Agent: CouchDB
```

Response:

```
HTTP/1.1 200 OK
Cache-Control: must-revalidate
```

```
Content-Type: application/json
Date: Sat, 05 Oct 2013 08:50:20 GMT
Server: CouchDB (Erlang/OTP)
```

Check Target Existence

Request:

```
HEAD /target HTTP/1.1
Host: localhost:5984
User-Agent: CouchDB
```

Response:

```
HTTP/1.1 200 OK
Cache-Control: must-revalidate
Content-Type: application/json
Date: Sat, 05 Oct 2013 08:51:11 GMT
Server: CouchDB (Erlang/OTP)
```

Create Target?

In case of a non-existent Target, the Replicator MAY make a *PUT /{db}* request to create the Target:

Request:

```
PUT /target HTTP/1.1
Accept: application/json
Host: localhost:5984
User-Agent: CouchDB
```

Response:

```
HTTP/1.1 201 Created
Content-Length: 12
Content-Type: application/json
Date: Sat, 05 Oct 2013 08:58:41 GMT
Server: CouchDB (Erlang/OTP)

{
    "ok": true
}
```

However, the Replicator's PUT request MAY NOT succeeded due to insufficient privileges (which are granted by the provided credential) and so receive a 401 Unauthorized or a 403 Forbidden error. Such errors SHOULD be expected and well handled:

```
HTTP/1.1 500 Internal Server Error
Cache-Control: must-revalidate
Content-Length: 108
Content-Type: application/json
Date: Fri, 09 May 2014 13:50:32 GMT
Server: CouchDB (Erlang OTP)

{
    "error": "unauthorized",
    "reason": "unauthorized to access or create database http://localhost:5984/target
}
```

Abort

In case of a non-existent Source or Target, Replication SHOULD be aborted with an HTTP error response:

```
HTTP/1.1 500 Internal Server Error
Cache-Control: must-revalidate
Content-Length: 56
Content-Type: application/json
Date: Sat, 05 Oct 2013 08:55:29 GMT
Server: CouchDB (Erlang OTP)

{
    "error": "db_not_found",
    "reason": "could not open source"
}
```

Get Peers Information

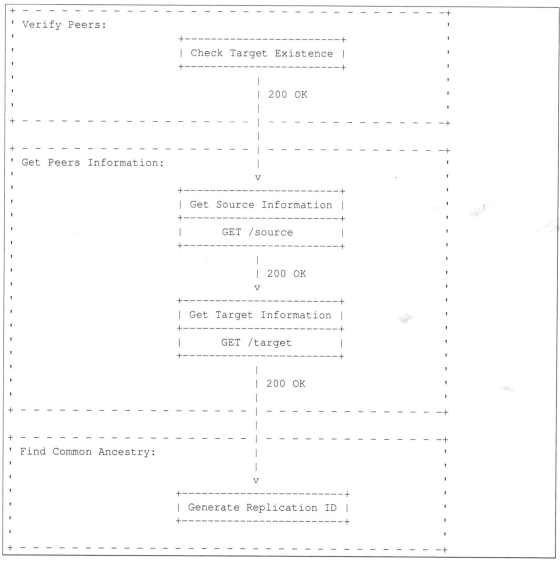

The Replicator retrieves basic information both from Source and Target using *GET /{db}* requests. The GET response MUST contain JSON objects with the following mandatory fields:

- **instance_start_time** (*string*): Timestamp when the Database was opened, expressed in *microseconds* since the epoch

- **update_seq** (*number* / *string*): The current database Sequence ID.

Any other fields are optional. The information that the Replicator needs is the `update_seq` field: this value will be used to define a *temporary* (because Database data is subject to change) upper bound for changes feed listening and statistic calculating to show proper Replication progress.

Get Source Information

Request:

```
GET /source HTTP/1.1
Accept: application/json
Host: localhost:5984
User-Agent: CouchDB
```

Response:

```
HTTP/1.1 200 OK
Cache-Control: must-revalidate
Content-Length: 256
Content-Type: application/json
Date: Tue, 08 Oct 2013 07:53:08 GMT
Server: CouchDB (Erlang OTP)

{
    "committed_update_seq": 61772,
    "compact_running": false,
    "data_size": 70781613961,
    "db_name": "source",
    "disk_format_version": 6,
    "disk_size": 79132913799,
    "doc_count": 41961,
    "doc_del_count": 3807,
    "instance_start_time": "1380901070238216",
    "purge_seq": 0,
    "update_seq": 61772
}
```

Get Target Information

Request:

```
GET /target/ HTTP/1.1
Accept: application/json
Host: localhost:5984
User-Agent: CouchDB
```

Response:

```
HTTP/1.1 200 OK
Content-Length: 363
Content-Type: application/json
Date: Tue, 08 Oct 2013 12:37:01 GMT
Server: CouchDB (Erlang/OTP)

{
    "compact_running": false,
    "db_name": "target",
    "disk_format_version": 5,
```

```
    "disk_size": 77001455,
    "doc_count": 1832,
    "doc_del_count": 1,
    "instance_start_time": "0",
    "other": {
        "data_size": 50829452
    },
    "purge_seq": 0,
    "update_seq": "1841-g1AAAADveJzLYWBgYMlgTmGQT0lKzi9KdUhJMtbLSs1LLUst0k"
}
```

Find Common Ancestry

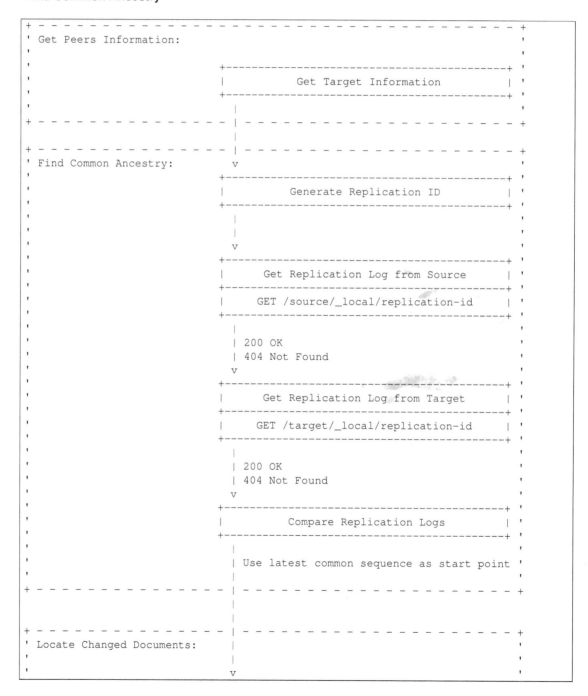

```
'                            +--------------------------------------+  '
'                            |         Listen Source Changes Feed   |  '
'                            +--------------------------------------+  '
'                                                                      '
+ - - - - - - - - - - - - - - - - - - - - - - - - - - - - - - - - - +
```

Generate Replication ID

Before Replication is started, the Replicator MUST generate a Replication ID. This value is used to track Replication History, resume and continue previously interrupted Replication process.

The Replication ID generation algorithm is implementation specific. Whatever algorithm is used it MUST uniquely identify the Replication process. CouchDB's Replicator, for example, uses the following factors in generating a Replication ID:

- Persistent Peer UUID value. For CouchDB, the local *Server UUID* is used
- Source and Target URI and if Source or Target are local or remote Databases
- If Target needed to be created
- If Replication is Continuous
- OAuth headers if any
- Any custom headers
- *Filter function* code if used
- Changes Feed query parameters, if any

Note: See couch_replicator_utils.erl for an example of a Replication ID generation implementation.

Retrieve Replication Logs from Source and Target

Once the Replication ID has been generated, the Replicator SHOULD retrieve the Replication Log from both Source and Target using *GET /{db}/_local/{docid}*:

Request:

```
GET /source/_local/b3e44b920ee2951cb2e123b63044427a HTTP/1.1
Accept: application/json
Host: localhost:5984
User-Agent: CouchDB
```

Response:

```
HTTP/1.1 200 OK
Cache-Control: must-revalidate
Content-Length: 1019
Content-Type: application/json
Date: Thu, 10 Oct 2013 06:18:56 GMT
ETag: "0-8"
Server: CouchDB (Erlang OTP)

{
    "_id": "_local/b3e44b920ee2951cb2e123b63044427a",
    "_rev": "0-8",
    "history": [
        {
            "doc_write_failures": 0,
            "docs_read": 2,
            "docs_written": 2,
```

```
            "end_last_seq": 5,
            "end_time": "Thu, 10 Oct 2013 05:56:38 GMT",
            "missing_checked": 2,
            "missing_found": 2,
            "recorded_seq": 5,
            "session_id": "d5a34cbbdafa70e0db5cb57d02a6b955",
            "start_last_seq": 3,
            "start_time": "Thu, 10 Oct 2013 05:56:38 GMT"
        },
        {
            "doc_write_failures": 0,
            "docs_read": 1,
            "docs_written": 1,
            "end_last_seq": 3,
            "end_time": "Thu, 10 Oct 2013 05:56:12 GMT",
            "missing_checked": 1,
            "missing_found": 1,
            "recorded_seq": 3,
            "session_id": "11a79cdae1719c362e9857cd1ddff09d",
            "start_last_seq": 2,
            "start_time": "Thu, 10 Oct 2013 05:56:12 GMT"
        },
        {
            "doc_write_failures": 0,
            "docs_read": 2,
            "docs_written": 2,
            "end_last_seq": 2,
            "end_time": "Thu, 10 Oct 2013 05:56:04 GMT",
            "missing_checked": 2,
            "missing_found": 2,
            "recorded_seq": 2,
            "session_id": "77cdf93cde05f15fcb710f320c37c155",
            "start_last_seq": 0,
            "start_time": "Thu, 10 Oct 2013 05:56:04 GMT"
        }
    ],
    "replication_id_version": 3,
    "session_id": "d5a34cbbdafa70e0db5cb57d02a6b955",
    "source_last_seq": 5
}
```

The Replication Log SHOULD contain the following fields:

- **history** (*array* of *object*): Replication history. **Required**

    - **doc_write_failures** (*number*): Number of failed writes

    - **docs_read** (*number*): Number of read documents

    - **docs_written** (*number*): Number of written documents

    - **end_last_seq** (*number*): Last processed Update Sequence ID

    - **end_time** (*string*): Replication completion datetime in **RFC 5322** format

    - **missing_checked** (*number*): Number of checked revisions on Source

    - **missing_found** (*number*): Number of missing revisions found on Target

    - **recorded_seq** (*number*): Recorded intermediate Checkpoint. **Required**

    - **session_id** (*string*): Unique session ID. Commonly, a random UUID value is used. **Required**

    - **start_last_seq** (*number*): Start update Sequence ID

    - **start_time** (*string*): Replication start datetime in **RFC 5322** format

- **replication_id_version** (*number*): Replication protocol version. Defines Replication ID calculation algorithm, HTTP API calls and the others routines. **Required**

- **session_id** (*string*): Unique ID of the last session. Shortcut to the `session_id` field of the latest `history` object. **Required**

- **source_last_seq** (*number*): Last processed Checkpoint. Shortcut to the `recorded_seq` field of the latest `history` object. **Required**

This request MAY fall with a 404 Not Found response:

Request:

```
GET /source/_local/b6cef528f67aa1a8a014dd1144b10e09 HTTP/1.1
Accept: application/json
Host: localhost:5984
User-Agent: CouchDB
```

Response:

```
HTTP/1.1 404 Object Not Found
Cache-Control: must-revalidate
Content-Length: 41
Content-Type: application/json
Date: Tue, 08 Oct 2013 13:31:10 GMT
Server: CouchDB (Erlang OTP)

{
    "error": "not_found",
    "reason": "missing"
}
```

That's OK. This means that there is no information about the current Replication so it must not have been run previously and as such the Replicator MUST run a Full Replication.

Compare Replication Logs

If the Replication Logs are successfully retrieved from both Source and Target then the Replicator MUST determine their common ancestry by following the next algorithm:

- Compare `session_id` values for the chronological last session - if they match both Source and Target have a common Replication history and it seems to be valid. Use `source_last_seq` value for the startup Checkpoint

- In case of mismatch, iterate over the `history` collection to search for the latest (chronologically) common `session_id` for Source and Target. Use value of `recorded_seq` field as startup Checkpoint

If Source and Target has no common ancestry, the Replicator MUST run Full Replication.

Locate Changed Documents

```
+ - - - - - - - - - - - - - - - - - - - - - - - - - - - - - - - - - - - +
' Find Common Ancestry:                                                  '
'                                                                        '
'               +-------------------------------+                        '
'               |    Compare Replication Logs   |                        '
'               +-------------------------------+                        '
'                               |                                        '
'                               |                                        '
+ - - - - - - - - - - - - - - - | - - - - - - - - - - - - - - - - - - - +
                                |
+ - - - - - - - - - - - - - - - | - - - - - - - - - - - - - - - - - - - +
' Locate Changed Documents:     |                                        '
```

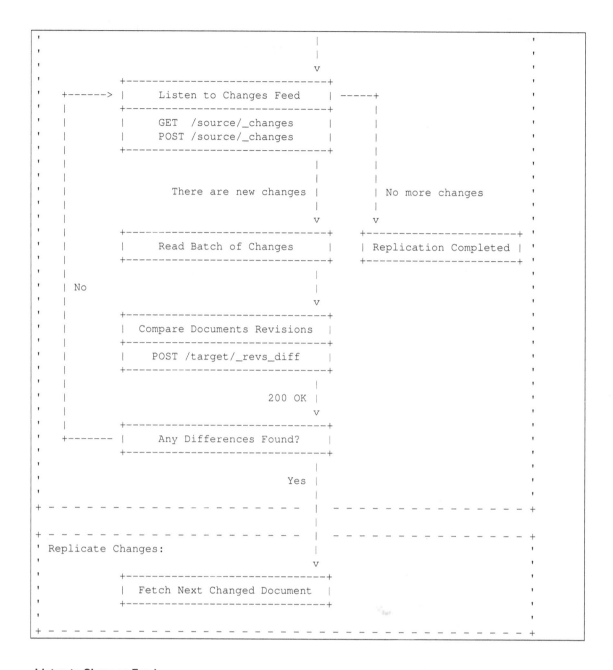

Listen to Changes Feed

When the start up Checkpoint has been defined, the Replicator SHOULD read the Source's *Changes Feed* by using a `GET /{db}/_changes` request. This request MUST be made with the following query parameters:

- `feed` parameter defines the Changes Feed response style: for Continuous Replication the `continuous` value SHOULD be used, otherwise - `normal`.

- `style=all_docs` query parameter tells the Source that it MUST include all Revision leaves for each document's event in output.

- For Continuous Replication the `heartbeat` parameter defines the heartbeat period in *milliseconds*. The RECOMMENDED value by default is `10000` (10 seconds).

- If a startup Checkpoint was found during the Replication Logs comparison, the `since` query parameter MUST be passed with this value. In case of Full Replication it MAY be 0 (number zero) or be omitted.

Additionally, the `filter` query parameter MAY be specified to enable a *filter function* on Source side. Other custom parameters MAY also be provided.

Read Batch of Changes

Reading the whole feed in a single shot may not be an optimal use of resources. It is RECOMMENDED to process the feed in small chunks. However, there is no specific recommendation on chunk size since it is heavily dependent on available resources: large chunks requires more memory while they reduce I/O operations and vice versa.

Note, that Changes Feed output format is different for a request with *feed=normal* and with *feed=continuous* query parameter.

Normal Feed:

Request:

```
GET /source/_changes?feed=normal&style=all_docs&heartbeat=10000 HTTP/1.1
Accept: application/json
Host: localhost:5984
User-Agent: CouchDB
```

Response:

```
HTTP/1.1 200 OK
Cache-Control: must-revalidate
Content-Type: application/json
Date: Fri, 09 May 2014 16:20:41 GMT
Server: CouchDB (Erlang OTP)
Transfer-Encoding: chunked

{"results":[
{"seq":14,"id":"f957f41e","changes":[{"rev":"3-46a3"}],"deleted":true}
{"seq":29,"id":"ddf339dd","changes":[{"rev":"10-304b"}]}
{"seq":37,"id":"d3cc62f5","changes":[{"rev":"2-eec2"}],"deleted":true}
{"seq":39,"id":"f13bd08b","changes":[{"rev":"1-b35d"}]}
{"seq":41,"id":"e0a99867","changes":[{"rev":"2-c1c6"}]}
{"seq":42,"id":"a75bdfc5","changes":[{"rev":"1-967a"}]}
{"seq":43,"id":"a5f467a0","changes":[{"rev":"1-5575"}]}
{"seq":45,"id":"470c3004","changes":[{"rev":"11-c292"}]}
{"seq":46,"id":"b1cb8508","changes":[{"rev":"10-ABC"}]}
{"seq":47,"id":"49ec0489","changes":[{"rev":"157-b01f"},{"rev":"123-6f7c"}]}
{"seq":49,"id":"dad10379","changes":[{"rev":"1-9346"},{"rev":"6-5b8a"}]}
{"seq":50,"id":"73464877","changes":[{"rev":"1-9f08"}]}
{"seq":51,"id":"7ae19302","changes":[{"rev":"1-57bf"}]}
{"seq":63,"id":"6a7a6c86","changes":[{"rev":"5-acf6"}],"deleted":true}
{"seq":64,"id":"dfb9850a","changes":[{"rev":"1-102f"}]}
{"seq":65,"id":"c532afa7","changes":[{"rev":"1-6491"}]}
{"seq":66,"id":"af8a9508","changes":[{"rev":"1-3db2"}]}
{"seq":67,"id":"caa3dded","changes":[{"rev":"1-6491"}]}
{"seq":68,"id":"79f3b4e9","changes":[{"rev":"1-102f"}]}
{"seq":69,"id":"1d89d16f","changes":[{"rev":"1-3db2"}]}
{"seq":71,"id":"abae7348","changes":[{"rev":"2-7051"}]}
{"seq":77,"id":"6c25534f","changes":[{"rev":"9-CDE"},{"rev":"3-00e7"},{"rev":"1-ABC"}]}
{"seq":78,"id":"SpaghettiWithMeatballs","changes":[{"rev":"22-5f95"}]}
],
"last_seq":78}
```

Continuous Feed:

Request:

```
GET /source/_changes?feed=continuous&style=all_docs&heartbeat=10000 HTTP/1.1
Accept: application/json
Host: localhost:5984
User-Agent: CouchDB
```

Response:

```
HTTP/1.1 200 OK
Cache-Control: must-revalidate
Content-Type: application/json
Date: Fri, 09 May 2014 16:22:22 GMT
Server: CouchDB (Erlang OTP)
Transfer-Encoding: chunked

{"seq":14,"id":"f957f41e","changes":[{"rev":"3-46a3"}],"deleted":true}
{"seq":29,"id":"ddf339dd","changes":[{"rev":"10-304b"}]}
{"seq":37,"id":"d3cc62f5","changes":[{"rev":"2-eec2"}],"deleted":true}
{"seq":39,"id":"f13bd08b","changes":[{"rev":"1-b35d"}]}
{"seq":41,"id":"e0a99867","changes":[{"rev":"2-c1c6"}]}
{"seq":42,"id":"a75bdfc5","changes":[{"rev":"1-967a"}]}
{"seq":43,"id":"a5f467a0","changes":[{"rev":"1-5575"}]}
{"seq":45,"id":"470c3004","changes":[{"rev":"11-c292"}]}
{"seq":46,"id":"b1cb8508","changes":[{"rev":"10-ABC"}]}
{"seq":47,"id":"49ec0489","changes":[{"rev":"157-b01f"},{"rev":"123-6f7c"}]}
{"seq":49,"id":"dad10379","changes":[{"rev":"1-9346"},{"rev":"6-5b8a"}]}
{"seq":50,"id":"73464877","changes":[{"rev":"1-9f08"}]}
{"seq":51,"id":"7ae19302","changes":[{"rev":"1-57bf"}]}
{"seq":63,"id":"6a7a6c86","changes":[{"rev":"5-acf6"}],"deleted":true}
{"seq":64,"id":"dfb9850a","changes":[{"rev":"1-102f"}]}
{"seq":65,"id":"c532afa7","changes":[{"rev":"1-6491"}]}
{"seq":66,"id":"af8a9508","changes":[{"rev":"1-3db2"}]}
{"seq":67,"id":"caa3dded","changes":[{"rev":"1-6491"}]}
{"seq":68,"id":"79f3b4e9","changes":[{"rev":"1-102f"}]}
{"seq":69,"id":"1d89d16f","changes":[{"rev":"1-3db2"}]}
{"seq":71,"id":"abae7348","changes":[{"rev":"2-7051"}]}
{"seq":75,"id":"SpaghettiWithMeatballs","changes":[{"rev":"21-5949"}]}
{"seq":77,"id":"6c255","changes":[{"rev":"9-CDE"},{"rev":"3-00e7"},{"rev":"1-ABC"}]}
{"seq":78,"id":"SpaghettiWithMeatballs","changes":[{"rev":"22-5f95"}]}
```

For both Changes Feed formats record-per-line style is preserved to simplify iterative fetching and decoding JSON objects with less memory footprint.

Calculate Revision Difference

After reading the batch of changes from the Changes Feed, the Replicator forms a JSON mapping object for Document ID and related leaf Revisions and sends the result to Target via a *POST /{db}/_revs_diff* request:

Request:

```
POST /target/_revs_diff HTTP/1.1
Accept: application/json
Content-Length: 287
Content-Type: application/json
Host: localhost:5984
User-Agent: CouchDB

{
    "baz": [
        "2-7051cbe5c8faecd085a3fa619e6e6337"
    ],
    "foo": [
        "3-6a540f3d701ac518d3b9733d673c5484"
```

```
        ],
        "bar": [
            "1-d4e501ab47de6b2000fc8a02f84a0c77",
            "1-967a00dff5e02add41819138abb3284d"
        ]
}
```

Response:

```
HTTP/1.1 200 OK
Cache-Control: must-revalidate
Content-Length: 88
Content-Type: application/json
Date: Fri, 25 Oct 2013 14:44:41 GMT
Server: CouchDB (Erlang/OTP)


{
    "baz": {
        "missing": [
            "2-7051cbe5c8faecd085a3fa619e6e6337"
        ]
    },
    "bar": {
        "missing": [
            "1-d4e501ab47de6b2000fc8a02f84a0c77"
        ]
    }
}
```

In the response the Replicator receives a Document ID – Revisions mapping, but only for Revisions that do not exist in Target and are REQUIRED to be transferred from Source.

If all Revisions in the request match the current state of the Documents then the response will contain an empty JSON object:

Request

```
POST /target/_revs_diff HTTP/1.1
Accept: application/json
Content-Length: 160
Content-Type: application/json
Host: localhost:5984
User-Agent: CouchDB


{
    "foo": [
        "3-6a540f3d701ac518d3b9733d673c5484"
    ],
    "bar": [
        "1-967a00dff5e02add41819138abb3284d"
    ]
}
```

Response:

```
HTTP/1.1 200 OK
Cache-Control: must-revalidate
Content-Length: 2
Content-Type: application/json
Date: Fri, 25 Oct 2013 14:45:00 GMT
Server: CouchDB (Erlang/OTP)


{}
```

Replication Completed

When there are no more changes left to process and no more Documents left to replicate, the Replicator finishes the Replication process. If Replication wasn't Continuous, the Replicator MAY return a response to client with statistics about the process.

```
HTTP/1.1 200 OK
Cache-Control: must-revalidate
Content-Length: 414
Content-Type: application/json
Date: Fri, 09 May 2014 15:14:19 GMT
Server: CouchDB (Erlang OTP)

{
    "history": [
        {
            "doc_write_failures": 2,
            "docs_read": 2,
            "docs_written": 0,
            "end_last_seq": 2939,
            "end_time": "Fri, 09 May 2014 15:14:19 GMT",
            "missing_checked": 1835,
            "missing_found": 2,
            "recorded_seq": 2939,
            "session_id": "05918159f64842f1fe73e9e2157b2112",
            "start_last_seq": 0,
            "start_time": "Fri, 09 May 2014 15:14:18 GMT"
        }
    ],
    "ok": true,
    "replication_id_version": 3,
    "session_id": "05918159f64842f1fe73e9e2157b2112",
    "source_last_seq": 2939
}
```

Replicate Changes

```
+ - - - - - - - - - - - - - - - - - - - - - - - - - - - - - - - - - - - +
' Locate Changed Documents:                                             '
'                                                                       '
'                  +------------------------------------+              '
'                  |        Any Differences Found?       |              '
'                  +------------------------------------+              '
'                                              |                        '
'                                              |                        '
'                                              |                        '
+ - - - - - - - - - - - - - - - - - - - - - - |- - - - - - - - - - - - +
                                               |
+ - - - - - - - - - - - - - - - - - - - - - - |- - - - - - - - - - - - +
' Replicate Changes:                           |                        '
'                                              v                        '
'                  +------------------------------------+              '
'   +--------> |     Fetch Next Changed Document    | <-------------------+  '
'   |              +------------------------------------+                |  '
'   |              |        GET /source/docid           |                |  '
'   |              +------------------------------------+                |  '
'   |                  |                                                  |  '
'   |                  |                                                  |  '
'   |                  |                               201 Created     |  '
'   |              | 200 OK                            401 Unauthorized |  '
'   |              |                                   403 Forbidden    |  '
```

```
  |            |                                                |       |
  |            v                                                |       |
  |          +------------------------------------+            |       |
  |  +------ | Document Has Changed Attachments?  |            |       |
  |  |       +------------------------------------+            |       |
  |  |            |                                            |       |
  |  |            |                                            |       |
  |  |            | Yes                                        |       |
  |  |            |                                            |       |
  |  |            v                                            |       |
  |  |          +----------------------+  Yes  +----------------------------+
  |  | No       | Are They Big Enough? | ------> | Update Document on Target |
  |  |          +----------------------+        +----------------------------+
  |  |            |                              |     PUT /target/docid     |
  |  |            |                              +----------------------------+
  |  |            |                              |
  |  |            | No                           |
  |  |            |                              |
  |  |            v                              |
  |  |          +------------------------------------+
  |  +------>  |       Put Document Into the Stack   |
  |  |         +------------------------------------+
  |  |            |
  |  |            |
  |  |            v
  |  No        +------------------------------------+
  +----------  |            Stack is Full?           |
  |            +------------------------------------+
  |              |
  |              | Yes
  |              |
  |              v
  |            +------------------------------------+
  |            | Upload Stack of Documents to Target |
  |            +------------------------------------+
  |            |         POST /target/_bulk_docs     |
  |            +------------------------------------+
  |              |
  |              | 201 Created
  |              v
  |            +------------------------------------+
  |            |            Ensure in Commit          |
  |            +------------------------------------+
  |            |  POST /target/_ensure_full_commit    |
  |            +------------------------------------+
  |              |
  |              | 201 Created
  |              v
  |            +------------------------------------+
  |            |      Record Replication Checkpoint   |
  |            +------------------------------------+
  |            |  PUT /source/_local/replication-id   |
  |            |  PUT /target/_local/replication-id   |
  |            +------------------------------------+
  |              |
  |              | 201 Created
  |              v
  |  No        +------------------------------------+
  +----------  | All Documents from Batch Processed? |
  |            +------------------------------------+
  |                                              |
  |                                         Yes  |
  |                                              |
```

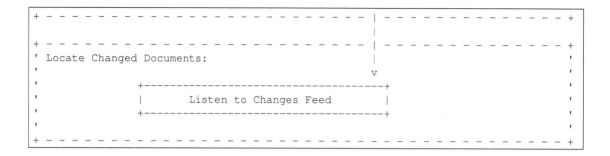

```
+ - - - - - - - - - - - - - - - - - - - - - - | - - - - - - - - - - - - - - +
                                              |                             |
+ - - - - - - - - - - - - - - - - - - - - - - | - - - - - - - - - - - - - - +
'  Locate Changed Documents:                  |                             '
'                                             v                             '
'              +----------------------------------------+                   '
'              |          Listen to Changes Feed        |                   '
'              +----------------------------------------+                   '
'                                                                           '
+ - - - - - - - - - - - - - - - - - - - - - - - - - - - - - - - - - - - - - +
```

Fetch Changed Documents

At this step the Replicator MUST fetch all Document Leaf Revisions from Source that are missed at Target. This operation is effective if Replication WILL use previously calculated Revision differences since they define missing Documents and their Revisions.

To fetch the Document the Replicator will make a *GET /{db}/{docid}* request with the following query parameters:

- revs=true: Instructs the Source to include the list of all known revisions into the Document in the _revisions field. This information is needed to synchronize the Document's ancestors history between Source and Target

- The open_revs query parameter contains a JSON array with a list of Leaf Revisions that are needed to be fetched. If the specified Revision exists then the Document MUST be returned for this Revision. Otherwise, Source MUST return an object with the single field missing with the missed Revision as the value. In case the Document contains attachments, Source MUST return information only for those ones that had been changed (added or updated) since the specified Revision values. If an attachment was deleted, the Document MUST NOT have stub information for it

- latest=true: Ensures, that Source will return the latest Document Revision regardless of which one was specified in the open_revs query parameter. This parameter solves a race condition problem where the requested Document may be changed in between this step and handling related events on the Changes Feed

In the response Source SHOULD return *multipart/mixed* or respond instead with *application/json* unless the Accept header specifies a different mime type. The *multipart/mixed* content type allows handling the response data as a stream, since there could be multiple documents (one per each Leaf Revision) plus several attachments. These attachments are mostly binary and JSON has no way to handle such data except as base64 encoded strings which are very ineffective for transfer and processing operations.

With a *multipart/mixed* response the Replicator handles multiple Document Leaf Revisions and their attachments one by one as raw data without any additional encoding applied. There is also one agreement to make data processing more effective: the Document ALWAYS goes before its attachments, so the Replicator has no need to process all the data to map related Documents-Attachments and may handle it as stream with lesser memory footprint.

Request:

```
GET /source/SpaghettiWithMeatballs?revs=true&open_revs=[%225-00ecbbc%22,%221-917fa23
Accept: multipart/mixed
Host: localhost:5984
User-Agent: CouchDB
```

Response:

```
HTTP/1.1 200 OK
Content-Type: multipart/mixed; boundary="7b1596fc4940bc1be725ad67f11ec1c4"
Date: Thu, 07 Nov 2013 15:10:16 GMT
Server: CouchDB (Erlang OTP)
Transfer-Encoding: chunked
```

```
--7b1596fc4940bc1be725ad67f11ec1c4
Content-Type: application/json

{
    "_id": "SpaghettiWithMeatballs",
    "_rev": "1-917fa23",
    "_revisions": {
        "ids": [
            "917fa23"
        ],
        "start": 1
    },
    "description": "An Italian-American delicious dish",
    "ingredients": [
        "spaghetti",
        "tomato sauce",
        "meatballs"
    ],
    "name": "Spaghetti with meatballs"
}
--7b1596fc4940bc1be725ad67f11ec1c4
Content-Type: multipart/related; boundary="a81a77b0ca68389dda3243a43ca946f2"

--a81a77b0ca68389dda3243a43ca946f2
Content-Type: application/json

{
    "_attachments": {
      "recipe.txt": {
          "content_type": "text/plain",
          "digest": "md5-R5CrCb6fX10Y46AqtNn0oQ==",
          "follows": true,
          "length": 87,
          "revpos": 7
      }
    },
    "_id": "SpaghettiWithMeatballs",
    "_rev": "7-474f12e",
    "_revisions": {
        "ids": [
            "474f12e",
            "5949cfc",
            "00ecbbc",
            "fc997b6",
            "3552c87",
            "404838b",
            "5defd9d",
            "dc1e4be"
        ],
        "start": 7
    },
    "description": "An Italian-American delicious dish",
    "ingredients": [
        "spaghetti",
        "tomato sauce",
        "meatballs",
        "love"
    ],
    "name": "Spaghetti with meatballs"
}
--a81a77b0ca68389dda3243a43ca946f2
Content-Disposition: attachment; filename="recipe.txt"
```

```
Content-Type: text/plain
Content-Length: 87

1. Cook spaghetti
2. Cook meetballs
3. Mix them
4. Add tomato sauce
5. ...
6. PROFIT!

--a81a77b0ca68389dda3243a43ca946f2--
--7b1596fc4940bc1be725ad67f11ec1c4
Content-Type: application/json; error="true"

{"missing":"3-6bcedf1"}
--7b1596fc4940bc1be725ad67f11ec1c4--
```

After receiving the response, the Replicator puts all the received data into a local stack for further bulk upload to utilize network bandwidth effectively. The local stack size could be limited by number of Documents or bytes of handled JSON data. When the stack is full the Replicator uploads all the handled Document in bulk mode to the Target. While bulk operations are highly RECOMMENDED to be used, in certain cases the Replicator MAY upload Documents to Target one by one.

Note: Alternative Replicator implementations MAY use alternative ways to retrieve Documents from Source. For instance, PouchDB doesn't uses Multipart API and fetches only latest Document Revision with inline attachments as single JSON object. While this is still valid CouchDB HTTP API usage, such solutions MAY require a different API implementation for non-CouchDB Peers.

Upload Batch of Changed Documents

To upload multiple Documents in a single shot the Replicator sends a `POST /{db}/_bulk_docs` request to Target with payload containing a JSON object with the following mandatory fields:

- **docs** (*array* of *objects*): List of Document objects to update on Target. These Documents MUST contain the `_revisions` field that holds a list of the full Revision history to let Target create Leaf Revisions that correctly preserve ancestry

- **new_edits** (*boolean*): Special flag that instructs Target to store Documents with the specified Revision (field `_rev`) value as-is without generating a new revision. Always `false`

The request also MAY contain **X-Couch-Full-Commit** that controls CouchDB `commit policy`. Other Peers MAY ignore this header or use it to control similar local feature.

Request:

```
POST /target/_bulk_docs HTTP/1.1
Accept: application/json
Content-Length: 826
Content-Type:application/json
Host: localhost:5984
User-Agent: CouchDB
X-Couch-Full-Commit: false

{
    "docs": [
        {
            "_id": "SpaghettiWithMeatballs",
            "_rev": "1-917fa2381192822767f010b95b45325b",
            "_revisions": {
                "ids": [
                    "917fa2381192822767f010b95b45325b"
```

```
            ],
            "start": 1
        },
        "description": "An Italian-American delicious dish",
        "ingredients": [
            "spaghetti",
            "tomato sauce",
            "meatballs"
        ],
        "name": "Spaghetti with meatballs"
    },
    {

        "_id": "LambStew",
        "_rev": "1-34c318924a8f327223eed702ddfdc66d",
        "_revisions": {
            "ids": [
                "34c318924a8f327223eed702ddfdc66d"
            ],
            "start": 1
        },
        "servings": 6,
        "subtitle": "Delicious with scone topping",
        "title": "Lamb Stew"
    },
    {

        "_id": "FishStew",
        "_rev": "1-9c65296036141e575d32ba9c034dd3ee",
        "_revisions": {
            "ids": [
                "9c65296036141e575d32ba9c034dd3ee"
            ],
            "start": 1
        },
        "servings": 4,
        "subtitle": "Delicious with fresh bread",
        "title": "Fish Stew"
    }
    ],
    "new_edits": false
}
```

In its response Target MUST return a JSON array with a list of Document update statuses. If the Document has been stored successfully, the list item MUST contain the field `ok` with `true` value. Otherwise it MUST contain `error` and `reason` fields with error type and a human-friendly reason description.

Document updating failure isn't fatal as Target MAY reject the update for its own reasons. It's RECOMMENDED to use error type `forbidden` for rejections, but other error types can also be used (like invalid field name etc.). The Replicator SHOULD NOT retry uploading rejected documents unless there are good reasons for doing so (e.g. there is special error type for that).

Note that while a update may fail for one Document in the response, Target can still return a 201 Created response. Same will be true if all updates fail for all uploaded Documents.

Response:

```
HTTP/1.1 201 Created
Cache-Control: must-revalidate
Content-Length: 246
Content-Type: application/json
Date: Sun, 10 Nov 2013 19:02:26 GMT
Server: CouchDB (Erlang/OTP)


[
    {
```

```
            "ok": true,
            "id": "SpaghettiWithMeatballs",
            "rev":" 1-917fa2381192822767f010b95b45325b"
        },
        {

            "ok": true,
            "id": "FishStew",
            "rev": "1-9c65296036141e575d32ba9c034dd3ee"
        },
        {

            "error": "forbidden",
            "id": "LambStew",
            "reason": "sorry",
            "rev": "1-34c318924a8f327223eed702ddfdc66d"
        }
    ]
```

Upload Document with Attachments

There is a special optimization case when then Replicator WILL NOT use bulk upload of changed Documents. This case is applied when Documents contain a lot of attached files or the files are too big to be efficiently encoded with Base64.

Note: CouchDB defines a limit of 8 attachments per Document and each attached file size should not be greater than 64 KiB. While this is a RECOMMENDED limitation, other Replicator implementations MAY have their own values.

For this case the Replicator issues a */{db}/{docid}?new_edits=false* request with *multipart/related* content type. Such a request allows one to easily stream the Document and all its attachments one by one without any serialization overhead.

Request:

```
PUT /target/SpaghettiWithMeatballs?new_edits=false HTTP/1.1
Accept: application/json
Content-Length: 1030
Content-Type: multipart/related; boundary="864d690aeb91f25d469dec6851fb57f2"
Host: localhost:5984
User-Agent: CouchDB

--2fa48cba80d0cdba7829931fe8acce9d
Content-Type: application/json

{
    "_attachments": {
        "recipe.txt": {
            "content_type": "text/plain",
            "digest": "md5-R5CrCb6fX10Y46AqtNn0oQ==",
            "follows": true,
            "length": 87,
            "revpos": 7
        }
    },
    "_id": "SpaghettiWithMeatballs",
    "_rev": "7-474f12eb068c717243487a9505f6123b",
    "_revisions": {
        "ids": [
            "474f12eb068c717243487a9505f6123b",
            "5949cfcd437e3ee22d2d98a26d1a83bf",
            "00ecbbc54e2a171156ec345b77dfdf59",
            "fc997b62794a6268f2636a4a176efcd6",
```

```
            "7552c87351aadc1e4bea2461a1e8113a",
            "404838bc2862ce76c6ebed046f9eb542",
            "5defd9d813628cea6e98196eb0ee8594"
        ],
        "start": 7
    },
    "description": "An Italian-American delicious dish",
    "ingredients": [
        "spaghetti",
        "tomato sauce",
        "meatballs",
        "love"
    ],
    "name": "Spaghetti with meatballs"
}
--2fa48cba80d0cdba7829931fe8acce9d
Content-Disposition: attachment; filename="recipe.txt"
Content-Type: text/plain
Content-Length: 87

1. Cook spaghetti
2. Cook meetballs
3. Mix them
4. Add tomato sauce
5. ...
6. PROFIT!

--2fa48cba80d0cdba7829931fe8acce9d--
```

Response:

```
HTTP/1.1 201 Created
Cache-Control: must-revalidate
Content-Length: 105
Content-Type: application/json
Date: Fri, 08 Nov 2013 16:35:27 GMT
Server: CouchDB (Erlang/OTP)


{
    "ok": true,
    "id": "SpaghettiWithMeatballs",
    "rev": "7-474f12eb068c717243487a9505f6123b"
}
```

Unlike bulk updating via *POST /{db}/_bulk_docs* endpoint, the response MAY come with a different status code. For instance, in the case when the Document is rejected, Target SHOULD respond with a 403 Forbidden:

Response:

```
HTTP/1.1 403 Forbidden
Cache-Control: must-revalidate
Content-Length: 39
Content-Type: application/json
Date: Fri, 08 Nov 2013 16:35:27 GMT
Server: CouchDB (Erlang/OTP)


{
    "error": "forbidden",
    "reason": "sorry"
}
```

Replicator SHOULD NOT retry requests in case of a 401 Unauthorized, 403 Forbidden, 409 Conflict or 412 Precondition Failed since repeating the request couldn't solve the issue with user credentials or uploaded data.

Ensure In Commit

Once a batch of changes has been successfully uploaded to Target, the Replicator issues a *POST /{db}/_ensure_full_commit* request to ensure that every transferred bit is laid down on disk or other *persistent* storage place. Target MUST return 201 Created response with a JSON object containing the following mandatory fields:

- **instance_start_time** (*string*): Timestamp of when the database was opened, expressed in *microseconds* since the epoch

- **ok** (*boolean*): Operation status. Constantly true

Request:

```
POST /target/_ensure_full_commit HTTP/1.1
Accept: application/json
Content-Type: application/json
Host: localhost:5984
```

Response:

```
HTTP/1.1 201 Created
Cache-Control: must-revalidate
Content-Length: 53
Content-Type: application/json
Date: Web, 06 Nov 2013 18:20:43 GMT
Server: CouchDB (Erlang/OTP)

{
    "instance_start_time": "1381218659871282",
    "ok": true
}
```

Record Replication Checkpoint

Since batches of changes were uploaded and committed successfully, the Replicator updates the Replication Log both on Source and Target recording the current Replication state. This operation is REQUIRED so that in the case of Replication failure the replication can resume from last point of success, not from the very beginning.

Replicator updates Replication Log on Source:

Request:

```
PUT /source/_local/afa899a9e59589c3d4ce5668e3218aef HTTP/1.1
Accept: application/json
Content-Length: 591
Content-Type: application/json
Host: localhost:5984
User-Agent: CouchDB

{
    "_id": "_local/afa899a9e59589c3d4ce5668e3218aef",
    "_rev": "0-1",
    "_revisions": {
        "ids": [
            "31f36e40158e717fbe9842e227b389df"
        ],
        "start": 1
    },
    "history": [
        {
            "doc_write_failures": 0,
            "docs_read": 6,
```

```
            "docs_written": 6,
            "end_last_seq": 26,
            "end_time": "Thu, 07 Nov 2013 09:42:17 GMT",
            "missing_checked": 6,
            "missing_found": 6,
            "recorded_seq": 26,
            "session_id": "04bf15bf1d9fa8ac1abc67d0c3e04f07",
            "start_last_seq": 0,
            "start_time": "Thu, 07 Nov 2013 09:41:43 GMT"
        }
    ],
    "replication_id_version": 3,
    "session_id": "04bf15bf1d9fa8ac1abc67d0c3e04f07",
    "source_last_seq": 26
}
```

Response:

```
HTTP/1.1 201 Created
Cache-Control: must-revalidate
Content-Length: 75
Content-Type: application/json
Date: Thu, 07 Nov 2013 09:42:17 GMT
Server: CouchDB (Erlang/OTP)

{
    "id": "_local/afa899a9e59589c3d4ce5668e3218aef",
    "ok": true,
    "rev": "0-2"
}
```

...and on Target too:

Request:

```
PUT /target/_local/afa899a9e59589c3d4ce5668e3218aef HTTP/1.1
Accept: application/json
Content-Length: 591
Content-Type: application/json
Host: localhost:5984
User-Agent: CouchDB

{
    "_id": "_local/afa899a9e59589c3d4ce5668e3218aef",
    "_rev": "1-31f36e40158e717fbe9842e227b389df",
    "_revisions": {
        "ids": [
            "31f36e40158e717fbe9842e227b389df"
        ],
        "start": 1
    },
    "history": [
        {
            "doc_write_failures": 0,
            "docs_read": 6,
            "docs_written": 6,
            "end_last_seq": 26,
            "end_time": "Thu, 07 Nov 2013 09:42:17 GMT",
            "missing_checked": 6,
            "missing_found": 6,
            "recorded_seq": 26,
            "session_id": "04bf15bf1d9fa8ac1abc67d0c3e04f07",
            "start_last_seq": 0,
            "start_time": "Thu, 07 Nov 2013 09:41:43 GMT"
```

```
        }
    ],
    "replication_id_version": 3,
    "session_id": "04bf15bf1d9fa8ac1abc67d0c3e04f07",
    "source_last_seq": 26
}
```

Response:

```
HTTP/1.1 201 Created
Cache-Control: must-revalidate
Content-Length: 106
Content-Type: application/json
Date: Thu, 07 Nov 2013 09:42:17 GMT
Server: CouchDB (Erlang/OTP)

{
    "id": "_local/afa899a9e59589c3d4ce5668e3218aef",
    "ok": true,
    "rev": "2-9b5d1e36bed6ae08611466e30af1259a"
}
```

Continue Reading Changes

Once a batch of changes had been processed and transferred to Target successfully, the Replicator can continue to listen to the Changes Feed for new changes. If there are no new changes to process the Replication is considered to be done.

For Continuous Replication, the Replicator MUST continue to wait for new changes from Source.

4.2.3 Protocol Robustness

Since the *CouchDB Replication Protocol* works on top of HTTP, which is based on TCP/IP, the Replicator SHOULD expect to be working within an unstable environment with delays, losses and other bad surprises that might eventually occur. The Replicator SHOULD NOT count every HTTP request failure as a *fatal error*. It SHOULD be smart enough to detect timeouts, repeat failed requests, be ready to process incomplete or malformed data and so on. *Data must flow* - that's the rule.

4.2.4 Error Responses

In case something goes wrong the Peer MUST respond with a JSON object with the following REQUIRED fields:

- **error** (*string*): Error type for programs and developers
- **reason** (*string*): Error description for humans

Bad Request

If a request contains malformed data (like invalid JSON) the Peer MUST respond with a HTTP 400 Bad Request and `bad_request` as error type:

```
{
    "error": "bad_request",
    "reason": "invalid json"
}
```

Unauthorized

If a Peer REQUIRES credentials be included with the request and the request does not contain acceptable credentials then the Peer MUST respond with the HTTP 401 Unauthorized and unauthorized as error type:

```
{
    "error": "unauthorized",
    "reason": "Name or password is incorrect"
}
```

Forbidden

If a Peer receives valid user credentials, but the requester does not have sufficient permissions to perform the operation then the Peer MUST respond with a HTTP 403 Forbidden and forbidden as error type:

```
{
    "error": "forbidden",
    "reason": "You may only update your own user document."
}
```

Resource Not Found

If the requested resource, Database or Document wasn't found on a Peer, the Peer MUST respond with a HTTP 404 Not Found and not_found as error type:

```
{
    "error": "not_found",
    "reason": "database \"target\" does not exists"
}
```

Method Not Allowed

If an unsupported method was used then the Peer MUST respond with a HTTP 405 Method Not Allowed and method_not_allowed as error type:

```
{
    "error": "method_not_allowed",
    "reason": "Only GET, PUT, DELETE allowed"
}
```

Resource Conflict

A resource conflict error occurs when there are concurrent updates of the same resource by multiple clients. In this case the Peer MUST respond with a HTTP 409 Conflict and conflict as error type:

```
{
    "error": "conflict",
    "reason": "document update conflict"
}
```

Precondition Failed

The HTTP 412 Precondition Failed response may be sent in case of an attempt to create a Database (error type db_exists) that already exists or some attachment information is missing (error type missing_stub). There is no explicit error type restrictions, but it is RECOMMEND to use error types that are previously mentioned:

```
{
    "error": "db_exists",
    "reason": "database \"target\" exists"
}
```

Server Error

Raised in case an error is *fatal* and the Replicator cannot do anything to continue Replication. In this case the Replicator MUST return a HTTP 500 Internal Server Error response with an error description (no restrictions on error type applied):

```
{
    "error": "worker_died",
    "reason": "kaboom!"
}
```

4.2.5 Optimisations

There are RECOMMENDED approaches to optimize the Replication process:

- Keep the number of HTTP requests at a reasonable minimum
- Try to work with a connection pool and make parallel/multiple requests whenever possible
- Don't close sockets after each request: respect the keep-alive option
- Use continuous sessions (cookies, etc.) to reduce authentication overhead
- Try to use bulk requests for every operations with Documents
- Find out optimal batch size for Changes feed processing
- Preserve Replication Logs and resume Replication from the last Checkpoint whenever possible
- Optimize filter functions: let them run as fast as possible
- Get ready for surprises: networks are very unstable environments

4.2.6 API Reference

Common Methods

- *HEAD /{db}* – Check Database existence
- *GET /{db}* – Retrieve Database information
- *GET /{db}/_local/{docid}* – Read the last Checkpoint
- *PUT /{db}/_local/{docid}* – Save a new Checkpoint

For Target

- *PUT /{db}* – Create Target if it not exists and the option was provided
- *POST /{db}/_revs_diff* – Locate Revisions that are not known to Target
- *POST /{db}/_bulk_docs* – Upload Revisions to Target
- *PUT /{db}/{docid}* – Upload a single Document with attachments to Target
- *POST /{db}/_ensure_full_commit* – Ensure that all changes are stored on disk

For Source

- `GET /{db}/_changes` – Fetch changes since the last pull of Source
- `POST /{db}/_changes` – Fetch changes for specified Document IDs since the last pull of Source
- `GET /{db}/{docid}` – Retrieve a single Document from Source with attachments

4.2.7 Reference

- Refuge RCouch wiki
- CouchBase Lite IOS wiki
- CouchDB documentation

4.3 Replicator Database

The `_replicator` database works like any other in CouchDB, but documents added to it will trigger replications. Create (`PUT` or `POST`) a document to start replication. `DELETE` a replication document to cancel an ongoing replication.

These documents have exactly the same content as the JSON objects we used to `POST` to `_replicate` (fields `source`, `target`, `create_target`, `continuous`, `doc_ids`, `filter`, `query_params`, `use_checkpoints`, `checkpoint_interval`).

Replication documents can have a user defined `_id` (handy for finding a specific replication request later). Design Documents (and `_local` documents) added to the replicator database are ignored.

The default name of this database is `_replicator`. The name can be changed in the `local.ini` configuration, section `[replicator]`, parameter `db`.

4.3.1 Basics

Let's say you POST the following document into `_replicator`:

```
{
    "_id": "my_rep",
    "source":  "http://myserver.com:5984/foo",
    "target":  "bar",
    "create_target":  true
}
```

In the couch log you'll see 2 entries like these:

```
[Thu, 17 Feb 2011 19:43:59 GMT] [info] [<0.291.0>] Document `my_rep` triggered replicatio
[Thu, 17 Feb 2011 19:44:37 GMT] [info] [<0.124.0>] Replication `c0ebe9256695ff083347cbf95
```

As soon as the replication is triggered, the document will be updated by CouchDB with 3 new fields:

```
{
    "_id": "my_rep",
    "source":  "http://myserver.com:5984/foo",
    "target":  "bar",
    "create_target":  true,
    "_replication_id":  "c0ebe9256695ff083347cbf95f93e280",
    "_replication_state":  "triggered",
    "_replication_state_time":  1297974122
}
```

Special fields set by the replicator start with the prefix `_replication_`.

- _replication_id

  The ID internally assigned to the replication. This is also the ID exposed by /_active_tasks.

- _replication_state

  The current state of the replication.

- _replication_state_time

  A Unix timestamp (number of seconds since 1 Jan 1970) that tells us when the current replication state (marked in _replication_state) was set.

- _replication_state_reason

  If replication_state is error, this field contains the reason.

```
{
    "_id": "my_rep",
    "_rev": "2-9f2c0d9372f4ee4dc75652ab8f8e7c70",
    "source": "foodb",
    "target": "bardb",
    "_replication_state": "error",
    "_replication_state_time": "2013-12-13T18:48:00+01:00",
    "_replication_state_reason": "db_not_found: could not open foodb",
    "_replication_id": "fe965cdc47b4d5f6c02811d9d351ac3d"
}
```

When the replication finishes, it will update the _replication_state field (and _replication_state_time) with the value completed, so the document will look like:

```
{
    "_id": "my_rep",
    "source":  "http://myserver.com:5984/foo",
    "target":  "bar",
    "create_target": true,
    "_replication_id":  "c0ebe9256695ff083347cbf95f93e280",
    "_replication_state":  "completed",
    "_replication_state_time":  1297974122
}
```

When an error happens during replication, the _replication_state field is set to error (and _replication_state_reason and _replication_state_time are updated).

When you PUT/POST a document to the _replicator database, CouchDB will attempt to start the replication up to 10 times (configurable under [replicator], parameter max_replication_retry_count). If it fails on the first attempt, it waits 5 seconds before doing a second attempt. If the second attempt fails, it waits 10 seconds before doing a third attempt. If the third attempt fails, it waits 20 seconds before doing a fourth attempt (each attempt doubles the previous wait period). When an attempt fails, the Couch log will show you something like:

```
[error] [<0.149.0>] Error starting replication `67c1bb92010e7abe35d7d629635f18b6+create_t
```

Note: The _replication_state field is only set to error when all the attempts were unsuccessful.

There are only 3 possible values for the _replication_state field: triggered, completed and error. Continuous replications never get their state set to completed.

4.3.2 Documents describing the same replication

Lets suppose 2 documents are added to the _replicator database in the following order:

```
{
    "_id": "doc_A",
    "source":  "http://myserver.com:5984/foo",
    "target":  "bar"
}
```

and

```
{
    "_id": "doc_B",
    "source":  "http://myserver.com:5984/foo",
    "target":  "bar"
}
```

Both describe exactly the same replication (only their _ids differ). In this case document doc_A triggers the replication, getting updated by CouchDB with the fields _replication_state, _replication_state_time and _replication_id, just like it was described before. Document doc_B however, is only updated with one field, the _replication_id so it will look like this:

```
{
    "_id": "doc_B",
    "source":  "http://myserver.com:5984/foo",
    "target":  "bar",
    "_replication_id":  "c0ebe9256695ff083347cbf95f93e280"
}
```

While document doc_A will look like this:

```
{
    "_id": "doc_A",
    "source":  "http://myserver.com:5984/foo",
    "target":  "bar",
    "_replication_id":  "c0ebe9256695ff083347cbf95f93e280",
    "_replication_state":  "triggered",
    "_replication_state_time":  1297974122
}
```

Note that both document get exactly the same value for the _replication_id field. This way you can identify which documents refer to the same replication - you can for example define a view which maps replication IDs to document IDs.

4.3.3 Canceling replications

To cancel a replication simply DELETE the document which triggered the replication. The Couch log will show you an entry like the following:

```
[Thu, 17 Feb 2011 20:16:29 GMT] [info] [<0.125.0>] Stopped replication `c0ebe9256695ff083
```

Note: You need to DELETE the document that triggered the replication. DELETE-ing another document that describes the same replication but did not trigger it, will not cancel the replication.

4.3.4 Server restart

When CouchDB is restarted, it checks its _replicator database and restarts any replication that is described by a document that either has its _replication_state field set to triggered or it doesn't have yet the _replication_state field set.

Note: Continuous replications always have a _replication_state field with the value triggered, therefore they're always restarted when CouchDB is restarted.

4.3.5 Updating Documents in the Replicator Database

Once the replicator has started work on a job defined in the `_replicator` database, modifying the replication document is no longer allowed. Attempting to do this will result in the following response

```
{
    "error": "forbidden",
    "reason": "Only the replicator can edit replication documents that are in the trigger
}
```

The way to accomplish this is to first delete the old version and then insert the new one.

4.3.6 Changing the Replicator Database

Imagine your replicator database (default name is `_replicator`) has the two following documents that represent pull replications from servers A and B:

```
{
    "_id": "rep_from_A",
    "source":  "http://aserver.com:5984/foo",
    "target":  "foo_a",
    "continuous": true,
    "_replication_id":  "c0ebe9256695ff083347cbf95f93e280",
    "_replication_state":  "triggered",
    "_replication_state_time":  1297971311
}
```

```
{
    "_id": "rep_from_B",
    "source":  "http://bserver.com:5984/foo",
    "target":  "foo_b",
    "continuous": true,
    "_replication_id":  "231bb3cf9d48314eaa8d48a9170570d1",
    "_replication_state":  "triggered",
    "_replication_state_time":  1297974122
}
```

Now without stopping and restarting CouchDB, you change the name of the replicator database to `another_replicator_db`:

```
$ curl -X PUT http://localhost:5984/_config/replicator/db -d '"another_replicator_db"'
"_replicator"
```

As soon as this is done, both pull replications defined before, are stopped. This is explicitly mentioned in CouchDB's log:

```
[Fri, 11 Mar 2011 07:44:20 GMT] [info] [<0.104.0>] Stopping all ongoing replications beca
[Fri, 11 Mar 2011 07:44:20 GMT] [info] [<0.127.0>] 127.0.0.1 - - PUT /_config/replicator/
```

Imagine now you add a replication document to the new replicator database named `another_replicator_db`:

```
{
    "_id": "rep_from_X",
    "source":  "http://xserver.com:5984/foo",
    "target":  "foo_x",
    "continuous": true
}
```

From now own you have a single replication going on in your system: a pull replication pulling from server X. Now you change back the replicator database to the original one `_replicator`:

```
$ curl -X PUT http://localhost:5984/_config/replicator/db -d '"_replicator"'
"another_replicator_db"
```

Immediately after this operation, the replication pulling from server X will be stopped and the replications defined in the `_replicator` database (pulling from servers A and B) will be resumed.

Changing again the replicator database to `another_replicator_db` will stop the pull replications pulling from servers A and B, and resume the pull replication pulling from server X.

4.3.7 Replicating the replicator database

Imagine you have in server C a replicator database with the two following pull replication documents in it:

```
{
    "_id": "rep_from_A",
    "source":  "http://aserver.com:5984/foo",
    "target":  "foo_a",
    "continuous": true,
    "_replication_id":  "c0ebe9256695ff083347cbf95f93e280",
    "_replication_state":  "triggered",
    "_replication_state_time": 1297971311
}
```

```
{
    "_id": "rep_from_B",
    "source":  "http://bserver.com:5984/foo",
    "target":  "foo_b",
    "continuous": true,
    "_replication_id":  "231bb3cf9d48314eaa8d48a9170570d1",
    "_replication_state":  "triggered",
    "_replication_state_time": 1297974122
}
```

Now you would like to have the same pull replications going on in server D, that is, you would like to have server D pull replicating from servers A and B. You have two options:

- Explicitly add two documents to server's D replicator database
- Replicate server's C replicator database into server's D replicator database

Both alternatives accomplish exactly the same goal.

4.3.8 Delegations

Replication documents can have a custom `user_ctx` property. This property defines the user context under which a replication runs. For the old way of triggering a replication (POSTing to `/_replicate/`), this property is not needed. That's because information about the authenticated user is readily available during the replication, which is not persistent in that case. Now, with the replicator database, the problem is that information about which user is starting a particular replication is only present when the replication document is written. The information in the replication document and the replication itself are persistent, however. This implementation detail implies that in the case of a non-admin user, a `user_ctx` property containing the user's name and a subset of their roles must be defined in the replication document. This is enforced by the document update validation function present in the default design document of the replicator database. The validation function also ensures that non-admin users are unable to set the value of the user context's `name` property to anything other than their own user name. The same principle applies for roles.

For admins, the `user_ctx` property is optional, and if it's missing it defaults to a user context with name `null` and an empty list of roles, which means design documents won't be written to local targets. If writing design documents to local targets is desired, the role `_admin` must be present in the user context's list of roles.

Also, for admins the `user_ctx` property can be used to trigger a replication on behalf of another user. This is the user context that will be passed to local target database document validation functions.

Note: The `user_ctx` property only has effect for local endpoints.

Example delegated replication document:

```
{
    "_id": "my_rep",
    "source":  "http://bserver.com:5984/foo",
    "target":  "bar",
    "continuous": true,
    "user_ctx": {
        "name": "joe",
        "roles": ["erlanger", "researcher"]
    }
}
```

As stated before, the `user_ctx` property is optional for admins, while being mandatory for regular (non-admin) users. When the roles property of `user_ctx` is missing, it defaults to the empty list `[]`.

4.4 Replication and conflict model

Let's take the following example to illustrate replication and conflict handling.

- Alice has a document containing Bob's business card;

- She synchronizes it between her desktop PC and her laptop;

- On the desktop PC, she updates Bob's E-mail address; Without syncing again, she updates Bob's mobile number on the laptop;

- Then she replicates the two to each other again.

So on the desktop the document has Bob's new E-mail address and his old mobile number, and on the laptop it has his old E-mail address and his new mobile number.

The question is, what happens to these conflicting updated documents?

4.4.1 CouchDB replication

CouchDB works with JSON documents inside databases. Replication of databases takes place over HTTP, and can be either a "pull" or a "push", but is unidirectional. So the easiest way to perform a full sync is to do a "push" followed by a "pull" (or vice versa).

So, Alice creates v1 and sync it. She updates to v2a on one side and v2b on the other, and then replicates. What happens?

The answer is simple: both versions exist on both sides!

```
   DESKTOP                      LAPTOP
+---------+
| /db/bob |                              INITIAL
|   v1    |                              CREATION
+---------+


+---------+                  +---------+
| /db/bob |  --------------->  | /db/bob |    PUSH
|   v1    |                  |   v1    |
+---------+                  +---------+


+---------+                  +---------+  INDEPENDENT
| /db/bob |                  | /db/bob |    LOCAL
|   v2a   |                  |   v2b   |    EDITS
```

```
+--------+                      +--------+
+--------+                      +--------+
| /db/bob |  ------------------>  | /db/bob |      PUSH
|   v2a   |                      |   v2a   |
+--------+                      |   v2b   |
                                +--------+


+--------+                      +--------+
| /db/bob |  <------------------  | /db/bob |      PULL
|   v2a   |                      |   v2a   |
|   v2b   |                      |   v2b   |
+--------+                      +--------+
```

After all, this is not a filesystem, so there's no restriction that only one document can exist with the name /db/bob. These are just "conflicting" revisions under the same name.

Because the changes are always replicated, the data is safe. Both machines have identical copies of both documents, so failure of a hard drive on either side won't lose any of the changes.

Another thing to notice is that peers do not have to be configured or tracked. You can do regular replications to peers, or you can do one-off, ad-hoc pushes or pulls. After the replication has taken place, there is no record kept of which peer any particular document or revision came from.

So the question now is: what happens when you try to read /db/bob? By default, CouchDB picks one arbitrary revision as the "winner", using a deterministic algorithm so that the same choice will be made on all peers. The same happens with views: the deterministically-chosen winner is the only revision fed into your map function.

Let's say that the winner is v2a. On the desktop, if Alice reads the document she'll see v2a, which is what she saved there. But on the laptop, after replication, she'll also see only v2a. It could look as if the changes she made there have been lost - but of course they have not, they have just been hidden away as a conflicting revision. But eventually she'll need these changes merged into Bob's business card, otherwise they will effectively have been lost.

Any sensible business-card application will, at minimum, have to present the conflicting versions to Alice and allow her to create a new version incorporating information from them all. Ideally it would merge the updates itself.

4.4.2 Conflict avoidance

When working on a single node, CouchDB will avoid creating conflicting revisions by returning a 409 Conflict error. This is because, when you PUT a new version of a document, you must give the _rev of the previous version. If that _rev has already been superseded, the update is rejected with a 409 Conflict response.

So imagine two users on the same node are fetching Bob's business card, updating it concurrently, and writing it back:

```
USER1    ----------->   GET /db/bob
         <-----------   {"_rev":"1-aaa", ...}

USER2    ----------->   GET /db/bob
         <-----------   {"_rev":"1-aaa", ...}

USER1    ----------->   PUT /db/bob?rev=1-aaa
         <-----------   {"_rev":"2-bbb", ...}

USER2    ----------->   PUT /db/bob?rev=1-aaa
         <-----------   409 Conflict   (not saved)
```

User2's changes are rejected, so it's up to the app to fetch /db/bob again, and either:

1. apply the same changes as were applied to the earlier revision, and submit a new PUT

2. redisplay the document so the user has to edit it again

---

3. just overwrite it with the document being saved before (which is not advisable, as user1's changes will be silently lost)

So when working in this mode, your application still has to be able to handle these conflicts and have a suitable retry strategy, but these conflicts never end up inside the database itself.

4.4.3 Conflicts in batches

There are two different ways that conflicts can end up in the database:

- Conflicting changes made on different databases, which are replicated to each other, as shown earlier.

- Changes are written to the database using _bulk_docs and all_or_nothing, which bypasses the 409 mechanism.

The _bulk_docs API lets you submit multiple updates (and/or deletes) in a single HTTP POST. Normally, these are treated as independent updates; some in the batch may fail because the _rev is stale (just like a 409 from a PUT) whilst others are written successfully. The response from _bulk_docs lists the success/fail separately for each document in the batch.

However there is another mode of working, whereby you specify { "all_or_nothing":true} as part of the request. This is CouchDB's nearest equivalent of a "transaction", but it's not the same as a database transaction which can fail and roll back. Rather, it means that all of the changes in the request will be forcibly applied to the database, even if that introduces conflicts.

So this gives you a way to introduce conflicts within a single database instance. If you choose to do this instead of PUT, it means you don't have to write any code for the possibility of getting a 409 response, because you will never get one. Rather, you have to deal with conflicts appearing later in the database, which is what you'd have to do in a multi-master application anyway.

```
POST /db/_bulk_docs
```

```
{
    "all_or_nothing": true,
    "docs": [
        {"_id":"x", "_rev":"1-xxx", ...},
        {"_id":"y", "_rev":"1-yyy", ...},
        ...
    ]
}
```

4.4.4 Revision tree

When you update a document in CouchDB, it keeps a list of the previous revisions. In the case where conflicting updates are introduced, this history branches into a tree, where the current conflicting revisions for this document form the tips (leaf nodes) of this tree:

```
   ,--> r2a
r1 --> r2b
   `--> r2c
```

Each branch can then extend its history - for example if you read revision r2b and then PUT with ?rev=r2b then you will make a new revision along that particular branch.

```
   ,--> r2a -> r3a -> r4a
r1 --> r2b -> r3b
   `--> r2c -> r3c
```

Here, (r4a, r3b, r3c) are the set of conflicting revisions. The way you resolve a conflict is to delete the leaf nodes along the other branches. So when you combine (r4a+r3b+r3c) into a single merged document, you would replace r4a and delete r3b and r3c.

```
  ,    )  iΩu   )  ωдα   )  rɅд  -)  r5д
r1 --> r2b -> r3b -> (r4b deleted)
  `--> r2c -> r3c -> (r4c deleted)
```

Note that r4b and r4c still exist as leaf nodes in the history tree, but as deleted docs. You can retrieve them but they will be marked "_deleted":true.

When you compact a database, the bodies of all the non-leaf documents are discarded. However, the list of historical _revs is retained, for the benefit of later conflict resolution in case you meet any old replicas of the database at some time in future. There is "revision pruning" to stop this getting arbitrarily large.

4.4.5 Working with conflicting documents

The basic *:get:'/{doc}/{docid}'* operation will not show you any information about conflicts. You see only the deterministically-chosen winner, and get no indication as to whether other conflicting revisions exist or not:

```
{
    "_id":"test",
    "_rev":"2-b91bb807b4685080c6a651115ff558f5",
    "hello":"bar"
}
```

If you do GET /db/test?conflicts=true, and the document is in a conflict state, then you will get the winner plus a _conflicts member containing an array of the revs of the other, conflicting revision(s). You can then fetch them individually using subsequent GET /db/test?rev=xxxx operations:

```
{
    "_id":"test",
    "_rev":"2-b91bb807b4685080c6a651115ff558f5",
    "hello":"bar",
    "_conflicts":[
        "2-65db2a11b5172bf928e3bcf59f728970",
        "2-5bc3c6319edf62d4c624277fdd0ae191"
    ]
}
```

If you do GET /db/test?open_revs=all then you will get all the leaf nodes of the revision tree. This will give you all the current conflicts, but will also give you leaf nodes which have been deleted (i.e. parts of the conflict history which have since been resolved). You can remove these by filtering out documents with "_deleted":true:

```
[
    {"ok":{"_id":"test","_rev":"2-5bc3c6319edf62d4c624277fdd0ae191","hello":"foo"}},
    {"ok":{"_id":"test","_rev":"2-65db2a11b5172bf928e3bcf59f728970","hello":"baz"}},
    {"ok":{"_id":"test","_rev":"2-b91bb807b4685080c6a651115ff558f5","hello":"bar"}}
]
```

The "ok" tag is an artifact of open_revs, which also lets you list explicit revisions as a JSON array, e.g. open_revs=[rev1,rev2,rev3]. In this form, it would be possible to request a revision which is now missing, because the database has been compacted.

Note: The order of revisions returned by open_revs=all is **NOT** related to the deterministic "winning" algorithm. In the above example, the winning revision is 2-b91b... and happens to be returned last, but in other cases it can be returned in a different position.

Once you have retrieved all the conflicting revisions, your application can then choose to display them all to the user. Or it could attempt to merge them, write back the merged version, and delete the conflicting versions - that is, to resolve the conflict permanently.

As described above, you need to update one revision and delete all the conflicting revisions explicitly. This can be done using a single *POST* to _bulk_docs, setting "_deleted":true on those revisions you wish to delete.

4.4.6 Multiple document API

You can fetch multiple documents at once using `include_docs=true` on a view. However, a `conflicts=true` request is ignored; the "doc" part of the value never includes a `_conflicts` member. Hence you would need to do another query to determine for each document whether it is in a conflicting state:

```
$ curl 'http://127.0.0.1:5984/conflict_test/_all_docs?include_docs=true&conflicts=true'
```

```
{
    "total_rows":1,
    "offset":0,
    "rows":[
        {
            "id":"test",
            "key":"test",
            "value":{"rev":"2-b91bb807b4685080c6a651115ff558f5"},
            "doc":{
                "_id":"test",
                "_rev":"2-b91bb807b4685080c6a651115ff558f5",
                "hello":"bar"
            }
        }
    ]
}
```

```
$ curl 'http://127.0.0.1:5984/conflict_test/test?conflicts=true'
```

```
{
    "_id":"test",
    "_rev":"2-b91bb807b4685080c6a651115ff558f5",
    "hello":"bar",
    "_conflicts":[
        "2-65db2a11b5172bf928e3bcf59f728970",
        "2-5bc3c6319edf62d4c624277fdd0ae191"
    ]
}
```

4.4.7 View map functions

Views only get the winning revision of a document. However they do also get a `_conflicts` member if there are any conflicting revisions. This means you can write a view whose job is specifically to locate documents with conflicts. Here is a simple map function which achieves this:

```
function(doc) {
    if (doc._conflicts) {
        emit(null, [doc._rev].concat(doc._conflicts));
    }
}
```

which gives the following output:

```
{
    "total_rows":1,
    "offset":0,
    "rows":[
        {
            "id":"test",
            "key":null,
            "value":[
                "2-b91bb807b4685080c6a651115ff558f5",
                "2-65db2a11b5172bf928e3bcf59f728970",
                "2-5bc3c6319edf62d4c624277fdd0ae191"
```

```
            ]
        }
    ]
}
```

If you do this, you can have a separate "sweep" process which periodically scans your database, looks for documents which have conflicts, fetches the conflicting revisions, and resolves them.

Whilst this keeps the main application simple, the problem with this approach is that there will be a window between a conflict being introduced and it being resolved. From a user's viewpoint, this may appear that the document they just saved successfully may suddenly lose their changes, only to be resurrected some time later. This may or may not be acceptable.

Also, it's easy to forget to start the sweeper, or not to implement it properly, and this will introduce odd behaviour which will be hard to track down.

CouchDB's "winning" revision algorithm may mean that information drops out of a view until a conflict has been resolved. Consider Bob's business card again; suppose Alice has a view which emits mobile numbers, so that her telephony application can display the caller's name based on caller ID. If there are conflicting documents with Bob's old and new mobile numbers, and they happen to be resolved in favour of Bob's old number, then the view won't be able to recognise his new one. In this particular case, the application might have preferred to put information from both the conflicting documents into the view, but this currently isn't possible.

Suggested algorithm to fetch a document with conflict resolution:

1. Get document via `GET docid?conflicts=true` request;

2. For each member in the `_conflicts` array call `GET docid?rev=xxx`. If any errors occur at this stage, restart from step 1. (There could be a race where someone else has already resolved this conflict and deleted that rev)

3. Perform application-specific merging

4. Write `_bulk_docs` with an update to the first rev and deletes of the other revs.

This could either be done on every read (in which case you could replace all calls to GET in your application with calls to a library which does the above), or as part of your sweeper code.

And here is an example of this in Ruby using the low-level RestClient:

```ruby
require 'rubygems'
require 'rest_client'
require 'json'
    ="http://127.0.0.1:5984/conflict_test"

# Write multiple documents as all_or_nothing, can introduce conflicts
def writem(docs)
        .parse(        .post("#    /_bulk_docs", {
        "all_or_nothing" => true,
        "docs" => docs,
    }.to_json))
end

# Write one document, return the rev
def write1(doc, id=nil, rev=nil)
    doc['_id'] = id if id
    doc['_rev'] = rev if rev
    writem([doc]).first['rev']
end

# Read a document, return *all* revs
def read1(id)
    retries = 0
    loop do
        # FIXME: escape id
```

```
            res = [JSON.parse(RestClient.get("#{DB}/#{id}?conflicts=true"))]
        if revs = res.first.delete('_conflicts')
            begin
                revs.each do |rev|
                    res << JSON.parse(RestClient.get("#{DB}/#{id}?rev=#{rev}"))
                end
            rescue
                retries += 1
                raise if retries >= 5
                next
            end
        end
    end
    return res
  end
end

# Create DB
RestClient.delete DB rescue nil
RestClient.put DB, {}.to_json

# Write a document
rev1 = write1({"hello"=>"xxx"},"test")
p read1("test")

# Make three conflicting versions
write1({"hello"=>"foo"},"test",rev1)
write1({"hello"=>"bar"},"test",rev1)
write1({"hello"=>"baz"},"test",rev1)

res = read1("test")
p res

# Now let's replace these three with one
res.first['hello'] = "foo+bar+baz"
res.each_with_index do |r,i|
    unless i == 0
        r.replace({'_id'=>r['_id'], '_rev'=>r['_rev'], '_deleted'=>true})
    end
end
writem(res)

p read1("test")
```

An application written this way never has to deal with a PUT 409, and is automatically multi-master capable.

You can see that it's straightforward enough when you know what you're doing. It's just that CouchDB doesn't currently provide a convenient HTTP API for "fetch all conflicting revisions", nor "PUT to supersede these N revisions", so you need to wrap these yourself. I also don't know of any client-side libraries which provide support for this.

4.4.8 Merging and revision history

Actually performing the merge is an application-specific function. It depends on the structure of your data. Sometimes it will be easy: e.g. if a document contains a list which is only ever appended to, then you can perform a union of the two list versions.

Some merge strategies look at the changes made to an object, compared to its previous version. This is how git's merge function works.

For example, to merge Bob's business card versions v2a and v2b, you could look at the differences between v1 and v2b, and then apply these changes to v2a as well.

With CouchDB, you can sometimes get hold of old revisions of a document. For example, if you fetch /db/bob?rev=v2b&revs_info=true you'll get a list of the previous revision Ids which ended up with revision v2b. Doing the same for v2a you can find their common ancestor revision. However if the database has been compacted, the content of that document revision will have been lost. `revs_info` will still show that v1 was an ancestor, but report it as "missing":

```
BEFORE COMPACTION            AFTER COMPACTION

    ,-> v2a                      v2a
  v1
    `-> v2b                      v2b
```

So if you want to work with diffs, the recommended way is to store those diffs within the new revision itself. That is: when you replace v1 with v2a, include an extra field or attachment in v2a which says which fields were changed from v1 to v2a. This unfortunately does mean additional book-keeping for your application.

4.4.9 Comparison with other replicating data stores

The same issues arise with other replicating systems, so it can be instructive to look at these and see how they compare with CouchDB. Please feel free to add other examples.

Unison

Unison is a bi-directional file synchronisation tool. In this case, the business card would be a file, say *bob.vcf.*

When you run unison, changes propagate both ways. If a file has changed on one side but not the other, the new replaces the old. Unison maintains a local state file so that it knows whether a file has changed since the last successful replication.

In our example it has changed on both sides. Only one file called *bob.vcf* can exist within the filesystem. Unison solves the problem by simply ducking out: the user can choose to replace the remote version with the local version, or vice versa (both of which would lose data), but the default action is to leave both sides unchanged.

From Alice's point of view, at least this is a simple solution. Whenever she's on the desktop she'll see the version she last edited on the desktop, and whenever she's on the laptop she'll see the version she last edited there.

But because no replication has actually taken place, the data is not protected. If her laptop hard drive dies, she'll lose all her changes made on the laptop; ditto if her desktop hard drive dies.

It's up to her to copy across one of the versions manually (under a different filename), merge the two, and then finally push the merged version to the other side.

Note also that the original file (version v1) has been lost by this point. So it's not going to be known from inspection alone which of v2a and v2b has the most up-to-date E-mail address for Bob, and which has the most up-to-date mobile number. Alice has to remember which she entered last.

Git

Git is a well-known distributed source control system. Like Unison, git deals with files. However, git considers the state of a whole set of files as a single object, the "tree". Whenever you save an update, you create a "commit" which points to both the updated tree and the previous commit(s), which in turn point to the previous tree(s). You therefore have a full history of all the states of the files. This forms a branch, and a pointer is kept to the tip of the branch, from which you can work backwards to any previous state. The "pointer" is actually an SHA1 hash of the tip commit.

If you are replicating with one or more peers, a separate branch is made for each of the peers. For example, you might have:

```
master                 -- my local branch
remotes/foo/master     -- branch on peer 'foo'
remotes/bar/master     -- branch on peer 'bar'
```

In the normal way of working, replication is a "pull", importing changes from a remote peer into the local repository. A "pull" does two things: first "fetch" the state of the peer into the remote tracking branch for that peer; and then attempt to "merge" those changes into the local branch.

Now let's consider the business card. Alice has created a git repo containing `bob.vcf`, and cloned it across to the other machine. The branches look like this, where AAAAAAAA is the SHA1 of the commit:

```
---------- desktop ----------          ---------- laptop ----------
master: AAAAAAAA                        master: AAAAAAAA
remotes/laptop/master: AAAAAAAA         remotes/desktop/master: AAAAAAAA
```

Now she makes a change on the desktop, and commits it into the desktop repo; then she makes a different change on the laptop, and commits it into the laptop repo:

```
---------- desktop ----------          ---------- laptop ----------
master: BBBBBBBB                        master: CCCCCCCC
remotes/laptop/master: AAAAAAAA         remotes/desktop/master: AAAAAAAA
```

Now on the desktop she does `git pull laptop`. Firstly, the remote objects are copied across into the local repo and the remote tracking branch is updated:

```
---------- desktop ----------          ---------- laptop ----------
master: BBBBBBBB                        master: CCCCCCCC
remotes/laptop/master: CCCCCCCC         remotes/desktop/master: AAAAAAAA
```

Note: repo still contains AAAAAAAA because commits BBBBBBBB and CCCCCCCC point to it

---

Then git will attempt to merge the changes in. It can do this because it knows the parent commit to CCCCCCCC is AAAAAAAA, so it takes a diff between AAAAAAAA and CCCCCCCC and tries to apply it to BBBBBBBB.

If this is successful, then you'll get a new version with a merge commit:

```
---------- desktop ----------          ---------- laptop ----------
master: DDDDDDDD                        master: CCCCCCCC
remotes/laptop/master: CCCCCCCC         remotes/desktop/master: AAAAAAAA
```

Then Alice has to logon to the laptop and run `git pull desktop`. A similar process occurs. The remote tracking branch is updated:

```
---------- desktop ----------          ---------- laptop ----------
master: DDDDDDDD                        master: CCCCCCCC
remotes/laptop/master: CCCCCCCC         remotes/desktop/master: DDDDDDDD
```

Then a merge takes place. This is a special-case: CCCCCCCC one of the parent commits of DDDDDDDD, so the laptop can *fast forward* update from CCCCCCCC to DDDDDDDD directly without having to do any complex merging. This leaves the final state as:

```
---------- desktop ----------          ---------- laptop ----------
master: DDDDDDDD                        master: DDDDDDDD
remotes/laptop/master: CCCCCCCC         remotes/desktop/master: DDDDDDDD
```

Now this is all and good, but you may wonder how this is relevant when thinking about CouchDB.

Firstly, note what happens in the case when the merge algorithm fails. The changes are still propagated from the remote repo into the local one, and are available in the remote tracking branch; so unlike Unison, you know the data is protected. It's just that the local working copy may fail to update, or may diverge from the remote version. It's up to you to create and commit the combined version yourself, but you are guaranteed to have all the history you might need to do this.

Note that whilst it's possible to build new merge algorithms into Git, the standard ones are focused on line-based changes to source code. They don't work well for XML or JSON if it's presented without any line breaks.

The other interesting consideration is multiple peers. In this case you have multiple remote tracking branches, some of which may match your local branch, some of which may be behind you, and some of which may be ahead of you (i.e. contain changes that you haven't yet merged):

```
master: AAAAAAAA
remotes/foo/master: BBBBBBBB
remotes/bar/master: CCCCCCCC
remotes/baz/master: AAAAAAAA
```

Note that each peer is explicitly tracked, and therefore has to be explicitly created. If a peer becomes stale or is no longer needed, it's up to you to remove it from your configuration and delete the remote tracking branch. This is different to CouchDB, which doesn't keep any peer state in the database.

Another difference with git is that it maintains all history back to time zero - git compaction keeps diffs between all those versions in order to reduce size, but CouchDB discards them. If you are constantly updating a document, the size of a git repo would grow forever. It is possible (with some effort) to use "history rewriting" to make git forget commits earlier than a particular one.

What is the CouchDB replication protocol? Is it like Git?

> **Author** Jason Smith
>
> **Date** 2011-01-29
>
> **Source** StackOverflow

Key points

If you know Git, then you know how Couch replication works. Replicating is *very* similar to pushing or pulling with distributed source managers like Git.

CouchDB replication does not have its own protocol. A replicator simply connects to two DBs as a client, then reads from one and writes to the other. Push replication is reading the local data and updating the remote DB; pull replication is vice versa.

- **Fun fact 1**: The replicator is actually an independent Erlang application, in its own process. It connects to both couches, then reads records from one and writes them to the other.

- **Fun fact 2**: CouchDB has no way of knowing who is a normal client and who is a replicator (let alone whether the replication is push or pull). It all looks like client connections. Some of them read records. Some of them write records.

Everything flows from the data model

The replication algorithm is trivial, uninteresting. A trained monkey could design it. It's simple because the cleverness is the data model, which has these useful characteristics:

1. Every record in CouchDB is completely independent of all others. That sucks if you want to do a JOIN or a transaction, but it's awesome if you want to write a replicator. Just figure out how to replicate one record, and then repeat that for each record.

2. Like Git, records have a linked-list revision history. A record's revision ID is the checksum of its own data. Subsequent revision IDs are checksums of: the new data, plus the revision ID of the previous.

3. In addition to application data (`{"name": "Jason", "awesome": true}`), every record stores the evolutionary timeline of all previous revision IDs leading up to itself.

   - Exercise: Take a moment of quiet reflection. Consider any two different records, A and B. If A's revision ID appears in B's timeline, then B definitely evolved from A. Now consider Git's fast-forward merges. Do you hear that? That is the sound of your mind being blown.

4. Git isn't really a linear list. It has forks, when one parent has multiple children. CouchDB has that too.

   - Exercise: Compare two different records, A and B. A's revision ID does not appear in B's timeline; however, one revision ID, C, is in both A's and B's timeline. Thus A didn't evolve from B. B didn't evolve from A. But rather, A and B have a common ancestor C. In Git, that is a "fork." In CouchDB, it's a "conflict."

   - In Git, if both children go on to develop their timelines independently, that's cool. Forks totally support that.

- In CouchDB, if both children go on to develop their timelines independently, that cool too. Conflicts totally support that.

- **Fun fact 3**: CouchDB "conflicts" do not correspond to Git "conflicts." A Couch conflict is a divergent revision history, what Git calls a "fork." For this reason the CouchDB community pronounces "conflict" with a silent *n*: "co-flicked."

5. Git also has merges, when one child has multiple parents. CouchDB *sort* of has that too.

- **In the data model, there is no merge.** The client simply marks one timeline as deleted and continues to work with the only extant timeline.

- **In the application, it feels like a merge.** Typically, the client merges the *data* from each timeline in an application-specific way. Then it writes the new data to the timeline. In Git, this is like copying and pasting the changes from branch A into branch B, then commiting to branch B and deleting branch A. The data was merged, but there was no *git merge*.

- These behaviors are different because, in Git, the timeline itself is important; but in CouchDB, the data is important and the timeline is incidental—it's just there to support replication. That is one reason why CouchDB's built-in revisioning is inappropriate for storing revision data like a wiki page.

Final notes

At least one sentence in this writeup (possibly this one) is complete BS.

## CHAPTER 5

CouchDB Maintenance

5.1 Compaction

The *compaction* operation is the way to reduce disk space usage by removing unused and old data from database or view index files. This operation is a very similar to the *vacuum* (SQLite ex.) available for other database management systems.

During compaction of the *target* CouchDB creates new file with the `.compact` extension and transfers only actual data into. Because of this, CouchDB checks first for the available disk space - it should be *twice greater* than the compacted file's data.

When all actual data is successfully transferred to the *compacted* file CouchDB replaces the *target* with the *compacted* file.

5.1.1 Database Compaction

Database compaction compresses the database file by removing unused file sections created during updates. Old documents revisions are replaced with small amount of metadata called *tombstone* which are used for conflicts resolution during replication. The number of stored revisions (and their *tombstones*) can be configured by using the `_revs_limit` URL endpoint.

Compaction is manually triggered operation per database and runs as a background task. To start it for specific database there is need to send HTTP `POST /{db}/_compact` sub-resource of the target database:

```
curl -H "Content-Type: application/json" -X POST http://localhost:5984/my_db/_compact
```

On success, HTTP status 202 Accepted is returned immediately:

```
HTTP/1.1 202 Accepted
Cache-Control: must-revalidate
Content-Length: 12
Content-Type: text/plain; charset=utf-8
Date: Wed, 19 Jun 2013 09:43:52 GMT
Server: CouchDB (Erlang/OTP)
```

```
{"ok":true}
```

Although the request body is not used you must still specify Content-Type header with `application/json` value for the request. If you don't, you will be aware about with HTTP status 415 Unsupported Media Type response:

```
HTTP/1.1 415 Unsupported Media Type
Cache-Control: must-revalidate
Content-Length: 78
Content-Type: application/json
Date: Wed, 19 Jun 2013 09:43:44 GMT
Server: CouchDB (Erlang/OTP)
```

```
{"error":"bad_content_type","reason":"Content-Type must be application/json"}
```

When the compaction is successful started and running it is possible to get information about it via *database information resource*:

```
curl http://localhost:5984/my_db
```

```
HTTP/1.1 200 OK
Cache-Control: must-revalidate
Content-Length: 246
Content-Type: application/json
Date: Wed, 19 Jun 2013 16:51:20 GMT
Server: CouchDB (Erlang/OTP)

{
    "committed_update_seq": 76215,
    "compact_running": true,
    "data_size": 3787996,
    "db_name": "my_db",
    "disk_format_version": 6,
    "disk_size": 17703025,
    "doc_count": 5091,
    "doc_del_count": 0,
    "instance_start_time": "1371660751878859",
    "purge_seq": 0,
    "update_seq": 76215
}
```

Note that `compaction_running` field is `true` indicating that compaction is actually running. To track the compaction progress you may query the `_active_tasks` resource:

```
curl http://localhost:5984/my_db
```

```
HTTP/1.1 200 OK
Cache-Control: must-revalidate
Content-Length: 175
Content-Type: application/json
Date: Wed, 19 Jun 2013 16:27:23 GMT
Server: CouchDB (Erlang/OTP)

[
    {
        "changes_done": 44461,
        "database": "my_db",
        "pid": "<0.218.0>",
        "progress": 58,
        "started_on": 1371659228,
        "total_changes": 76215,
        "type": "database_compaction",
        "updated_on": 1371659241
    }
]
```

5.1.2 Views Compaction

Views are also need compaction like databases, unlike databases views are compacted by groups per *design document*. To start their compaction there is need to send HTTP *POST /{db}/_compact/{ddoc}* request:

```
curl -H "Content-Type: application/json" -X POST http://localhost:5984/dbname/_compact/de
```

```
{"ok":true}
```

This compacts the view index from the current version of the specified design document. The HTTP response code is 202 Accepted (like *compaction for databases*) and a compaction background task will be created.

Views cleanup

View indexes on disk are named after their *MD5* hash of the view definition. When you change a view, old indexes remain on disk. To clean up all outdated view indexes (files named after the MD5 representation of views, that does not exist anymore) you can trigger a *view cleanup*:

```
curl -H "Content-Type: application/json" -X POST http://localhost:5984/dbname/_view_clean
```

```
{"ok":true}
```

5.1.3 Automatic Compaction

While both *database* and *views* compactions are required be manually triggered, it is also possible to configure automatic compaction, so that compaction of databases and views is automatically triggered based on various criteria. Automatic compaction is configured in CouchDB's *configuration files*.

The `daemons/compaction_daemon` is responsible for triggering the compaction. It is automatically started, but disabled by default. The criteria for triggering the compactions is configured in the `compactions` section.

5.2 Performance

With up to tens of thousands of documents you will generally find CouchDB to perform well no matter how you write your code. Once you start getting into the millions of documents you need to be a lot more careful.

5.2.1 Disk I/O

File Size

The smaller your file size, the less *I/O* operations there will be, the more of the file can be cached by CouchDB and the operating system, the quicker it is to replicate, backup etc. Consequently you should carefully examine the data you are storing. For example it would be silly to use keys that are hundreds of characters long, but your program would be hard to maintain if you only used single character keys. Carefully consider data that is duplicated by putting it in views.

Disk and File System Performance

Using faster disks, striped RAID arrays and modern file systems can all speed up your CouchDB deployment. However, there is one option that can increase the responsiveness of your CouchDB server when disk performance is a bottleneck. From the Erlang documentation for the file module:

> On operating systems with thread support, it is possible to let file operations be performed in threads of their own, allowing other Erlang processes to continue executing in parallel with the file operations. See the command line flag +A in erl(1).

Setting this argument to a number greater than zero can keep your CouchDB installation responsive even during periods of heavy disk utilization. The easiest way to set this option is through the `ERL_FLAGS` environment variable. For example, to give Erlang four threads with which to perform I/O operations add the following to `(prefix)/etc/defaults/couchdb` (or equivalent):

```
export ERL_FLAGS="+A 4"
```

5.2.2 System Resource Limits

One of the problems that administrators run into as their deployments become large are resource limits imposed by the system and by the application configuration. Raising these limits can allow your deployment to grow beyond what the default configuration will support.

CouchDB Configuration Options

delayed_commits

The `delayed commits` allows to achieve better write performance for some workloads while sacrificing a small amount of durability. The setting causes CouchDB to wait up to a full second before committing new data after an update. If the server crashes before the header is written then any writes since the last commit are lost. Keep this option enabled on your own risk.

max_dbs_open

In your *configuration* (local.ini or similar) familiarize yourself with the `couchdb/max_dbs_open`:

```
[couchdb]
max_dbs_open = 100
```

This option places an upper bound on the number of databases that can be open at one time. CouchDB reference counts database accesses internally and will close idle databases when it must. Sometimes it is necessary to keep more than the default open at once, such as in deployments where many databases will be continuously replicating.

Erlang

Even if you've increased the maximum connections CouchDB will allow, the Erlang runtime system will not allow more than 1024 connections by default. Adding the following directive to `(prefix)/etc/default/couchdb` (or equivalent) will increase this limit (in this case to 4096):

```
export ERL_MAX_PORTS=4096
```

CouchDB versions up to 1.1.x also create Erlang Term Storage (ETS) tables for each replication. If you are using a version of CouchDB older than 1.2 and must support many replications, also set the ERL_MAX_ETS_TABLES variable. The default is approximately 1400 tables.

Note that on Mac OS X, Erlang will not actually increase the file descriptor limit past 1024 (i.e. the system header–defined value of FD_SETSIZE). See this tip for a possible workaround and this thread for a deeper explanation.

PAM and ulimit

Finally, most *nix operating systems impose various resource limits on every process. If your system is set up to use the Pluggable Authentication Modules (PAM) system, increasing this limit is straightforward. For example, creating a file named `/etc/security/limits.d/100-couchdb.conf` with the following contents will ensure that CouchDB can open enough file descriptors to service your increased maximum open databases and Erlang ports:

```
#<domain>      <type>    <item>     <value>
couchdb        hard      nofile     4096
couchdb        soft      nofile     4096
```

If your system does not use PAM, a *ulimit* command is usually available for use in a custom script to launch CouchDB with increased resource limits. If necessary, feel free to increase this limits as long as your hardware can handle the load.

5.2.3 Network

There is latency overhead making and receiving each request/response. In general you should do your requests in batches. Most APIs have some mechanism to do batches, usually by supplying lists of documents or keys in the request body. Be careful what size you pick for the batches. The larger batch requires more time your client has to spend encoding the items into JSON and more time is spent decoding that number of responses. Do some benchmarking with your own configuration and typical data to find the sweet spot. It is likely to be between one and ten thousand documents.

If you have a fast I/O system then you can also use concurrency - have multiple requests/responses at the same time. This mitigates the latency involved in assembling JSON, doing the networking and decoding JSON.

As of CouchDB 1.1.0, users often report lower write performance of documents compared to older releases. The main reason is that this release ships with the more recent version of the HTTP server library Mochiweb, which by default sets the TCP socket option SO_NODELAY to false. This means that small data sent to the TCP socket, like the reply to a document write request (or reading a very small document), will not be sent immediately to the network - TCP will buffer it for a while hoping that it will be asked to send more data through the same socket and then send all the data at once for increased performance. This TCP buffering behaviour can be disabled via `httpd/socket_options`:

```
[httpd]
socket_options = [{nodelay, true}]
```

See also:

Bulk *load* and *store* API.

5.2.4 CouchDB

DELETE operation

When you DELETE a document the database will create a new revision which contains the _id and _rev fields as well as the *_deleted* flag. This revision will remain even after a *database compaction* so that the deletion can be replicated. Deleted documents, like non-deleted documents, can affect view build times, PUT and DELETE requests time and size of database on disk, since they increase the size of the B+Tree's. You can see the number of deleted documents in `database information`. If your use case creates lots of deleted documents (for example, if you are storing short-term data like logfile entries, message queues, etc), you might want to periodically switch to a new database and delete the old one (once the entries in it have all expired).

Document's ID

The db file size is derived from your document and view sizes but also on a multiple of your _id sizes. Not only is the _id present in the document, but it and parts of it are duplicated in the binary tree structure CouchDB uses to navigate the file to find the document in the first place. As a real world example for one user switching from 16 byte ids to 4 byte ids made a database go from 21GB to 4GB with 10 million documents (the raw JSON text when from 2.5GB to 2GB).

Inserting with sequential (and at least sorted) ids is faster than random ids. Consequently you should consider generating ids yourself, allocating them sequentially and using an encoding scheme that consumes fewer bytes. For example, something that takes 16 hex digits to represent can be done in 4 base 62 digits (10 numerals, 26 lower case, 26 upper case).

5.2.5 Views

Views Generation

Views with the JavaScript query server are extremely slow to generate when there are a non-trivial number of documents to process. The generation process won't even saturate a single CPU let alone your I/O. The cause is the latency involved in the CouchDB server and separate *couchjs* query server, dramatically indicating how important it is to take latency out of your implementation.

You can let view access be "stale" but it isn't practical to determine when that will occur giving you a quick response and when views will be updated which will take a long time. (A 10 million document database took about 10 minutes to load into CouchDB but about 4 hours to do view generation).

View information isn't replicated - it is rebuilt on each database so you can't do the view generation on a separate sever.

Builtin Reduce Functions

If you're using a very simple view function that only performs a sum or count reduction, you can call native Erlang implementations of them by simply writing _sum or _count in place of your function declaration. This will speed up things dramatically, as it cuts down on IO between CouchDB and the *JavaScript query server*. For example, as mentioned on the mailing list, the time for outputting an (already indexed and cached) view with about 78,000 items went down from 60 seconds to 4 seconds.

Before:

```
{
    "_id": "_design/foo",
    "views": {
        "bar": {
            "map": "function (doc) { emit(doc.author, 1); }",
            "reduce": "function (keys, values, rereduce) { return sum(values); }"
        }
    }
}
```

After:

```
{
    "_id": "_design/foo",
    "views": {
        "bar": {
            "map": "function (doc) { emit(doc.author, 1); }",
            "reduce": "_sum"
        }
    }
}
```

See also:

Builtin reduce functions

## CHAPTER 6

CouchApp

CouchApps are web applications served directly from CouchDB, mostly driven by JavaScript and HTML5. If you can fit your application into those constraints, then you get CouchDB's scalability and flexibility "for free" (and deploying your app is as simple as replicating it to the production server).

6.1 Design Functions

In this section we'll show how to write design documents, using the built-in *JavaScript Query Server*.

But before we start to write our first function, let's take a look at the list of common objects that will be used during our code journey - we'll be using them extensively within each function:

- *Database information object*
- *Request object*
- *Response object*
- *UserCtx object*
- *Database Security object*
- *Guide to JavaScript Query Server*

6.1.1 View functions

Views are the primary tool used for querying and reporting on CouchDB databases.

Map functions

mapfun (*doc*)

> **Arguments**
>
> > - **doc** – Processed document object.

Map functions accept a single document as the argument and (optionally) *emit ()* key/value pairs that are stored in a view.

```
function (doc) {
  if (doc.type === 'post' && doc.tags && Array.isArray(doc.tags)) {
    doc.tags.forEach(function (tag) {
      emit(tag.toLowerCase(), 1);
    });
  }
}
```

In this example a key/value pair is emitted for each value in the *tags* array of a document with a *type* of "post". Note that `emit ()` may be called many times for a single document, so the same document may be available by several different keys.

Also keep in mind that each document is *sealed* to prevent the situation where one map function changes document state and another receives a modified version.

For efficiency reasons, documents are passed to a group of map functions - each document is processed by group of map functions from all views of related design document. This means that if you trigger index update for one view in ddoc, all others will get updated too.

Since version *1.1.0*, *map* supports *CommonJS* modules and the `require ()` function.

Reduce and rereduce functions

redfun (*keys*, *values*[, *rereduce*])

> **Arguments**
>
> > * **keys** – Array of pairs of docid-key for related map function results. Always `null` if rereduce is running (has `true` value).
> >
> > * **values** – Array of map function result values.
> >
> > * **rereduce** – Boolean sign of rereduce run.
>
> **Returns** Reduces *values*

Reduce functions takes two required arguments of keys and values lists - the result of the related map function - and an optional third value which indicates if *rereduce* mode is active or not. *Rereduce* is used for additional reduce values list, so when it is `true` there is no information about related *keys* (first argument is `null`).

Note that if the result of a *reduce* function is longer than the initial values list then a Query Server error will be raised. However, this behavior can be disabled by setting `reduce_limit` config option to `false`:

```
[query_server_config]
reduce_limit = false
```

While disabling `reduce_limit` might be useful for debug proposes, remember that the main task of reduce functions is to *reduce* the mapped result, not to make it bigger. Generally, your reduce function should converge rapidly to a single value - which could be an array or similar object.

Builtin reduce functions

Additionally, CouchDB has three built-in reduce functions. These are implemented in Erlang and run inside CouchDB, so they are much faster than the equivalent JavaScript functions: `_sum`, `_count` and `_stats`. Their equivalents in JavaScript:

```
// could be replaced by _sum
function(keys, values) {
    return sum(values);
}

// could be replaced by _count
function(keys, values, rereduce) {
    if (rereduce) {
        return sum(values);
    } else {
        return values.length;
    }
}

// could be replaced by _stats
```

```
function(keys, values, rereduce) {
    if (rereduce) {
        return {
            'sum': values.reduce(function(a, b) { return a + b.sum }, 0),
            'min': values.reduce(function(a, b) { return Math.min(a, b.min) }, Infinity),
            'max': values.reduce(function(a, b) { return Math.max(a, b.max) }, -Infinity)
            'count': values.reduce(function(a, b) { return a + b.count }, 0),
            'sumsqr': values.reduce(function(a, b) { return a + b.sumsqr }, 0)
        }
    } else {
        return {
            'sum': sum(values),
            'min': Math.min.apply(null, values),
            'max': Math.max.apply(null, values),
            'count': values.length,
            'sumsqr': (function() {
            var sumsqr = 0;

            values.forEach(function (value) {
                sumsqr += value * value;
            });

            return sumsqr;
            })(),
        }
    }
}
```

Note: Why don't reduce functions support CommonJS modules?

While *map* functions have limited access to stored modules through `require()`, there is no such feature for *reduce* functions. The reason lies deep inside the way *map* and *reduce* functions are processed by the Query Server. Let's take a look at *map* functions first:

1. CouchDB sends all *map* functions for a processed design document to Query Server.

2. Query Server handles them one by one, compiles and puts them onto an internal stack.

3. After all *map* functions have been processed, CouchDB will send the remaining documents to index, one by one.

4. Query Server receives the document object and applies it to every function from the stack. The emitted results are then joined into a single array and sent back to CouchDB.

Now let's see how *reduce* functions are handled:

1. CouchDB sends *as single command* list of available *reduce* functions with result list of key-value pairs that was previously received as the result of *map* functions' work.

2. Query Server compiles reduce functions and applies them to key-value lists. Reduced result is sent back to CouchDB.

As you may note, *reduce* functions are applied in a single shot to the map results while the *map* functions are applied in an iterative way to one document at a time. This means that it's possible for *map* functions to precompile CommonJS libraries and use them during the entire view processing, but for *reduce* functions they would be compiled again and again for each view result reduction, which would lead to performance degradation (*reduce* function are already working hard to make large results smaller).

6.1.2 Show functions

showfun (*doc*, *req*)

        Arguments

- **doc** – Processed document, may be omitted.
- **req** – *Request object*.

Returns *Response object*

Return type object or string

Show functions are used to represent documents in various formats, commonly as HTML pages with nice formatting. They can also be used to run server-side functions without requiring a pre-existing document.

Basic example of show function could be:

```
function(doc, req){
    if (doc) {
        return "Hello from " + doc._id + "!";
    } else {
        return "Hello, world!";
    }
}
```

Also, there is more simple way to return json encoded data:

```
function(doc, req){
    return {
        'json': {
            'id': doc['_id'],
            'rev': doc['_rev']
        }
    }
}
```

and even files (this one is CouchDB logo):

```
function(doc, req){
    return {
        'headers': {
            'Content-Type' : 'image/png',
        },
        'base64': ''.concat(
            'iVBORw0KGgoAAAANSUhEUgAAABAAAAAQCAMAAAAoLQ9TAAAAsV',
            'BMVEUAAAD//////////////////////5ur3rEBn///////////wDBL/',
            'AADuBAe9EB3IEBz/7+//X1/qBQn2AgP/f3/ilpzsDxfpChDtDhXeCA76AQH/v7',
            '/84eLyWV/uc3bJPEf/Dw/uw8bRWmP1h4zxSlD6YGHuQ0f6g4XyQkXvCA36MDH6',
            'wMH/z8/yAwX64ODeh47BHiv/Ly/20dLQLTj98PDXWmP/Pz//39/wGyJ7Iy9JAA',
            'AADHRSTlMAbw8vf08/bz+Pv19jK/W3AAAAgOlEQVR4Xp3LRQ4DQRBD0QqTm4Y5',
            'zMxw/4OleiJlHeUtv2X6RbNO1Uqj9g0RMCuQO0vBIg4vMFeOpCWIWmDOw82fZx',
            'vaND1c8OG4vrdOqD8YwgpDYDxRgkSm5rwu0nQVBJuMg++pLXZyr5jnc1BaH4GT',
            'LvEliY253nA3pVhQqdPt0f/erJkMGMB8xucAAAAASUVORK5CYII=')
    }
}
```

But what if you need to represent data in different formats via a single function? Functions `registerType()` and `provides()` are your the best friends in that question:

```
function(doc, req){
    provides('json', function(){
        return {'json': doc}
    });
    provides('html', function(){
        return '<pre>' + toJSON(doc) + '</pre>'
    })
    provides('xml', function(){
        return {
            'headers': {'Content-Type': 'application/xml'},
            'body' : ''.concat(
```

```
                    '<?xml version="1.0" encoding="utf-8"?>\n',
                    '<doc>',
                    (function(){
                        escape = function(s){
                            return s.replace(/&quot;/g, '"')
                                    .replace(/&gt;/g, '>')
                                    .replace(/&lt;/g, '<')
                                    .replace(/&amp;/g, '&');
                        };
                        var content = '';
                        for(var key in doc){
                            if(!doc.hasOwnProperty(key)) continue;
                            var value = escape(toJSON(doc[key]));
                            var key = escape(key);
                            content += ''.concat(
                                '<' + key + '>',
                                value
                                '</' + key + '>'
                            )
                        }
                        return content;
                    })(),
                    '</doc>'
                )
            }
        })
    registerType('text-json', 'text/json')
    provides('text-json', function(){
        return toJSON(doc);
    })
}
```

This function may return *html*, *json* , *xml* or our custom *text json* format representation of same document object with same processing rules. Probably, the *xml* provider in our function needs more care to handle nested objects correctly, and keys with invalid characters, but you've got the idea!

See also:

CouchDB Wiki:

- Showing Documents

CouchDB Guide:

- Show Functions

6.1.3 List functions

`listfun` (*head, req*)

> **Arguments**
>
> > - **head** – *View Head Information*
> >
> > - **req** – *Request object.*
>
> **Returns** Last chunk.
>
> **Return type** string

While *Show functions* are used to customize document presentation, *List functions* are used for same purpose, but against *View functions* results.

The next list function formats view and represents it as a very simple HTML page:

```
function(head, req){
    start({
        'headers': {
            'Content-Type': 'text/html'
        }
    });
    send('<html><body><table>');
    send('<tr><th>ID</th><th>Key</th><th>Value</th></tr>')
    while(row = getRow()){
        send(''.concat(
            '<tr>',
            '<td>' + toJSON(row.id) + '</td>',
            '<td>' + toJSON(row.key) + '</td>',
            '<td>' + toJSON(row.value) + '</td>',
            '</tr>'
        ));
    }
    send('</table></body></html>');
}
```

Templates and styles could obviously be used to present data in a nicer fashion, but this is an excellent starting point. Note that you may also use *registerType()* and *provides()* functions in the same way as for *Show functions*!

See also:

CouchDB Wiki:

- Listing Views with CouchDB 0.10 and later

CouchDB Guide:

- Transforming Views with List Functions

6.1.4 Update functions

updatefun (*doc*, *req*)

> **Arguments**
>
> > - **doc** – Update function target document.
> >
> > - **req** – *Request object*
>
> **Returns** Two-element array: the first element is the (updated or new) document, which is committed to the database. If the first element is `null` no document will be committed to the database. If you are updating an existing document, it should already have an `_id` set, and if you are creating a new document, make sure to set its `_id` to something, either generated based on the input or the `req.uuid` provided. The second element is the response that will be sent back to the caller.

Update handlers are functions that clients can request to invoke server-side logic that will create or update a document. This feature allows a range of use cases such as providing a server-side last modified timestamp, updating individual fields in a document without first getting the latest revision, etc.

When the request to an update handler includes a document ID in the URL, the server will provide the function with the most recent version of that document. You can provide any other values needed by the update handler function via the `POST/PUT` entity body or query string parameters of the request.

The basic example that demonstrates all use-cases of update handlers below:

```
function(doc, req){
    if (!doc){
        if ('id' in req && req['id']){
            // create new document
```

```
            return [{'_id': req['id']}, 'New World']
        }
        // change nothing in database
        return [null, 'Empty World']
    }
    doc['world'] = 'hello';
    doc['edited_by'] = req['userCtx']['name']
    return [doc, 'Edited World!']
}
```

See also:

CouchDB Wiki:

> • Document Update Handlers

6.1.5 Filter functions

filterfun (*doc*, *req*)

> **Arguments**
>
> > • **doc** – Processed document object.
> >
> > • **req** – *Request object*
>
> **Returns** Boolean value: `true` means that *doc* passes the filter rules, `false` means that it does not.

Filter functions mostly act like *Show functions* and *List functions*: they format, or *filter* the *changes feed*.

Classic filters

By default the changes feed emits all database documents changes. But if you're waiting for some special changes, processing all documents is inefficient.

Filters are special design document functions that allow the changes feed to emit only specific documents that pass filter rules.

Let's assume that our database is a mailbox and we need to handle only new mail events (documents with status *new*). Our filter function will look like this:

```
function(doc, req){
    // we need only 'mail' documents
    if (doc.type != 'mail'){
        return false;
    }
    // we're interested only in 'new' ones
    if (doc.status != 'new'){
        return false;
    }
    return true; // passed!
}
```

Filter functions must return `true` if a document passed all defined rules. Now, if you apply this function to the changes feed it will emit only changes about "new mails":

```
GET /somedatabase/_changes?filter=mailbox/new_mail HTTP/1.1
```

```
{"results":[
{"seq":1,"id":"df8eca9da37dade42ee4d7aa3401f1dd","changes":[{"rev":"1-c2e0085a21d34f1cec
{"seq":7,"id":"df8eca9da37dade42ee4d7aa34024714","changes":[{"rev":"1-29d748a6e87b43db967
],
"last_seq":27}
```

Note that the value of last_seq is 27, but we received only two records. Seems like any other changes were for documents that haven't passed our filter.

We probably need to filter the changes feed of our mailbox by more than a single status value. We're also interested in statuses like "spam" to update spam-filter heuristic rules, "outgoing" to let a mail daemon actually send mails, and so on. Creating a lot of similar functions that actually do similar work isn't good idea - so we need a dynamic filter.

You may have noticed that filter functions take a second argument named *request*. This allows the creation of dynamic filters based on query parameters, *user context* and more.

The dynamic version of our filter looks like this:

```
function(doc, req){
    // we need only `mail` documents
    if (doc.type != 'mail'){
        return false;
    }
    // we're interested only in requested status
    if (doc.status != req.query.status){
        return false;
    }
    return true; // passed!
}
```

and now we have passed the *status* query parameter in request to let our filter match only required documents:

```
GET /somedatabase/_changes?filter=mailbox/by_status&status=new HTTP/1.1
```

```
{"results":[
{"seq":1,"id":"df8eca9da37dade42ee4d7aa3401f1dd","changes":[{"rev":"1-c2e0085a21d34f1cec
{"seq":7,"id":"df8eca9da37dade42ee4d7aa34024714","changes":[{"rev":"1-29d748a6e87b43db967
],
"last_seq":27}
```

and we can easily change filter behavior with:

```
GET /somedatabase/_changes?filter=mailbox/by_status&status=spam HTTP/1.1
```

```
{"results":[
{"seq":11,"id":"8960e91220798fc9f9d29d24ed612e0d","changes":[{"rev":"3-cc6ff71af716ddc2ba
],
"last_seq":27}
```

Combining filters with a *continuous* feed allows creating powerful event-driven systems.

View filters

View filters are the same as above, with one small difference: they use views *map* function instead to *filter* one to process the changes feed. Each time a key-value pair could be emitted, a change is returned. This allows us to avoid creating filter functions that mostly do the same works as views.

To use them just specify _view value for filter parameter and *designdoc/viewname* for view one:

```
GET /somedatabase/_changes?filter=_view&view=dname/viewname  HTTP/1.1
```

Note: Since view filters uses *map* functions as filters, they can't show any dynamic behavior since *request object* is not available.

See also:

CouchDB Guide:

- Guide to filter change notification

CouchDB Wiki:

- Filtered replication

6.1.6 Validate document update functions

validatefun (*newDoc, oldDoc, userCtx, secObj*)

> **Arguments**
>
> - **newDoc** – New version of document that will be stored.
> - **oldDoc** – Previous version of document that is already stored.
> - **userCtx** – *User Context Object*
> - **secObj** – *Security Object*
>
> **Throws** forbidden error to gracefully prevent document storing.
>
> **Throws** unauthorized error to prevent storage and allow the user to re-auth.

A design document may contain a function named *validate_doc_update* which can be used to prevent invalid or unauthorized document update requests from being stored. The function is passed the new document from the update request, the current document stored in the database, a *User Context Object* containing information about the user writing the document (if present), and a *Security Object* with lists of database security roles.

Validation functions typically examine the structure of the new document to ensure that required fields are present and to verify that the requesting user should be allowed to make changes to the document properties. For example, an application may require that a user must be authenticated in order to create a new document or that specific document fields be present when a document is updated. The validation function can abort the pending document write by throwing one of two error objects:

```
// user is not authorized to make the change but may re-authenticate
throw({ unauthorized: 'Error message here.' });

// change is not allowed
throw({ forbidden: 'Error message here.' });
```

Document validation is optional, and each design document in the database may have at most one validation function. When a write request is received for a given database, the validation function in each design document in that database is called in an unspecified order. If any of the validation functions throw an error, the write will not succeed.

Example: The _design/_auth ddoc from *_users* database uses a validation function to ensure that documents contain some required fields and are only modified by a user with the _admin role:

```
function(newDoc, oldDoc, userCtx, secObj) {
    if (newDoc._deleted === true) {
        // allow deletes by admins and matching users
        // without checking the other fields
        if ((userCtx.roles.indexOf('_admin') !== -1) ||
            (userCtx.name == oldDoc.name)) {
            return;
        } else {
            throw({forbidden: 'Only admins may delete other user docs.'});
        }
    }

    if ((oldDoc && oldDoc.type !== 'user') || newDoc.type !== 'user') {
        throw({forbidden : 'doc.type must be user'});
    } // we only allow user docs for now

    if (!newDoc.name) {
        throw({forbidden: 'doc.name is required'});
```

```
    }

    if (!newDoc.roles) {
        throw({forbidden: 'doc.roles must exist'});
    }

    if (!isArray(newDoc.roles)) {
        throw({forbidden: 'doc.roles must be an array'});
    }

    if (newDoc._id !== ('org.couchdb.user:' + newDoc.name)) {
        throw({
            forbidden: 'Doc ID must be of the form org.couchdb.user:name'
        });
    }

    if (oldDoc) { // validate all updates
        if (oldDoc.name !== newDoc.name) {
            throw({forbidden: 'Usernames can not be changed.'});
        }
    }

    if (newDoc.password_sha && !newDoc.salt) {
        throw({
            forbidden: 'Users with password_sha must have a salt.' +
                'See /_utils/script/couch.js for example code.'
        });
    }

    var is_server_or_database_admin = function(userCtx, secObj) {
        // see if the user is a server admin
        if(userCtx.roles.indexOf('_admin') !== -1) {
            return true; // a server admin
        }

        // see if the user a database admin specified by name
        if(secObj && secObj.admins && secObj.admins.names) {
            if(secObj.admins.names.indexOf(userCtx.name) !== -1) {
                return true; // database admin
            }
        }

        // see if the user a database admin specified by role
        if(secObj && secObj.admins && secObj.admins.roles) {
            var db_roles = secObj.admins.roles;
            for(var idx = 0; idx < userCtx.roles.length; idx++) {
                var user_role = userCtx.roles[idx];
                if(db_roles.indexOf(user_role) !== -1) {
                    return true; // role matches!
                }
            }
        }

        return false; // default to no admin
    }

    if (!is_server_or_database_admin(userCtx, secObj)) {
        if (oldDoc) { // validate non-admin updates
            if (userCtx.name !== newDoc.name) {
                throw({
                    forbidden: 'You may only update your own user document.'
                });
            }
```

```
                // validate role updates
        var oldRoles = oldDoc.roles.sort();
        var newRoles = newDoc.roles.sort();

        if (oldRoles.length !== newRoles.length) {
            throw({forbidden: 'Only _admin may edit roles'});
        }

        for (var i = 0; i < oldRoles.length; i++) {
            if (oldRoles[i] !== newRoles[i]) {
                throw({forbidden: 'Only _admin may edit roles'});
            }
        }
    } else if (newDoc.roles.length > 0) {
        throw({forbidden: 'Only _admin may set roles'});
    }
}

// no system roles in users db
for (var i = 0; i < newDoc.roles.length; i++) {
    if (newDoc.roles[i][0] === '_') {
        throw({
            forbidden:
            'No system roles (starting with underscore) in users db.'
        });
    }
}

// no system names as names
if (newDoc.name[0] === '_') {
    throw({forbidden: 'Username may not start with underscore.'});
}

var badUserNameChars = [':'];

for (var i = 0; i < badUserNameChars.length; i++) {
    if (newDoc.name.indexOf(badUserNameChars[i]) >= 0) {
        throw({forbidden: 'Character `' + badUserNameChars[i] +
                '` is not allowed in usernames.'});
    }
}
}
```

Note: The `return` statement is used only for function, it has no impact on the validation process.

See also:

CouchDB Guide:

  • Validation Functions

CouchDB Wiki:

  • Document Update Validation

6.2 Guide to Views

Views are the primary tool used for querying and reporting on CouchDB documents. There you'll learn how they works and how to use them to build effective applications with CouchDB

6.2.1 Introduction to Views

Views are useful for many purposes:

- Filtering the documents in your database to find those relevant to a particular process.

- Extracting data from your documents and presenting it in a specific order.

- Building efficient indexes to find documents by any value or structure that resides in them.

- Use these indexes to represent relationships among documents.

- Finally, with views you can make all sorts of calculations on the data in your documents. For example, if documents represent your company's financial transactions, a view can answer the question of what the spending was in the last week, month, or year.

What Is a View?

Let's go through the different use cases. First is extracting data that you might need for a special purpose in a specific order. For a front page, we want a list of blog post titles sorted by date. We'll work with a set of example documents as we walk through how views work:

```
{
    "_id":"biking",
    "_rev":"AE19EBC7654",

    "title":"Biking",
    "body":"My biggest hobby is mountainbiking. The other day...",
    "date":"2009/01/30 18:04:11"
}
```

```
{
    "_id":"bought-a-cat",
    "_rev":"4A3BBEE711",

    "title":"Bought a Cat",
    "body":"I went to the the pet store earlier and brought home a little kitty...",
    "date":"2009/02/17 21:13:39"
}
```

```
{
    "_id":"hello-world",
    "_rev":"43FBA4E7AB",

    "title":"Hello World",
    "body":"Well hello and welcome to my new blog...",
    "date":"2009/01/15 15:52:20"
}
```

Three will do for the example. Note that the documents are sorted by "_id", which is how they are stored in the database. Now we define a view. Bear with us without an explanation while we show you some code:

```
function(doc) {
    if(doc.date && doc.title) {
        emit(doc.date, doc.title);
    }
}
```

This is a *map function*, and it is written in JavaScript. If you are not familiar with JavaScript but have used C or any other C-like language such as Java, PHP, or C#, this should look familiar. It is a simple function definition.

You provide CouchDB with view functions as strings stored inside the `views` field of a design document. You don't run it yourself. Instead, when you *query your view*, CouchDB takes the source code and runs it for you on every document in the database your view was defined in. You *query your view* to retrieve the *view result*.

All map functions have a single parameter doc. This is a single document in the database. Our map function checks whether our document has a `date` and a `title` attribute — luckily, all of our documents have them — and then calls the built-in `emit()` function with these two attributes as arguments.

The `emit()` function always takes two arguments: the first is `key`, and the second is `value`. The `emit(key, value)` function creates an entry in our *view result*. One more thing: the `emit()` function can be called multiple times in the map function to create multiple entries in the view results from a single document, but we are not doing that yet.

CouchDB takes whatever you pass into the emit() function and puts it into a list (see Table 1, "View results" below). Each row in that list includes the *key* and *value*. More importantly, the list is sorted by key (by `doc.date` in our case). The most important feature of a view result is that it is sorted by *key*. We will come back to that over and over again to do neat things. Stay tuned.

Table 1. View results:

Key	Value
"2009/01/15 15:52:20"	"Hello World"
"2009/01/30 18:04:11"	"Biking"
"2009/02/17 21:13:39"	"Bought a Cat"

When you query your view, CouchDB takes the source code and runs it for you on every document in the database. If you have a lot of documents, that takes quite a bit of time and you might wonder if it is not horribly inefficient to do this. Yes, it would be, but CouchDB is designed to avoid any extra costs: it only runs through all documents once, when you first query your view. If a document is changed, the map function is only run once, to recompute the keys and values for that single document.

The view result is stored in a B-tree, just like the structure that is responsible for holding your documents. View B-trees are stored in their own file, so that for high-performance CouchDB usage, you can keep views on their own disk. The B-tree provides very fast lookups of rows by key, as well as efficient streaming of rows in a key range. In our example, a single view can answer all questions that involve time: "Give me all the blog posts from last week" or "last month" or "this year." Pretty neat.

When we query our view, we get back a list of all documents sorted by date. Each row also includes the post title so we can construct links to posts. Table 1 is just a graphical representation of the view result. The actual result is JSON-encoded and contains a little more metadata:

```
{
    "total_rows": 3,
    "offset": 0,
    "rows": [
        {
            "key": "2009/01/15 15:52:20",
            "id": "hello-world",
            "value": "Hello World"
        },

        {
            "key": "2009/01/30 18:04:11",
            "id": "biking",
            "value": "Biking"
        },

        {
            "key": "2009/02/17 21:13:39",
            "id": "bought-a-cat",
            "value": "Bought a Cat"
        }

    ]
}
```

Now, the actual result is not as nicely formatted and doesn't include any superfluous whitespace or newlines, but this is better for you (and us!) to read and understand. Where does that "id" member in the result rows come from? That wasn't there before. That's because we omitted it earlier to avoid confusion. CouchDB automatically includes the document ID of the document that created the entry in the view result. We'll use this as well when constructing links to the blog post pages.

Efficient Lookups

Let's move on to the second use case for views: "building efficient indexes to find documents by any value or structure that resides in them." We already explained the efficient indexing, but we skipped a few details. This is a good time to finish this discussion as we are looking at map functions that are a little more complex.

First, back to the B-trees! We explained that the B-tree that backs the key-sorted view result is built only once, when you first query a view, and all subsequent queries will just read the B-tree instead of executing the map function for all documents again. What happens, though, when you change a document, add a new one, or delete one? Easy: CouchDB is smart enough to find the rows in the view result that were created by a specific document. It marks them invalid so that they no longer show up in view results. If the document was deleted, we're good — the resulting B-tree reflects the state of the database. If a document got updated, the new document is run through the map function and the resulting new lines are inserted into the B-tree at the correct spots. New documents are handled in the same way. The B-tree is a very efficient data structure for our needs, and the crash-only design of CouchDB databases is carried over to the view indexes as well.

To add one more point to the efficiency discussion: usually multiple documents are updated between view queries. The mechanism explained in the previous paragraph gets applied to all changes in the database since the last time the view was queried in a batch operation, which makes things even faster and is generally a better use of your resources.

Find One

On to more complex map functions. We said "find documents by any value or structure that resides in them." We already explained how to extract a value by which to sort a list of views (our date field). The same mechanism is used for fast lookups. The URI to query to get a view's result is `/database/_design/designdocname/_view/viewname`. This gives you a list of all rows in the view. We have only three documents, so things are small, but with thousands of documents, this can get long. You can add view parameters to the URI to constrain the result set. Say we know the date of a blog post. To find a single document, we would use `/blog/_design/docs/_view/by_date?key="2009/01/30 18:04:11"` to get the "Biking" blog post. Remember that you can place whatever you like in the key parameter to the emit() function. Whatever you put in there, we can now use to look up exactly — and fast.

Note that in the case where multiple rows have the same key (perhaps we design a view where the key is the name of the post's author), key queries can return more than one row.

Find Many

We talked about "getting all posts for last month." If it's February now, this is as easy as:

```
/blog/_design/docs/_view/by_date?startkey="2010/01/01 00:00:00"&endkey="2010/02/00 00:00:
```

The `startkey` and `endkey` parameters specify an inclusive range on which we can search.

To make things a little nicer and to prepare for a future example, we are going to change the format of our date field. Instead of a string, we are going to use an array, where individual members are part of a timestamp in decreasing significance. This sounds fancy, but it is rather easy. Instead of:

```
{
    "date": "2009/01/31 00:00:00"
}
```

we use:

```
{
    "date": [2009, 1, 31, 0, 0, 0]
}
```

Our map function does not have to change for this, but our view result looks a little different:

Table 2. New view results:

Key	Value
[2009, 1, 15, 15, 52, 20]	"Hello World"
[2009, 2, 17, 21, 13, 39]	"Biking"
[2009, 1, 30, 18, 4, 11]	"Bought a Cat"

And our queries change to:

```
/blog/_design/docs/_view/by_date?startkey=[2010, 1, 1, 0, 0, 0]&endkey=[2010, 2, 1, 0, 0,
```

For all you care, this is just a change in syntax, not meaning. But it shows you the power of views. Not only can you construct an index with scalar values like strings and integers, you can also use JSON structures as keys for your views. Say we tag our documents with a list of tags and want to see all tags, but we don't care for documents that have not been tagged.

```
{
    ...
    tags: ["cool", "freak", "plankton"],
    ...
}
```

```
{
    ...
    tags: [],
    ...
}
```

```
function(doc) {
    if(doc.tags.length > 0) {
        for(var idx in doc.tags) {
            emit(doc.tags[idx], null);
        }
    }
}
```

This shows a few new things. You can have conditions on structure (if(doc.tags.length > 0)) instead of just values. This is also an example of how a map function calls *emit()* multiple times per document. And finally, you can pass null instead of a value to the value parameter. The same is true for the key parameter. We'll see in a bit how that is useful.

Reversed Results

To retrieve view results in reverse order, use the descending=true query parameter. If you are using a startkey parameter, you will find that CouchDB returns different rows or no rows at all. What's up with that?

It's pretty easy to understand when you see how view query options work under the hood. A view is stored in a tree structure for fast lookups. Whenever you query a view, this is how CouchDB operates:

1. Starts reading at the top, or at the position that startkey specifies, if present.

2. Returns one row at a time until the end or until it hits endkey, if present.

If you specify descending=true, the reading direction is reversed, not the sort order of the rows in the view. In addition, the same two-step procedure is followed.

Say you have a view result that looks like this:

Key	Value
0	"foo"
1	"bar"
2	"baz"

Here are potential query options: `?startkey=1&descending=true`. What will CouchDB do? See #1 above: it jumps to `startkey`, which is the row with the key 1, and starts reading backward until it hits the end of the view. So the particular result would be:

Key	Value
1	"bar"
0	"foo"

This is very likely not what you want. To get the rows with the indexes 1 and 2 in reverse order, you need to switch the `startkey` to `endkey`: `endkey=1&descending=true`:

Key	Value
2	"baz"
1	"bar"

Now that looks a lot better. CouchDB started reading at the bottom of the view and went backward until it hit `endkey`.

The View to Get Comments for Posts

We use an array key here to support the `group_level` reduce query parameter. CouchDB's views are stored in the B-tree file structure. Because of the way B-trees are structured, we can cache the intermediate reduce results in the non-leaf nodes of the tree, so reduce queries can be computed along arbitrary key ranges in logarithmic time. See Figure 1, "Comments map function".

In the blog app, we use `group_level` reduce queries to compute the count of comments both on a per-post and total basis, achieved by querying the same view index with different methods. With some array keys, and assuming each key has the value 1:

```
["a","b","c"]
["a","b","e"]
["a","c","m"]
["b","a","c"]
["b","a","g"]
```

the reduce view:

```
function(keys, values, rereduce) {
    return sum(values)
}
```

returns the total number of rows between the start and end key. So with `startkey=["a","b"]&endkey=["b"]` (which includes the first three of the above keys) the result would equal 3. The effect is to count rows. If you'd like to count rows without depending on the row value, you can switch on the `rereduce` parameter:

```
function(keys, values, rereduce) {
    if (rereduce) {
        return sum(values);
    } else {
        return values.length;
    }
}
```

Note: The JavaScript function above could be effectively replaced by the builtin `_count`.

This is the reduce view used by the example app to count comments, while utilizing the map to output the comments, which are more useful than just 1 over and over. It pays to spend some time playing around with map

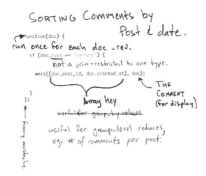

Fig. 6.1: Figure 1. Comments map function

and reduce functions. Futon is OK for this, but it doesn't give full access to all the query parameters. Writing your own test code for views in your language of choice is a great way to explore the nuances and capabilities of CouchDB's incremental MapReduce system.

Anyway, with a `group_level` query, you're basically running a series of reduce range queries: one for each group that shows up at the level you query. Let's reprint the key list from earlier, grouped at level 1:

```
["a"]    3
["b"]    2
```

And at `group_level=2`:

```
["a","b"]    2
["a","c"]    1
["b","a"]    2
```

Using the parameter `group=true` makes it behave as though it were `group_level=999`, so in the case of our current example, it would give the number 1 for each key, as there are no exactly duplicated keys.

Reduce/Rereduce

We briefly talked about the `rereduce` parameter to the reduce function. We'll explain what's up with it in this section. By now, you should have learned that your view result is stored in B-tree index structure for efficiency. The existence and use of the `rereduce` parameter is tightly coupled to how the B-tree index works.

Consider the map result are:

```
"afrikaans", 1
"afrikaans", 1
"chinese", 1
"chinese", 1
"chinese", 1
"chinese", 1
"french", 1
"italian", 1
"italian", 1
"spanish", 1
"vietnamese", 1
"vietnamese", 1
```

Example 1. Example view result (mmm, food)

When we want to find out how many dishes there are per origin, we can reuse the simple reduce function shown earlier:

```
function(keys, values, rereduce) {
    return sum(values);
}
```

Figure 2, "The B-tree index" shows a simplified version of what the B-tree index looks like. We abbreviated the key strings.

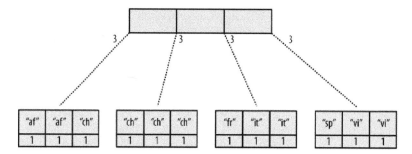

Fig. 6.2: Figure 2. The B-tree index

The view result is what computer science grads call a "pre-order" walk through the tree. We look at each element in each node starting from the left. Whenever we see that there is a subnode to descend into, we descend and start reading the elements in that subnode. When we have walked through the entire tree, we're done.

You can see that CouchDB stores both keys and values inside each leaf node. In our case, it is simply always 1, but you might have a value where you count other results and then all rows have a different value. What's important is that CouchDB runs all elements that are within a node into the reduce function (setting the `rereduce` parameter to false) and stores the result inside the parent node along with the edge to the subnode. In our case, each edge has a 3 representing the reduce value for the node it points to.

Note: In reality, nodes have more than 1,600 elements in them. CouchDB computes the result for all the elements in multiple iterations over the elements in a single node, not all at once (which would be disastrous for memory consumption).

Now let's see what happens when we run a query. We want to know how many "chinese" entries we have. The query option is simple: `?key="chinese"`. See Figure 3, "The B-tree index reduce result".

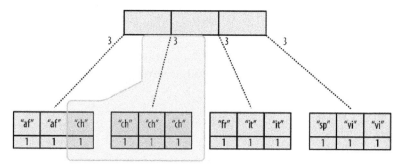

Fig. 6.3: Figure 3. The B-tree index reduce result

CouchDB detects that all values in the subnode include the "chinese" key. It concludes that it can take just the 3 values associated with that node to compute the final result. It then finds the node left to it and sees that it's a node with keys outside the requested range (`key=` requests a range where the beginning and the end are the same value). It concludes that it has to use the "chinese" element's value and the other node's value and run them through the reduce function with the `rereduce` parameter set to true.

The reduce function effectively calculates 3 + 1 at query time and returns the desired result. The next example shows some pseudocode that shows the last invocation of the reduce function with actual values:

```
function(null, [3, 1], true) {
    return sum([3, 1]);
}
```

Now, we said your reduce function must actually reduce your values. If you see the B-tree, it should become obvious what happens when you don't reduce your values. Consider the following map result and reduce function. This time we want to get a list of all the unique labels in our view:

```
"abc", "afrikaans"
"cef", "afrikaans"
"fhi", "chinese"
"hkl", "chinese"
"ino", "chinese"
"lqr", "chinese"
"mtu", "french"
"owx", "italian"
"qza", "italian"
"tdx", "spanish"
"xfg", "vietnamese"
"zul", "vietnamese"
```

We don't care for the key here and only list all the labels we have. Our reduce function removes duplicates:

```
function(keys, values, rereduce) {
    var unique_labels = {};
    values.forEach(function(label) {
        if(!unique_labels[label]) {
            unique_labels[label] = true;
        }
    });

    return unique_labels;
}
```

This translates to Figure 4, "An overflowing reduce index".

We hope you get the picture. The way the B-tree storage works means that if you don't actually reduce your data in the reduce function, you end up having CouchDB copy huge amounts of data around that grow linearly, if not faster, with the number of rows in your view.

CouchDB will be able to compute the final result, but only for views with a few rows. Anything larger will experience a ridiculously slow view build time. To help with that, CouchDB since version 0.10.0 will throw an error if your reduce function does not reduce its input values.

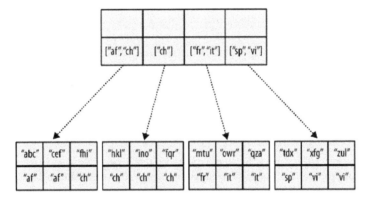

Fig. 6.4: Figure 4. An overflowing reduce index

Lessons Learned

- If you don't use the key field in the map function, you are probably doing it wrong.

- If you are trying to make a list of values unique in the reduce functions, you are probably doing it wrong.

- If you don't reduce your values to a single scalar value or a small fixed-sized object or array with a fixed number of scalar values of small sizes, you are probably doing it wrong.

Wrapping Up

Map functions are side effect–free functions that take a document as argument and *emit* key/value pairs. CouchDB stores the emitted rows by constructing a sorted B-tree index, so row lookups by key, as well as streaming operations across a range of rows, can be accomplished in a small memory and processing footprint, while writes avoid seeks. Generating a view takes $O(N)$, where N is the total number of rows in the view. However, querying a view is very quick, as the B-tree remains shallow even when it contains many, many keys.

Reduce functions operate on the sorted rows emitted by map view functions. CouchDB's reduce functionality takes advantage of one of the fundamental properties of B-tree indexes: for every leaf node (a sorted row), there is a chain of internal nodes reaching back to the root. Each leaf node in the B-tree carries a few rows (on the order of tens, depending on row size), and each internal node may link to a few leaf nodes or other internal nodes.

The reduce function is run on every node in the tree in order to calculate the final reduce value. The end result is a reduce function that can be incrementally updated upon changes to the map function, while recalculating the reduction values for a minimum number of nodes. The initial reduction is calculated once per each node (inner and leaf) in the tree.

When run on leaf nodes (which contain actual map rows), the reduce function's third parameter, `rereduce`, is false. The arguments in this case are the keys and values as output by the map function. The function has a single returned reduction value, which is stored on the inner node that a working set of leaf nodes have in common, and is used as a cache in future reduce calculations.

When the reduce function is run on inner nodes, the `rereduce` flag is `true`. This allows the function to account for the fact that it will be receiving its own prior output. When `rereduce` is true, the values passed to the function are intermediate reduction values as cached from previous calculations. When the tree is more than two levels deep, the *rereduce* phase is repeated, consuming chunks of the previous level's output until the final reduce value is calculated at the root node.

A common mistake new CouchDB users make is attempting to construct complex aggregate values with a reduce function. Full reductions should result in a scalar value, like 5, and not, for instance, a JSON hash with a set of unique keys and the count of each. The problem with this approach is that you'll end up with a very large final value. The number of unique keys can be nearly as large as the number of total keys, even for a large set. It is fine to combine a few scalar calculations into one reduce function; for instance, to find the total, average, and standard deviation of a set of numbers in a single function.

If you're interested in pushing the edge of CouchDB's incremental reduce functionality, have a look at Google's paper on Sawzall, which gives examples of some of the more exotic reductions that can be accomplished in a system with similar constraints.

6.2.2 Views Collation

Basics

View functions specify a key and a value to be returned for each row. CouchDB collates the view rows by this key. In the following example, the `LastName` property serves as the key, thus the result will be sorted by `LastName`:

```
function(doc) {
    if (doc.Type == "customer") {
        emit(doc.LastName, {FirstName: doc.FirstName, Address: doc.Address});
    }
}
```

CouchDB allows arbitrary JSON structures to be used as keys. You can use JSON arrays as keys for fine-grained control over sorting and grouping.

Examples

The following clever trick would return both customer and order documents. The key is composed of a customer _id and a sorting token. Because the key for order documents begins with the _id of a customer document, all the orders will be sorted by customer. Because the sorting token for customers is lower than the token for orders, the customer document will come before the associated orders. The values 0 and 1 for the sorting token are arbitrary.

```
function(doc) {
    if (doc.Type == "customer") {
        emit([doc._id, 0], null);
    } else if (doc.Type == "order") {
        emit([doc.customer_id, 1], null);
    }
}
```

To list a specific customer with _id XYZ, and all of that customer's orders, limit the startkey and endkey ranges to cover only documents for that customer's _id:

```
startkey=["XYZ"]&endkey=["XYZ", {}]
```

It is not recommended to emit the document itself in the view. Instead, to include the bodies of the documents when requesting the view, request the view with ?include_docs=true.

Sorting by Dates

It maybe be convenient to store date attributes in a human readable format (i.e. as a *string*), but still sort by date. This can be done by converting the date to a *number* in the emit() function. For example, given a document with a created_at attribute of 'Wed Jul 23 16:29:21 +0100 2013', the following emit function would sort by date:

```
emit(Date.parse(doc.created_at).getTime(), null);
```

Alternatively, if you use a date format which sorts lexicographically, such as "2013/06/09 13:52:11 +0000" you can just

```
emit(doc.created_at, null);
```

and avoid the conversion. As a bonus, this date format is compatible with the JavaScript date parser, so you can use new Date(doc.created_at) in your client side JavaScript to make date sorting easy in the browser.

String Ranges

If you need start and end keys that encompass every string with a given prefix, it is better to use a high value unicode character, than to use a 'ZZZZ' suffix.

That is, rather than:

```
startkey="abc"&endkey="abcZZZZZZZZZ"
```

You should use:

```
startkey="abc"&endkey="abc\ufff0"
```

Collation Specification

This section is based on the view_collation function in view_collation.js:

```
// special values sort before all other types
null
false
true

// then numbers
1
2
3.0
4

// then text, case sensitive
"a"
"A"
"aa"
"b"
"B"
"ba"
"bb"

// then arrays. compared element by element until different.
// Longer arrays sort after their prefixes
["a"]
["b"]
["b","c"]
["b","c", "a"]
["b","d"]
["b","d", "e"]

// then object, compares each key value in the list until different.
// larger objects sort after their subset objects.
{a:1}
{a:2}
{b:1}
{b:2}
{b:2, a:1} // Member order does matter for collation.
           // CouchDB preserves member order
           // but doesn't require that clients will.
           // this test might fail if used with a js engine
           // that doesn't preserve order
{b:2, c:2}
```

Comparison of strings is done using ICU which implements the Unicode Collation Algorithm, giving a dictionary sorting of keys. This can give surprising results if you were expecting ASCII ordering. Note that:

- All symbols sort before numbers and letters (even the "high" symbols like tilde, 0x7e)

- Differing sequences of letters are compared without regard to case, so a < aa but also A < aa and a < AA

- Identical sequences of letters are compared with regard to case, with lowercase before uppercase, so a < A

You can demonstrate the collation sequence for 7-bit ASCII characters like this:

```
require 'rubygems'
require 'restclient'
require 'json'

DB="http://127.0.0.1:5984/collator"

RestClient.delete DB rescue nil
RestClient.put "#{DB}",""
```

```
(32..126).each do |c|
            .put "#    //#.c.to_s(16) ", {"x"=>c.chr}.to_json
end

         .put "#   /_design/test", <<

{
    "views":{
        "one":{
            "map":"function (doc) { emit(doc.x,null); }"
        }
    }
}

puts           .get("# / /_design/test/_view/one")
```

This shows the collation sequence to be:

```
` ^ _ - , ; : ! ? . ' " ( ) [ ] { } @ * / \ & # % + < = > | ~ $ 0 1 2 3 4 5 6 7 8 9
a A b B c C d D e E f F g G h H i I j J k K l L m M n N o O p P q Q r R s S t T u U v V w
```

Key ranges

Take special care when querying key ranges. For example: the query:

```
startkey="Abc"&endkey="AbcZZZZ"
```

will match "ABC" and "abc1", but not "abc". This is because UCA sorts as:

```
abc < Abc < ABC < abc1 < AbcZZZZZ
```

For most applications, to avoid problems you should lowercase the *startkey*:

```
startkey="abc"&endkey="abcZZZZZZZ"
```

will match all keys starting with [aA][bB][cC]

Complex keys

The query `startkey=["foo"]&endkey=["foo",{}]` will match most array keys with "foo" in the first element, such as `["foo","bar"]` and `["foo",["bar","baz"]]`. However it will not match `["foo",{"an":"object"}]`

_all_docs

The *_all_docs* view is a special case because it uses ASCII collation for doc ids, not UCA:

```
startkey="_design/"&endkey="_design/ZZZZZZZZ"
```

will not find _design/abc because 'Z' comes before 'a' in the ASCII sequence. A better solution is:

```
startkey="_design/"&endkey="_design0"
```

Raw collation

To squeeze a little more performance out of views, you can specify `"options":{"collation":"raw"}` within the view definition for native Erlang collation, especially if you don't require UCA. This gives a different collation sequence:

```
1
false
null
true
{"a":"a"},
["a"]
"a"
```

Beware that { } is no longer a suitable "high" key sentinel value. Use a string like "\ufff0" instead.

6.2.3 Joins With Views

Linked Documents

If your *map function* emits an object value which has {'_id': XXX} and you *query view* with include_docs=true parameter, then CouchDB will fetch the document with id XXX rather than the document which was processed to emit the key/value pair.

This means that if one document contains the ids of other documents, it can cause those documents to be fetched in the view too, adjacent to the same key if required.

For example, if you have the following hierarchically-linked documents:

```
[
    { "_id": "11111" },
    { "_id": "22222", "ancestors": ["11111"], "value": "hello" },
    { "_id": "33333", "ancestors": ["22222","11111"], "value": "world" }
]
```

You can emit the values with the ancestor documents adjacent to them in the view like this:

```
function(doc) {
    if (doc.value) {
        emit([doc.value, 0], null);
        if (doc.ancestors) {
            for (var i in doc.ancestors) {
                emit([doc.value, Number(i)+1], {_id: doc.ancestors[i]});
            }
        }
    }
}
```

The result you get is:

```
{
    "total_rows": 5,
    "offset": 0,
    "rows": [
        {
            "id": "22222",
            "key": [
                "hello",
                0
            ],
            "value": null,
            "doc": {
                "_id": "22222",
                "_rev": "1-0eee81fecb5aa4f51e285c621271ff02",
                "ancestors": [
                    "11111"
                ],
                "value": "hello"
            }
        }
```

```
        },
        {
            "id": "22222",
            "key": [
                "hello",
                1
            ],
            "value": {
                "_id": "11111"
            },
            "doc": {
                "_id": "11111",
                "_rev": "1-967a00dff5e02add41819138abb3284d"
            }
        },
        {
            "id": "33333",
            "key": [
                "world",
                0
            ],
            "value": null,
            "doc": {
                "_id": "33333",
                "_rev": "1-11e42b44fdb3d3784602eca7c0332a43",
                "ancestors": [
                    "22222",
                    "11111"
                ],
                "value": "world"
            }
        },
        {
            "id": "33333",
            "key": [
                "world",
                1
            ],
            "value": {
                "_id": "22222"
            },
            "doc": {
                "_id": "22222",
                "_rev": "1-0eee81fecb5aa4f51e285c621271ff02",
                "ancestors": [
                    "11111"
                ],
                "value": "hello"
            }
        },
        {
            "id": "33333",
            "key": [
                "world",
                2
            ],
            "value": {
                "_id": "11111"
            },
            "doc": {
                "_id": "11111",
                "_rev": "1-967a00dff5e02add41819138abb3284d"
            }
```

```
        }
    ]
}
```

which makes it very cheap to fetch a document plus all its ancestors in one query.

Note that the `"id"` in the row is still that of the originating document. The only difference is that `include_docs` fetches a different doc.

The current revision of the document is resolved at query time, not at the time the view is generated. This means that if a new revision of the linked document is added later, it will appear in view queries even though the view itself hasn't changed. To force a specific revision of a linked document to be used, emit a `"_rev"` property as well as `"_id"`.

Using View Collation

Author Christopher Lenz

Date 2007-10-05

Source http://www.cmlenz.net/archives/2007/10/couchdb-joins

Just today, there was a discussion on IRC on how you'd go about modeling a simple blogging system with "post" and "comment" entities, where any blog post might have N comments. If you'd be using an SQL database, you'd obviously have two tables with foreign keys and you'd be using joins. (At least until you needed to add some denormalization).

But what would the "obvious" approach in CouchDB look like?

Approach #1: Comments Inlined

A simple approach would be to have one document per blog post, and store the comments inside that document:

```
{
    "_id": "myslug",
    "_rev": "123456",
    "author": "john",
    "title": "My blog post",
    "content": "Bla bla bla ...",
    "comments": [
        {"author": "jack", "content": "..."},
        {"author": "jane", "content": "..."}
    ]
}
```

Note: Of course the model of an actual blogging system would be more extensive, you'd have tags, timestamps, etc, etc. This is just to demonstrate the basics.

The obvious advantage of this approach is that the data that belongs together is stored in one place. Delete the post, and you automatically delete the corresponding comments, and so on.

You may be thinking that putting the comments inside the blog post document would not allow us to query for the comments themselves, but you'd be wrong. You could trivially write a CouchDB view that would return all comments across all blog posts, keyed by author:

```
function(doc) {
    for (var i in doc.comments) {
        emit(doc.comments[i].author, doc.comments[i].content);
    }
}
```

Now you could list all comments by a particular user by invoking the view and passing it a `?key="username"` query string parameter.

However, this approach has a drawback that can be quite significant for many applications: To add a comment to a post, you need to:

- Fetch the blog post document

- Add the new comment to the JSON structure

- Send the updated document to the server

Now if you have multiple client processes adding comments at roughly the same time, some of them will get a *HTTP 409 Conflict* error on step 3 (that's optimistic concurrency in action). For some applications this makes sense, but in many other apps, you'd want to append new related data regardless of whether other data has been added in the meantime.

The only way to allow non-conflicting addition of related data is by putting that related data into separate documents.

Approach #2: Comments Separate

Using this approach you'd have one document per blog post, and one document per comment. The comment documents would have a "backlink" to the post they belong to.

The blog post document would look similar to the above, minus the comments property. Also, we'd now have a type property on all our documents so that we can tell the difference between posts and comments:

```
{
    "_id": "myslug",
    "_rev": "123456",
    "type": "post",
    "author": "john",
    "title": "My blog post",
    "content": "Bla bla bla ..."
}
```

The comments themselves are stored in separate documents, which also have a type property (this time with the value "comment"), and additionally feature a post property containing the ID of the post document they belong to:

```
{
    "_id": "ABCDEF",
    "_rev": "123456",
    "type": "comment",
    "post": "myslug",
    "author": "jack",
    "content": "..."
}
```

```
{
    "_id": "DEFABC",
    "_rev": "123456",
    "type": "comment",
    "post": "myslug",
    "author": "jane",
    "content": "..."
}
```

To list all comments per blog post, you'd add a simple view, keyed by blog post ID:

```
function(doc) {
    if (doc.type == "comment") {
        emit(doc.post, {author: doc.author, content: doc.content});
    }
}
```

And you'd invoke that view passing it a `?key="post_id"` query string parameter.

Viewing all comments by author is just as easy as before:

```
function(doc) {
    if (doc.type == "comment") {
        emit(doc.author, {post: doc.post, content: doc.content});
    }
}
```

So this is better in some ways, but it also has a disadvantage. Imagine you want to display a blog post with all the associated comments on the same web page. With our first approach, we needed just a single request to the CouchDB server, namely a `GET` request to the document. With this second approach, we need two requests: a `GET` request to the post document, and a `GET` request to the view that returns all comments for the post.

That is okay, but not quite satisfactory. Just imagine you wanted to add threaded comments: you'd now need an additional fetch per comment. What we'd probably want then would be a way to join the blog post and the various comments together to be able to retrieve them with a single HTTP request.

This was when Damien Katz, the author of CouchDB, chimed in to the discussion on IRC to show us the way.

Optimization: Using the Power of View Collation

Obvious to Damien, but not at all obvious to the rest of us: it's fairly simple to make a view that includes both the content of the blog post document, and the content of all the comments associated with that post. The way you do that is by using *complex keys*. Until now we've been using simple string values for the view keys, but in fact they can be arbitrary JSON values, so let's make some use of that:

```
function(doc) {
    if (doc.type == "post") {
        emit([doc._id, 0], doc);
    } else if (doc.type == "comment") {
        emit([doc.post, 1], doc);
    }
}
```

Okay, this may be confusing at first. Let's take a step back and look at what views in CouchDB are really about.

CouchDB views are basically highly efficient on-disk dictionaries that map keys to values, where the key is automatically indexed and can be used to filter and/or sort the results you get back from your views. When you "invoke" a view, you can say that you're only interested in a subset of the view rows by specifying a `?key=foo` query string parameter. Or you can specify `?startkey=foo` and/or `?endkey=bar` query string parameters to fetch rows over a range of keys.

It's also important to note that keys are always used for collating (i.e. sorting) the rows. CouchDB has well defined (but as of yet undocumented) rules for comparing arbitrary JSON objects for collation. For example, the JSON value `["foo", 2]` is sorted after (considered "greater than") the values `["foo"]` or `["foo", 1, "bar"]`, but before e.g. `["foo", 2, "bar"]`. This feature enables a whole class of tricks that are rather non-obvious...

See also:

Views Collation

With that in mind, let's return to the view function above. First note that, unlike the previous view functions we've used here, this view handles both "post" and "comment" documents, and both of them end up as rows in the same view. Also, the key in this view is not just a simple string, but an array. The first element in that array is always the ID of the post, regardless of whether we're processing an actual post document, or a comment associated with a post. The second element is 0 for post documents, and 1 for comment documents.

Let's assume we have two blog posts in our database. Without limiting the view results via `key`, `startkey`, or `endkey`, we'd get back something like the following:

```
{
    "total_rows": 5, "offset": 0, "rows": [{
            "id": "myslug",
            "key": ["myslug", 0],
            "value": {...}
        }, {
            "id": "ABCDEF",
            "key": ["myslug", 1],
            "value": {...}
        }, {
            "id": "DEFABC",
            "key": ["myslug", 1],
            "value": {...}
        }, {
            "id": "other_slug",
            "key": ["other_slug", 0],
            "value": {...}
        }, {
            "id": "CDEFAB",
            "key": ["other_slug", 1],
            "value": {...}
        },
    ]
}
```

Note: The `...` placeholders here would contain the complete JSON encoding of the corresponding documents

Now, to get a specific blog post and all associated comments, we'd invoke that view with the query string:

```
?startkey=["myslug"]&endkey;=["myslug", 2]
```

We'd get back the first three rows, those that belong to the `myslug` post, but not the others. Et voila, we now have the data we need to display a post with all associated comments, retrieved via a single `GET` request.

You may be asking what the 0 and 1 parts of the keys are for. They're simply to ensure that the post document is always sorted before the the associated comment documents. So when you get back the results from this view for a specific post, you'll know that the first row contains the data for the blog post itself, and the remaining rows contain the comment data.

One remaining problem with this model is that comments are not ordered, but that's simply because we don't have date/time information associated with them. If we had, we'd add the timestamp as third element of the key array, probably as ISO date/time strings. Now we would continue using the query string `?startkey=["myslug"]&endkey=["myslug", 2]` to fetch the blog post and all associated comments, only now they'd be in chronological order.

6.2.4 View Cookbook for SQL Jockeys

This is a collection of some common SQL queries and how to get the same result in CouchDB. The key to remember here is that CouchDB does not work like an SQL database at all, and that best practices from the SQL world do not translate well or at all to CouchDB. This document's "cookbook" assumes that you are familiar with the CouchDB basics such as creating and updating databases and documents.

Using Views

How you would do this in SQL:

```
CREATE TABLE
```

or:

```
ALTER TABLE
```

How you can do this in CouchDB?

Using views is a two-step process. First you define a view; then you query it. This is analogous to defining a table structure (with indexes) using CREATE TABLE or ALTER TABLE and querying it using an SQL query.

Defining a View

Defining a view is done by creating a special document in a CouchDB database. The only real specialness is the _id of the document, which starts with _design/ — for example, _design/application. Other than that, it is just a regular CouchDB document. To make sure CouchDB understands that you are defining a view, you need to prepare the contents of that design document in a special format. Here is an example:

```
{
    "_id": "_design/application",
    "_rev": "1-C1687D17",
    "views": {
        "viewname": {
            "map": "function(doc) { ... }",
            "reduce": "function(keys, values) { ... }"
        }
    }
}
```

We are defining a view *viewname*. The definition of the view consists of two functions: the map function and the reduce function. Specifying a reduce function is optional. We'll look at the nature of the functions later. Note that *viewname* can be whatever you like: users, by-name, or by-date are just some examples.

A single design document can also include multiple view definitions, each identified by a unique name:

```
{
    "_id": "_design/application",
    "_rev": "1-C1687D17",
    "views": {
        "viewname": {
            "map": "function(doc) { ... }",
            "reduce": "function(keys, values) { ... }"
        },
        "anotherview": {
            "map": "function(doc) { ... }",
            "reduce": "function(keys, values) { ... }"
        }
    }
}
```

Querying a View

The name of the design document and the name of the view are significant for querying the view. To query the view *viewname*, you perform an HTTP GET request to the following URI:

```
/database/_design/application/_view/viewname
```

database is the name of the database you created your design document in. Next up is the design document name, and then the view name prefixed with _view/. To query *anotherview*, replace *viewname* in that URI with *anotherview*. If you want to query a view in a different design document, adjust the design document name.

MapReduce Functions

MapReduce is a concept that solves problems by applying a two-step process, aptly named the map phase and the reduce phase. The map phase looks at all documents in CouchDB separately one after the other and creates a *map result*. The map result is an ordered list of key/value pairs. Both key and value can be specified by the user writing the map function. A map function may call the built-in `emit(key, value)` function 0 to N times per document, creating a row in the map result per invocation.

CouchDB is smart enough to run a map function only once for every document, even on subsequent queries on a view. Only changes to documents or new documents need to be processed anew.

Map functions

Map functions run in isolation for every document. They can't modify the document, and they can't talk to the outside world—they can't have side effects. This is required so that CouchDB can guarantee correct results without having to recalculate a complete result when only one document gets changed.

The map result looks like this:

```
{"total_rows":3,"offset":0,"rows":[
{"id":"fc2636bf50556346f1ce46b4bc01fe30","key":"Lena","value":5},
{"id":"1fb2449f9b9d4e466dbfa47ebe675063","key":"Lisa","value":4},
{"id":"8ede09f6f6aeb35d948485624b28f149","key":"Sarah","value":6}
]}
```

It is a list of rows sorted by the value of key. The id is added automatically and refers back to the document that created this row. The value is the data you're looking for. For example purposes, it's the girl's age.

The map function that produces this result is:

```
function(doc) {
    if(doc.name && doc.age) {
        emit(doc.name, doc.age);
    }
}
```

It includes the if statement as a sanity check to ensure that we're operating on the right fields and calls the emit function with the name and age as the key and value.

Look Up by Key

How you would do this in SQL:

```
SELECT field FROM table WHERE value="searchterm"
```

How you can do this in CouchDB?

Use case: get a result (which can be a record or set of records) associated with a key ("searchterm").

To look something up quickly, regardless of the storage mechanism, an index is needed. An index is a data structure optimized for quick search and retrieval. CouchDB's map result is stored in such an index, which happens to be a B+ tree.

To look up a value by "searchterm", we need to put all values into the key of a view. All we need is a simple map function:

```
function(doc) {
    if(doc.value) {
        emit(doc.value, null);
    }
}
```

This creates a list of documents that have a value field sorted by the data in the value field. To find all the records that match "searchterm", we query the view and specify the search term as a query parameter:

```
/database/_design/application/_view/viewname?key="searchterm"
```

Consider the documents from the previous section, and say we're indexing on the age field of the documents to find all the five-year-olds:

```
function(doc) {
    if(doc.age && doc.name) {
        emit(doc.age, doc.name);
    }
}
```

Query:

```
/ladies/_design/ladies/_view/age?key=5
```

Result:

```
{"total_rows":3,"offset":1,"rows":[
{"id":"fc2636bf50556346f1ce46b4bc01fe30","key":5,"value":"Lena"}
]}
```

Easy.

Note that you have to emit a value. The view result includes the associated document ID in every row. We can use it to look up more data from the document itself. We can also use the `?include_docs=true` parameter to have CouchDB fetch the individual documents for us.

Look Up by Prefix

How you would do this in SQL:

```
SELECT field FROM table WHERE value LIKE "searchterm%"
```

How you can do this in CouchDB?

Use case: find all documents that have a field value that starts with *searchterm*. For example, say you stored a MIME type (like *text/html* or *image/jpg*) for each document and now you want to find all documents that are images according to the MIME type.

The solution is very similar to the previous example: all we need is a map function that is a little more clever than the first one. But first, an example document:

```
{
    "_id": "Hugh Laurie",
    "_rev": "1-9fded7deef52ac373119d05435581edf",
    "mime-type": "image/jpg",
    "description": "some dude"
}
```

The clue lies in extracting the prefix that we want to search for from our document and putting it into our view index. We use a regular expression to match our prefix:

```
function(doc) {
    if(doc["mime-type"]) {
        // from the start (^) match everything that is not a slash ([^\/]+) until
        // we find a slash (\/). Slashes needs to be escaped with a backslash (\/)
        var prefix = doc["mime-type"].match(/^[^\/]+\//);
        if(prefix) {
            emit(prefix, null);
        }
    }
}
```

We can now query this view with our desired MIME type prefix and not only find all images, but also text, video, and all other formats:

```
/files/_design/finder/_view/by-mime-type?key="image/"
```

Aggregate Functions

How you would do this in SQL:

```
SELECT COUNT(field) FROM table
```

How you can do this in CouchDB?

Use case: calculate a derived value from your data.

We haven't explained reduce functions yet. Reduce functions are similar to aggregate functions in SQL. They compute a value over multiple documents.

To explain the mechanics of reduce functions, we'll create one that doesn't make a whole lot of sense. But this example is easy to understand. We'll explore more useful reductions later.

Reduce functions operate on the output of the map function (also called the map result or intermediate result). The reduce function's job, unsurprisingly, is to reduce the list that the map function produces.

Here's what our summing reduce function looks like:

```
function(keys, values) {
    var sum = 0;
    for(var idx in values) {
        sum = sum + values[idx];
    }
    return sum;
}
```

Here's an alternate, more idiomatic JavaScript version:

```
function(keys, values) {
    var sum = 0;
    values.forEach(function(element) {
        sum = sum + element;
    });
    return sum;
}
```

Note: Don't miss effective builtin *reduce functions* like _sum and _count

This reduce function takes two arguments: a list of keys and a list of values. For our summing purposes we can ignore the keys-list and consider only the value list. We're looping over the list and add each item to a running total that we're returning at the end of the function.

You'll see one difference between the map and the reduce function. The map function uses emit() to create its result, whereas the reduce function returns a value.

For example, from a list of integer values that specify the age, calculate the sum of all years of life for the news headline, *"786 life years present at event."* A little contrived, but very simple and thus good for demonstration purposes. Consider the documents and the map view we used earlier in this document.

The reduce function to calculate the total age of all girls is:

```
function(keys, values) {
    return sum(values);
}
```

Note that, instead of the two earlier versions, we use CouchDB's predefined *sum()* function. It does the same thing as the other two, but it is such a common piece of code that CouchDB has it included.

The result for our reduce view now looks like this:

```
{"rows":[
    {"key":null,"value":15}
]}
```

The total sum of all age fields in all our documents is 15. Just what we wanted. The key member of the result object is null, as we can't know anymore which documents took part in the creation of the reduced result. We'll cover more advanced reduce cases later on.

As a rule of thumb, the reduce function should reduce to a single scalar value. That is, an integer; a string; or a small, fixed-size list or object that includes an aggregated value (or values) from the values argument. It should never just return values or similar. CouchDB will give you a warning if you try to use reduce "the wrong way":

```
{
    "error":"reduce_overflow_error",
    "message":"Reduce output must shrink more rapidly: Current output: ..."
}
```

Get Unique Values

How you would do this in SQL:

```
SELECT DISTINCT field FROM table
```

How you can do this in CouchDB?

Getting unique values is not as easy as adding a keyword. But a reduce view and a special query parameter give us the same result. Let's say you want a list of tags that your users have tagged themselves with and no duplicates.

First, let's look at the source documents. We punt on _id and _rev attributes here:

```
{
    "name":"Chris",
    "tags":["mustache", "music", "couchdb"]
}
```

```
{
    "name":"Noah",
    "tags":["hypertext", "philosophy", "couchdb"]
}
```

```
{
    "name":"Jan",
    "tags":["drums", "bike", "couchdb"]
}
```

Next, we need a list of all tags. A map function will do the trick:

```
function(doc) {
    if(doc.name && doc.tags) {
        doc.tags.forEach(function(tag) {
            emit(tag, null);
        });
    }
}
```

The result will look like this:

```
{"total_rows":9,"offset":0,"rows":[
{"id":"3525ab874bc4965fa3cda7c549e92d30","key":"bike","value":null},
```

```
{"id":"3525ab874bc4965fa3cda7c549e92d30","key":"couchdb","value":null},
{"id":"53f82b1f0ff49a08ac79a9dff41d7860","key":"couchdb","value":null},
{"id":"da5ea89448a4506925823f4d985aabbd","key":"couchdb","value":null},
{"id":"3525ab874bc4965fa3cda7c549e92d30","key":"drums","value":null},
{"id":"53f82b1f0ff49a08ac79a9dff41d7860","key":"hypertext","value":null},
{"id":"da5ea89448a4506925823f4d985aabbd","key":"music","value":null},
{"id":"da5ea89448a4506925823f4d985aabbd","key":"mustache","value":null},
{"id":"53f82b1f0ff49a08ac79a9dff41d7860","key":"philosophy","value":null}
]}
```

As promised, these are all the tags, including duplicates. Since each document gets run through the map function in isolation, it cannot know if the same key has been emitted already. At this stage, we need to live with that. To achieve uniqueness, we need a reduce:

```
function(keys, values) {
    return true;
}
```

This reduce doesn't do anything, but it allows us to specify a special query parameter when querying the view:

```
/dudes/_design/dude-data/_view/tags?group=true
```

CouchDB replies:

```
{"rows":[
{"key":"bike","value":true},
{"key":"couchdb","value":true},
{"key":"drums","value":true},
{"key":"hypertext","value":true},
{"key":"music","value":true},
{"key":"mustache","value":true},
{"key":"philosophy","value":true}
]}
```

In this case, we can ignore the value part because it is always true, but the result includes a list of all our tags and no duplicates!

With a small change we can put the reduce to good use, too. Let's see how many of the non-unique tags are there for each tag. To calculate the tag frequency, we just use the summing up we already learned about. In the map function, we emit a 1 instead of null:

```
function(doc) {
    if(doc.name && doc.tags) {
        doc.tags.forEach(function(tag) {
            emit(tag, 1);
        });
    }
}
```

In the reduce function, we return the sum of all values:

```
function(keys, values) {
    return sum(values);
}
```

Now, if we query the view with the `?group=true` parameter, we get back the count for each tag:

```
{"rows":[
{"key":"bike","value":1},
{"key":"couchdb","value":3},
{"key":"drums","value":1},
{"key":"hypertext","value":1},
{"key":"music","value":1},
{"key":"mustache","value":1},
```

```
{"key":"philosophy","value":1}
]}
```

Enforcing Uniqueness

How you would do this in SQL:

```
UNIQUE KEY(column)
```

How you can do this in CouchDB?

Use case: your applications require that a certain value exists only once in a database.

This is an easy one: within a CouchDB database, each document must have a unique `_id` field. If you require unique values in a database, just assign them to a document's `_id` field and CouchDB will enforce uniqueness for you.

There's one caveat, though: in the distributed case, when you are running more than one CouchDB node that accepts write requests, uniqueness can be guaranteed only per node or outside of CouchDB. CouchDB will allow two identical IDs to be written to two different nodes. On replication, CouchDB will detect a conflict and flag the document accordingly.

6.2.5 Pagination Recipe

This recipe explains how to paginate over view results. Pagination is a user interface (UI) pattern that allows the display of a large number of rows (*the result set*) without loading all the rows into the UI at once. A fixed-size subset, the *page*, is displayed along with next and previous links or buttons that can move the *viewport* over the result set to an adjacent page.

We assume you're familiar with creating and querying documents and views as well as the multiple view query options.

Example Data

To have some data to work with, we'll create a list of bands, one document per band:

```
{ "name":"Biffy Clyro" }

{ "name":"Foo Fighters" }

{ "name":"Tool" }

{ "name":"Nirvana" }

{ "name":"Helmet" }

{ "name":"Tenacious D" }

{ "name":"Future of the Left" }

{ "name":"A Perfect Circle" }

{ "name":"Silverchair" }

{ "name":"Queens of the Stone Age" }

{ "name":"Kerub" }
```

A View

We need a simple map function that gives us an alphabetical list of band names. This should be easy, but we're adding extra smarts to filter out "The" and "A" in front of band names to put them into the right position:

```
function(doc) {
    if(doc.name) {
        var name = doc.name.replace(/^(A|The) /, "");
        emit(name, null);
    }
}
```

The views result is an alphabetical list of band names. Now say we want to display band names five at a time and have a link pointing to the next five names that make up one page, and a link for the previous five, if we're not on the first page.

We learned how to use the `startkey`, `limit`, and `skip` parameters in earlier documents. We'll use these again here. First, let's have a look at the full result set:

```
{"total_rows":11,"offset":0,"rows":[
    {"id":"a0746072bba60a62b01209f467ca4fe2","key":"Biffy Clyro","value":null},
    {"id":"b47d82284969f10cd1b6ea460ad62d00","key":"Foo Fighters","value":null},
    {"id":"45ccde324611f86ad4932555dea7fce0","key":"Tenacious D","value":null},
    {"id":"d7ab24bb3489a9010c7d1a2087a4a9e4","key":"Future of the Left","value":null},
    {"id":"ad2f85ef87f5a9a65db5b3a75a03cd82","key":"Helmet","value":null},
    {"id":"a2f31cfa68118a6ae9d35444fcb1a3cf","key":"Nirvana","value":null},
    {"id":"67373171d0f626b811bdc34e92e77901","key":"Kerub","value":null},
    {"id":"3e1b84630c384f6aef1a5c50a81e4a34","key":"Perfect Circle","value":null},
    {"id":"84a371a7b8414237fad1b6aaf68cd16a","key":"Queens of the Stone Age","value":null
    {"id":"dcdaf08242a4be7da1a36e25f4f0b022","key":"Silverchair","value":null},
    {"id":"fd590d4ad53771db47b0406054f02243","key":"Tool","value":null}
]}
```

Setup

The mechanics of paging are very simple:

- Display first page
- If there are more rows to show, show next link
- Draw subsequent page
- If this is not the first page, show a previous link
- If there are more rows to show, show next link

Or in a pseudo-JavaScript snippet:

```
var result = new Result();
var page = result.getPage();

page.display();

if(result.hasPrev()) {
    page.display_link('prev');
}

if(result.hasNext()) {
    page.display_link('next');
}
```

Paging

To get the first five rows from the view result, you use the `?limit=5` query parameter:

```
curl -X GET http://127.0.0.1:5984/artists/_design/artists/_view/by-name?limit=5
```

The result:

```
{"total_rows":11,"offset":0,"rows":[
    {"id":"a0746072bba60a62b01209f467ca4fe2","key":"Biffy Clyro","value":null},
    {"id":"b47d82284969f10cd1b6ea460ad62d00","key":"Foo Fighters","value":null},
    {"id":"45ccde324611f86ad4932555dea7fce0","key":"Tenacious D","value":null},
    {"id":"d7ab24bb3489a9010c7d1a2087a4a9e4","key":"Future of the Left","value":null},
    {"id":"ad2f85ef87f5a9a65db5b3a75a03cd82","key":"Helmet","value":null}
]}
```

By comparing the `total_rows` value to our `limit` value, we can determine if there are more pages to display. We also know by the *offset* member that we are on the first page. We can calculate the value for `skip=` to get the results for the next page:

```
var rows_per_page = 5;
var page = (offset / rows_per_page) + 1; // == 1
var skip = page * rows_per_page; // == 5 for the first page, 10 for the second ...
```

So we query CouchDB with:

```
curl -X GET 'http://127.0.0.1:5984/artists/_design/artists/_view/by-name?limit=5&skip=5'
```

Note we have to use ' (single quotes) to escape the & character that is special to the shell we execute curl in.

The result:

```
{"total_rows":11,"offset":5,"rows":[
    {"id":"a2f31cfa68118a6ae9d35444fcb1a3cf","key":"Nirvana","value":null},
    {"id":"67373171d0f626b811bdc34e92e77901","key":"Kerub","value":null},
    {"id":"3e1b84630c384f6aef1a5c50a81e4a34","key":"Perfect Circle","value":null},
    {"id":"84a371a7b8414237fad1b6aaf68cd16a","key":"Queens of the Stone Age",
    "value":null},
    {"id":"dcdaf08242a4be7da1a36e25f4f0b022","key":"Silverchair","value":null}
]}
```

Implementing the `hasPrev()` and `hasNext()` method is pretty straightforward:

```
function hasPrev()
{
    return page > 1;
}

function hasNext()
{
    var last_page = Math.floor(total_rows / rows_per_page) +
        (total_rows % rows_per_page);
    return page != last_page;
}
```

Paging (Alternate Method)

The method described above performed poorly with large skip values until CouchDB 1.2. Additionally, some use cases may call for the following alternate method even with newer versions of CouchDB. One such case is when duplicate results should be prevented. Using skip alone it is possible for new documents to be inserted during pagination which could change the offset of the start of the subsequent page.

A correct solution is not much harder. Instead of slicing the result set into equally sized pages, we look at 10 rows at a time and use `startkey` to jump to the next 10 rows. We even use skip, but only with the value 1.

Here is how it works:

- Request *rows_per_page* + *1* rows from the view

- Display *rows_per_page* rows, *store* + *1* row as *next_startkey* and *next_startkey_docid*

- As page information, keep `startkey` and *next_startkey*

- Use the *next_** values to create the next link, and use the others to create the previous link

The trick to finding the next page is pretty simple. Instead of requesting 10 rows for a page, you request 11 rows, but display only 10 and use the values in the 11th row as the `startkey` for the next page. Populating the link to the previous page is as simple as carrying the current `startkey` over to the next page. If there's no previous `startkey`, we are on the first page. We stop displaying the link to the next page if we get *rows_per_page* or less rows back. This is called linked list pagination, as we go from page to page, or list item to list item, instead of jumping directly to a pre-computed page. There is one caveat, though. Can you spot it?

CouchDB view keys do not have to be unique; you can have multiple index entries read. What if you have more index entries for a key than rows that should be on a page? `startkey` jumps to the first row, and you'd be screwed if CouchDB didn't have an additional parameter for you to use. All view keys with the same value are internally sorted by *docid*, that is, the ID of the document that created that view row. You can use the `startkey_docid` and `endkey_docid` parameters to get subsets of these rows. For pagination, we still don't need `endkey_docid`, but `startkey_docid` is very handy. In addition to `startkey` and `limit`, you also use `startkey_docid` for pagination if, and only if, the extra row you fetch to find the next page has the same key as the current `startkey`.

It is important to note that the **_docid* parameters only work in addition to the **key* parameters and are only useful to further narrow down the result set of a view for a single key. They do not work on their own (the one exception being the built-in *_all_docs view* that already sorts by document ID).

The advantage of this approach is that all the key operations can be performed on the super-fast B-tree index behind the view. Looking up a page doesn't include scanning through hundreds and thousands of rows unnecessarily.

Jump to Page

One drawback of the linked list style pagination is that you can't pre-compute the rows for a particular page from the page number and the rows per page. Jumping to a specific page doesn't really work. Our gut reaction, if that concern is raised, is, "Not even Google is doing that!" and we tend to get away with it. Google always pretends on the first page to find 10 more pages of results. Only if you click on the second page (something very few people actually do) might Google display a reduced set of pages. If you page through the results, you get links for the previous and next 10 pages, but no more. Pre-computing the necessary `startkey` and `startkey_docid` for 20 pages is a feasible operation and a pragmatic optimization to know the rows for every page in a result set that is potentially tens of thousands of rows long, or more.

If you really do need to jump to a page over the full range of documents (we have seen applications that require that), you can still maintain an integer value index as the view index and take a hybrid approach at solving pagination.

## CHAPTER 7

CouchDB Externals API

Author Paul Joseph Davis

Date 2010-09-26

Source http://davispj.com/2010/09/26/new-couchdb-externals-api.html

For a bit of background, CouchDB has had an API for managing external OS processes that are capable of handling HTTP requests for a given URL prefix. These OS processes communicate with CouchDB using JSON over stdio. They're dead simple to write and provide CouchDB users an easy way to extend CouchDB functionality.

Even though they're dead simple to write, there are a few issues. The implementation in CouchDB does not provide fancy pooling semantics. The current API is explicitly synchronous which prevents people from writing event driven code in an external handler. In the end, they may be simple, but their simplicity is also quite limiting.

During CouchCamp a few weeks ago I had multiple discussions with various people that wanted to see the _externals API modified in slight ways that weren't mutually compatible. After having multiple discussions with multiple people we formed a general consensus on what a new API could look like.

7.1 The New Hotness

So the first idea for improving the _external API was to make CouchDB act as a reverse proxy. This would allow people to write an HTTP server that was as simple or as complicated as they wanted. It will allow people to change their networking configuration more easily and also allow for external processes to be hosted on nodes other than the one running CouchDB. Bottom line, it not only allows us to have similar semantics as _externals, it provides a lot more fringe benefits as well. I'm always a fan of extra awesomeness.

After hitting on the idea of adding a reverse proxy, people quickly pointed out that it would require users to start manually managing their external processes using something like Runit or Supervisord. After some more discussions I ran into people that wanted something like _externals that didn't handle HTTP requests. After that it was easy to see that adding a second feature that managed OS processes was the way to go.

I spent this weekend implementing both of these features. Both are at the stage of working but requiring more testing. In the case of the HTTP proxy I have no tests because I can't decide how to test the thing. If you have ideas, I'd sure like to hear them.

[**Update**]: I woke up the other morning realizing that I was being an idiot and that Erlang is awesome. There's no reason that I can't have an HTTP client, proxy, and server all hosted in the same process. So that's what I did. It turns out to be a fairly nice way of configuring matching assertions between the client and the server to test the proxy transmissions.

7.2 How does it work? - HTTP Proxying

To configure a *proxy handler*, edit your *local.ini* and add a section like such:

```
[httpd_global_handlers]
_fti = {couch_httpd_proxy, handle_proxy_req, <<"http://127.0.0.1:5985">>}
```

This would be approximately what you'd need to do to get CouchDB-Lucene handled through this interface. The URL you use to access a query would be:

http://127.0.0.1:5984/_fti/db_name/_design/foo/by_content?q=hello

A couple things to note here. Anything in the path after the configured proxy name ("_fti" in this case) will be appended to the configured destination URL ("http://127.0.0.1:5985" in this case). The query string and any associated body will also be proxied transparently.

Also, of note is that there's nothing that limits on what resources can be proxied. You're free to choose any destination that the CouchDB node is capable of communicating with.

7.3 How does it work? - OS Daemons

The second part of the new API gives CouchDB simple OS process management. When CouchDB boots it will start each configured OS daemon. If one of these daemons fails at some point, it will be restarted. If one of these daemons fails too often, CouchDB will stop attempting to start it.

OS daemons are one-to-one. For each daemon, CouchDB will make sure that exactly one instance of it is alive. If you have something where you want multiple processes, you need to either tell CouchDB about each one, or have a main process that forks off the required sub-processes.

To configure an *OS daemon*, add this to your *local.ini*:

```
[os_daemons]
my_daemon = /path/to/command -with args
```

7.3.1 Configuration API

As an added benefit, because stdio is now free, I implemented a simple API that OS daemons can use to read the configuration of their CouchDB host. This way you can have them store their configuration inside CouchDB's config system if you desire. Or they can peek at things like the *httpd/bind_address* and *httpd/port* that CouchDB is using.

A request for a config section looks like this:

```
["get", "os_daemons"]\n
```

And the response:

```
{"my_daemon": "/path/to/command -with args"}\n
```

Or to get a specific key:

```
["get", "os_daemons", "my_daemon"]\n
```

And the response:

```
"/path/to/command -with args"\n
```

All requests and responses are terminated with a newline (indicated by \n).

7.3.2 Logging API

There's also an API for adding messages to CouchDB's logs. Its simply:

```
["log", $MESG]\n
```

Where $MESG is any arbitrary JSON. There is no response from this command. As with the config API, the trailing \n represents a newline byte.

7.3.3 Dynamic Daemons

The OS daemons react in real time to changes to the configuration system. If you set or delete keys in the os_daemons section, the corresponding daemons will be started or killed as appropriate.

7.4 Neat. But So What?

It was suggested that a good first demo would be a Node.js handler. So, I present to you a "Hello, World" Node.js handler. Also, remember that this currently relies on code in my fork on GitHub.

File *node-hello-world.js*:

```
var http = require('http');
var sys = require('sys');

// Send a log message to be included in CouchDB's
// log files.

var log = function(mesg) {
    console.log(JSON.stringify(["log", mesg]));
}

// The Node.js example HTTP server

var server = http.createServer(function (req, resp) {
    resp.writeHead(200, {'Content-Type': 'text/plain'});
    resp.end('Hello World\n');
    log(req.method + " " + req.url);
})

// We use stdin in a couple ways. First, we
// listen for data that will be the requested
// port information. We also listen for it
// to close which indicates that CouchDB has
// exited and that means its time for us to
// exit as well.

var stdin = process.openStdin();

stdin.on('data', function(d) {
    server.listen(parseInt(JSON.parse(d)));
});

stdin.on('end', function () {
    process.exit(0);
});

// Send the request for the port to listen on.

console.log(JSON.stringify(["get", "node_hello", "port"]));
```

File *local.ini* (Just add these to what you have):

```
[log]
level = info
```

```
[os_daemons]
node_hello = /path/to/node-hello-world.js

[node_hello]
port = 8000

[httpd_global_handlers]
_hello = {couch_httpd_proxy, handle_proxy_req, <<"http://127.0.0.1:8000">>}
```

And then start CouchDB and try:

```
$ curl -v http://127.0.0.1:5984/_hello
* About to connect() to 127.0.0.1 port 5984 (#0)
*   Trying 127.0.0.1... connected
* Connected to 127.0.0.1 (127.0.0.1) port 5984 (#0)
> GET /_hello HTTP/1.1
> User-Agent: curl/7.19.7 (universal-apple-darwin10.0) libcurl/7.19.7 OpenSSL/0.9.81 zlib
> Host: 127.0.0.1:5984
> Accept: */*
>
< HTTP/1.1 200
< Transfer-Encoding: chunked
< Server: CouchDB (Erlang/OTP)
< Date: Mon, 27 Sep 2010 01:13:37 GMT
< Content-Type: text/plain
< Connection: keep-alive
<
Hello World
* Connection #0 to host 127.0.0.1 left intact
* Closing connection #0
```

The corresponding CouchDB logs look like:

```
Apache CouchDB 1.5.0 (LogLevel=info) is starting.
Apache CouchDB has started. Time to relax.
[info] [<0.31.0>] Apache CouchDB has started on http://127.0.0.1:5984/
[info] [<0.105.0>] 127.0.0.1 - - 'GET' /_hello 200
[info] [<0.95.0>] Daemon "node-hello" :: GET /
```

## CHAPTER 8

Query Server

The *Query server* is an external process that communicates with CouchDB by JSON protocol through stdio interface and processed all *design functions* calls: *views*, *shows*, *lists* and more.

The default query server is written in *JavaScript*, running via Mozilla SpiderMonkey. You can use other languages by setting a Query server key in the language property of a design document or the *Content-Type* header of a *temporary view*. Design documents that do not specify a language property are assumed to be of type *javascript*, as are ad hoc queries that are POSTed to *_temp_view* without a *Content-Type* header.

8.1 Query Server Protocol

The *Query Server* is an external process that communicates with CouchDB via a JSON protocol over stdio and processes all design functions calls: *views*, *shows*, *lists*, *filters*, *updates* and *validate_doc_update*.

CouchDB communicates with the Query Server process though stdio interface by JSON messages that terminated by newline character. Messages that are sent to the Query Server are always *array*-typed that could be matched by the pattern [<command>, <*arguments>]\n.

Note: To simplify examples reading we omitted trailing \n character to let Sphinx highlight them well. Also, all examples contain formatted JSON values while real data transfers in compact mode without formatting spaces.

8.1.1 `reset`

Command reset

Arguments *Query server state* (optional)

Returns true

This resets the state of the Query Server and makes it forget all previous input. If applicable, this is the point to run garbage collection.

CouchDB sends:

```
["reset"]
```

The Query Server answers:

```
true
```

To set up new Query Server state the second argument is used with object data. This argument is used

CouchDB sends:

```
["reset", {"reduce_limit": true, "timeout": 5000}]
```

The Query Server answers:

```
true
```

8.1.2 add_lib

> **Command** add_lib
>
> **Arguments** CommonJS library object by views/lib path
>
> **Returns** true

Adds *CommonJS* library to Query Server state for further usage in *map* functions.

CouchDB sends:

```
[
    "add_lib",
    {
        "utils": "exports.MAGIC = 42;"
    }
]
```

The Query Server answers:

```
true
```

Note: This library shouldn't have any side effects nor track its own state or you'll have a lot of happy debugging time if something went wrong. Remember that a complete index rebuild is a heavy operation and this is the only way to fix your mistakes with shared state.

---

add_fun

> **Command** add_fun
>
> **Arguments** Map function source code.
>
> **Returns** true

When creating or updating a view the Query Server gets sent the view function for evaluation. The Query Server should parse, compile and evaluate the function it receives to make it callable later. If this fails, the Query Server returns an error. CouchDB might store several functions before sending in any actual documents.

CouchDB sends:

```
[
    "add_fun",
    "function(doc) { if(doc.score > 50) emit(null, {'player_name': doc.name}); }"
]
```

The Query Server answers:

```
true
```

8.1.3 map_doc

> **Command** map_doc
>
> **Arguments** Document object
>
> **Returns** Array of key-value pairs per applied *function*

When the view function is stored in the Query Server, CouchDB starts sending in all the documents in the database, one at a time. The Query Server calls the previously stored functions one after another with a document and stores its result. When all functions have been called, the result is returned as a JSON string.

CouchDB sends:

```
[
    "map_doc",
    {
        "_id": "8877AFF9789988EE",
        "_rev": "3-235256484",
        "name": "John Smith",
        "score": 60
    }
]
```

If the function above is the only function stored, the Query Server answers:

```
[
    [
        [null, {"player_name": "John Smith"}]
    ]
]
```

That is, an array with the result for every function for the given document.

If a document is to be excluded from the view, the array should be empty.

CouchDB sends:

```
[
    "map_doc",
    {
        "_id": "9590AEB4585637FE",
        "_rev": "1-674684684",
        "name": "Jane Parker",
        "score": 43
    }
]
```

The Query Server answers:

```
[[]]
```

8.1.4 reduce

Command reduce

Arguments

- Reduce function source

- Array of *map function* results where each item represented in format [[key, id-of-doc], value]

Returns Array with pair values: true and another array with reduced result

If the view has a reduce function defined, CouchDB will enter into the reduce phase. The view server will receive a list of reduce functions and some map results on which it can apply them.

CouchDB sends:

```
[
    "reduce",
    [
        "function(k, v) { return sum(v); }"
```

```
    ],
    [
        [[1, "699b524273605d5d3e9d4fd0ff2cb272"], 10],
        [[2, "c081d0f69c13d2ce2050d684c7ba2843"], 20],
        [[null, "foobar"], 3]
    ]
]
```

The Query Server answers:

```
[
    true,
    [33]
]
```

Note that even though the view server receives the map results in the form `[[key, id-of-doc], value]`, the function may receive them in a different form. For example, the JavaScript Query Server applies functions on the list of keys and the list of values.

8.1.5 rereduce

Command rereduce

Arguments

- Reduce function source

- List of values

When building a view, CouchDB will apply the reduce step directly to the output of the map step and the rereduce step to the output of a previous reduce step.

CouchDB will send a list of reduce functions and a list of values, with no keys or document ids, to the rereduce step.

CouchDB sends:

```
[
    "rereduce",
    [
        "function(k, v, r) { return sum(v); }"
    ],
    [
        33,
        55,
        66
    ]
]
```

The Query Server answers:

```
[
    true,
    [154]
]
```

8.1.6 ddoc

Command ddoc

Arguments Array of objects.

- First phase (ddoc initialization):

– "new"

– Design document `_id`

– Design document object

- Second phase (design function execution):

– Design document `_id`

– Function path as an array of object keys

– Array of function arguments

Returns

- First phase (ddoc initialization): `true`

- Second phase (design function execution): custom object depending on executed function

This command acts in two phases: *ddoc* registration and *design function* execution.

In the first phase CouchDB sends a full design document content to the Query Server to let it cache it by `_id` value for further function execution.

To do this, CouchDB sends:

```
[
    "ddoc",
    "new",
    "_design/temp",
    {
        "_id": "_design/temp",
        "_rev": "8-d7379de23a751dc2a19e5638a7bbc5cc",
        "language": "javascript",
        "shows": {
            "request": "function(doc,req){ return {json: req}; }",
            "hello": "function(doc,req){ return {body: 'Hello, ' + (doc || {})._id + '!'}
        }
    }
]
```

The Query Server answers:

```
true
```

After than this design document is ready to serve next subcommands - that's the second phase.

Note: Each `ddoc` subcommand is the root design document key, so they are not actually subcommands, but first elements of the JSON path that may be handled and processed.

The pattern for subcommand execution is common:

```
["ddoc", <design_doc_id>, [<subcommand>, <funcname>], [<argument1>,
<argument2>, ...]]
```

---

shows

> **Command** `ddoc`
>
> **SubCommand** `shows`
>
> **Arguments**
>
> - Document object or `null` if document *id* wasn't specified in request
>
> - *Request object*
>
> **Returns** Array with two elements:

- `"resp"`

- *Response object*

Executes *show function*.

Couchdb sends:

```
[
    "ddoc",
    "_design/temp",
    [
        "shows",
        "doc"
    ],
    [
        null,
        {
            "info": {
                "db_name": "test",
                "doc_count": 8,
                "doc_del_count": 0,
                "update_seq": 105,
                "purge_seq": 0,
                "compact_running": false,
                "disk_size": 15818856,
                "data_size": 1535048,
                "instance_start_time": "1359952188595857",
                "disk_format_version": 6,
                "committed_update_seq": 105
            },
            "id": null,
            "uuid": "169cb4cc82427cc7322cb4463d0021bb",
            "method": "GET",
            "requested_path": [
                "api",
                "_design",
                "temp",
                "_show",
                "request"
            ],
            "path": [
                "api",
                "_design",
                "temp",
                "_show",
                "request"
            ],
            "raw_path": "/api/_design/temp/_show/request",
            "query": {},
            "headers": {
                "Accept": "*/*",
                "Host": "localhost:5984",
                "User-Agent": "curl/7.26.0"
            },
            "body": "undefined",
            "peer": "127.0.0.1",
            "form": {},
            "cookie": {},
            "userCtx": {
                "db": "api",
                "name": null,
                "roles": [
                    "_admin"
```

```
            ]
        },
        "secObj": {}
    }
]
]
```

The Query Server sends:

```
[
    "resp",
    {
        "body": "Hello, undefined!"
    }
]
```

lists

> **Command** ddoc
>
> **SubCommand** lists
>
> **Arguments**
>
> > • *View Head Information*:
> >
> > • *Request object*
>
> **Returns** Array. See below for details.

Executes *list function*.

The communication protocol for *list* functions is a bit complex so let's use an example for illustration.

Let's assume that we have view a function that emits *id-rev* pairs:

```
function(doc) {
    emit(doc._id, doc._rev);
}
```

And we'd like to emulate `_all_docs` JSON response with list function. Our *first* version of the list functions looks like this:

```
function(head, req){
    start({'headers': {'Content-Type': 'application/json'}});
    var resp = head;
    var rows = [];
    while(row=getRow()){
        rows.push(row);
    }
    resp.rows = rows;
    return toJSON(resp);
}
```

The whole communication session during list function execution could be divided on three parts:

1. Initialization

   The first returned object from list function is an array of next structure:

   ```
   ["start", <chunks>, <headers>]
   ```

   Where `<chunks>` is an array of text chunks that will be sent to client and `<headers>` is an object with response HTTP headers.

   This message is sent from the Query Server to CouchDB on the `start()` call which initialize HTTP response to the client:

```
[
    "start",
    [],
    {
        "headers": {
            "Content-Type": "application/json"
        }
    }
]
```

After this, the list function may start to process view rows.

2. View Processing

Since view results can be extremely large, it is not wise to pass all its rows in a single command. Instead, CouchDB can send view rows one by one to the Query Server allowing processing view and output generation in a streaming way.

CouchDB sends a special array that carries view row data:

```
[
    "list_row",
    {
        "id": "0cb42c267fe32d4b56b3500bc503e030",
        "key": "0cb42c267fe32d4b56b3500bc503e030",
        "value": "1-967a00dff5e02add41819138abb3284d"
    }
]
```

If Query Server has something to return on this, it returns an array with a "chunks" item in the head and an array of data in the tail. Now, for our case it has nothing to return, so the response will be:

```
[
    "chunks",
    []
]
```

When there is no more view rows to process, CouchDB sends special message, that signs about that there is no more data to send from its side:

```
["list_end"]
```

3. Finalization

The last stage of the communication process is the returning *list tail*: the last data chunk. After this, processing list function will be completed and client will receive complete response.

For our example the last message will be the next:

```
[
    "end",
    [
        "{\"total_rows\":2,\"offset\":0,\"rows\":[{\"id\":\"0cb42c267fe32d4b56b3500bc
    ]
]
```

There, we had made a big mistake: we had returned out result in a single message from the Query Server. That's ok when there are only a few rows in the view result, but it's not acceptable for millions documents and millions view rows

Let's fix our list function and see the changes in communication:

```
function(head, req){
    start({'headers': {'Content-Type': 'application/json'}});
    send('{');
    send('"total_rows":' + toJSON(head.total_rows) + ',');
```

```
    send('"offset":' + toJSON(head.offset) + ',');
    send('"rows":[');
    if (row=getRow()){
        send(toJSON(row));
    }
    while(row=getRow()){
        send(',' + toJSON(row));
    }
    send(']');
    return '}';
}
```

"Wait, what?" - you'd like to ask. Yes, we'd build JSON response manually by string chunks, but let's take a look on logs:

```
[Wed, 24 Jul 2013 05:45:30 GMT] [debug] [<0.19191.1>] OS Process #Port<0.4444> Output ::
[Wed, 24 Jul 2013 05:45:30 GMT] [info] [<0.18963.1>] 127.0.0.1 - - GET /blog/_design/post
[Wed, 24 Jul 2013 05:45:30 GMT] [debug] [<0.19191.1>] OS Process #Port<0.4444> Input ::
[Wed, 24 Jul 2013 05:45:30 GMT] [debug] [<0.19191.1>] OS Process #Port<0.4444> Output ::
[Wed, 24 Jul 2013 05:45:30 GMT] [debug] [<0.19191.1>] OS Process #Port<0.4444> Input ::
[Wed, 24 Jul 2013 05:45:30 GMT] [debug] [<0.19191.1>] OS Process #Port<0.4444> Output ::
[Wed, 24 Jul 2013 05:45:30 GMT] [debug] [<0.19191.1>] OS Process #Port<0.4444> Input ::
[Wed, 24 Jul 2013 05:45:30 GMT] [debug] [<0.19191.1>] OS Process #Port<0.4444> Output ::
```

Note, that now the Query Server sends response by lightweight chunks and if our communication process was extremely slow, the client will see how response data appears on their screen. Chunk by chunk, without waiting for the complete result, like they have for our previous list function.

updates

Command ddoc

SubCommand updates

Arguments

- Document object or null if document *id* wasn't specified in request

- *Request object*

Returns Array with there elements:

- "up"

- Document object or null if nothing should be stored

- *Response object*

Executes *update function*.

CouchDB sends:

```
[
    "ddoc",
    "_design/id",
    [
        "updates",
        "nothing"
    ],
    [
        null,
        {
            "info": {
                "db_name": "test",
                "doc_count": 5,
                "doc_del_count": 0,
```

```
                    "update_seq": 16,
                    "purge_seq": 0,
                    "compact_running": false,
                    "disk_size": 8044648,
                    "data_size": 7979601,
                    "instance_start_time": "1374612186131612",
                    "disk_format_version": 6,
                    "committed_update_seq": 16
                },
                "id": null,
                "uuid": "7b695cb34a03df0316c15ab529002e69",
                "method": "POST",
                "requested_path": [
                    "test",
                    "_design",
                    "1139",
                    "_update",
                    "nothing"
                ],
                "path": [
                    "test",
                    "_design",
                    "1139",
                    "_update",
                    "nothing"
                ],
                "raw_path": "/test/_design/1139/_update/nothinq",
                "query": {},
                "headers": {
                    "Accept": "*/*",
                    "Accept-Encoding": "identity, gzip, deflate, compress",
                    "Content-Length": "0",
                    "Host": "localhost:5984"
                },
                "body": "",
                "peer": "127.0.0.1",
                "form": {},
                "cookie": {},
                "userCtx": {
                    "db": "test",
                    "name": null,
                    "roles": [
                        "_admin"
                    ]
                },
                "secObj": {}
        }
    ]
]
```

The Query Server answers:

```
[
    "up",
    null,
    {"body": "document id wasn't provided"}
]
```

or in case of successful update:

```
[
    "up",
    {
```

```
        "_id": "7b695cb34a03df0316c15ab529002e69",
        "hello": "world!"
    },
    {"body": "document was updated"}
]
```

filters

Command `ddoc`

SubCommand `filters`

Arguments

- Array of document objects

- *Request object*

Returns Array of two elements:

- `true`

- Array of booleans in the same order of input documents.

Executes *filter function*.

CouchDB sends:

```
[
    "ddoc",
    "_design/test",
    [
        "filters",
        "random"
    ],
    [
        [
            {
                "_id": "431926a69504bde41851eb3c18a27b1f",
                "_rev": "1-967a00dff5e02add41819138abb3284d",
                "_revisions": {
                    "start": 1,
                    "ids": [
                        "967a00dff5e02add41819138abb3284d"
                    ]
                }
            },
            {
                "_id": "0cb42c267fe32d4b56b3500bc503e030",
                "_rev": "1-967a00dff5e02add41819138abb3284d",
                "_revisions": {
                    "start": 1,
                    "ids": [
                        "967a00dff5e02add41819138abb3284d"
                    ]
                }
            }
        ],
        {
            "info": {
                "db_name": "test",
                "doc_count": 5,
                "doc_del_count": 0,
                "update_seq": 19,
                "purge_seq": 0,
```

```
                 "compact_running": false,
                 "disk_size": 8056936,
                 "data_size": 7979745,
                 "instance_start_time": "1374612186131612",
                 "disk_format_version": 6,
                 "committed_update_seq": 19
             },
             "id": null,
             "uuid": "7b695cb34a03df0316c15ab529023a81",
             "method": "GET",
             "requested_path": [
                 "test",
                 "_changes?filter=test",
                 "random"
             ],
             "path": [
                 "test",
                 "_changes"
             ],
             "raw_path": "/test/_changes?filter=test/random",
             "query": {
                 "filter": "test/random"
             },
             "headers": {
                 "Accept": "application/json",
                 "Accept-Encoding": "identity, gzip, deflate, compress",
                 "Content-Length": "0",
                 "Content-Type": "application/json; charset=utf-8",
                 "Host": "localhost:5984"
             },
             "body": "",
             "peer": "127.0.0.1",
             "form": {},
             "cookie": {},
             "userCtx": {
                 "db": "test",
                 "name": null,
                 "roles": [
                     "_admin"
                 ]
             },
             "secObj": {}
         }
     ]
]
```

The Query Server answers:

```
[
    true,
    [
        true,
        false
    ]
]
```

views

Command ddoc

SubCommand views

Arguments Array of document objects

Returns Array of two elements:

- `true`
- Array of booleans in the same order of input documents.

New in version 1.2.

Executes *view function* in place of the filter.

Acts in the same way as *filters* command.

validate_doc_update

Command `ddoc`

SubCommand `validate_doc_update`

Arguments

- Document object that will be stored
- Document object that will be replaced
- *User Context Object*
- *Security Object*

Returns `1`

Executes *validation function*.

CouchDB send:

```
[
    "ddoc",
    "_design/id",
    ["validate_doc_update"],
    [
        {
            "_id": "docid",
            "_rev": "2-e0165f450f6c89dc6b071c075dde3c4d",
            "score": 10
        },
        {
            "_id": "docid",
            "_rev": "1-9f798c6ad72a406afdbf470b9eea8375",
            "score": 4
        },
        {
            "name": "Mike",
            "roles": ["player"]
        },
        {
            "admins": {},
            "members": []
        }
    ]
]
```

The Query Server answers:

```
1
```

Note: While the only valid response for this command is `true` to prevent document save the Query Server need to raise an error: `forbidden` or `unauthorized` - these errors will be turned into correct `HTTP 403` and `HTTP 401` responses respectively.

8.1.7 Raising errors

When something went wrong the Query Server is able to inform CouchDB about such a situation by sending special message in response of received command.

Error messages prevent further command execution and return an error description to CouchDB. All errors are logically divided into two groups:

- *Common errors.* These errors only break the current Query Server command and return the error info to the CouchDB instance *without* terminating the Query Server process.

- *Fatal errors.* The fatal errors signal about something really bad that hurts the overall Query Server process stability and productivity. For instance, if you're using Python Query Server and some design function is unable to import some third party module, it's better to count such error as fatal and terminate whole process or you still have to do the same after import fixing, but manually.

error

To raise an error, the Query Server have to answer:

```
["error", "error_name", "reason why"]
```

The "error_name" helps to classify problems by their type e.g. if it's "value_error" so probably user have entered wrong data, "not_found" notifies about missed resource and "type_error" definitely says about invalid and non expected input from user.

The "reason why" is the error message that explains why it raised and, if possible, what is needed to do to fix it.

For example, calling *Update functions* against non existent document could produce next error message:

```
["error", "not_found", "Update function requires existent document"]
```

forbidden

The *forbidden* error is widely used by *Validate document update functions* to stop further function processing and prevent on disk store of the new document version. Since this error actually is not an error, but an assertion against user actions, CouchDB doesn't log it at *"error"* level, but returns *HTTP 403 Forbidden* response with error information object.

To raise this error, the Query Server have to answer:

```
{"forbidden": "reason why"}
```

unauthorized

The *unauthorized* error mostly acts like *forbidden* one, but with the meaning of *please authorize first*. This small difference helps end users to understand what they can do to solve the problem. CouchDB doesn't log it at *"error"* level, but returns *HTTP 401 Unauthorized* response with error information object.

To raise this error, the Query Server have to answer:

```
{"unauthorized": "reason why"}
```

8.1.8 Logging

At any time, the Query Server may send some information that will be saved in CouchDB's log file. This is done by sending a special object with just one field, log, on a separate line:

```
["log", "some message"]
```

CouchDB responds nothing, but writes received message into log file:

```
[Sun, 13 Feb 2009 23:31:30 GMT] [info] [<0.72.0>] Query Server Log Message: some message
```

These messages are only logged at *info level*.

8.2 JavaScript

Note: While every design function has access to all JavaScript objects, the table below describes appropriate usage cases. For example, you may use *emit ()* in *List functions*, but *getRow ()* is not permitted during *Map functions*.

JS Function	Reasonable to use in design doc functions
emit ()	*Map functions*
getRow ()	*List functions*
JSON	any
isArray ()	any
log ()	any
provides ()	*Show functions*, *List functions*
registerType ()	*Show functions*, *List functions*
require ()	any, except *Reduce and rereduce functions*
send ()	*List functions*
start ()	*List functions*
sum ()	any
toJSON ()	any

8.2.1 Design functions context

Each design function executes in a special context of predefined objects, modules and functions:

emit (*key*, *value*)
> Emits a *key-value* pair for further processing by CouchDB after the map function is done.

> **Arguments**

> * **key** – The view key
> * **value** – The *key*'s associated value

```
function(doc){
    emit(doc._id, doc._rev);
}
```

getRow ()
> Extracts the next row from a related view result.

> **Returns** View result row

> **Return type** object

```
function(head, req){
    send('[');
    row = getRow();
    if (row){
        send(toJSON(row));
        while(row = getRow()){
            send(',');
            send(toJSON(row));
```

```
        }
    }
    return ']';
}
```

JSON

JSON2 object.

isArray (*obj*)

A helper function to check if the provided value is an *Array*.

Arguments

- **obj** – Any JavaScript value

Returns `true` if *obj* is *Array*-typed, `false` otherwise

Return type boolean

log (*message*)

Log a message to the CouchDB log (at the *INFO* level).

Arguments

- **message** – Message to be logged

```
function(doc){
    log('Procesing doc ' + doc['_id']);
    emit(doc['_id'], null);
}
```

After the map function has run, the following line can be found in CouchDB logs (e.g. at */var/log/couchdb/couch.log*):

```
[Sat, 03 Nov 2012 17:38:02 GMT] [info] [<0.7543.0>] OS Process #Port<0.3289> Log :: F
```

provides (*key*, *func*)

Registers callable handler for specified MIME key.

Arguments

- **key** – MIME key previously defined by `registerType()`

- **func** – MIME type handler

registerType (*key*, **mimes*)

Registers list of MIME types by associated *key*.

Arguments

- **key** – MIME types

- **mimes** – MIME types enumeration

Predefined mappings (*key-array*):

- **all**: `*/*`

- **text**: `text/plain; charset=utf-8`, `txt`

- **html**: `text/html; charset=utf-8`

- **xhtml**: `application/xhtml+xml`, `xhtml`

- **xml**: `application/xml`, `text/xml`, `application/x-xml`

- **js**: `text/javascript`, `application/javascript`, `application/x-javascript`

- **css**: `text/css`

- **ics**: `text/calendar`

•**csv**: `text/csv`

•**rss**: `application/rss+xml`

•**atom**: `application/atom+xml`

•**yaml**: `application/x-yaml`, `text/yaml`

•**multipart_form**: `multipart/form-data`

•**url_encoded_form**: `application/x-www-form-urlencoded`

•**json**: `application/json`, `text/x-json`

`require` (*path*)

Loads CommonJS module by a specified *path*. The path should not start with a slash.

Arguments

     • `path` – A CommonJS module path started from design document root

Returns Exported statements

`send` (*chunk*)

Sends a single string *chunk* in response.

Arguments

     • `chunk` – Text chunk

```
function(head, req){
    send('Hello,');
    send(' ');
    send('Couch');
    return !
}
```

`start` (*init_resp*)

Initiates chunked response. As an option, a custom *response* object may be sent at this point. For *list-*functions only!

Note: list functions may set the *HTTP response code* and *headers* by calling this function. This function must be called before `send()`, `getRow()` or a *return* statement; otherwise, the query server will implicitly call this function with the empty object (`{ }`).

```
function(head, req){
    start({
        "code": 302,
        "headers": {
            "Location": "http://couchdb.apache.org"
        }
    });
    return "Relax!";
}
```

`sum` (*arr*)

Sum *arr*'s items.

Arguments

     • `arr` – Array of numbers

Return type number

`toJSON` (*obj*)

Encodes *obj* to JSON string. This is an alias for the `JSON.stringify` method.

Arguments

- **obj** – JSON encodable object

Returns JSON string

8.2.2 CommonJS Modules

Support for CommonJS Modules (introduced in CouchDB 0.11.0) allows you to create modular design functions without the need for duplication of functionality.

Here's a CommonJS module that checks user permissions:

```
function user_context(userctx, secobj) {
    var is_admin = function() {
        return userctx.indexOf('_admin') != -1;
    }
    return {'is_admin': is_admin}
}

exports['user'] = user_context
```

Each module has access to additional global variables:

- **module** (*object*): Contains information about the stored module
    - **id** (*string*): The module id; a JSON path in ddoc context
    - **current** (*code*): Compiled module code object
    - **parent** (*object*): Parent frame
    - **exports** (*object*): Export statements
- **exports** (*object*): Shortcut to the `module.exports` object

The CommonJS module can be added to a design document, like so:

```
{
    "views": {
        "lib": {
            "security": "function user_context(userctx, secobj) { ... }"
        }
    },
    "validate_doc_update": "function(newdoc, olddoc, userctx, secobj) {
        user = require('lib/security').user(userctx, secobj);
        return user.is_admin();
    }"
    "_id": "_design/test"
}
```

Modules paths are relative to the design document's `views` object, but modules can only be loaded from the object referenced via `lib`. The `lib` structure can still be used for view functions as well, by simply storing view functions at e.g. `views.lib.map`, `views.lib.reduce`, etc.

8.3 Erlang

Note: The Erlang query server is disabled by default. Read *configuration guide* about reasons why and how to enable it.

Emit (*Id*, *Value*)

Emits *key-value* pairs to view indexer process.

```
fun({Doc}) ->
    <<K,_/binary>> = proplists:get_value(<<"_rev">>, Doc, null),
    V = proplists:get_value(<<"_id">>, Doc, null),
    Emit(<<K>>, V)
end.
```

FoldRows (*Fun*, *Acc*)

Helper to iterate over all rows in a list function.

Arguments

- **Fun** – Function object.

- **Acc** – The value previously returned by *Fun*.

```
fun(Head, {Req}) ->
    Fun = fun({Row}, Acc) ->
        Id = couch_util:get_value(<<"id">>, Row),
        Send(list_to_binary(io_lib:format("Previous doc id: ~p", [Acc]))),
        Send(list_to_binary(io_lib:format("Current  doc id: ~p", [Id]))),
        {ok, Id}
    end,
    FoldRows(Fun, nil),
    ""
end.
```

GetRow ()

Retrieves the next row from a related view result.

```
%% FoldRows background implementation.
%% https://git-wip-us.apache.org/repos/asf?p=couchdb.git;a=blob;f=src/couchdb/couch_
%%
foldrows(GetRow, ProcRow, Acc) ->
    case GetRow() of
        nil ->
            {ok, Acc};
        Row ->
            case (catch ProcRow(Row, Acc)) of
                {ok, Acc2} ->
                    foldrows(GetRow, ProcRow, Acc2);
                {stop, Acc2} ->
                    {ok, Acc2}
            end
end.
```

Log (*Msg*)

Arguments

- **Msg** – Log a message at the *INFO* level.

```
fun({Doc}) ->
    <<K,_/binary>> = proplists:get_value(<<"_rev">>, Doc, null),
    V = proplists:get_value(<<"_id">>, Doc, null),
    Log(lists:flatten(io_lib:format("Hello from ~s doc!", [V]))),
    Emit(<<K>>, V)
end.
```

After the map function has run, the following line can be found in CouchDB logs (e.g. at */var/log/couchdb/couch.log*):

```
[Sun, 04 Nov 2012 11:33:58 GMT] [info] [<0.9144.2>] Hello from 8d300b86622d67953d102
```

Send (*Chunk*)

Sends a single string *Chunk* in response.

```
fun(Head, {Req}) ->
    Send("Hello,"),
    Send(" "),
    Send("Couch"),
    "!"
end.
```

The function above produces the following response:

```
Hello, Couch!
```

Start (*Headers*)

Arguments

- **Headers** – Proplist of *response object*.

Initialize *List functions* response. At this point, response code and headers may be defined. For example, this function redirects to the CouchDB web site:

```
fun(Head, {Req}) ->
    Start({[{<<"code">>, 302},
            {<<"headers">>, {[
                {<<"Location">>, <<"http://couchdb.apache.org">>}]
            }}
        ]}),
    "Relax!"
end.
```

## CHAPTER 9

Fauxton

9.1 Installation

Recent versions of node.js and npm are required.

9.1.1 Get the source

Clone the CouchDB repo:

```
$ git clone http://git-wip-us.apache.org/repos/asf/couchdb.git
$ cd couchdb
```

9.1.2 Fauxton Setup

Install all dependencies:

```
couchdb/ $ cd src/fauxton
couchdb/src/fauxton/ $ npm install
```

Note: To avoid a npm global install add node_modules/.bin to your path:

```
export PATH=./node_modules/.bin:$PATH
```

Or just use the wrappers in ./bin/.

Development mode, non minified files:

```
./bin/grunt couchdebug
```

Or fully compiled install:

```
./bin/grunt couchdb
```

9.1.3 Dev Server

Using the dev server is the easiest way to use Fauxton, specially when developing for it:

```
grunt dev
```

9.1.4 Deploy Fauxton

Deploy Fauxton to your local CouchDB instance:

> ./bin/grunt couchapp_deploy

The Fauxton be available by /fauxton/_design/fauxton/index.html

Understanding Fauxton Code layout

Each bit of functionality is its own separate module or addon.

All core modules are stored under *app/module* and any addons that are optional are under *app/addons*.

We use backbone.js and Backbone.layoutmanager quite heavily, so best to get an idea how they work. Its best at this point to read through a couple of the modules and addons to get an idea of how they work.

Two good starting points are *app/addon/config* and *app/modules/databases*.

Each module must have a *base.js* file, this is read and compile when Fauxton is deployed.

The *resource.js* file is usually for your `Backbone.Models` and `Backbone.Collections`, *view.js* for your `Backbone.Views`.

The *routes.js* is used to register a url path for your view along with what layout, data, breadcrumbs and api point is required for the view.

ToDo items

Checkout JIRA for a list of items to do.

9.2 Writing Addons

Addons allow you to extend Fauxton for a specific use case. Usually, they have the following structure:

```
+ my_addon/
| ---+ assets [optional]
|    \ ---+ less
|         \ ---- my_addon.less
| ---+ templates/
|    \ ---- my_addon.html - underscore template fragments
| ---- resources.js - models and collections of the addon
| ---- routes.js - URL routing for the addon
| ---- views.js - views that the model provides
```

9.2.1 Generating an Addon

We have a *grunt-init* template that lets you create a skeleton addon, including all the boiler plate code. Run `grunt-init tasks/addon` and answer the questions it asks to create an addon:

```
± grunt-init tasks/addon
path.existsSync is now called `fs.existsSync`.
Running "addon" task

Please answer the following:
[?] Add on Name (WickedCool) SuperAddon
[?] Location of add ons (app/addons)
[?] Do you need an assets folder?(for .less) (y/N)
[?] Do you need to make any changes to the above before continuing? (y/N)
```

```
Created addon SuperAddon in app/addons

Done, without errors.
```

Once the addon is created add the name to the settings.json file to get it compiled and added on the next install.

9.2.2 Routes and hooks

An addon can insert itself into Fauxton in two ways; via a route or via a hook.

Routes

An addon will override an existing route should one exist, but in all other ways is just a normal backbone *route/view*. This is how you would add a whole new feature.

Hooks

Hooks let you modify/extend an existing feature. They modify a DOM element by selector for a named set of routes, for example:

```
var Search = new FauxtonAPI.addon();
Search.hooks = {
    // Render additional content into the sidebar
    "#sidebar-content": {
      routes:[
          "database/:database/_design/:ddoc/_search/:search",
          "database/:database/_design/:ddoc/_view/:view",
          "database/:database/_:handler"],
      callback: searchSidebar
    }
};
return Search;
```

adds the *searchSidebar* callback to *#sidebar-content* for three routes.

9.2.3 Hello world Addon

First create the addon skeleton:

```
± bbb addon
path.existsSync is now called `fs.existsSync`.
Running "addon" task

Please answer the following:
[?] Add on Name (WickedCool) Hello
[?] Location of add ons (app/addons)
[?] Do you need to make any changes to the above before continuing? (y/N)

Created addon Hello in app/addons

Done, without errors.
```

In *app/addons/hello/templates/hello.html* place:

```
<h1>Hello!</h1>
```

Next, we'll defined a simple view in *resources.js* (for more complex addons you may want to have a views.js) that renders that template:

```
define([
    "app",
    "api"
],

function (app, FauxtonAPI) {
    var Resources = {};

    Resources.Hello = FauxtonAPI.View.extend({
        template: "addons/hello/templates/hello"
    });

    return Resources;
});
```

Then define a route in *routes.js* that the addon is accessible at:

```
define([
    "app",
    "api",
    "addons/hello/resources"
],

function(app, FauxtonAPI, Resources) {
    var helloRoute = function () {
        console.log('helloRoute callback yo');
        return {
            layout: "one_pane",
            crumbs: [
                {"name": "Hello","link": "_hello"}
            ],
            views: {
                "#dashboard-content": new Resources.Hello({})
            },
            apiUrl: 'hello'
        };
    };

    Routes = {
        "_hello": helloRoute
    };

    return Routes;
});
```

Then wire it all together in base.js:

```
define([
    "app",
    "api",
    "addons/hello/routes"
],

function(app, FauxtonAPI, HelloRoutes) {
    var Hello = new FauxtonAPI.addon();
    console.log('hello from hello');

    Hello.initialize = function() {
        FauxtonAPI.addHeaderLink({title: "Hello", href: "#_hello"});
    };

    Hello.Routes = HelloRoutes;
    console.log(Hello);
```

```
    return Hello;
});
```

Once the code is in place include the add on in your *settings.json* so that it gets included by the *require* task. Your addon is included in one of three ways; a local path, a git URL or a name. Named plugins assume the plugin is in the Fauxton base directory, addons with a git URL will be cloned into the application, local paths will be copied. Addons included from a local path will be cleaned out by the clean task, others are left alone.

## CHAPTER 10

API Reference

The components of the API URL path help determine the part of the CouchDB server that is being accessed. The result is the structure of the URL request both identifies and effectively describes the area of the database you are accessing.

As with all URLs, the individual components are separated by a forward slash.

As a general rule, URL components and JSON fields starting with the _ (underscore) character represent a special component or entity within the server or returned object. For example, the URL fragment /_all_dbs gets a list of all of the databases in a CouchDB instance.

This reference is structured according to the URL structure, as below.

10.1 API Basics

The CouchDB API is the primary method of interfacing to a CouchDB instance. Requests are made using HTTP and requests are used to request information from the database, store new data, and perform views and formatting of the information stored within the documents.

Requests to the API can be categorised by the different areas of the CouchDB system that you are accessing, and the HTTP method used to send the request. Different methods imply different operations, for example retrieval of information from the database is typically handled by the GET operation, while updates are handled by either a POST or PUT request. There are some differences between the information that must be supplied for the different methods. For a guide to the basic HTTP methods and request structure, see *Request Format and Responses*.

For nearly all operations, the submitted data, and the returned data structure, is defined within a JavaScript Object Notation (JSON) object. Basic information on the content and data types for JSON are provided in *JSON Basics*.

Errors when accessing the CouchDB API are reported using standard HTTP Status Codes. A guide to the generic codes returned by CouchDB are provided in *HTTP Status Codes*.

When accessing specific areas of the CouchDB API, specific information and examples on the HTTP methods and request, JSON structures, and error codes are provided.

10.1.1 Request Format and Responses

CouchDB supports the following HTTP request methods:

- GET

  Request the specified item. As with normal HTTP requests, the format of the URL defines what is returned. With CouchDB this can include static items, database documents, and configuration and statistical information. In most cases the information is returned in the form of a JSON document.

- HEAD

  The HEAD method is used to get the HTTP header of a GET request without the body of the response.

- POST

  Upload data. Within CouchDB POST is used to set values, including uploading documents, setting document values, and starting certain administration commands.

- PUT

  Used to put a specified resource. In CouchDB PUT is used to create new objects, including databases, documents, views and design documents.

- DELETE

  Deletes the specified resource, including documents, views, and design documents.

- COPY

  A special method that can be used to copy documents and objects.

If you use an unsupported HTTP request type with an URL that does not support the specified type then a 405 - Resource Not Allowed will be returned, listing the supported HTTP methods. For example:

```
{
    "error":"method_not_allowed",
    "reason":"Only GET,HEAD allowed"
}
```

The CouchDB design document API and the functions when returning HTML (for example as part of a show or list) enables you to include custom HTTP headers through the headers block of the return object.

10.1.2 HTTP Headers

Because CouchDB uses HTTP for all communication, you need to ensure that the correct HTTP headers are supplied (and processed on retrieval) so that you get the right format and encoding. Different environments and clients will be more or less strict on the effect of these HTTP headers (especially when not present). Where possible you should be as specific as possible.

Request Headers

- Accept

  Specifies the list of accepted data types to be returned by the server (i.e. that are accepted/understandable by the client). The format should be a list of one or more MIME types, separated by colons.

  For the majority of requests the definition should be for JSON data (application/json). For attachments you can either specify the MIME type explicitly, or use */* to specify that all file types are supported. If the Accept header is not supplied, then the */* MIME type is assumed (i.e. client accepts all formats).

  The use of Accept in queries for CouchDB is not required, but is highly recommended as it helps to ensure that the data returned can be processed by the client.

  If you specify a data type using the Accept header, CouchDB will honor the specified type in the Content-type header field returned. For example, if you explicitly request application/json in the Accept of a request, the returned HTTP headers will use the value in the returned Content-type field.

  For example, when sending a request without an explicit Accept header, or when specifying */*:

```
GET /recipes HTTP/1.1
Host: couchdb:5984
Accept: */*
```

The returned headers are:

```
Server: CouchDB (Erlang/OTP)
Date: Thu, 13 Jan 2011 13:39:34 GMT
Content-Type: text/plain;charset=utf-8
Content-Length: 227
Cache-Control: must-revalidate
```

Note: The returned content type is `text/plain` even though the information returned by the request is in JSON format.

Explicitly specifying the `Accept` header:

```
GET /recipes HTTP/1.1
Host: couchdb:5984
Accept: application/json
```

The headers returned include the `application/json` content type:

```
Server: CouchDB (Erlang/OTP)
Date: Thu, 13 Jan 2013 13:40:11 GMT
Content-Type: application/json
Content-Length: 227
Cache-Control: must-revalidate
```

- `Content-type`

  Specifies the content type of the information being supplied within the request. The specification uses MIME type specifications. For the majority of requests this will be JSON (`application/json`). For some settings the MIME type will be plain text. When uploading attachments it should be the corresponding MIME type for the attachment or binary (`application/octet-stream`).

  The use of the `Content-type` on a request is highly recommended.

Response Headers

Response headers are returned by the server when sending back content and include a number of different header fields, many of which are standard HTTP response header and have no significance to CouchDB operation. The list of response headers important to CouchDB are listed below.

- `Cache-control`

  The cache control HTTP response header provides a suggestion for client caching mechanisms on how to treat the returned information. CouchDB typically returns the `must-revalidate`, which indicates that the information should be revalidated if possible. This is used to ensure that the dynamic nature of the content is correctly updated.

- `Content-length`

  The length (in bytes) of the returned content.

- `Content-type`

  Specifies the MIME type of the returned data. For most request, the returned MIME type is `text/plain`. All text is encoded in Unicode (UTF-8), and this is explicitly stated in the returned `Content-type`, as `text/plain;charset=utf-8`.

- `Etag`

  The `Etag` HTTP header field is used to show the revision for a document, or a view.

  ETags have been assigned to a map/reduce group (the collection of views in a single design document). Any change to any of the indexes for those views would generate a new ETag for all view URLs in a single design doc, even if that specific view's results had not changed.

Each _view URL has its own ETag which only gets updated when changes are made to the database that effect that index. If the index for that specific view does not change, that view keeps the original ETag head (therefore sending back 304 - Not Modified more often).

- Transfer-Encoding

If the response uses an encoding, then it is specified in this header field.

Transfer-Encoding: chunked means that the response is sent in parts, a method known as chunked transfer encoding. This is used when CouchDB does not know beforehand the size of the data it will send (for example, the *changes feed*).

10.1.3 JSON Basics

The majority of requests and responses to CouchDB use the JavaScript Object Notation (JSON) for formatting the content and structure of the data and responses.

JSON is used because it is the simplest and easiest solution for working with data within a web browser, as JSON structures can be evaluated and used as JavaScript objects within the web browser environment. JSON also integrates with the server-side JavaScript used within CouchDB.

JSON supports the same basic types as supported by JavaScript, these are:

- Array - a list of values enclosed in square brackets. For example:

```
["one", "two", "three"]
```

- Boolean - a true or false value. You can use these strings directly. For example:

```
{ "value": true}
```

- Number - an integer or floating-point number.

- Object - a set of key/value pairs (i.e. an associative array, or hash). The key must be a string, but the value can be any of the supported JSON values. For example:

```
{
    "servings" : 4,
    "subtitle" : "Easy to make in advance, and then cook when ready",
    "cooktime" : 60,
    "title" : "Chicken Coriander"
}
```

In CouchDB, the JSON object is used to represent a variety of structures, including the main CouchDB document.

- String - this should be enclosed by double-quotes and supports Unicode characters and backslash escaping. For example:

```
"A String"
```

Parsing JSON into a JavaScript object is supported through the JSON.parse() function in JavaScript, or through various libraries that will perform the parsing of the content into a JavaScript object for you. Libraries for parsing and generating JSON are available in many languages, including Perl, Python, Ruby, Erlang and others.

> **Warning:** Care should be taken to ensure that your JSON structures are valid, invalid structures will cause CouchDB to return an HTTP status code of 500 (server error).

Number Handling

Developers and users new to computer handling of numbers often encounter suprises when expecting that a number stored in JSON format does not necessarily return as the same number as compared character by character.

Any numbers defined in JSON that contain a decimal point or exponent will be passed through the Erlang VM's idea of the "double" data type. Any numbers that are used in views will pass through the view server's idea of a number (the common JavaScript case means even integers pass through a double due to JavaScript's definition of a number).

Consider this document that we write to CouchDB:

```
{
    "_id":"30b3b38cdbd9e3a587de9b8122000cff",
    "number": 1.1
}
```

Now let's read that document back from CouchDB:

```
{
    "_id":"30b3b38cdbd9e3a587de9b8122000cff",
    "_rev":"1-f065cee7c3fd93aa50f6c97acde93030",
    "number":1.1000000000000000888
}
```

What happens is CouchDB is changing the textual representation of the result of decoding what it was given into some numerical format. In most cases this is an IEEE 754 double precision floating point number which is exactly what almost all other languages use as well.

What Erlang does a bit differently than other languages is that it does not attempt to pretty print the resulting output to use the shortest number of characters. For instance, this is why we have this relationship:

```
ejson:encode(ejson:decode(<<"1.1">>)).
<<"1.1000000000000000888">>
```

What can be confusing here is that internally those two formats decode into the same IEEE-754 representation. And more importantly, it will decode into a fairly close representation when passed through all major parsers that we know about.

While we've only been discussing cases where the textual representation changes, another important case is when an input value contains more precision than can actually represented in a double. (You could argue that this case is actually "losing" data if you don't accept that numbers are stored in doubles).

Here's a log for a couple of the more common JSON libraries that happen to be on the author's machine:

Ejson (CouchDB's current parser) at CouchDB sha 168a663b:

```
$ ./utils/run -i
Erlang R14B04 (erts-5.8.5) [source] [64-bit] [smp:2:2] [rq:2]
[async-threads:4] [hipe] [kernel-poll:true]

Eshell V5.8.5  (abort with ^G)
1> ejson:encode(ejson:decode(<<"1.01234567890123456789012345678901234567890">>)).
<<"1.0123456789012346135">>
2> F = ejson:encode(ejson:decode(<<"1.01234567890123456789012345678901234567890">>)).
<<"1.0123456789012346135">>
3> ejson:encode(ejson:decode(F)).
<<"1.0123456789012346135">>
```

Node:

```
$ node -v
v0.6.15
$ node
JSON.stringify(JSON.parse("1.01234567890123456789012345678901234567890"))
'1.0123456789012346'
var f = JSON.stringify(JSON.parse("1.01234567890123456789012345678901234567890"))
undefined
JSON.stringify(JSON.parse(f))
'1.0123456789012346'
```

Python:

```
$ python
Python 2.7.2 (default, Jun 20 2012, 16:23:33)
[GCC 4.2.1 Compatible Apple Clang 4.0 (tags/Apple/clang-418.0.60)] on darwin
Type "help", "copyright", "credits" or "license" for more information.
import json
json.dumps(json.loads("1.0123456789012345678901234567890123456789"))
'1.0123456789012346'
f = json.dumps(json.loads("1.0123456789012345678901234567890123456789"))
json.dumps(json.loads(f))
'1.0123456789012346'
```

Ruby:

```
$ irb --version
irb 0.9.5(05/04/13)
require 'JSON'
=> true
JSON.dump(JSON.load("[1.0123456789012345678901234567890123456789]"))
=> "[1.01234567890123]"
f = JSON.dump(JSON.load("[1.0123456789012345678901234567890123456789]"))
=> "[1.01234567890123]"
JSON.dump(JSON.load(f))
=> "[1.01234567890123]"
```

Note: A small aside on Ruby, it requires a top level object or array, so I just wrapped the value. Should be obvious it doesn't affect the result of parsing the number though.

Spidermonkey:

```
$ js -h 2>&1 | head -n 1
JavaScript-C 1.8.5 2011-03-31
$ js
js> JSON.stringify(JSON.parse("1.0123456789012345678901234567890123456789"))
"1.0123456789012346"
js> var f = JSON.stringify(JSON.parse("1.0123456789012345678901234567890123456789")
js> JSON.stringify(JSON.parse(f))
"1.0123456789012346"
```

As you can see they all pretty much behave the same except for Ruby actually does appear to be losing some precision over the other libraries.

The astute observer will notice that ejson (the CouchDB JSON library) reported an extra three digits. While its tempting to think that this is due to some internal difference, its just a more specific case of the 1.1 input as described above.

The important point to realize here is that a double can only hold a finite number of values. What we're doing here is generating a string that when passed through the "standard" floating point parsing algorithms (ie, strtod) will result in the same bit pattern in memory as we started with. Or, slightly different, the bytes in a JSON serialized number are chosen such that they refer to a single specific value that a double can represent.

The important point to understand is that we're mapping from one infinite set onto a finite set. An easy way to see this is by reflecting on this:

```
1.0 == 1.00 == 1.000 = 1.(infinite zeroes)
```

Obviously a computer can't hold infinite bytes so we have to decimate our infinitely sized set to a finite set that can be represented concisely.

The game that other JSON libraries are playing is merely:

"How few characters do I have to use to select this specific value for a double"

And that game has lots and lots of subtle details that are difficult to duplicate in C without a significant amount of effort (it took Python over a year to get it sorted with their fancy build systems that automatically run on a number of different architectures).

Hopefully we've shown that CouchDB is not doing anything "funky" by changing input. Its behaving the same as any other common JSON library does, its just not pretty printing its output.

On the other hand, if you actually are in a position where an IEEE-754 double is not a satisfactory datatype for your numbers, then the answer as has been stated is to not pass your numbers through this representation. In JSON this is accomplished by encoding them as a string or by using integer types (although integer types can still bite you if you use a platform that has a different integer representation than normal, ie, JavaScript).

Further information can be found easily, including the Floating Point Guide, and David Goldberg's Reference.

Also, if anyone is really interested in changing this behavior, we're all ears for contributions to jiffy (which is theoretically going to replace ejson when we get around to updating the build system). The places we've looked for inspiration are TCL and Python. If you know a decent implementation of this float printing algorithm give us a holler.

10.1.4 HTTP Status Codes

With the interface to CouchDB working through HTTP, error codes and statuses are reported using a combination of the HTTP status code number, and corresponding data in the body of the response data.

A list of the error codes returned by CouchDB, and generic descriptions of the related errors are provided below. The meaning of different status codes for specific request types are provided in the corresponding API call reference.

- `200 - OK`

  Request completed successfully.

- `201 - Created`

  Document created successfully.

- `202 - Accepted`

  Request has been accepted, but the corresponding operation may not have completed. This is used for background operations, such as database compaction.

- `304 - Not Modified`

  The additional content requested has not been modified. This is used with the ETag system to identify the version of information returned.

- `400 - Bad Request`

  Bad request structure. The error can indicate an error with the request URL, path or headers. Differences in the supplied MD5 hash and content also trigger this error, as this may indicate message corruption.

- `401 - Unauthorized`

  The item requested was not available using the supplied authorization, or authorization was not supplied.

- `403 - Forbidden`

  The requested item or operation is forbidden.

- `404 - Not Found`

  The requested content could not be found. The content will include further information, as a JSON object, if available. The structure will contain two keys, `error` and `reason`. For example:

```
{"error":"not_found","reason":"no_db_file"}
```

- 405 - Resource Not Allowed

 A request was made using an invalid HTTP request type for the URL requested. For example, you have requested a PUT when a POST is required. Errors of this type can also triggered by invalid URL strings.

- 406 - Not Acceptable

 The requested content type is not supported by the server.

- 409 - Conflict

 Request resulted in an update conflict.

- 412 - Precondition Failed

 The request headers from the client and the capabilities of the server do not match.

- 415 - Bad Content Type

 The content types supported, and the content type of the information being requested or submitted indicate that the content type is not supported.

- 416 - Requested Range Not Satisfiable

 The range specified in the request header cannot be satisfied by the server.

- 417 - Expectation Failed

 When sending documents in bulk, the bulk load operation failed.

- 500 - Internal Server Error

 The request was invalid, either because the supplied JSON was invalid, or invalid information was supplied as part of the request.

10.2 Server

The CouchDB server interface provides the basic interface to a CouchDB server for obtaining CouchDB information and getting and setting configuration information.

10.2.1 /

GET /

 Accessing the root of a CouchDB instance returns meta information about the instance. The response is a JSON structure containing information about the server, including a welcome message and the version of the server.

 Request Headers

 - Accept –
 - *application/json*
 - *text/plain*

 Response Headers

 - Content-Type –
 - *application/json*
 - *text/plain; charset=utf-8*

 Status Codes

 - 200 OK – Request completed successfully

 Request:

```
GET / HTTP/1.1
Accept: application/json
Host: localhost:5984
```

Response:

```
HTTP/1.1 200 OK
Cache-Control: must-revalidate
Content-Length: 179
Content-Type: application/json
Date: Sat, 10 Aug 2013 06:33:33 GMT
Server: CouchDB (Erlang/OTP)

{
    "couchdb": "Welcome",
    "uuid": "85fb71bf700c17267fef77535820e371",
    "vendor": {
        "name": "The Apache Software Foundation",
        "version": "1.3.1"
    },
    "version": "1.3.1"
}
```

10.2.2 /_active_tasks

GET /_active_tasks

List of running tasks, including the task type, name, status and process ID. The result is a JSON array of the currently running tasks, with each task being described with a single object. Depending on operation type set of response object fields might be different.

Request Headers

- Accept –

  - *application/json*

  - *text/plain*

Response Headers

- Content-Type –

  - *application/json*

  - *text/plain; charset=utf-8*

Response JSON Object

- **changes_done** (*number*) – Processed changes

- **database** (*string*) – Source database

- **pid** (*string*) – Process ID

- **progress** (*number*) – Current percentage progress

- **started_on** (*number*) – Task start time as unix timestamp

- **status** (*string*) – Task status message

- **task** (*string*) – Task name

- **total_changes** (*number*) – Total changes to process

- **type** (*string*) – Operation Type

- **updated_on** (*number*) – Unix timestamp of last operation update

Status Codes

- 200 OK – Request completed successfully

- 401 Unauthorized – CouchDB Server Administrator privileges required

Request:

```
GET /_active_tasks HTTP/1.1
Accept: application/json
Host: localhost:5984
```

Response:

```
HTTP/1.1 200 OK
Cache-Control: must-revalidate
Content-Length: 1690
Content-Type: application/json
Date: Sat, 10 Aug 2013 06:37:31 GMT
Server: CouchDB (Erlang/OTP)

[
    {
        "changes_done": 64438,
        "database": "mailbox",
        "pid": "<0.12986.1>",
        "progress": 84,
        "started_on": 1376116576,
        "total_changes": 76215,
        "type": "database_compaction",
        "updated_on": 1376116619
    },
    {
        "changes_done": 14443,
        "database": "mailbox",
        "design_document": "c9753817b3ba7c674d92361f24f59b9f",
        "pid": "<0.10461.3>",
        "progress": 18,
        "started_on": 1376116621,
        "total_changes": 76215,
        "type": "indexer",
        "updated_on": 1376116650
    },
    {
        "changes_done": 5454,
        "database": "mailbox",
        "design_document": "_design/meta",
        "pid": "<0.6838.4>",
        "progress": 7,
        "started_on": 1376116632,
        "total_changes": 76215,
        "type": "indexer",
        "updated_on": 1376116651
    },
    {
        "checkpointed_source_seq": 68585,
        "continuous": false,
        "doc_id": null,
        "doc_write_failures": 0,
        "docs_read": 4524,
        "docs_written": 4524,
        "missing_revisions_found": 4524,
        "pid": "<0.1538.5>",
        "progress": 44,
        "replication_id": "9bc1727d74d49d9e157e260bb8bbd1d5",
        "revisions_checked": 4524,
        "source": "mailbox",
```

```
        "source_seq": 154419,
        "started_on": 1376116644,
        "target": "http://mailsrv:5984/mailbox",
        "type": "replication",
        "updated_on": 1376116651
    }
]
```

10.2.3 /_all_dbs

GET /_all_dbs
Returns a list of all the databases in the CouchDB instance.

Request Headers

- Accept –
  - *application/json*
  - *text/plain*

Response Headers

- Content-Type –
  - *application/json*
  - *text/plain; charset=utf-8*

Status Codes

- 200 OK – Request completed successfully

Request:

```
GET /_all_dbs HTTP/1.1
Accept: application/json
Host: localhost:5984
```

Response:

```
HTTP/1.1 200 OK
Cache-Control: must-revalidate
Content-Length: 52
Content-Type: application/json
Date: Sat, 10 Aug 2013 06:57:48 GMT
Server: CouchDB (Erlang/OTP)

[
   "_users",
   "contacts",
   "docs",
   "invoices",
   "locations"
]
```

10.2.4 /_db_updates

New in version 1.4.

GET /_db_updates
Returns a list of all database events in the CouchDB instance.

Request Headers

- Accept –
  - *application/json*
  - *text/plain*

Query Parameters

- **feed** (*string*) –
  - **longpoll**: Closes the connection after the first event.
  - **continuous**: Send a line of JSON per event. Keeps the socket open until `timeout`.
  - **eventsource**: Like, `continuous`, but sends the events in EventSource format.
- **timeout** (*number*) – Number of seconds until CouchDB closes the connection. Default is `60`.
- **heartbeat** (*boolean*) – Whether CouchDB will send a newline character (`\n`) on `timeout`. Default is `true`.

Response Headers

- Content-Type –
  - *application/json*
  - *text/plain; charset=utf-8*
- Transfer-Encoding – `chunked`

Response JSON Object

- **db_name** (*string*) – Database name
- **ok** (*boolean*) – Event operation status
- **type** (*string*) – A database event is one of `created`, `updated`, `deleted`

Status Codes

- 200 OK – Request completed successfully
- 401 Unauthorized – CouchDB Server Administrator privileges required

Request:

```
GET /_db_updates HTTP/1.1
Accept: application/json
Host: localhost:5984
```

Response:

```
HTTP/1.1 200 OK
Cache-Control: must-revalidate
Content-Type: application/json
Date: Sat, 10 Aug 2013 07:02:41 GMT
Server: CouchDB (Erlang/OTP)
Transfer-Encoding: chunked

{
    "db_name": "mailbox",
    "ok": true,
    "type": "created"
}
```

10.2.5 /_membership

New in version 2.0.

`GET /_membership`
Displays the nodes that are part of the cluster as `cluster_nodes`. The field `all_nodes` displays all nodes this node knows about, including the ones that are part of the cluster. The endpoint is useful when setting up a cluster, see *Node Management*

Request Headers

- Accept –

  - *application/json*

  - *text/plain*

Response Headers

- Content-Type –

  - *application/json*

  - *text/plain; charset=utf-8*

Status Codes

- 200 OK – Request completed successfully

Request:

```
GET /_membership HTTP/1.1
Accept: application/json
Host: localhost:5984
```

Response:

```
HTTP/1.1 200 OK
Cache-Control: must-revalidate
Content-Type: application/json
Date: Sat, 11 Jul 2015 07:02:41 GMT
Server: CouchDB (Erlang/OTP)
Content-Length: 142

{
    "all_nodes": [
        "node1@127.0.0.1",
        "node2@127.0.0.1",
        "node3@127.0.0.1"
    ],
    "cluster_nodes": [
        "node1@127.0.0.1",
        "node2@127.0.0.1",
        "node3@127.0.0.1"
    ]
}
```

10.2.6 /_log

`GET /_log`
Gets the CouchDB log, equivalent to accessing the local log file of the corresponding CouchDB instance.

Request Headers

- Accept –

  - *text/plain*

Query Parameters

- **bytes** (*number*) – Bytes to be returned. Default is `1000`.

- **offset** (*number*) – Offset in bytes where the log tail should be started. Default is 0.

Response Headers

- Content-Type – `text/plain; charset=utf-8`

- Transfer-Encoding – `chunked`

Status Codes

- 200 OK – Request completed successfully

- 401 Unauthorized – CouchDB Server Administrator privileges required

Request:

```
GET /_log HTTP/1.1
Accept: application/json
Host: localhost:5984
```

Response:

```
[Wed, 27 Oct 2010 10:49:42 GMT] [info] [<0.23338.2>] 192.168.0.2 - - 'PUT' /authdb 4(
[Wed, 27 Oct 2010 11:02:19 GMT] [info] [<0.23428.2>] 192.168.0.116 - - 'GET' /recipe:
[Wed, 27 Oct 2010 11:02:19 GMT] [info] [<0.23428.2>] 192.168.0.116 - - 'GET' /_sessic
[Wed, 27 Oct 2010 11:02:19 GMT] [info] [<0.24199.2>] 192.168.0.116 - - 'GET' / 200
[Wed, 27 Oct 2010 13:03:38 GMT] [info] [<0.24207.2>] 192.168.0.116 - - 'GET' /_log?o1
```

If you want to pick out specific parts of the log information you can use the `bytes` argument, which specifies the number of bytes to be returned, and `offset`, which specifies where the reading of the log should start, counted back from the end. For example, if you use the following request:

```
GET /_log?bytes=500&offset=2000
```

Reading of the log will start at 2000 bytes from the end of the log, and 500 bytes will be shown.

How bytes/offset works?

CouchDB reads specified amount of `bytes` from the end of log file, jumping to `offset` bytes towards the beginning of the file first:

```
Log File     FilePos
----------
|          |  10
|          |  20
|          |  30
|          |  40
|          |  50
|          |  60
|          |  70 -- Bytes = 20   --
|          |  80                 | Chunk
|          |  90 -- Offset = 10 --
|_____|  100
```

10.2.7 /_replicate

POST /_replicate

Request, configure, or stop, a replication operation.

Request Headers

- Accept –

  - *application/json*

  - *text/plain*

- Content-Type – *application/json*

Request JSON Object

- **cancel** (*boolean*) – Cancels the replication
- **continuous** (*boolean*) – Configure the replication to be continuous
- **create_target** (*boolean*) – Creates the target database. Required administrator's privileges on target server.
- **doc_ids** (*array*) – Array of document IDs to be synchronized
- **proxy** (*string*) – Address of a proxy server through which replication should occur (protocol can be "http" or "socks5")
- **source** (*string*) – Source database name or URL
- **target** (*string*) – Target database name or URL

Response Headers

- Content-Type –
  - *application/json*
  - *text/plain; charset=utf-8*

Response JSON Object

- **history** (*array*) – Replication history (see below)
- **ok** (*boolean*) – Replication status
- **replication_id_version** (*number*) – Replication protocol version
- **session_id** (*string*) – Unique session ID
- **source_last_seq** (*number*) – Last sequence number read from source database

Status Codes

- 200 OK – Replication request successfully completed
- 202 Accepted – Continuous replication request has been accepted
- 400 Bad Request – Invalid JSON data
- 401 Unauthorized – CouchDB Server Administrator privileges required
- 404 Not Found – Either the source or target DB is not found or attempt to cancel unknown replication task
- 500 Internal Server Error – JSON specification was invalid

The specification of the replication request is controlled through the JSON content of the request. The JSON should be an object with the fields defining the source, target and other options.

The *Replication history* is an array of objects with following structure:

JSON Object

- **doc_write_failures** (*number*) – Number of document write failures
- **docs_read** (*number*) – Number of documents read
- **docs_written** (*number*) – Number of documents written to target
- **end_last_seq** (*number*) – Last sequence number in changes stream
- **end_time** (*string*) – Date/Time replication operation completed in RFC 2822 format
- **missing_checked** (*number*) – Number of missing documents checked
- **missing_found** (*number*) – Number of missing documents found
- **recorded_seq** (*number*) – Last recorded sequence number

- **session_id** (*string*) – Session ID for this replication operation
- **start_last_seq** (*number*) – First sequence number in changes stream
- **start_time** (*string*) – Date/Time replication operation started in RFC 2822 format

Request

```
POST /_replicate HTTP/1.1
Accept: application/json
Content-Length: 36
Content-Type: application/json
Host: localhost:5984


{
    "source": "db_a",
    "target": "db_b"
}
```

Response

```
HTTP/1.1 200 OK
Cache-Control: must-revalidate
Content-Length: 692
Content-Type: application/json
Date: Sun, 11 Aug 2013 20:38:50 GMT
Server: CouchDB (Erlang/OTP)


{
    "history": [
        {
            "doc_write_failures": 0,
            "docs_read": 10,
            "docs_written": 10,
            "end_last_seq": 28,
            "end_time": "Sun, 11 Aug 2013 20:38:50 GMT",
            "missing_checked": 10,
            "missing_found": 10,
            "recorded_seq": 28,
            "session_id": "142a35854a08e205c47174d91b1f9628",
            "start_last_seq": 1,
            "start_time": "Sun, 11 Aug 2013 20:38:50 GMT"
        },
        {
            "doc_write_failures": 0,
            "docs_read": 1,
            "docs_written": 1,
            "end_last_seq": 1,
            "end_time": "Sat, 10 Aug 2013 15:41:54 GMT",
            "missing_checked": 1,
            "missing_found": 1,
            "recorded_seq": 1,
            "session_id": "6314f35c51de3ac408af79d6ee0c1a09",
            "start_last_seq": 0,
            "start_time": "Sat, 10 Aug 2013 15:41:54 GMT"
        }
    ],
    "ok": true,
    "replication_id_version": 3,
    "session_id": "142a35854a08e205c47174d91b1f9628",
    "source_last_seq": 28
}
```

Replication Operation

The aim of the replication is that at the end of the process, all active documents on the source database are also in the destination database and all documents that were deleted in the source databases are also deleted (if they exist) on the destination database.

Replication can be described as either push or pull replication:

- *Pull replication* is where the `source` is the remote CouchDB instance, and the `target` is the local database.

  Pull replication is the most useful solution to use if your source database has a permanent IP address, and your destination (local) database may have a dynamically assigned IP address (for example, through DHCP). This is particularly important if you are replicating to a mobile or other device from a central server.

- *Push replication* is where the `source` is a local database, and `target` is a remote database.

Specifying the Source and Target Database

You must use the URL specification of the CouchDB database if you want to perform replication in either of the following two situations:

- Replication with a remote database (i.e. another instance of CouchDB on the same host, or a different host)

- Replication with a database that requires authentication

For example, to request replication between a database local to the CouchDB instance to which you send the request, and a remote database you might use the following request:

```
POST http://couchdb:5984/_replicate
Content-Type: application/json
Accept: application/json

{
    "source" : "recipes",
    "target" : "http://coucdb-remote:5984/recipes",
}
```

In all cases, the requested databases in the `source` and `target` specification must exist. If they do not, an error will be returned within the JSON object:

```
{
    "error" : "db_not_found"
    "reason" : "could not open http://couchdb-remote:5984/ollka/",
}
```

You can create the target database (providing your user credentials allow it) by adding the `create_target` field to the request object:

```
POST http://couchdb:5984/_replicate
Content-Type: application/json
Accept: application/json

{
    "create_target" : true
    "source" : "recipes",
    "target" : "http://couchdb-remote:5984/recipes",
}
```

The `create_target` field is not destructive. If the database already exists, the replication proceeds as normal.

Single Replication

You can request replication of a database so that the two databases can be synchronized. By default, the replication process occurs one time and synchronizes the two databases together. For example, you can request a single synchronization between two databases by supplying the `source` and `target` fields within the request JSON content.

```
POST http://couchdb:5984/_replicate
Accept: application/json
Content-Type: application/json


{
    "source" : "recipes",
    "target" : "recipes-snapshot",
}
```

In the above example, the databases `recipes` and `recipes-snapshot` will be synchronized. These databases are local to the CouchDB instance where the request was made. The response will be a JSON structure containing the success (or failure) of the synchronization process, and statistics about the process:

```
{
    "ok" : true,
    "history" : [
        {
            "docs_read" : 1000,
            "session_id" : "52c2370f5027043d286daca4de247db0",
            "recorded_seq" : 1000,
            "end_last_seq" : 1000,
            "doc_write_failures" : 0,
            "start_time" : "Thu, 28 Oct 2010 10:24:13 GMT",
            "start_last_seq" : 0,
            "end_time" : "Thu, 28 Oct 2010 10:24:14 GMT",
            "missing_checked" : 0,
            "docs_written" : 1000,
            "missing_found" : 1000
        }
    ],
    "session_id" : "52c2370f5027043d286daca4de247db0",
    "source_last_seq" : 1000
}
```

Continuous Replication

Synchronization of a database with the previously noted methods happens only once, at the time the replicate request is made. To have the target database permanently replicated from the source, you must set the `continuous` field of the JSON object within the request to true.

With continuous replication changes in the source database are replicated to the target database in perpetuity until you specifically request that replication ceases.

```
POST http://couchdb:5984/_replicate
Accept: application/json
Content-Type: application/json


{
    "continuous" : true
    "source" : "recipes",
    "target" : "http://couchdb-remote:5984/recipes",
}
```

Changes will be replicated between the two databases as long as a network connection is available between the two instances.

Note: Two keep two databases synchronized with each other, you need to set replication in both directions; that is, you must replicate from `source` to `target`, and separately from `target` to `source`.

Canceling Continuous Replication

You can cancel continuous replication by adding the `cancel` field to the JSON request object and setting the value to true. Note that the structure of the request must be identical to the original for the cancellation request to be honoured. For example, if you requested continuous replication, the cancellation request must also contain the `continuous` field.

For example, the replication request:

```
POST http://couchdb:5984/_replicate
Content-Type: application/json
Accept: application/json

{
    "source" : "recipes",
    "target" : "http://couchdb-remote:5984/recipes",
    "create_target" : true,
    "continuous" : true
}
```

Must be canceled using the request:

```
POST http://couchdb:5984/_replicate
Accept: application/json
Content-Type: application/json

{
    "cancel" : true,
    "continuous" : true
    "create_target" : true,
    "source" : "recipes",
    "target" : "http://couchdb-remote:5984/recipes",
}
```

Requesting cancellation of a replication that does not exist results in a 404 error.

10.2.8 /_restart

POST /_restart
> Restarts the CouchDB instance. You must be authenticated as a user with administration privileges for this to work.
>
> > **Request Headers**
> >
> > > - Accept –
> > >
> > >   - *application/json*
> > >
> > >   - *text/plain*
> > >
> > > - Content-Type – *application/json*
> >
> > **Response Headers**
> >
> > > - Content-Type –
> > >
> > >   - *application/json*
> > >
> > >   - *text/plain; charset=utf-8*

Status Codes

- 202 Accepted – Server goes to restart (there is no guarantee that it will be alive after)
- 401 Unauthorized – **CouchDB Server Administrator privileges required**
- 415 Unsupported Media Type – **Bad request's** Content-Type

Request:

```
POST /_restart HTTP/1.1
Accept: application/json
Host: localhost:5984
```

Response:

```
HTTP/1.1 202 Accepted
Cache-Control: must-revalidate
Content-Length: 12
Content-Type: application/json
Date: Sat, 10 Aug 2013 11:33:50 GMT
Server: CouchDB (Erlang/OTP)


{
    "ok": true
}
```

10.2.9 /_stats

GET /_stats

The _stats resource returns a JSON object containing the statistics for the running server. The object is structured with top-level sections collating the statistics for a range of entries, with each individual statistic being easily identified, and the content of each statistic is self-describing

Request Headers

- Accept –
  - *application/json*
  - *text/plain*

Response Headers

- Content-Type –
  - *application/json*
  - *text/plain; charset=utf-8*

Status Codes

- 200 OK – Request completed successfully

Request:

```
GET /_stats/couchdb/request_time HTTP/1.1
Accept: application/json
Host: localhost:5984
```

Response:

```
HTTP/1.1 200 OK
Cache-Control: must-revalidate
Content-Length: 187
Content-Type: application/json
Date: Sat, 10 Aug 2013 11:41:11 GMT
Server: CouchDB (Erlang/OTP)
```

```
{
    "couchdb": {
        "request_time": {
            "current": 21.0,
            "description": "length of a request inside CouchDB without MochiWeb",
            "max": 19.0,
            "mean": 7.0,
            "min": 1.0,
            "stddev": 10.392,
            "sum": 21.0
        }
    }
}
```

The fields provide the current, minimum and maximum, and a collection of statistical means and quantities. The quantity in each case is not defined, but the descriptions below provide

The statistics are divided into the following top-level sections:

couchdb

Describes statistics specific to the internals of CouchDB

Statistic ID	Description	Unit
auth_cache_hits	Number of authentication cache hits	number
auth_cache_misses	Number of authentication cache misses	number
database_reads	Number of times a document was read from a database	number
database_writes	Number of times a database was changed	number
open_databases	Number of open databases	number
open_os_files	Number of file descriptors CouchDB has open	number
request_time	Length of a request inside CouchDB without MochiWeb	milliseconds

httpd_request_methods

Statistic ID	Description	Unit
COPY	Number of HTTP COPY requests	number
DELETE	Number of HTTP DELETE requests	number
GET	Number of HTTP GET requests	number
HEAD	Number of HTTP HEAD requests	number
POST	Number of HTTP POST requests	number
PUT	Number of HTTP PUT requests	number

`httpd_status_codes`

Statistic ID	Description	Unit
200	Number of HTTP 200 OK responses	number
201	Number of HTTP 201 Created responses	number
202	Number of HTTP 202 Accepted responses	number
301	Number of HTTP 301 Moved Permanently responses	number
304	Number of HTTP 304 Not Modified responses	number
400	Number of HTTP 400 Bad Request responses	number
401	Number of HTTP 401 Unauthorized responses	number
403	Number of HTTP 403 Forbidden responses	number
404	Number of HTTP 404 Not Found responses	number
405	Number of HTTP 405 Method Not Allowed responses	number
409	Number of HTTP 409 Conflict responses	number
412	Number of HTTP 412 Precondition Failed responses	number
500	Number of HTTP 500 Internal Server Error responses	number

`httpd`

Statistic ID	Description	Unit
`bulk_requests`	Number of bulk requests	number
`clients_requesting_changes`	Number of clients for continuous _changes	number
`requests`	Number of HTTP requests	number
`temporary_view_reads`	Number of temporary view reads	number
`view_reads`	Number of view reads	number

You can also access individual statistics by quoting the statistics sections and statistic ID as part of the URL path. For example, to get the `request_time` statistics, you can use:

```
GET /_stats/couchdb/request_time
```

This returns an entire statistics object, as with the full request, but containing only the request individual statistic. Hence, the returned structure is as follows:

```
{
    "couchdb" : {
        "request_time" : {
            "stddev" : 7454.305,
            "min" : 1,
            "max" : 34185,
            "current" : 34697.803,
            "mean" : 1652.276,
            "sum" : 34697.803,
            "description" : "length of a request inside CouchDB without MochiWeb"
        }
    }
}
```

10.2.10 /_utils

GET /_utils

Accesses the built-in Futon administration interface for CouchDB.

Response Headers

- Location – New URI location

Status Codes

- 301 Moved Permanently – Redirects to `GET /_utils/`

`GET /_utils/`

Response Headers

- Content-Type – `text/html`

- Last-Modified – Static files modification timestamp

Status Codes

- 200 OK – Request completed successfully

10.2.11 /_uuids

Changed in version 1.5.1.

`GET /_uuids`

Requests one or more Universally Unique Identifiers (UUIDs) from the CouchDB instance. The response is a JSON object providing a list of UUIDs.

Request Headers

- Accept –

  - `application/json`

  - `text/plain`

Query Parameters

- **count** (*number*) – Number of UUIDs to return. Default is 1.

Response Headers

- Content-Type –

  - `application/json`

  - `text/plain; charset=utf-8`

- ETag – Response hash

Status Codes

- 200 OK – Request completed successfully

- 403 Forbidden – Requested more UUIDs than is `allowed` to retrieve

Request:

```
GET /_uuids?count=10 HTTP/1.1
Accept: application/json
Host: localhost:5984
```

Response:

```
HTTP/1.1 200 OK
Content-Length: 362
Content-Type: application/json
Date: Sat, 10 Aug 2013 11:46:25 GMT
ETag: "DGRWWQFLUDWN5MRKSLKQ425XV"
Expires: Fri, 01 Jan 1990 00:00:00 GMT
Pragma: no-cache
Server: CouchDB (Erlang/OTP)

{
    "uuids": [
        "75480ca477454894678e22eec6002413",
        "75480ca477454894678e22eec600250b",
        "75480ca477454894678e22eec6002c41",
```

```
            "75480ca477454894678e22eec6003b90",
            "75480ca477454894678e22eec6003fca",
            "75480ca477454894678e22eec6004bef",
            "75480ca477454894678e22eec600528f",
            "75480ca477454894678e22eec6005e0b",
            "75480ca477454894678e22eec6006158",
            "75480ca477454894678e22eec6006161"
        ]
    }
```

The UUID type is determined by the *UUID algorithm* setting in the CouchDB configuration.

The UUID type may be changed at any time through the *Configuration API*. For example, the UUID type could be changed to random by sending this HTTP request:

```
PUT http://couchdb:5984/_config/uuids/algorithm
Content-Type: application/json
Accept: */*

"random"
```

You can verify the change by obtaining a list of UUIDs:

```
{
    "uuids" : [
        "031aad7b469956cf2826fcb2a9260492",
        "6ec875e15e6b385120938df18ee8e496",
        "cff9e881516483911aa2f0e98949092d",
        "b89d37509d39dd712546f9510d4a9271",
        "2e0dbf7f6c4ad716f21938a016e4e59f"
    ]
}
```

10.2.12 /favicon.ico

GET /favicon.ico
   Binary content for the *favicon.ico* site icon.

   Response Headers

   • Content-Type – *image/x-icon*

   Status Codes

   • 200 OK – Request completed successfully

   • 404 Not Found – The requested content could not be found

10.2.13 Authentication

Interfaces for obtaining session and authorization data.

Note: We also strongly recommend you *set up SSL* to improve all authentication methods' security.

Basic Authentication

Basic authentication (**RFC 2617**) is a quick and simple way to authenticate with CouchDB. The main drawback is the need to send user credentials with each request which may be insecure and could hurt operation performance (since CouchDB must compute the password hash with every request):

Request:

```
GET / HTTP/1.1
Accept: application/json
Authorization: Basic cm9vdDpyZWxheheA==
Host: localhost:5984
```

Response:

```
HTTP/1.1 200 OK
Cache-Control: must-revalidate
Content-Length: 177
Content-Type: application/json
Date: Mon, 03 Dec 2012 00:44:47 GMT
Server: CouchDB (Erlang/OTP)

{
    "couchdb":"Welcome",
    "uuid":"0a959b9b8227188afc2ac26ccdf345a6",
    "version":"1.3.0",
    "vendor": {
        "version":"1.3.0",
        "name":"The Apache Software Foundation"
    }
}
```

Cookie Authentication

For cookie authentication (RFC 2109) CouchDB generates a token that the client can use for the next few requests to CouchDB. Tokens are valid until a timeout. When CouchDB sees a valid token in a subsequent request, it will authenticate the user by this token without requesting the password again. By default, cookies are valid for 10 minutes, but it's *adjustable*. Also it's possible to make cookies *persistent*.

To obtain the first token and thus authenticate a user for the first time, the *username* and *password* must be sent to the *_session API*.

/_session

POST /_session
  Initiates new session for specified user credentials by providing *Cookie* value.

  Request Headers

  - Content-Type –
    - *application/x-www-form-urlencoded*
    - *application/json*

  Query Parameters

  - **next** (*string*) – Enforces redirect after successful login to the specified location. This location is relative from server root. *Optional*.

  Form Parameters

  - **name** – User name
  - **password** – Password

  Response Headers

  - Set-Cookie – Authorization token

  Response JSON Object

  - **ok** (*boolean*) – Operation status

- **name** (*string*) – Username

- **roles** (*array*) – List of user roles

Status Codes

- 200 OK – Successfully authenticated

- 302 Found – Redirect after successful authentication

- 401 Unauthorized – Username or password wasn't recognized

Request:

```
POST /_session HTTP/1.1
Accept: application/json
Content-Length: 24
Content-Type: application/x-www-form-urlencoded
Host: localhost:5984

name=root&password=relax
```

It's also possible to send data as JSON:

```
POST /_session HTTP/1.1
Accept: application/json
Content-Length: 37
Content-Type: application/json
Host: localhost:5984

{
    "name": "root",
    "password": "relax"
}
```

Response:

```
HTTP/1.1 200 OK
Cache-Control: must-revalidate
Content-Length: 43
Content-Type: application/json
Date: Mon, 03 Dec 2012 01:23:14 GMT
Server: CouchDB (Erlang/OTP)
Set-Cookie: AuthSession=cm9vdDo1MEJCRkYwMjq0LO0ylOIwShrgt8y-UkhI-c6BGw; Version=1; Pa

{"ok":true,"name":"root","roles":["_admin"]}
```

If next query parameter was provided the response will trigger redirection to the specified location in case of successful authentication:

Request:

```
POST /_session?next=/blog/_design/sofa/_rewrite/recent-posts HTTP/1.1
Accept: application/json
Content-Type: application/x-www-form-urlencoded
Host: localhost:5984

name=root&password=relax
```

Response:

```
HTTP/1.1 302 Moved Temporarily
Cache-Control: must-revalidate
Content-Length: 43
Content-Type: application/json
Date: Mon, 03 Dec 2012 01:32:46 GMT
Location: http://localhost:5984/blog/_design/sofa/_rewrite/recent-posts
```

```
Server: CouchDB (Erlang/OTP)
Set-Cookie: AuthSession=cm9vdDo1MEJDMDEzRTp7Vu5GKCkTxTVxwXbpXsBARQWnhQ; Version=1; Pa

{"ok":true,"name":null,"roles":["_admin"]}
```

GET /_session

Returns complete information about authenticated user. This information contains *User Context Object*, authentication method and available ones and authentication database.

Query Parameters

- **basic** (*boolean*) – Accept *Basic Auth* by requesting this resource. *Optional*.

Status Codes

- 200 OK – Successfully authenticated.

- 401 Unauthorized – Username or password wasn't recognized.

Request:

```
GET /_session HTTP/1.1
Host: localhost:5984
Accept: application/json
Cookie: AuthSession=cm9vdDo1MEJDMDQxRDpqb-Ta9QfP9hpdPjHLxNTKg_Hf9w
```

Response:

```
HTTP/1.1 200 OK
Cache-Control: must-revalidate
Content-Length: 175
Content-Type: application/json
Date: Fri, 09 Aug 2013 20:27:45 GMT
Server: CouchDB (Erlang/OTP)
Set-Cookie: AuthSession=cm9vdDo1MjA1NTBDMTqmX2qKt1KDR--GUC80DQ6-Ew_XIw; Version=1; Pa

{
    "info": {
        "authenticated": "cookie",
        "authentication_db": "_users",
        "authentication_handlers": [
            "oauth",
            "cookie",
            "default"
        ]
    },
    "ok": true,
    "userCtx": {
        "name": "root",
        "roles": [
            "_admin"
        ]
    }
}
```

DELETE /_session

Closes user's session.

Status Codes

- 200 OK – Successfully close session.

- 401 Unauthorized – User wasn't authenticated.

Request:

```
DELETE /_session HTTP/1.1
Accept: application/json
Cookie: AuthSession=cm9vdDo1MjA1NEVGMDo1QXNQkqC_0Qmgrk8Fw61_AzDeXw
Host: localhost:5984
```

Response:

```
HTTP/1.1 200 OK
Cache-Control: must-revalidate
Content-Length: 12
Content-Type: application/json
Date: Fri, 09 Aug 2013 20:30:12 GMT
Server: CouchDB (Erlang/OTP)
Set-Cookie: AuthSession=; Version=1; Path=/; HttpOnly

{
    "ok": true
}
```

Proxy Authentication

Note: To use this authentication method make sure that the `{couch_httpd_auth, proxy_authentication_handler}` value in added to the list of the active *httpd/authentication_handlers*:

```
[httpd]
authentication_handlers = {couch_httpd_oauth, oauth_authentication_handler}, {couch_httpd
```

Proxy authentication is very useful in case your application already uses some external authentication service and you don't want to duplicate users and their roles in CouchDB.

This authentication method allows creation of a *User Context Object* for remotely authenticated user. By default, the client just need to pass specific headers to CouchDB with related request:

- *X-Auth-CouchDB-UserName*: username;

- *X-Auth-CouchDB-Roles*: list of user roles separated by a comma (,);

- *X-Auth-CouchDB-Token*: authentication token. Optional, but strongly recommended to *force token be required* to prevent requests from untrusted sources.

Request:

```
GET /_session HTTP/1.1
Host: localhost:5984
Accept: application/json
Content-Type: application/json; charset=utf-8
X-Auth-CouchDB-Roles: users,blogger
X-Auth-CouchDB-UserName: foo
```

Response:

```
HTTP/1.1 200 OK
Cache-Control: must-revalidate
Content-Length: 190
Content-Type: application/json
Date: Fri, 14 Jun 2013 10:16:03 GMT
Server: CouchDB (Erlang/OTP)

{
    "info": {
        "authenticated": "proxy",
        "authentication_db": "_users",
```

```
        "authentication_handlers": [
            "oauth",
            "cookie",
            "proxy",
            "default"
        ]
    },
    "ok": true,
    "userCtx": {
        "name": "foo",
        "roles": [
            "users",
            "blogger"
        ]
    }
}
```

Note that you don't need to request *session* to be authenticated by this method if all required HTTP headers are provided.

OAuth Authentication

CouchDB supports OAuth 1.0 authentication (RFC 5849). OAuth provides a method for clients to access server resources without sharing real credentials (username and password).

First, *configure oauth*, by setting consumer and token with their secrets and binding token to real CouchDB username.

Probably, it's not good idea to work with plain curl, let use some scripting language like Python:

```python
#!/usr/bin/env python2
from oauth import oauth # pip install oauth
import httplib

URL = 'http://localhost:5984/_session'
CONSUMER_KEY = 'consumer1'
CONSUMER_SECRET = 'sekr1t'
TOKEN = 'token1'
SECRET = 'tokensekr1t'

consumer = oauth.OAuthConsumer(CONSUMER_KEY, CONSUMER_SECRET)
token = oauth.OAuthToken(TOKEN, SECRET)
req = oauth.OAuthRequest.from_consumer_and_token(
    consumer,
    token=token,
    http_method='GET',
    http_url=URL,
    parameters={}
)
req.sign_request(oauth.OAuthSignatureMethod_HMAC_SHA1(), consumer,token)

headers = req.to_header()
headers['Accept'] = 'application/json'

con = httplib.HTTPConnection('localhost', 5984)
con.request('GET', URL, headers=headers)
resp = con.getresponse()
print resp.read()
```

or Ruby:

```ruby
#!/usr/bin/env ruby
```

```
require 'oauth' # gem install oauth

URL = 'http://localhost:5984'
CONSUMER_KEY = 'consumer1'
CONSUMER_SECRET = 'sekr1t'
TOKEN = 'token1'
SECRET = 'tokensekr1t'

@consumer = OAuth::Consumer.new CONSUMER_KEY,
                                CONSUMER_SECRET,
                                {:site => URL}

@access_token = OAuth::AccessToken.new(@consumer, TOKEN, SECRET)

puts @access_token.get('/_session').body
```

Both snippets produces similar request and response pair:

```
GET /_session HTTP/1.1
Host: localhost:5984
Accept: application/json
Authorization: OAuth realm="", oauth_nonce="81430018", oauth_timestamp="1374561749", oaut
```

```
HTTP/1.1 200 OK
Cache-Control : must-revalidate
Content-Length : 167
Content-Type : application/json
Date : Tue, 23 Jul 2013 06:51:15 GMT
Server: CouchDB (Erlang/OTP)

{
    "ok": true,
    "info": {
        "authenticated": "oauth",
        "authentication_db": "_users",
        "authentication_handlers": ["oauth", "cookie", "default"]
    },
    "userCtx": {
        "name": "couchdb_username",
        "roles": []
    }
}
```

There we request the _session_ resource to ensure that authentication was successful and the target CouchDB username is correct. Change the target URL to request required resource.

10.2.14 Configuration

The CouchDB Server Configuration API provide an interface to query and update the various configuration values within a running CouchDB instance.

`/_config`

GET /_config
    Returns the entire CouchDB server configuration as a JSON structure. The structure is organized by different configuration sections, with individual values.

    Request Headers

    - Accept –

        – application/json

– *text/plain*

Response Headers

- Content-Type –

  – *application/json*

  – *text/plain; charset=utf-8*

Status Codes

- 200 OK – Request completed successfully

- 401 Unauthorized – CouchDB Server Administrator privileges required

Request

```
GET /_config HTTP/1.1
Accept: application/json
Host: localhost:5984
```

Response:

```
HTTP/1.1 200 OK
Cache-Control: must-revalidate
Content-Length: 4148
Content-Type: application/json
Date: Sat, 10 Aug 2013 12:01:42 GMT
Server: CouchDB (Erlang/OTP)

{
    "attachments": {
        "compressible_types": "text/*, application/javascript, application/json,  app
        "compression_level": "8"
    },
    "couch_httpd_auth": {
        "auth_cache_size": "50",
        "authentication_db": "_users",
        "authentication_redirect": "/_utils/session.html",
        "require_valid_user": "false",
        "timeout": "600"
    },
    "couchdb": {
        "database_dir": "/var/lib/couchdb",
        "delayed_commits": "true",
        "max_attachment_chunk_size": "4294967296",
        "max_dbs_open": "100",
        "max_document_size": "4294967296",
        "os_process_timeout": "5000",
        "uri_file": "/var/lib/couchdb/couch.uri",
        "util_driver_dir": "/usr/lib64/couchdb/erlang/lib/couch-1.5.0/priv/lib",
        "view_index_dir": "/var/lib/couchdb"
    },
    "daemons": {
        "auth_cache": "{couch_auth_cache, start_link, []}",
        "db_update_notifier": "{couch_db_update_notifier_sup, start_link, []}",
        "external_manager": "{couch_external_manager, start_link, []}",
        "httpd": "{couch_httpd, start_link, []}",
        "query_servers": "{couch_query_servers, start_link, []}",
        "stats_aggregator": "{couch_stats_aggregator, start, []}",
        "stats_collector": "{couch_stats_collector, start, []}",
        "uuids": "{couch_uuids, start, []}",
        "view_manager": "{couch_view, start_link, []}"
    },
    "httpd": {
        "allow_jsonp": "false",
```

```
        "authentication_handlers": "{couch_httpd_oauth, oauth_authentication_handler}
        "bind_address": "192.168.0.2",
        "default_handler": "{couch_httpd_db, handle_request}",
        "max_connections": "2048",
        "port": "5984",
        "secure_rewrites": "true",
        "vhost_global_handlers": "_utils, _uuids, _session, _oauth, _users"
    },
    "httpd_db_handlers": {
        "_changes": "{couch_httpd_db, handle_changes_req}",
        "_compact": "{couch_httpd_db, handle_compact_req}",
        "_design": "{couch_httpd_db, handle_design_req}",
        "_temp_view": "{couch_httpd_view, handle_temp_view_req}",
        "_view_cleanup": "{couch_httpd_db, handle_view_cleanup_req}"
    },
    "httpd_design_handlers": {
        "_info": "{couch_httpd_db,   handle_design_info_req}",
        "_list": "{couch_httpd_show, handle_view_list_req}",
        "_rewrite": "{couch_httpd_rewrite, handle_rewrite_req}",
        "_show": "{couch_httpd_show, handle_doc_show_req}",
        "_update": "{couch_httpd_show, handle_doc_update_req}",
        "_view": "{couch_httpd_view, handle_view_req}"
    },
    "httpd_global_handlers": {
        "/": "{couch_httpd_misc_handlers, handle_welcome_req, <<\"Welcome\">>}",
        "_active_tasks": "{couch_httpd_misc_handlers, handle_task_status_req}",
        "_all_dbs": "{couch_httpd_misc_handlers, handle_all_dbs_req}",
        "_config": "{couch_httpd_misc_handlers, handle_config_req}",
        "_log": "{couch_httpd_misc_handlers, handle_log_req}",
        "_oauth": "{couch_httpd_oauth, handle_oauth_req}",
        "_replicate": "{couch_httpd_misc_handlers, handle_replicate_req}",
        "_restart": "{couch_httpd_misc_handlers, handle_restart_req}",
        "_session": "{couch_httpd_auth, handle_session_req}",
        "_stats": "{couch_httpd_stats_handlers, handle_stats_req}",
        "_utils": "{couch_httpd_misc_handlers, handle_utils_dir_req, \"/usr/share/cou
        "_uuids": "{couch_httpd_misc_handlers, handle_uuids_req}",
        "favicon.ico": "{couch_httpd_misc_handlers, handle_favicon_req, \"/usr/share/
    },
    "log": {
        "file": "/var/log/couchdb/couch.log",
        "include_sasl": "true",
        "level": "info"
    },
    "query_server_config": {
        "reduce_limit": "true"
    },
    "query_servers": {
        "javascript": "/usr/bin/couchjs /usr/share/couchdb/server/main.js"
    },
    "replicator": {
        "max_http_pipeline_size": "10",
        "max_http_sessions": "10"
    },
    "stats": {
        "rate": "1000",
        "samples": "[0, 60, 300, 900]"
    },
    "uuids": {
        "algorithm": "utc_random"
    }
}
```

`/_config/section`

GET /_config/{section}

Gets the configuration structure for a single section.

> **Parameters**
>
> > • **section** – Configuration section name
>
> **Request Headers**
>
> > • Accept –
> >
> > > – *application/json*
> > >
> > > – *text/plain*
>
> **Response Headers**
>
> > • Content-Type –
> >
> > > – *application/json*
> > >
> > > – *text/plain; charset=utf-8*
>
> **Status Codes**
>
> > • 200 OK – Request completed successfully
> >
> > • 401 Unauthorized – CouchDB Server Administrator privileges required

Request:

```
GET /_config/httpd HTTP/1.1
Accept: application/json
Host: localhost:5984
```

Response:

```
HTTP/1.1 200 OK
Cache-Control: must-revalidate
Content-Length: 444
Content-Type: application/json
Date: Sat, 10 Aug 2013 12:10:40 GMT
Server: CouchDB (Erlang/OTP)

{
    "allow_jsonp": "false",
    "authentication_handlers": "{couch_httpd_oauth, oauth_authentication_handler}, {c
    "bind_address": "127.0.0.1",
    "default_handler": "{couch_httpd_db, handle_request}",
    "enable_cors": "false",
    "log_max_chunk_size": "1000000",
    "port": "5984",
    "secure_rewrites": "true",
    "vhost_global_handlers": "_utils, _uuids, _session, _oauth, _users"
}
```

`/_config/section/key`

GET /_config/{section}/{key}

Gets a single configuration value from within a specific configuration section.

> **Parameters**
>
> > • **section** – Configuration section name
> >
> > • **key** – Configuration option name

Request Headers

- Accept –

    - *application/json*

    - *text/plain*

Response Headers

- Content-Type –

    - *application/json*

    - *text/plain; charset=utf-8*

Status Codes

- 200 OK – Request completed successfully

- 401 Unauthorized – CouchDB Server Administrator privileges required

Request:

```
GET /_config/log/level HTTP/1.1
Accept: application/json
Host: localhost:5984
```

Response:

```
HTTP/1.1 200 OK
Cache-Control: must-revalidate
Content-Length: 8
Content-Type: application/json
Date: Sat, 10 Aug 2013 12:12:59 GMT
Server: CouchDB (Erlang/OTP)

"debug"
```

Note: The returned value will be the JSON of the value, which may be a string or numeric value, or an array or object. Some client environments may not parse simple strings or numeric values as valid JSON.

PUT /_config/{section}/{key}
Updates a configuration value. The new value should be supplied in the request body in the corresponding JSON format. If you are setting a string value, you must supply a valid JSON string. In response CouchDB sends old value for target section key.

Parameters

- **section** – Configuration section name

- **key** – Configuration option name

Request Headers

- Accept –

    - *application/json*

    - *text/plain*

- Content-Type – *application/json*

Response Headers

- Content-Type –

    - *application/json*

    - *text/plain; charset=utf-8*

Status Codes

- 200 OK – Request completed successfully
- 400 Bad Request – Invalid JSON request body
- 401 Unauthorized – CouchDB Server Administrator privileges required
- 500 Internal Server Error – Error setting configuration

Request:

```
PUT /_config/log/level HTTP/1.1
Accept: application/json
Content-Length: 7
Content-Type: application/json
Host: localhost:5984

"info"
```

Response:

```
HTTP/1.1 200 OK
Cache-Control: must-revalidate
Content-Length: 8
Content-Type: application/json
Date: Sat, 10 Aug 2013 12:12:59 GMT
Server: CouchDB (Erlang/OTP)

"debug"
```

DELETE /_config/{section}/{key}

Deletes a configuration value. The returned JSON will be the value of the configuration parameter before it was deleted.

Parameters

- **section** – Configuration section name
- **key** – Configuration option name

Request Headers

- Accept –
  - *application/json*
  - *text/plain*

Response Headers

- Content-Type –
  - *application/json*
  - *text/plain; charset=utf-8*

Status Codes

- 200 OK – Request completed successfully
- 401 Unauthorized – CouchDB Server Administrator privileges required
- 404 Not Found – Specified configuration option not found

Request:

```
DELETE /_config/log/level HTTP/1.1
Accept: application/json
Host: localhost:5984
```

Response:

```
HTTP/1.1 200 OK
Cache-Control: must-revalidate
Content-Length: 7
Content-Type: application/json
Date: Sat, 10 Aug 2013 12:29:03 GMT
Server: CouchDB (Erlang/OTP)

"info"
```

10.3 Databases

The Database endpoint provides an interface to an entire database with in CouchDB. These are database-level, rather than document-level requests.

For all these requests, the database name within the URL path should be the database name that you wish to perform the operation on. For example, to obtain the meta information for the database `recipes`, you would use the HTTP request:

```
GET /recipes
```

For clarity, the form below is used in the URL paths:

```
GET /db
```

Where db is the name of any database.

10.3.1 /db

HEAD /{db}

Returns the HTTP Headers containing a minimal amount of information about the specified database. Since the response body is empty, using the HEAD method is a lightweight way to check if the database exists already or not.

Parameters

- **db** – Database name

Status Codes

- 200 OK – Database exists

- 404 Not Found – Requested database not found

Request:

```
HEAD /test HTTP/1.1
Host: localhost:5984
```

Response:

```
HTTP/1.1 200 OK
Cache-Control: must-revalidate
Content-Type: application/json
Date: Mon, 12 Aug 2013 01:27:41 GMT
Server: CouchDB (Erlang/OTP)
```

GET /{db}

Gets information about the specified database.

Parameters

- **db** – Database name

Request Headers

- Accept –

  - *application/json*

  - *text/plain*

Response Headers

- Content-Type –

  - *application/json*

  - *text/plain; charset=utf-8*

Response JSON Object

- **committed_update_seq** (*number*) – The number of committed update.

- **compact_running** (*boolean*) – Set to `true` if the database compaction routine is operating on this database.

- **db_name** (*string*) – The name of the database.

- **disk_format_version** (*number*) – The version of the physical format used for the data when it is stored on disk.

- **data_size** (*number*) – The number of bytes of live data inside the database file.

- **disk_size** (*number*) – The length of the database file on disk. Views indexes are not included in the calculation.

- **doc_count** (*number*) – A count of the documents in the specified database.

- **doc_del_count** (*number*) – Number of deleted documents

- **instance_start_time** (*string*) – Timestamp of when the database was opened, expressed in microseconds since the epoch.

- **purge_seq** (*number*) – The number of purge operations on the database.

- **update_seq** (*number*) – The current number of updates to the database.

Status Codes

- 200 OK – Request completed successfully

- 404 Not Found – Requested database not found

Request:

```
GET /receipts HTTP/1.1
Accept: application/json
Host: localhost:5984
```

Response:

```
HTTP/1.1 200 OK
Cache-Control: must-revalidate
Content-Length: 258
Content-Type: application/json
Date: Mon, 12 Aug 2013 01:38:57 GMT
Server: CouchDB (Erlang/OTP)

{
    "committed_update_seq": 292786,
    "compact_running": false,
    "data_size": 65031503,
    "db_name": "receipts",
    "disk_format_version": 6,
    "disk_size": 137433211,
```

```
        "doc_count": 6146,
        "doc_del_count": 64637,
        "instance_start_time": "1376269325408900",
        "purge_seq": 0,
        "update_seq": 292786
}
```

PUT /{db}

Creates a new database. The database name {db} must be composed by following next rules:

•Name must begin with a lowercase letter (a-z)

•Lowercase characters (a-z)

•Digits (0-9)

•Any of the characters _, $, (,), +, -, and /.

If you're familiar with Regular Expressions, the rules above could be written as ^[a-z][a-z0-9_$()+/-]*$.

Parameters

   • **db** – Database name

Request Headers

   • Accept –

      – application/json

      – text/plain

Response Headers

   • Content-Type –

      – application/json

      – text/plain; charset=utf-8

   • Location – Database URI location

Response JSON Object

   • **ok** (*boolean*) – Operation status. Available in case of success

   • **error** (*string*) – Error type. Available if response code is 4xx

   • **reason** (*string*) – Error description. Available if response code is 4xx

Status Codes

   • 201 Created – Database created successfully

   • 400 Bad Request – Invalid database name

   • 401 Unauthorized – CouchDB Server Administrator privileges required

   • 412 Precondition Failed – Database already exists

Request:

```
PUT /db HTTP/1.1
Accept: application/json
Host: localhost:5984
```

Response:

```
HTTP/1.1 201 Created
Cache-Control: must-revalidate
Content-Length: 12
Content-Type: application/json
```

```
Date: Mon, 12 Aug 2013 08:01:45 GMT
Location: http://localhost:5984/db
Server: CouchDB (Erlang/OTP)

{
    "ok": true
}
```

If we repeat the same request to CouchDB, it will response with `412` since the database already exists:

Request:

```
PUT /db HTTP/1.1
Accept: application/json
Host: localhost:5984
```

Response:

```
HTTP/1.1 412 Precondition Failed
Cache-Control: must-revalidate
Content-Length: 95
Content-Type: application/json
Date: Mon, 12 Aug 2013 08:01:16 GMT
Server: CouchDB (Erlang/OTP)

{
    "error": "file_exists",
    "reason": "The database could not be created, the file already exists."
}
```

If an invalid database name is supplied, CouchDB returns response with `400`:

Request:

```
PUT /_db HTTP/1.1
Accept: application/json
Host: localhost:5984
```

Request:

```
HTTP/1.1 400 Bad Request
Cache-Control: must-revalidate
Content-Length: 194
Content-Type: application/json
Date: Mon, 12 Aug 2013 08:02:10 GMT
Server: CouchDB (Erlang/OTP)

{
    "error": "illegal_database_name",
    "reason": "Name: '_db'. Only lowercase characters (a-z), digits (0-9), and any o1
}
```

DELETE /{db}

Deletes the specified database, and all the documents and attachments contained within it.

Note: To avoid deleting a database, CouchDB will respond with the HTTP status code 400 when the request URL includes a ?rev= parameter. This suggests that one wants to delete a document but forgot to add the document id to the URL.

> **Parameters**
>
> > • **db** – Database name
>
> **Request Headers**

- Accept –
  - *application/json*
  - *text/plain*

Response Headers

- Content-Type –
  - *application/json*
  - *text/plain; charset=utf-8*

Response JSON Object

- **ok** (*boolean*) – Operation status

Status Codes

- 200 OK – Database removed successfully
- 400 Bad Request – Invalid database name or forgotten document id by accident
- 401 Unauthorized – CouchDB Server Administrator privileges required
- 404 Not Found – Database doesn't exist

Request:

```
DELETE /db HTTP/1.1
Accept: application/json
Host: localhost:5984
```

Response:

```
HTTP/1.1 200 OK
Cache-Control: must-revalidate
Content-Length: 12
Content-Type: application/json
Date: Mon, 12 Aug 2013 08:54:00 GMT
Server: CouchDB (Erlang/OTP)

{
    "ok": true
}
```

POST /{db}

Creates a new document in the specified database, using the supplied JSON document structure.

If the JSON structure includes the _id field, then the document will be created with the specified document ID.

If the _id field is not specified, a new unique ID will be generated, following whatever UUID algorithm is configured for that server.

Parameters

- **db** – Database name

Request Headers

- Accept –
  - *application/json*
  - *text/plain*
- Content-Type – *application/json*
- **X-Couch-Full-Commit** – Overrides server's *commit policy*. Possible values are: false and true. *Optional*.

Query Parameters

- **batch** (*string*) – Stores document in *batch mode* Possible values: ok. *Optional*

Response Headers

- Content-Type –
    - *application/json*
    - *text/plain; charset=utf-8*
- ETag – Quoted new document's revision
- Location – Document's URI

Response JSON Object

- **id** (*string*) – Document ID
- **ok** (*boolean*) – Operation status
- **rev** (*string*) – Revision info

Status Codes

- 201 Created – Document created and stored on disk
- 202 Accepted – Document data accepted, but not yet stored on disk
- 400 Bad Request – Invalid database name
- 401 Unauthorized – Write privileges required
- 404 Not Found – Database doesn't exist
- 409 Conflict – A Conflicting Document with same ID already exists

Request:

```
POST /db HTTP/1.1
Accept: application/json
Content-Length: 81
Content-Type: application/json

{
    "servings": 4,
    "subtitle": "Delicious with fresh bread",
    "title": "Fish Stew"
}
```

Response:

```
HTTP/1.1 201 Created
Cache-Control: must-revalidate
Content-Length: 95
Content-Type: application/json
Date: Tue, 13 Aug 2013 15:19:25 GMT
ETag: "1-9c65296036141e575d32ba9c034dd3ee"
Location: http://localhost:5984/db/ab39fe0993049b84cfa81acd6ebad09d
Server: CouchDB (Erlang/OTP)

{
    "id": "ab39fe0993049b84cfa81acd6ebad09d",
    "ok": true,
    "rev": "1-9c65296036141e575d32ba9c034dd3ee"
}
```

Specifying the Document ID

The document ID can be specified by including the _id field in the JSON of the submitted record. The following request will create the same document with the ID FishStew.

Request:

```
POST /db HTTP/1.1
Accept: application/json
Content-Length: 98
Content-Type: application/json

{
    "_id": "FishStew",
    "servings": 4,
    "subtitle": "Delicious with fresh bread",
    "title": "Fish Stew"
}
```

Response:

```
HTTP/1.1 201 Created
Cache-Control: must-revalidate
Content-Length: 71
Content-Type: application/json
Date: Tue, 13 Aug 2013 15:19:25 GMT
ETag: "1-9c65296036141e575d32ba9c034dd3ee"
Location: http://localhost:5984/db/FishStew
Server: CouchDB (Erlang/OTP)

{
    "id": "FishStew",
    "ok": true,
    "rev": "1-9c65296036141e575d32ba9c034dd3ee"
}
```

Batch Mode Writes

You can write documents to the database at a higher rate by using the batch option. This collects document writes together in memory (on a user-by-user basis) before they are committed to disk. This increases the risk of the documents not being stored in the event of a failure, since the documents are not written to disk immediately.

To use the batched mode, append the batch=ok query argument to the URL of the PUT or POST /{db} request. The CouchDB server will respond with a HTTP 202 Accepted response code immediately.

Note: Creating or updating documents with batch mode doesn't guarantee that all documents will be successfully stored on disk. For example, individual documents may not be saved due to conflicts, rejection by *validation function* or by other reasons, even if overall the batch was sucessfully submitted.

Request:

```
POST /db?batch=ok HTTP/1.1
Accept: application/json
Content-Length: 98
Content-Type: application/json

{
    "_id": "FishStew",
    "servings": 4,
    "subtitle": "Delicious with fresh bread",
    "title": "Fish Stew"
}
```

Response:

```
HTTP/1.1 202 Accepted
Cache-Control: must-revalidate
Content-Length: 28
Content-Type: application/json
Date: Tue, 13 Aug 2013 15:19:25 GMT
Location: http://localhost:5984/db/FishStew
Server: CouchDB (Erlang/OTP)

{
    "id": "FishStew",
    "ok": true
}
```

10.3.2 /db/_all_docs

GET /{db}/_all_docs

Returns a JSON structure of all of the documents in a given database. The information is returned as a JSON structure containing meta information about the return structure, including a list of all documents and basic contents, consisting the ID, revision and key. The key is the from the document's _id.

Parameters

- **db** – Database name

Request Headers

- Accept –
  - *application/json*
  - *text/plain*

Query Parameters

- **conflicts** (*boolean*) – Includes *conflicts* information in response. Ignored if *include_docs* isn't `true`. Default is `false`.

- **descending** (*boolean*) – Return the documents in descending by key order. Default is `false`.

- **endkey** (*string*) – Stop returning records when the specified key is reached. *Optional*.

- **end_key** (*string*) – Alias for *endkey* param.

- **endkey_docid** (*string*) – Stop returning records when the specified document ID is reached. *Optional*.

- **end_key_doc_id** (*string*) – Alias for *endkey_docid* param.

- **include_docs** (*boolean*) – Include the full content of the documents in the return. Default is `false`.

- **inclusive_end** (*boolean*) – Specifies whether the specified end key should be included in the result. Default is `true`.

- **key** (*string*) – Return only documents that match the specified key. *Optional*.

- **keys** (*string*) – Return only documents that match the specified keys. *Optional*.

- **limit** (*number*) – Limit the number of the returned documents to the specified number. *Optional*.

- **skip** (*number*) – Skip this number of records before starting to return the results. Default is `0`.

- **stale** (*string*) – Allow the results from a stale view to be used, without triggering a rebuild of all views within the encompassing design doc. Supported values: `ok` and `update_after`. *Optional*.
- **startkey** (*string*) – Return records starting with the specified key. *Optional*.
- **start_key** (*string*) – Alias for *startkey* param.
- **startkey_docid** (*string*) – Return records starting with the specified document ID. *Optional*.
- **start_key_doc_id** (*string*) – Alias for *startkey_docid* param.
- **update_seq** (*boolean*) – Response includes an `update_seq` value indicating which sequence id of the underlying database the view reflects. Default is `false`.

Response Headers

- Content-Type –
  - *application/json*
  - *text/plain; charset=utf-8*
- ETag – Response signature

Response JSON Object

- **offset** (*number*) – Offset where the document list started
- **rows** (*array*) – Array of view row objects. By default the information returned contains only the document ID and revision.
- **total_rows** (*number*) – Number of documents in the database/view. Note that this is not the number of rows returned in the actual query.
- **update_seq** (*number*) – Current update sequence for the database

Status Codes

- 200 OK – Request completed successfully

Request:

```
GET /db/_all_docs HTTP/1.1
Accept: application/json
Host: localhost:5984
```

Response:

```
HTTP/1.1 200 OK
Cache-Control: must-revalidate
Content-Type: application/json
Date: Sat, 10 Aug 2013 16:22:56 GMT
ETag: "1W2DJUZFZSZD9K78UFA3GZWB4"
Server: CouchDB (Erlang/OTP)
Transfer-Encoding: chunked

{
    "offset": 0,
    "rows": [
        {
            "id": "16e458537602f5ef2a710089dffd9453",
            "key": "16e458537602f5ef2a710089dffd9453",
            "value": {
                "rev": "1-967a00dff5e02add41819138abb3284d"
            }
        },
        {
            "id": "a4c51cdfa2069f3e905c431114001aff",
```

```
                "key": "a4c51cdfa2069f3e905c431114001aff",
                "value": {
                    "rev": "1-967a00dff5e02add41819138abb3284d"
                }
            },
            {
                "id": "a4c51cdfa2069f3e905c4311140034aa",
                "key": "a4c51cdfa2069f3e905c4311140034aa",
                "value": {
                    "rev": "5-6182c9c954200ab5e3c6bd5e76a1549f"
                }
            },
            {
                "id": "a4c51cdfa2069f3e905c431114003597",
                "key": "a4c51cdfa2069f3e905c431114003597",
                "value": {
                    "rev": "2-7051cbe5c8faecd085a3fa619e6e6337"
                }
            },
            {
                "id": "f4ca7773ddea715afebc4b4b15d4f0b3",
                "key": "f4ca7773ddea715afebc4b4b15d4f0b3",
                "value": {
                    "rev": "2-7051cbe5c8faecd085a3fa619e6e6337"
                }
            }
        ],
        "total_rows": 5
}
```

POST /{db}/_all_docs

The POST to _all_docs allows to specify multiple keys to be selected from the database. This enables you to request multiple documents in a single request, in place of multiple GET /{db}/{docid} requests.

The request body should contain a list of the keys to be returned as an array to a keys object. For example:

```
POST /db/_all_docs HTTP/1.1
Accept: application/json
Content-Length: 70
Content-Type: application/json
Host: localhost:5984

{
    "keys" : [
        "Zingylemontart",
        "Yogurtraita"
    ]
}
```

The returned JSON is the all documents structure, but with only the selected keys in the output:

```
{
    "total_rows" : 2666,
    "rows" : [
        {
            "value" : {
                "rev" : "1-a3544d296de19e6f5b932ea77d886942"
            },
            "id" : "Zingylemontart",
            "key" : "Zingylemontart"
        },
        {
            "value" : {
```

```
            "rev" : "1-91635098bfe7d40197a1b98d7ee085fc"
        },
        "id" : "Yogurtraita",
        "key" : "Yogurtraita"
    }
],
"offset" : 0
}
```

10.3.3 /db/_bulk_docs

POST /{db}/_bulk_docs

The bulk document API allows you to create and update multiple documents at the same time within a single request. The basic operation is similar to creating or updating a single document, except that you batch the document structure and information.

When creating new documents the document ID (_id) is optional.

For updating existing documents, you must provide the document ID, revision information (_rev), and new document values.

In case of batch deleting documents all fields as document ID, revision information and deletion status (_deleted) are required.

Parameters

- **db** – Database name

Request Headers

- Accept –

    - *application/json*

    - *text/plain*

- Content-Type – *application/json*

- **X-Couch-Full-Commit** – Overrides server's *commit policy*. Possible values are: false and true. *Optional*

Request JSON Object

- **all_or_nothing** (*boolean*) – Sets the database commit mode to use *all-or-nothing* semantics. Default is false. *Optional*

- **docs** (*array*) – List of documents objects

- **new_edits** (*boolean*) – If false, prevents the database from assigning them new revision IDs. Default is true. *Optional*

Response Headers

- Content-Type –

    - *application/json*

    - *text/plain; charset=utf-8*

Response JSON Array of Objects

- **id** (*string*) – Document ID

- **rev** (*string*) – New document revision token. Available if document have saved without errors. *Optional*

- **error** (*string*) – Error type. *Optional*

- **reason** (*string*) – Error reason. *Optional*

Status Codes

- 201 Created – Document(s) have been created or updated

- 400 Bad Request – The request provided invalid JSON data

- 417 Expectation Failed – Occurs when `all_or_nothing` option set as `true` and at least one document was rejected by *validation function*

- 500 Internal Server Error – Malformed data provided, while it's still valid JSON

Request:

```
POST /db/_bulk_docs HTTP/1.1
Accept: application/json
Content-Length: 109
Content-Type:application/json
Host: localhost:5984

{
    "docs": [
        {
            "_id": "FishStew"
        },
        {
            "_id": "LambStew",
            "_rev": "2-0786321986194c92dd3b57dfbfc741ce",
            "_deleted": true
        }
    ]
}
```

Response:

```
HTTP/1.1 201 Created
Cache-Control: must-revalidate
Content-Length: 144
Content-Type: application/json
Date: Mon, 12 Aug 2013 00:15:05 GMT
Server: CouchDB (Erlang/OTP)

[
    {
        "ok": true,
        "id": "FishStew",
        "rev":" 1-967a00dff5e02add41819138abb3284d"
    },
    {
        "ok": true,
        "id": "LambStew",
        "rev": "3-f9c62b2169d0999103e9f41949090807"
    }
]
```

Inserting Documents in Bulk

Each time a document is stored or updated in CouchDB, the internal B-tree is updated. Bulk insertion provides efficiency gains in both storage space, and time, by consolidating many of the updates to intermediate B-tree nodes.

It is not intended as a way to perform `ACID`-like transactions in CouchDB, the only transaction boundary within CouchDB is a single update to a single database. The constraints are detailed in *Bulk Documents Transaction Semantics*.

To insert documents in bulk into a database you need to supply a JSON structure with the array of documents that you want to add to the database. You can either include a document ID, or allow the document ID to be automatically generated.

For example, the following update inserts three new documents, two with the supplied document IDs, and one which will have a document ID generated:

```
POST /source/_bulk_docs HTTP/1.1
Accept: application/json
Content-Length: 323
Content-Type: application/json
Host: localhost:5984

{
    "docs": [
        {
            "_id": "FishStew",
            "servings": 4,
            "subtitle": "Delicious with freshly baked bread",
            "title": "FishStew"
        },
        {
            "_id": "LambStew",
            "servings": 6,
            "subtitle": "Serve with a whole meal scone topping",
            "title": "LambStew"
        },
        {
            "_id": "BeefStew",
            "servings": 8,
            "subtitle": "Hand-made dumplings make a great accompaniment",
            "title": "BeefStew"
        }
    ]
}
```

The return type from a bulk insertion will be 201 Created, with the content of the returned structure indicating specific success or otherwise messages on a per-document basis.

The return structure from the example above contains a list of the documents created, here with the combination and their revision IDs:

```
HTTP/1.1 201 Created
Cache-Control: must-revalidate
Content-Length: 215
Content-Type: application/json
Date: Sat, 26 Oct 2013 00:10:39 GMT
Server: CouchDB (Erlang OTP)

[
    {
        "id": "FishStew",
        "ok": true,
        "rev": "1-6a466d5dfda05e613ba97bd737829d67"
    },
    {
        "id": "LambStew",
        "ok": true,
        "rev": "1-648f1b989d52b8e43f05aa877092cc7c"
    },
    {
        "id": "BeefStew",
        "ok": true,
        "rev": "1-e4602845fc4c99674f50b1d5a804fdfa"
```

```
    }
]
```

The content and structure of the returned JSON will depend on the transaction semantics being used for the bulk update; see *Bulk Documents Transaction Semantics* for more information. Conflicts and validation errors when updating documents in bulk must be handled separately; see *Bulk Document Validation and Conflict Errors*.

Updating Documents in Bulk

The bulk document update procedure is similar to the insertion procedure, except that you must specify the document ID and current revision for every document in the bulk update JSON string.

For example, you could send the following request:

```
POST /recipes/_bulk_docs HTTP/1.1
Accept: application/json
Content-Length: 464
Content-Type: application/json
Host: localhost:5984

{
    "docs": [
        {
            "_id": "FishStew",
            "_rev": "1-6a466d5dfda05e613ba97bd737829d67",
            "servings": 4,
            "subtitle": "Delicious with freshly baked bread",
            "title": "FishStew"
        },
        {
            "_id": "LambStew",
            "_rev": "1-648f1b989d52b8e43f05aa877092cc7c",
            "servings": 6,
            "subtitle": "Serve with a whole meal scone topping",
            "title": "LambStew"
        },
        {
            "_id": "BeefStew",
            "_rev": "1-e4602845fc4c99674f50b1d5a804fdfa",
            "servings": 8,
            "subtitle": "Hand-made dumplings make a great accompaniment",
            "title": "BeefStew"
        }
    ]
}
```

The return structure is the JSON of the updated documents, with the new revision and ID information:

```
HTTP/1.1 201 Created
Cache-Control: must-revalidate
Content-Length: 215
Content-Type: application/json
Date: Sat, 26 Oct 2013 00:10:39 GMT
Server: CouchDB (Erlang OTP)

[
    {
        "id": "FishStew",
        "ok": true,
        "rev": "2-2bff94179917f1dec7cd7f0209066fb8"
    },
    {
```

```
        "id": "LambStew",
        "ok": true,
        "rev": "2-6a7aae7ac481aa98a2042718d09843c4"
    },
    {

        "id": "BeefStew",
        "ok": true,
        "rev": "2-9801936a42f06a16f16c30027980d96f"
    }
]
```

You can optionally delete documents during a bulk update by adding the _deleted field with a value of true to each document ID/revision combination within the submitted JSON structure.

The return type from a bulk insertion will be 201 Created, with the content of the returned structure indicating specific success or otherwise messages on a per-document basis.

The content and structure of the returned JSON will depend on the transaction semantics being used for the bulk update; see *Bulk Documents Transaction Semantics* for more information. Conflicts and validation errors when updating documents in bulk must be handled separately; see *Bulk Document Validation and Conflict Errors*.

Bulk Documents Transaction Semantics

CouchDB supports two different modes for updating (or inserting) documents using the bulk documentation system. Each mode affects both the state of the documents in the event of system failure, and the level of conflict checking performed on each document. The two modes are:

- **non-atomic**

  The default mode is *non-atomic*, that is, CouchDB will only guarantee that some of the documents will be saved when you send the request. The response will contain the list of documents successfully inserted or updated during the process. In the event of a crash, some of the documents may have been successfully saved, and some will have been lost.

  In this mode, the response structure will indicate whether the document was updated by supplying the new _rev parameter indicating a new document revision was created. If the update failed, then you will get an error of type conflict. For example:

```
[
    {
        "id" : "FishStew",
        "error" : "conflict",
        "reason" : "Document update conflict."
    },
    {
        "id" : "LambStew",
        "error" : "conflict",
        "reason" : "Document update conflict."
    },
    {
        "id" : "BeefStew",
        "error" : "conflict",
        "reason" : "Document update conflict."
    }
]
```

  In this case no new revision has been created and you will need to submit the document update, with the correct revision tag, to update the document.

- **all-or-nothing**

  In *all-or-nothing* mode, either all documents are written to the database, or no documents are written to the database, in the event of a system failure during commit.

In addition, the per-document conflict checking is not performed. Instead a new revision of the document is created, even if the new revision is in conflict with the current revision in the database. The returned structure contains the list of documents with new revisions:

```
HTTP/1.1 201 Created
Cache-Control: must-revalidate
Content-Length: 215
Content-Type: application/json
Date: Sat, 26 Oct 2013 00:13:33 GMT
Server: CouchDB (Erlang OTP)

[
    {
        "id": "FishStew",
        "ok": true,
        "rev": "1-6a466d5dfda05e613ba97bd737829d67"
    },
    {
        "id": "LambStew",
        "ok": true,
        "rev": "1-648f1b989d52b8e43f05aa877092cc7c"
    },
    {
        "id": "BeefStew",
        "ok": true,
        "rev": "1-e4602845fc4c99674f50b1d5a804fdfa"
    }
]
```

When updating documents using this mode the revision of a document included in views will be arbitrary. You can check the conflict status for a document by using the `conflicts=true` query argument when accessing the view. Conflicts should be handled individually to ensure the consistency of your database.

To use this mode, you must include the `all_or_nothing` field (set to true) within the main body of the JSON of the request.

The effects of different database operations on the different modes are summarized below:

- **Transaction Mode**: Non-atomic
  - **Transaction**: Insert
    * **Cause**: Requested document ID already exists
    * **Resolution**: Resubmit with different document ID, or update the existing document
  - **Transaction**: Update
    * **Cause**: Revision missing or incorrect
    * **Resolution**: Resubmit with correct revision
- **Transaction Mode**: All-or-nothing
  - **Transaction**: Insert / Update
    * **Cause**: Additional revision inserted
    * **Resolution**: Resolve conflicted revisions

Replication of documents is independent of the type of insert or update. The documents and revisions created during a bulk insert or update are replicated in the same way as any other document. This can mean that if you make use of the *all-or-nothing* mode the exact list of documents, revisions (and their conflict state) may or may not be replicated to other databases correctly.

Bulk Document Validation and Conflict Errors

The JSON returned by the `_bulk_docs` operation consists of an array of JSON structures, one for each document in the original submission. The returned JSON structure should be examined to ensure that all of the documents submitted in the original request were successfully added to the database.

When a document (or document revision) is not correctly committed to the database because of an error, you should check the `error` field to determine error type and course of action. Errors will be one of the following type:

- **conflict**

  The document as submitted is in conflict. If you used the default bulk transaction mode then the new revision will not have been created and you will need to re-submit the document to the database. If you used `all-or-nothing` mode then you will need to manually resolve the conflicted revisions of the document.

  Conflict resolution of documents added using the bulk docs interface is identical to the resolution procedures used when resolving conflict errors during replication.

- **forbidden**

  Entries with this error type indicate that the validation routine applied to the document during submission has returned an error.

  For example, if your *validation routine* includes the following:

  ```
  throw({forbidden: 'invalid recipe ingredient'});
  ```

  The error response returned will be:

  ```
  HTTP/1.1 417 Expectation Failed
  Cache-Control: must-revalidate
  Content-Length: 120
  Content-Type: application/json
  Date: Sat, 26 Oct 2013 00:05:17 GMT
  Server: CouchDB (Erlang OTP)

  {
      "error": "forbidden",
      "id": "LambStew",
      "reason": "invalid recipe ingredient",
      "rev": "1-34c318924a8f327223eed702ddfdc66d"
  }
  ```

10.3.4 `/db/_changes`

GET `/{db}/_changes`

Returns a sorted list of changes made to documents in the database, in time order of application, can be obtained from the database's `_changes` resource. Only the most recent change for a given document is guaranteed to be provided, for example if a document has had fields added, and then deleted, an API client checking for changes will not necessarily receive the intermediate state of added documents.

This can be used to listen for update and modifications to the database for post processing or synchronization, and for practical purposes, a continuously connected `_changes` feed is a reasonable approach for generating a real-time log for most applications.

Parameters

- **db** – Database name

Request Headers

- Accept –

  - *application/json*

– *text/event-stream*

– *text/plain*

- Last-Event-ID – ID of the last events received by the server on a previous connection. Overrides *since* query parameter.

Query Parameters

- **doc_ids** (*array*) – List of document IDs to filter the changes feed as valid JSON array. Used with *_doc_ids* filter. Since length of URL is limited, it is better to use *POST* */{db}/_changes* instead.

- **conflicts** (*boolean*) – Includes *conflicts* information in response. Ignored if *include_docs* isn't `true`. Default is `false`.

- **descending** (*boolean*) – Return the change results in descending sequence order (most recent change first). Default is `false`.

- **feed** (*string*) – see *Changes Feeds*. Default is `normal`.

- **filter** (*string*) – Reference to a *filter function* from a design document that will filter whole stream emitting only filtered events. See the section Change Notifications in the book CouchDB The Definitive Guide for more information.

- **heartbeat** (*number*) – Period in *milliseconds* after which an empty line is sent in the results. Only applicable for *longpoll* or *continuous* feeds. Overrides any timeout to keep the feed alive indefinitely. Default is `60000`. May be `true` to use default value.

- **include_docs** (*boolean*) – Include the associated document with each result. If there are conflicts, only the winning revision is returned. Default is `false`.

- **attachments** (*boolean*) – Include the Base64-encoded content of *attachments* in the documents that are included if *include_docs* is `true`. Ignored if *include_docs* isn't `true`. Default is `false`.

- **att_encoding_info** (*boolean*) – Include encoding information in attachment stubs if *include_docs* is `true` and the particular attachment is compressed. Ignored if *include_docs* isn't `true`. Default is `false`.

- **last-event-id** (*number*) – Alias of *Last-Event-ID* header.

- **limit** (*number*) – Limit number of result rows to the specified value (note that using `0` here has the same effect as `1`).

- **since** – Start the results from the change immediately after the given sequence number. Can be integer number or `now` value. Default is `0`.

- **style** (*string*) – Specifies how many revisions are returned in the changes array. The default, `main_only`, will only return the current "winning" revision; `all_docs` will return all leaf revisions (including conflicts and deleted former conflicts).

- **timeout** (*number*) – Maximum period in *milliseconds* to wait for a change before the response is sent, even if there are no results. Only applicable for *longpoll* or *continuous* feeds. Default value is specified by *httpd/changes_timeout* configuration option. Note that `60000` value is also the default maximum timeout to prevent undetected dead connections.

- **view** (*string*) – Allows to use view functions as filters. Documents counted as "passed" for view filter in case if map function emits at least one record for them. See *_view* for more info.

Response Headers

- Cache-Control – `no-cache` if changes feed is *eventsource*

- Content-Type –

– *application/json*

        – *text/event-stream*

        – *text/plain; charset=utf-8*

- ETag – Response hash is changes feed is *normal*

- Transfer-Encoding – chunked

Response JSON Object

- **last_seq** (*number*) – Last change sequence number

- **results** (*array*) – Changes made to a database

Status Codes

- 200 OK – Request completed successfully

- 400 Bad Request – Bad request

The result field of database changes

JSON Object

- **changes** (*array*) – List of document's leafs with single field rev

- **id** (*string*) – Document ID

- **seq** (*number*) – Update sequence number

Request:

```
GET /db/_changes?style=all_docs HTTP/1.1
Accept: application/json
Host: localhost:5984
```

Response:

```
HTTP/1.1 200 OK
Cache-Control: must-revalidate
Content-Type: application/json
Date: Mon, 12 Aug 2013 00:54:58 GMT
ETag: "6ASLEKEMSRABT005XY9UPO9Z"
Server: CouchDB (Erlang/OTP)
Transfer-Encoding: chunked

{
    "last_seq": 11,
    "results": [
        {
            "changes": [
                {
                    "rev": "2-7051cbe5c8faecd085a3fa619e6e6337"
                }
            ],
            "id": "6478c2ae800dfc387396d14e1fc39626",
            "seq": 6
        },
        {
            "changes": [
                {
                    "rev": "3-7379b9e515b161226c6559d90c4dc49f"
                }
            ],
            "deleted": true,
            "id": "5bbc9ca465f1b0fcd62362168a7c8831",
            "seq": 9
        },
        {
```

```
            "changes": [
                {
                    "rev": "6-460637e73a6288cb24d532bf91f32969"
                },
                {
                    "rev": "5-eeaa298781f60b7bcae0c91bdedd1b87"
                }
            ],
            "id": "729eb57437745e506b333068fff665ae",
            "seq": 11
        }
    ]
}
```

Changed in version 0.11.0: added `include_docs` parameter

Changed in version 1.2.0: added `view` parameter and special value _view_ for `filter` one

Changed in version 1.3.0: `since` parameter could take _now_ value to start listen changes since current seq number.

Changed in version 1.3.0: `eventsource` feed type added.

Changed in version 1.4.0: Support `Last-Event-ID` header.

Changed in version 1.6.0: added `attachments` and `att_encoding_info` parameters

> **Warning:** Using the `attachments` parameter to include attachments in the changes feed is not recommended for large attachment sizes. Also note that the Base64-encoding that is used leads to a 33% overhead (i.e. one third) in transfer size for attachments.

POST /{db}/_changes

Requests the database changes feed in the same way as `GET /{db}/_changes` does, but is widely used with `?filter=_doc_ids` query parameter and allows one to pass a larger list of document IDs to filter.

Request:

```
POST /recipes/_changes?filter=_doc_ids HTTP/1.1
Accept: application/json
Content-Length: 40
Content-Type: application/json
Host: localhost:5984

{
    "doc_ids": [
        "SpaghettiWithMeatballs"
    ]
}
```

Response:

```
HTTP/1.1 200 OK
Cache-Control: must-revalidate
Content-Type: application/json
Date: Sat, 28 Sep 2013 07:23:09 GMT
ETag: "ARIHFWL3I7PIS0SPVTFU6TLR2"
Server: CouchDB (Erlang OTP)
Transfer-Encoding: chunked

{
    "last_seq": 38,
    "results": [
        {
            "changes": [
                {
                    "rev": "13-bcb9d6388b60fd1e960d9ec4e8e3f29e"
```

```
                    }
            ],
            "id": "SpaghettiWithMeatballs",
            "seq": 38
        }
    ]
}
```

Changes Feeds

Polling

By default all changes are immediately returned within the JSON body:

```
GET /somedatabase/_changes HTTP/1.1
```

```
{"results":[
{"seq":1,"id":"fresh","changes":[{"rev":"1-967a00dff5e02add41819138abb3284d"}]},
{"seq":3,"id":"updated","changes":[{"rev":"2-7051cbe5c8faecd085a3fa619e6e6337"}]},
{"seq":5,"id":"deleted","changes":[{"rev":"2-eec205a9d413992850a6e32678485900"}],"deleted
],
"last_seq":5}
```

results is the list of changes in sequential order. New and changed documents only differ in the value of the rev; deleted documents include the "deleted": true attribute. (In the style=all_docs mode, deleted applies only to the current/winning revision. The other revisions listed might be deleted even if there is no deleted property; you have to GET them individually to make sure.)

last_seq is the sequence number of the last update returned. (Currently it will always be the same as the seq of the last item in results.)

Sending a since param in the query string skips all changes up to and including the given sequence number:

```
GET /somedatabase/_changes?since=3 HTTP/1.1
```

The return structure for normal and longpoll modes is a JSON array of changes objects, and the last update sequence number.

In the return format for continuous mode, the server sends a CRLF (carriage-return, linefeed) delimited line for each change. Each line contains the *JSON object* described above.

You can also request the full contents of each document change (instead of just the change notification) by using the include_docs parameter.

```
{
    "last_seq": 5
    "results": [
        {
            "changes": [
                {
                    "rev": "2-eec205a9d413992850a6e32678485900"
                }
            ],
            "deleted": true,
            "id": "deleted",
            "seq": 5,
        }
    ]
}
```

Long Polling

The *longpoll* feed, probably most applicable for a browser, is a more efficient form of polling that waits for a change to occur before the response is sent. *longpoll* avoids the need to frequently poll CouchDB to discover nothing has changed!

The request to the server will remain open until a change is made on the database and is subsequently transferred, and then the connection will close. This is low load for both server and client.

The response is basically the same JSON as is sent for the *normal* feed.

Because the wait for a change can be significant you can set a timeout before the connection is automatically closed (the `timeout` argument). You can also set a heartbeat interval (using the `heartbeat` query argument), which sends a newline to keep the connection active.

Continuous

Continually polling the CouchDB server is not ideal - setting up new HTTP connections just to tell the client that nothing happened puts unnecessary strain on CouchDB.

A continuous feed stays open and connected to the database until explicitly closed and changes are sent to the client as they happen, i.e. in near real-time.

As with the *longpoll* feed type you can set both the timeout and heartbeat intervals to ensure that the connection is kept open for new changes and updates.

The continuous feed's response is a little different than the other feed types to simplify the job of the client - each line of the response is either empty or a JSON object representing a single change, as found in the normal feed's results.

```
GET /somedatabase/_changes?feed=continuous HTTP/1.1
```

```
{"seq":1,"id":"fresh","changes":[{"rev":"1-967a00dff5e02add41819138abb3284d"}]}
{"seq":3,"id":"updated","changes":[{"rev":"2-7051cbe5c8faecd085a3fa619e6e6337"}]}
{"seq":5,"id":"deleted","changes":[{"rev":"2-eec205a9d413992850a6e32678485900"}],"deleted
... tum tee tum ...
{"seq":6,"id":"updated","changes":[{"rev":"3-825cb35de44c433bfb2df415563a19de"}]}
```

Obviously, ... *tum tee tum* ... does not appear in the actual response, but represents a long pause before the change with seq 6 occurred.

Event Source

The *eventsource* feed provides push notifications that can be consumed in the form of DOM events in the browser. Refer to the W3C eventsource specification for further details. CouchDB also honours the `Last-Event-ID` parameter.

```
GET /somedatabase/_changes?feed=eventsource HTTP/1.1
```

```
// define the event handling function
if (window.EventSource) {

    var source = new EventSource("/somedatabase/_changes?feed=eventsource");
    source.onerror = function(e) {
        alert('EventSource failed.');
    };

    var results = [];
    var sourceListener = function(e) {
        var data = JSON.parse(e.data);
        results.push(data);
```

```
    };

    // start listening for events
    source.addEventListener('message', sourceListener, false);

    // stop listening for events
    source.removeEventListener('message', sourceListener, false);

}
```

If you set a heartbeat interval (using the `heartbeat` query argument), CouchDB will send a `hearbeat` event that you can subscribe to with:

```
source.addEventListener('heartbeat', function () {}, false);
```

This can be monitored by the client application to restart the EventSource connection if needed (i.e. if the TCP connection gets stuck in a half-open state).

Note: EventSource connections are subject to cross-origin resource sharing restrictions. You might need to configure *CORS support* to get the EventSource to work in your application.

Filtering

You can filter the contents of the changes feed in a number of ways. The most basic way is to specify one or more document IDs to the query. This causes the returned structure value to only contain changes for the specified IDs. Note that the value of this query argument should be a JSON formatted array.

You can also filter the _changes feed by defining a filter function within a design document. The specification for the filter is the same as for replication filters. You specify the name of the filter function to the `filter` parameter, specifying the design document name and *filter name*. For example:

```
GET /db/_changes?filter=design_doc/filtername
```

Additionally, there are couple of builtin filters are available and described below.

_doc_ids

This filter accepts only changes for documents which ID in specified in `doc_ids` query parameter or payload's object array. See *POST /{db}/_changes* for an example.

_design

The `_design` filter accepts only changes for any design document within the requested database.

Request:

```
GET /recipes/_changes?filter=_design HTTP/1.1
Accept: application/json
Host: localhost:5984
```

Response:

```
HTTP/1.1 200 OK
Cache-Control: must-revalidate
Content-Type: application/json
Date: Sat, 28 Sep 2013 07:28:28 GMT
ETag: "ARIHFWL3I7PIS0SPVTFU6TLR2"
Server: CouchDB (Erlang OTP)
Transfer-Encoding: chunked
```

```
{
    "last_seq": 38,
    "results": [
        {
            "changes": [
                {
                    "rev": "10-304cae84fd862832ea9814f02920d4b2"
                }
            ],
            "id": "_design/ingredients",
            "seq": 29
        },
        {
            "changes": [
                {
                    "rev": "123-6f7c1b7c97a9e4f0d22bdf130e8fd817"
                }
            ],
            "deleted": true,
            "id": "_design/cookbook",
            "seq": 35
        },
        {
            "changes": [
                {
                    "rev": "6-5b8a52c22580e922e792047cff3618f3"
                }
            ],
            "deleted": true,
            "id": "_design/meta",
            "seq": 36
        }
    ]
}
```

_view

New in version 1.2.

The special filter _view allows to use existing *map function* as the *filter*. If the map function emits anything for the processed document it counts as accepted and the changes event emits to the feed. For most use-practice cases *filter* functions are very similar to *map* ones, so this feature helps to reduce amount of duplicated code.

> **Warning:** While *map functions* doesn't process the design documents, using _view filter forces them to do this. You need to be sure, that they are ready to handle documents with *alien* structure without panic crush.

Note: Using _view filter doesn't queries the view index files, so you cannot use common *view query parameters* to additionally filter the changes feed by index key. Also, CouchDB doesn't returns the result instantly as it does for views - it really uses the specified map function as filter.

Moreover, you cannot make such filters dynamic e.g. process the request query parameters or handle the *User Context Object* - the map function is only operates with the document.

Request:

```
GET /recipes/_changes?filter=_view&view=ingredients/by_recipe HTTP/1.1
Accept: application/json
Host: localhost:5984
```

Response:

```
HTTP/1.1 200 OK
Cache-Control: must-revalidate
Content-Type: application/json
Date: Sat, 28 Sep 2013 07:36:40 GMT
ETag: "ARIHFWL3I7PIS0SPVTFU6TLR2"
Server: CouchDB (Erlang OTP)
Transfer-Encoding: chunked

{
    "last_seq": 38,
    "results": [
        {
            "changes": [
                {
                    "rev": "13-bcb9d6388b60fd1e960d9ec4e8e3f29e"
                }
            ],
            "id": "SpaghettiWithMeatballs",
            "seq": 38
        }
    ]
}
```

10.3.5 /db/_compact

POST /{db}/_compact

Request compaction of the specified database. Compaction compresses the disk database file by performing the following operations:

- Writes a new, optimised, version of the database file, removing any unused sections from the new version during write. Because a new file is temporarily created for this purpose, you may require up to twice the current storage space of the specified database in order for the compaction routine to complete.

- Removes old revisions of documents from the database, up to the per-database limit specified by the _revs_limit database parameter.

Compaction can only be requested on an individual database; you cannot compact all the databases for a CouchDB instance. The compaction process runs as a background process.

You can determine if the compaction process is operating on a database by obtaining the database meta information, the compact_running value of the returned database structure will be set to true. See *GET /{db}*.

You can also obtain a list of running processes to determine whether compaction is currently running. See *_active_tasks*.

Parameters

- **db** – Database name

Request Headers

- Accept –
    - *application/json*
    - *text/plain*
- Content-Type – *application/json*

Response Headers

- Content-Type –
    - *application/json*

> – *text/plain; charset=utf-8*

Response JSON Object

- **ok** (*boolean*) – Operation status

Status Codes

- 202 Accepted – Compaction request has been accepted
- 400 Bad Request – Invalid database name
- 401 Unauthorized – CouchDB Server Administrator privileges required
- 415 Unsupported Media Type – Bad Content-Type value

Request:

```
POST /db/_compact HTTP/1.1
Accept: application/json
Content-Type: application/json
Host: localhost:5984
```

Response:

```
HTTP/1.1 202 Accepted
Cache-Control: must-revalidate
Content-Length: 12
Content-Type: application/json
Date: Mon, 12 Aug 2013 09:27:43 GMT
Server: CouchDB (Erlang/OTP)

{
    "ok": true
}
```

10.3.6 /db/_compact/design-doc

POST /{db}/_compact/{ddoc}

Compacts the view indexes associated with the specified design document. If may be that compacting a large view can return more storage than compacting the actual db. Thus, you can use this in place of the full database compaction if you know a specific set of view indexes have been affected by a recent database change.

Parameters

- **db** – Database name
- **ddoc** – Design document name

Request Headers

- Accept –
  - *application/json*
  - *text/plain*
- Content-Type – *application/json*

Response Headers

- Content-Type –
  - *application/json*
  - *text/plain; charset=utf-8*

Response JSON Object

- **ok** (*boolean*) – Operation status

Status Codes

- 202 Accepted – Compaction request has been accepted

- 400 Bad Request – Invalid database name

- 401 Unauthorized – CouchDB Server Administrator privileges required

- 404 Not Found – Design document not found

- 415 Unsupported Media Type – Bad Content-Type value

Request:

```
POST /db/_compact/posts HTTP/1.1
Accept: application/json
Content-Type: application/json
Host: localhost:5984
```

Response:

```
HTTP/1.1 202 Accepted
Cache-Control: must-revalidate
Content-Length: 12
Content-Type: application/json
Date: Mon, 12 Aug 2013 09:36:44 GMT
Server: CouchDB (Erlang/OTP)

{
    "ok": true
}
```

Note: View indexes are stored in a separate .couch file based on a hash of the design document's relevant functions, in a sub directory of where the main .couch database files are located.

10.3.7 /db/_ensure_full_commit

POST /{db}/_ensure_full_commit
Commits any recent changes to the specified database to disk. You should call this if you want to ensure that recent changes have been flushed. This function is likely not required, assuming you have the recommended configuration setting of delayed_commits=false, which requires CouchDB to ensure changes are written to disk before a 200 or similar result is returned.

Parameters

- **db** – Database name

Request Headers

- Accept –

    - *application/json*

    - *text/plain*

- Content-Type – *application/json*

Response Headers

- Content-Type –

    - *application/json*

    - *text/plain; charset=utf-8*

Response JSON Object

- **instance_start_time** (*string*) – Timestamp of when the database was opened, expressed in microseconds since the epoch.

- **ok** (*boolean*) – Operation status

Status Codes

- 201 Created – Commit completed successfully

- 400 Bad Request – Invalid database name

- 415 Unsupported Media Type – Bad Content-Type value

Request:

```
POST /db/_ensure_full_commit HTTP/1.1
Accept: application/json
Content-Type: application/json
Host: localhost:5984
```

Response:

```
HTTP/1.1 201 Created
Cache-Control: must-revalidate
Content-Length: 53
Content-Type: application/json
Date: Mon, 12 Aug 2013 10:22:19 GMT
Server: CouchDB (Erlang/OTP)

{
    "instance_start_time": "1376269047459338",
    "ok": true
}
```

10.3.8 /db/_view_cleanup

POST /{db}/_view_cleanup

Removes view index files that are no longer required by CouchDB as a result of changed views within design documents. As the view filename is based on a hash of the view functions, over time old views will remain, consuming storage. This call cleans up the cached view output on disk for a given view.

Parameters

- **db** – Database name

Request Headers

- Accept –
    - *application/json*
    - *text/plain*
- Content-Type – *application/json*

Response Headers

- Content-Type –
    - *application/json*
    - *text/plain; charset=utf-8*

Response JSON Object

- **ok** (*boolean*) – Operation status

Status Codes

- 202 Accepted – Compaction request has been accepted

- 400 Bad Request – Invalid database name
- 401 Unauthorized – CouchDB Server Administrator privileges required
- 415 Unsupported Media Type – Bad Content-Type value

Request:

```
POST /db/_view_cleanup HTTP/1.1
Accept: application/json
Content-Type: application/json
Host: localhost:5984
```

Response:

```
HTTP/1.1 202 Accepted
Cache-Control: must-revalidate
Content-Length: 12
Content-Type: application/json
Date: Mon, 12 Aug 2013 09:27:43 GMT
Server: CouchDB (Erlang/OTP)


{
    "ok": true
}
```

10.3.9 /db/_security

GET /{db}/_security

Returns the current security object from the specified database.

The security object consists of two compulsory elements, admins and members, which are used to specify the list of users and/or roles that have admin and members rights to the database respectively:

- members: they can read all types of documents from the DB, and they can write (and edit) documents to the DB except for design documents.

- admins: they have all the privileges of members plus the privileges: write (and edit) design documents, add/remove database admins and members, set the *database revisions limit* and execute *temporary views* against the database. They can not create a database nor delete a database.

Both members and admins objects are contains two array-typed fields:

- names: List of CouchDB user names

- roles: List of users roles

Any other additional fields in the security object are optional. The entire security object is made available to validation and other internal functions so that the database can control and limit functionality.

If both the names and roles fields of either the admins or members properties are empty arrays, it means the database has no admins or members.

Having no admins, only server admins (with the reserved _admin role) are able to update design document and make other admin level changes.

Having no members, any user can write regular documents (any non-design document) and read documents from the database.

If there are any member names or roles defined for a database, then only authenticated users having a matching name or role are allowed to read documents from the database (or do a GET /{db} call).

Note: If the security object for a database has never been set, then the value returned will be empty.

Also note, that security objects are not regular versioned documents (that is, they are not under MVCC rules). This is a design choice to speedup authorization checks (avoids traversing a database's documents B-Tree).

Parameters

- **db** – Database name

Request Headers

- Accept –

  - *application/json*

  - *text/plain*

Response Headers

- Content-Type –

  - *application/json*

  - *text/plain; charset=utf-8*

Response JSON Object

- **admins** (*object*) – Object with two fields as names and roles. See description above for more info.

- **members** (*object*) – Object with two fields as names and roles. See description above for more info.

Status Codes

- 200 OK – Request completed successfully

Request:

```
GET /db/_security HTTP/1.1
Accept: application/json
Host: localhost:5984
```

Response:

```
HTTP/1.1 200 OK
Cache-Control: must-revalidate
Content-Length: 109
Content-Type: application/json
Date: Mon, 12 Aug 2013 19:05:29 GMT
Server: CouchDB (Erlang/OTP)

{
    "admins": {
        "names": [
            "superuser"
        ],
        "roles": [
            "admins"
        ]
    },
    "members": {
        "names": [
            "user1",
            "user2"
        ],
        "roles": [
            "developers"
        ]
    }
}
```

PUT /{db}/_security
   Sets the security object for the given database.

   Parameters

   - **db** – Database name

   Request Headers

   - Accept –
     - *application/json*
     - *text/plain*
   - Content-Type – *application/json*

   Request JSON Object

   - **admins** (*object*) – Object with two fields as names and roles. *See description above for more info.*
   - **members** (*object*) – Object with two fields as names and roles. *See description above for more info.*

   Response Headers

   - Content-Type –
     - *application/json*
     - *text/plain; charset=utf-8*

   Response JSON Object

   - **ok** (*boolean*) – Operation status

   Status Codes

   - 200 OK – Request completed successfully
   - 401 Unauthorized – CouchDB Server Administrator privileges required

   Request:

```
PUT /db/_security HTTP/1.1
Accept: application/json
Content-Length: 121
Content-Type: application/json
Host: localhost:5984

{
    "admins": {
        "names": [
            "superuser"
        ],
        "roles": [
            "admins"
        ]
    },
    "members": {
        "names": [
            "user1",
            "user2"
        ],
        "roles": [
            "developers"
        ]
    }
}
```

Response:

```
HTTP/1.1 200 OK
Cache-Control: must-revalidate
Content-Length: 12
Content-Type: application/json
Date: Tue, 13 Aug 2013 11:26:28 GMT
Server: CouchDB (Erlang/OTP)

{
    "ok": true
}
```

10.3.10 /db/_temp_view

POST /{db}/_temp_view

Creates (and executes) a temporary view based on the view function supplied in the JSON request.

The arguments also available to standard view requests also apply to temporary views, but the execution of the view may take some time as it relies on being executed at the time of the request. This means that for every temporary view you create, the entire database will be read one doc at a time and passed through the view function.

This should not be used on production CouchDB instances, and is purely a convenience function for quick development testing. You should use a defined view if you want to achieve the best performance.

See */db/_design/design-doc/_view/view-name* for more info.

Request:

```
POST /db/_temp_view?group=true HTTP/1.1
Accept: application/json
Content-Length: 92
Content-Type: application/json
Host: localhost:5984

{
    "map": "function(doc) { if (doc.value) { emit(doc.value, null); } }",
    "reduce": "_count"
}
```

Response:

```
HTTP/1.1 200 OK
Cache-Control: must-revalidate
Content-Type: application/json
Date: Tue, 13 Aug 2013 12:28:12 GMT
ETag: "AU33B3N7S9K4SAZSFA048HVB4"
Server: CouchDB (Erlang/OTP)
Transfer-Encoding: chunked

{
    "rows": [
        {
            "key": -10,
            "value": 1
        },
        {
            "key": 10,
            "value": 2
        },
        {
            "key": 15,
```

```
            "value": 1
        }
    ]
}
```

10.3.11 /db/_purge

POST /{db}/_purge

A database purge permanently removes the references to deleted documents from the database. Normal deletion of a document within CouchDB does not remove the document from the database, instead, the document is marked as _deleted=true (and a new revision is created). This is to ensure that deleted documents can be replicated to other databases as having been deleted. This also means that you can check the status of a document and identify that the document has been deleted by its absence.

> **Warning:** Purging a document from a database should only be done as a last resort when sensitive information has been introduced inadvertently into a database. In clustered or replicated environments it is very difficult to guarantee that a particular purged document has been removed from all replicas. Do not rely on this API as a way of doing secure deletion.

The purge operation removes the references to the deleted documents from the database. The purging of old documents is not replicated to other databases. If you are replicating between databases and have deleted a large number of documents you should run purge on each database.

> **Note:** Purging documents does not remove the space used by them on disk. To reclaim disk space, you should run a database compact (see */db/_compact*), and compact views (see */db/_compact/design-doc*).

The format of the request must include the document ID and one or more revisions that must be purged.

The response will contain the purge sequence number, and a list of the document IDs and revisions successfully purged.

> **Parameters**
> - **db** – Database name

> **Request Headers**
> - Accept –
>   - *application/json*
>   - *text/plain*
> - Content-Type – *application/json*

> **Request JSON Object**
> - **object** – Mapping of document ID to list of revisions to purge

> **Response Headers**
> - Content-Type –
>   - *application/json*
>   - *text/plain; charset=utf-8*

> **Response JSON Object**
> - **purge_seq** (*number*) – Purge sequence number
> - **purged** (*object*) – Mapping of document ID to list of purged revisions

> **Status Codes**
> - 200 OK – Request completed successfully

- 400 Bad Request – Invalid database name or JSON payload

- 415 Unsupported Media Type – **Bad** Content-Type value

Request:

```
POST /db/_purge HTTP/1.1
Accept: application/json
Content-Length: 76
Content-Type: application/json
Host: localhost:5984

{
    "c6114c65e295552ab1019e2b046b10e": [
        "3-b06fcd1c1c9e0ec7c480ee8aa467bf3b",
        "3-0e871ef78849b0c206091f1a7af6ec41"
    ]
}
```

Response:

```
HTTP/1.1 200 OK
Cache-Control: must-revalidate
Content-Length: 103
Content-Type: application/json
Date: Mon, 12 Aug 2013 10:53:24 GMT
Server: CouchDB (Erlang/OTP)

{
    "purge_seq":3,
    "purged":{
        "c6114c65e295552ab1019e2b046b10e": [
            "3-b06fcd1c1c9e0ec7c480ee8aa467bf3b"
        ]
    }
}
```

Updating Indexes

The number of purges on a database is tracked using a purge sequence. This is used by the view indexer to optimize the updating of views that contain the purged documents.

When the indexer identifies that the purge sequence on a database has changed, it compares the purge sequence of the database with that stored in the view index. If the difference between the stored sequence and database is sequence is only 1, then the indexer uses a cached list of the most recently purged documents, and then removes these documents from the index individually. This prevents completely rebuilding the index from scratch.

If the difference between the stored sequence number and current database sequence is greater than 1, then the view index is entirely rebuilt. This is an expensive operation as every document in the database must be examined.

10.3.12 /db/_missing_revs

POST /{db}/_missing_revs
    With given a list of document revisions, returns the document revisions that do not exist in the database.

Parameters

- **db** – Database name

Request Headers

- Accept –

    - *application/json*

> – *text/plain*

- Content-Type – *application/json*

Request JSON Object

> - **object** – Mapping of document ID to list of revisions to lookup

Response Headers

> - Content-Type –
>
>> – *application/json*
>>
>> – *text/plain; charset=utf-8*

Response JSON Object

> - **missing_revs** (*object*) – Mapping of document ID to list of missed revisions

Status Codes

> - 200 OK – Request completed successfully
>
> - 400 Bad Request – Invalid database name or JSON payload

Request:

```
POST /db/_missing_revs HTTP/1.1
Accept: application/json
Content-Length: 76
Content-Type: application/json
Host: localhost:5984

{
    "c6114c65e295552ab1019e2b046b10e": [
        "3-b06fcd1c1c9e0ec7c480ee8aa467bf3b",
        "3-0e871ef78849b0c206091f1a7af6ec41"
    ]
}
```

Response:

```
HTTP/1.1 200 OK
Cache-Control: must-revalidate
Content-Length: 64
Content-Type: application/json
Date: Mon, 12 Aug 2013 10:53:24 GMT
Server: CouchDB (Erlang/OTP)

{
    "missed_revs":{
        "c6114c65e295552ab1019e2b046b10e": [
            "3-b06fcd1c1c9e0ec7c480ee8aa467bf3b"
        ]
    }
}
```

10.3.13 /db/_revs_diff

POST /{db}/_revs_diff

Given a set of document/revision IDs, returns the subset of those that do not correspond to revisions stored in the database.

Its primary use is by the replicator, as an important optimization: after receiving a set of new revision IDs from the source database, the replicator sends this set to the destination database's _revs_diff to find out which of them already exist there. It can then avoid fetching and sending already-known document bodies.

Both the request and response bodies are JSON objects whose keys are document IDs; but the values are structured differently:

- In the request, a value is an array of revision IDs for that document.

- In the response, a value is an object with a `missing`: key, whose value is a list of revision IDs for that document (the ones that are not stored in the database) and optionally a `possible_ancestors` key, whose value is an array of revision IDs that are known that might be ancestors of the missing revisions.

Parameters

- **db** – Database name

Request Headers

- Accept –
    - `application/json`
    - `text/plain`
- Content-Type – `application/json`

Request JSON Object

- **object** – Mapping of document ID to list of revisions to lookup

Response Headers

- Content-Type –
    - `application/json`
    - `text/plain; charset=utf-8`

Response JSON Object

- **missing** (*array*) – List of missed revisions for specified document

- **possible_ancestors** (*array*) – List of revisions that *may be* ancestors for specified document and its current revision in requested database

Status Codes

- 200 OK – Request completed successfully

- 400 Bad Request – Invalid database name or JSON payload

Request:

```
POST /db/_revs_diff HTTP/1.1
Accept: application/json
Content-Length: 113
Content-Type: application/json
Host: localhost:5984

{
    "190f721ca3411be7aa9477db5f948bbb": [
        "3-bb72a7682290f94a985f7afac8b27137",
        "4-10265e5a26d807a3cfa459cf1a82ef2e",
        "5-067a00dff5e02add41819138abb3284d"
    ]
}
```

Response:

```
HTTP/1.1 200 OK
Cache-Control: must-revalidate
Content-Length: 88
Content-Type: application/json
```

```
Date: Mon, 12 Aug 2013 16:56:02 GMT
Server: CouchDB (Erlang/OTP)

{
    "190f721ca3411be7aa9477db5f948bbb": {
        "missing": [
            "3-bb72a7682290f94a985f7afac8b27137",
            "5-067a00dff5e02add41819138abb3284d"
        ],
        "possible_ancestors": [
            "4-10265e5a26d807a3cfa459cf1a82ef2e"
        ]
    }
}
```

10.3.14 /db/_revs_limit

GET /{db}/_revs_limit

Gets the current revs_limit (revision limit) setting.

Parameters

- **db** – Database name

Request Headers

- Accept –
  - *application/json*
  - *text/plain*

Response Headers

- Content-Type –
  - *application/json*
  - *text/plain; charset=utf-8*

Status Codes

- 200 OK – Request completed successfully

Request:

```
GET /db/_revs_limit HTTP/1.1
Accept: application/json
Host: localhost:5984
```

Response:

```
HTTP/1.1 200 OK
Cache-Control: must-revalidate
Content-Length: 5
Content-Type: application/json
Date: Mon, 12 Aug 2013 17:27:30 GMT
Server: CouchDB (Erlang/OTP)

1000
```

PUT /{db}/_revs_limit

Sets the maximum number of document revisions that will be tracked by CouchDB, even after compaction has occurred. You can set the revision limit on a database with a scalar integer of the limit that you want to set as the request body.

Parameters

- **db** – Database name

Request Headers

- Accept –

  - *application/json*

  - *text/plain*

- Content-Type – *application/json*

Response Headers

- Content-Type –

  - *application/json*

  - *text/plain; charset=utf-8*

Response JSON Object

- **ok** (*boolean*) – Operation status

Status Codes

- 200 OK – Request completed successfully

- 400 Bad Request – Invalid JSON data

Request:

```
PUT /db/_revs_limit HTTP/1.1
Accept: application/json
Content-Length: 5
Content-Type: application/json
Host: localhost:5984

1000
```

Response:

```
HTTP/1.1 200 OK
Cache-Control: must-revalidate
Content-Length: 12
Content-Type: application/json
Date: Mon, 12 Aug 2013 17:47:52 GMT
Server: CouchDB (Erlang/OTP)

{
    "ok": true
}
```

10.4 Documents

Details on how to create, read, update and delete documents within a database.

10.4.1 /db/doc

HEAD /{db}/{docid}

Returns the HTTP Headers containing a minimal amount of information about the specified document. The method supports the same query arguments as the *GET /{db}/{docid}* method, but only the header information (including document size, and the revision as an ETag), is returned.

The ETag header shows the current revision for the requested document, and the Content-Length specifies the length of the data, if the document were requested in full.

Adding any of the query arguments (see *GET /{db}/{docid}*), then the resulting HTTP Headers will correspond to what would be returned.

Parameters

- **db** – Database name
- **docid** – Document ID

Request Headers

- If-None-Match – Double quoted document's revision token

Response Headers

- Content-Length – Document size
- ETag – Double quoted document's revision token

Status Codes

- 200 OK – Document exists
- 304 Not Modified – Document wasn't modified since specified revision
- 401 Unauthorized – Read privilege required
- 404 Not Found – Document not found

Request:

```
HEAD /db/SpaghettiWithMeatballs HTTP/1.1
Accept: application/json
Host: localhost:5984
```

Response:

```
HTTP/1.1 200 OK
Cache-Control: must-revalidate
Content-Length: 660
Content-Type: application/json
Date: Tue, 13 Aug 2013 21:35:37 GMT
ETag: "12-151bb8678d45aaa949ec3698ef1c7e78"
Server: CouchDB (Erlang/OTP)
```

GET /{db}/{docid}

Returns document by the specified docid from the specified db. Unless you request a specific revision, the latest revision of the document will always be returned.

Parameters

- **db** – Database name
- **docid** – Document ID

Request Headers

- Accept –
  - *application/json*
  - *multipart/mixed*
  - *text/plain*
- If-None-Match – Double quoted document's revision token

Query Parameters

- **attachments** (*boolean*) – Includes attachments bodies in response. Default is false

- **att_encoding_info** (*boolean*) – Includes encoding information in attachment stubs if the particular attachment is compressed. Default is `false`.

- **atts_since** (*array*) – Includes attachments only since specified revisions. Doesn't includes attachments for specified revisions. *Optional*

- **conflicts** (*boolean*) – Includes information about conflicts in document. Default is `false`

- **deleted_conflicts** (*boolean*) – Includes information about deleted conflicted revisions. Default is `false`

- **latest** (*boolean*) – Forces retrieving latest "leaf" revision, no matter what *rev* was requested. Default is `false`

- **local_seq** (*boolean*) – Includes last update sequence number for the document. Default is `false`

- **meta** (*boolean*) – Acts same as specifying all *conflicts*, *deleted_conflicts* and *open_revs* query parameters. Default is `false`

- **open_revs** (*array*) – Retrieves documents of specified leaf revisions. Additionally, it accepts value as `all` to return all leaf revisions. *Optional*

- **rev** (*string*) – Retrieves document of specified revision. *Optional*

- **revs** (*boolean*) – Includes list of all known document revisions. Default is `false`

- **revs_info** (*boolean*) – Includes detailed information for all known document revisions. Default is `false`

Response Headers

- Content-Type –

  - `application/json`

  - `multipart/mixed`

  - `text/plain; charset=utf-8`

- ETag – Double quoted document's revision token. Not available when retrieving conflicts-related information

- Transfer-Encoding – `chunked`. Available if requested with query parameter `open_revs`

Response JSON Object

- **_id** (*string*) – Document ID

- **_rev** (*string*) – Revision MVCC token

- **_deleted** (*boolean*) – Deletion flag. Available if document was removed

- **_attachments** (*object*) – Attachment's stubs. Available if document has any attachments

- **_conflicts** (*array*) – List of conflicted revisions. Available if requested with `conflicts=true` query parameter

- **_deleted_conflicts** (*array*) – List of deleted conflicted revisions. Available if requested with `deleted_conflicts=true` query parameter

- **_local_seq** (*number*) – Document's sequence number in current database. Available if requested with `local_seq=true` query parameter

- **_revs_info** (*array*) – List of objects with information about local revisions and their status. Available if requested with `open_revs` query parameter

- **_revisions** (*object*) – List of local revision tokens without. Available if requested with `revs=true` query parameter

---

Status Codes

- 200 OK – Request completed successfully

- 304 Not Modified – Document wasn't modified since specified revision

- 400 Bad Request – The format of the request or revision was invalid

- 401 Unauthorized – Read privilege required

- 404 Not Found – Document not found

Request:

```
GET /recipes/SpaghettiWithMeatballs HTTP/1.1
Accept: application/json
Host: localhost:5984
```

Response:

```
HTTP/1.1 200 OK
Cache-Control: must-revalidate
Content-Length: 660
Content-Type: application/json
Date: Tue, 13 Aug 2013 21:35:37 GMT
ETag: "1-917fa2381192822767f010b95b45325b"
Server: CouchDB (Erlang/OTP)

{
    "_id": "SpaghettiWithMeatballs",
    "_rev": "1-917fa2381192822767f010b95b45325b",
    "description": "An Italian-American dish that usually consists of spaghetti, toma
    "ingredients": [
        "spaghetti",
        "tomato sauce",
        "meatballs"
    ],
    "name": "Spaghetti with meatballs"
}
```

PUT /{db}/{docid}

The PUT method creates a new named document, or creates a new revision of the existing document. Unlike the *POST /{db}*, you must specify the document ID in the request URL.

Parameters

- **db** – Database name

- **docid** – Document ID

Request Headers

- Accept –

    - *application/json*

    - *text/plain*

- Content-Type – *application/json*

- If-Match – Document's revision. Alternative to *rev* query parameter

- **X-Couch-Full-Commit** – Overrides server's *commit policy*. Possible values are: false and true. *Optional*

Query Parameters

- **batch** (*string*) – Stores document in *batch mode* Possible values: ok. *Optional*

Response Headers

- Content-Type –
  - *application/json*
  - *text/plain; charset=utf-8*
- ETag – Quoted document's new revision
- Location – Document URI

Response JSON Object

- **id** (*string*) – Document ID
- **ok** (*boolean*) – Operation status
- **rev** (*string*) – Revision MVCC token

Status Codes

- 201 Created – Document created and stored on disk
- 202 Accepted – Document data accepted, but not yet stored on disk
- 400 Bad Request – Invalid request body or parameters
- 401 Unauthorized – Write privileges required
- 404 Not Found – Specified database or document ID doesn't exists
- 409 Conflict – Document with the specified ID already exists or specified revision is not latest for target document

Request:

```
PUT /recipes/SpaghettiWithMeatballs HTTP/1.1
Accept: application/json
Content-Length: 196
Content-Type: application/json
Host: localhost:5984

{
    "description": "An Italian-American dish that usually consists of spaghetti, toma
    "ingredients": [
        "spaghetti",
        "tomato sauce",
        "meatballs"
    ],
    "name": "Spaghetti with meatballs"
}
```

Response:

```
HTTP/1.1 201 Created
Cache-Control: must-revalidate
Content-Length: 85
Content-Type: application/json
Date: Wed, 14 Aug 2013 20:31:39 GMT
ETag: "1-917fa2381192822767f010b95b45325b"
Location: http://localhost:5984/recipes/SpaghettiWithMeatballs
Server: CouchDB (Erlang/OTP)

{
    "id": "SpaghettiWithMeatballs",
    "ok": true,
    "rev": "1-917fa2381192822767f010b95b45325b"
}
```

DELETE /{db}/{docid}

Marks the specified document as deleted by adding a field _deleted with the value true. Documents with this field will not be returned within requests anymore, but stay in the database. You must supply the current (latest) revision, either by using the `rev` parameter or by using the If-Match header to specify the revision.

Note: CouchDB doesn't completely delete the specified document. Instead, it leaves a tombstone with very basic information about the document. The tombstone is required so that the delete action can be replicated across databases.

See also:

Retrieving Deleted Documents

Parameters

- **db** – Database name
- **docid** – Document ID

Request Headers

- Accept –
  - *application/json*
  - *text/plain*
- If-Match – Document's revision. Alternative to *rev* query parameter
- **X-Couch-Full-Commit** – Overrides server's `commit policy`. Possible values are: `false` and `true`. *Optional*

Query Parameters

- **rev** (*string*) – Actual document's revision
- **batch** (*string*) – Stores document in *batch mode* Possible values: ok. *Optional*

Response Headers

- Content-Type –
  - *application/json*
  - *text/plain; charset=utf-8*
- ETag – Double quoted document's new revision

Response JSON Object

- **id** (*string*) – Document ID
- **ok** (*boolean*) – Operation status
- **rev** (*string*) – Revision MVCC token

Status Codes

- 200 OK – Document successfully removed
- 202 Accepted – Request was accepted, but changes are not yet stored on disk
- 400 Bad Request – Invalid request body or parameters
- 401 Unauthorized – Write privileges required
- 404 Not Found – Specified database or document ID doesn't exists
- 409 Conflict – Specified revision is not the latest for target document

Request:

```
DELETE /recipes/FishStew?rev=1-9c65296036141e575d32ba9c034dd3ee HTTP/1.1
Accept: application/json
Host: localhost:5984
```

Alternatively, instead of `rev` query parameter you may use If-Match header:

```
DELETE /recipes/FishStew HTTP/1.1
Accept: application/json
If-Match: 1-9c65296036141e575d32ba9c034dd3ee
Host: localhost:5984
```

Response:

```
HTTP/1.1 200 OK
Cache-Control: must-revalidate
Content-Length: 71
Content-Type: application/json
Date: Wed, 14 Aug 2013 12:23:13 GMT
ETag: "2-056f5f44046ecafc08a2bc2b9c229e20"
Server: CouchDB (Erlang/OTP)

{
    "id": "FishStew",
    "ok": true,
    "rev": "2-056f5f44046ecafc08a2bc2b9c229e20"
}
```

COPY /{db}/{docid}

The COPY (which is non-standard HTTP) copies an existing document to a new or existing document.

The source document is specified on the request line, with the Destination header of the request specifying the target document.

Parameters

- **db** – Database name
- **docid** – Document ID

Request Headers

- Accept –
    - *application/json*
    - *text/plain*
- Destination – Destination document
- If-Match – Source document's revision. Alternative to *rev* query parameter
- **X-Couch-Full-Commit** – Overrides server's `commit policy`. Possible values are: `false` and `true`. *Optional*

Query Parameters

- **rev** (*string*) – Revision to copy from. *Optional*
- **batch** (*string*) – Stores document in *batch mode* Possible values: `ok`. *Optional*

Response Headers

- Content-Type –
    - *application/json*
    - *text/plain; charset=utf-8*
- ETag – Double quoted document's new revision
- Location – Document URI

Response JSON Object

- **id** (*string*) – Document document ID
- **ok** (*boolean*) – Operation status
- **rev** (*string*) – Revision MVCC token

Status Codes

- 201 Created – Document successfully created
- 202 Accepted – Request was accepted, but changes are not yet stored on disk
- 400 Bad Request – Invalid request body or parameters
- 401 Unauthorized – Read or write privileges required
- 404 Not Found – Specified database, document ID or revision doesn't exists
- 409 Conflict – Document with the specified ID already exists or specified revision is not latest for target document

Request:

```
COPY /recipes/SpaghettiWithMeatballs HTTP/1.1
Accept: application/json
Destination: SpaghettiWithMeatballs_Italian
Host: localhost:5984
```

Response:

```
HTTP/1.1 201 Created
Cache-Control: must-revalidate
Content-Length: 93
Content-Type: application/json
Date: Wed, 14 Aug 2013 14:21:00 GMT
ETag: "1-e86fdf912560c2321a5fcefc6264e6d9"
Location: http://localhost:5984/recipes/SpaghettiWithMeatballs_Italian
Server: CouchDB (Erlang/OTP)

{
    "id": "SpaghettiWithMeatballs_Italian",
    "ok": true,
    "rev": "1-e86fdf912560c2321a5fcefc6264e6d9"
}
```

Attachments

If the document includes attachments, then the returned structure will contain a summary of the attachments associated with the document, but not the attachment data itself.

The JSON for the returned document will include the _attachments field, with one or more attachment definitions.

The _attachments object keys are attachments names while values are information objects with next structure:

- **content_type** (*string*): Attachment MIME type
- **data** (*string*): Base64-encoded content. Available if attachment content is requested by using the following query parameters:
  - attachments=true when querying a document
  - attachments=true&include_docs=true when querying a *changes feed* or a *view*
  - atts_since.

- **digest** (*string*): Content hash digest. It starts with prefix which announce hash type (md5-) and continues with Base64-encoded hash digest

- **encoded_length** (*number*): Compressed attachment size in bytes. Available if content_type is in *list of compressible types* when the attachment was added and the following query parameters are specified:

    - att_encoding_info=true when querying a document

    - att_encoding_info=true&include_docs=true when querying a *changes feed* or a *view*

- **encoding** (*string*): Compression codec. Available if content_type is in *list of compressible types* when the attachment was added and the following query parameters are specified:

    - att_encoding_info=true when querying a document

    - att_encoding_info=true&include_docs=true when querying a *changes feed* or a *view*

- **length** (*number*): Real attachment size in bytes. Not available if attachment content requested

- **revpos** (*number*): Revision *number* when attachment was added

- **stub** (*boolean*): Has true value if object contains stub info and no content. Otherwise omitted in response

Basic Attachments Info

Request:

```
GET /recipes/SpaghettiWithMeatballs HTTP/1.1
Accept: application/json
Host: localhost:5984
```

Response:

```
HTTP/1.1 200 OK
Cache-Control: must-revalidate
Content-Length: 660
Content-Type: application/json
Date: Tue, 13 Aug 2013 21:35:37 GMT
ETag: "5-fd96acb3256302bf0dd2f32713161f2a"
Server: CouchDB (Erlang/OTP)

{
    "_attachments": {
        "grandma_recipe.txt": {
            "content_type": "text/plain",
            "digest": "md5-Ids41vtv725jyrN7iUvMcQ==",
            "length": 1872,
            "revpos": 4,
            "stub": true
        },
        "my_recipe.txt": {
            "content_type": "text/plain",
            "digest": "md5-198BPPNiT5fqlLxoYYbjBA==",
            "length": 85,
            "revpos": 5,
            "stub": true
        },
        "photo.jpg": {
            "content_type": "image/jpeg",
            "digest": "md5-7Pv4HW2822WY1r/3WDbPug==",
            "length": 165504,
            "revpos": 2,
            "stub": true
        }
}
```

```
    },
    "_id": "SpaghettiWithMeatballs",
    "_rev": "5-fd96acb3256302bf0dd2f32713161f2a",
    "description": "An Italian-American dish that usually consists of spaghetti, tomato s
    "ingredients": [
        "spaghetti",
        "tomato sauce",
        "meatballs"
    ],
    "name": "Spaghetti with meatballs"
}
```

Retrieving Attachments Content

It's possible to retrieve document with all attached files content by using `attachements=true` query parameter:

Request:

```
GET /db/pixel?attachments=true HTTP/1.1
Accept: application/json
Host: localhost:5984
```

Response:

```
HTTP/1.1 200 OK
Cache-Control: must-revalidate
Content-Length: 553
Content-Type: application/json
Date: Wed, 14 Aug 2013 11:32:40 GMT
ETag: "4-f1bcae4bf7bbb92310079e632abfe3f4"
Server: CouchDB (Erlang/OTP)

{
    "_attachments": {
        "pixel.gif": {
            "content_type": "image/gif",
            "data": "R0lGOD1hAQABAIAAAAAAAP///yH5BAEAAAAALAAAAAABAAEAAAIBRAA7",
            "digest": "md5-2JdGiI2i2VELZKnwMers1Q==",
            "revpos": 2
        },
        "pixel.png": {
            "content_type": "image/png",
            "data": "iVBORw0KGgoAAAANSUhEUgAAAAEAAAABAQMAAAA121bKAAAAXNSR0IArs4c6QAAAANQ
            "digest": "md5-Dgf5zxgGuchWrve73evvGQ==",
            "revpos": 3
        }
    },
    "_id": "pixel",
    "_rev": "4-f1bcae4bf7bbb92310079e632abfe3f4"
}
```

Or retrieve attached files content since specific revision using `atts_since` query parameter:

Request:

```
GET /recipes/SpaghettiWithMeatballs?atts_since=[%224-874985bc28906155ba0e2e0538f67b05%22]
Accept: application/json
Host: localhost:5984
```

Response:

```
HTTP/1.1 200 OK
Cache-Control: must-revalidate
Content-Length: 760
Content-Type: application/json
Date: Tue, 13 Aug 2013 21:35:37 GMT
ETag: "5-fd96acb3256302bf0dd2f32713161f2a"
Server: CouchDB (Erlang/OTP)

{
    "_attachments": {
        "grandma_recipe.txt": {
            "content_type": "text/plain",
            "digest": "md5-Ids41vtv725jyrN7iUvMcQ==",
            "length": 1872,
            "revpos": 4,
            "stub": true
        },
        "my_recipe.txt": {
            "content_type": "text/plain",
            "data": "MS4gQ29vayBzcGFnaGV0dGkKMi4gQ29vayBtZWV0YmFsbHMKMy4gTW14IHRoZW0KNC4g
            "digest": "md5-198BPPNiT5fqlLxoYYbjBA==",
            "revpos": 5
        },
        "photo.jpg": {
            "content_type": "image/jpeg",
            "digest": "md5-7Pv4HW2822WY1r/3WDbPug==",
            "length": 165504,
            "revpos": 2,
            "stub": true
        }
    },
    "_id": "SpaghettiWithMeatballs",
    "_rev": "5-fd96acb3256302bf0dd2f32713161f2a",
    "description": "An Italian-American dish that usually consists of spaghetti, tomato s
    "ingredients": [
        "spaghetti",
        "tomato sauce",
        "meatballs"
    ],
    "name": "Spaghetti with meatballs"
}
```

Efficient Multiple Attachments Retrieving As you had noted above, retrieving document with `attachements=true` returns large JSON object where all attachments are included. While you document and files are smaller it's ok, but if you have attached something bigger like media files (audio/video), parsing such response might be very expensive.

To solve this problem, CouchDB allows to get documents in *multipart/related* format:

Request:

```
GET /recipes/secret?attachments=true HTTP/1.1
Accept: multipart/related
Host: localhost:5984
```

Response:

```
HTTP/1.1 200 OK
Content-Length: 538
Content-Type: multipart/related; boundary="e89b3e29388aef23453450d10e5aaed0"
Date: Sat, 28 Sep 2013 08:08:22 GMT
ETag: "2-c1c6c44c4bc3c9344b037c8690468605"
Server: CouchDB (Erlang OTP)
```

```
--e89b3e29388aef23453450d10e5aaed0
Content-Type: application/json

{"_id":"secret","_rev":"2-c1c6c44c4bc3c9344b037c8690468605","_attachments":{"recipe.txt":
--e89b3e29388aef23453450d10e5aaed0
Content-Disposition: attachment; filename="recipe.txt"
Content-Type: text/plain
Content-Length: 86

1. Take R
2. Take E
3. Mix with L
4. Add some A
5. Serve with X

--e89b3e29388aef23453450d10e5aaed0--
```

In this response the document contains only attachments stub information and quite short while all attachments goes as separate entities which reduces memory footprint and processing overhead (you'd noticed, that attachment content goes as raw data, not in base64 encoding, right?).

Retrieving Attachments Encoding Info

By using `att_encoding_info=true` query parameter you may retrieve information about compressed attachments size and used codec.

Request:

```
GET /recipes/SpaghettiWithMeatballs?att_encoding_info=true HTTP/1.1
Accept: application/json
Host: localhost:5984
```

Response:

```
HTTP/1.1 200 OK
Cache-Control: must-revalidate
Content-Length: 736
Content-Type: application/json
Date: Tue, 13 Aug 2013 21:35:37 GMT
ETag: "5-fd96acb3256302bf0dd2f32713161f2a"
Server: CouchDB (Erlang/OTP)

{
    "_attachments": {
        "grandma_recipe.txt": {
            "content_type": "text/plain",
            "digest": "md5-Ids41vtv725jyrN7iUvMcQ==",
            "encoded_length": 693,
            "encoding": "gzip",
            "length": 1872,
            "revpos": 4,
            "stub": true
        },
        "my_recipe.txt": {
            "content_type": "text/plain",
            "digest": "md5-198BPPNiT5fqlLxoYYbjBA==",
            "encoded_length": 100,
            "encoding": "gzip",
            "length": 85,
            "revpos": 5,
            "stub": true
        },
```

```
        "photo.jpg": {
            "content_type": "image/jpeg",
            "digest": "md5-7Pv4HW2822WY1r/3WDbPug==",
            "length": 165504,
            "revpos": 2,
            "stub": true
        }
    },
    "_id": "SpaghettiWithMeatballs",
    "_rev": "5-fd96acb3256302bf0dd2f32713161f2a",
    "description": "An Italian-American dish that usually consists of spaghetti, tomato s
    "ingredients": [
        "spaghetti",
        "tomato sauce",
        "meatballs"
    ],
    "name": "Spaghetti with meatballs"
}
```

Creating Multiple Attachments

To create a document with multiple attachments with single request you need just inline base64 encoded attachments data into the document body:

```
{
  "_id":"multiple_attachments",
  "_attachments":
  {
    "foo.txt":
    {
      "content_type":"text\/plain",
      "data": "VGhpcyBpcyBhIGJhc2U2NCBlbmNvZGVkIHRleHQ="
    },

    "bar.txt":
    {
      "content_type":"text\/plain",
      "data": "VGhpcyBpcyBhIGJhc2U2NCBlbmNvZGVkIHRleHQ="
    }
  }
}
```

Alternatively, you can upload a document with attachments more efficiently in *multipart/related* format. This avoids having to Base64-encode the attachments, saving CPU and bandwidth. To do this, set the Content-Type header of the *PUT /{db}/{docid}* request to *multipart/related*.

The first MIME body is the document itself, which should have its own Content-Type of *application/json"*. It also should include an _attachments metadata object in which each attachment object has a key follows with value true.

The subsequent MIME bodies are the attachments.

Request:

```
PUT /temp/somedoc HTTP/1.1
Accept: application/json
Content-Length: 372
Content-Type: multipart/related;boundary="abc123"
Host: localhost:5984
User-Agent: HTTPie/0.6.0

--abc123
```

```
Content-Type: application/json

{
    "body": "This is a body.",
    "_attachments": {
        "foo.txt": {
            "follows": true,
            "content_type": "text/plain",
            "length": 21
        },
        "bar.txt": {
            "follows": true,
            "content_type": "text/plain",
            "length": 20
        }
    }
}

--abc123

this is 21 chars long
--abc123

this is 20 chars lon
--abc123--
```

Response:

```
HTTP/1.1 201 Created
Cache-Control: must-revalidate
Content-Length: 72
Content-Type: application/json
Date: Sat, 28 Sep 2013 09:13:24 GMT
ETag: "1-5575e26acdeb1df561bb5b70b26ba151"
Location: http://localhost:5984/temp/somedoc
Server: CouchDB (Erlang OTP)

{
    "id": "somedoc",
    "ok": true,
    "rev": "1-5575e26acdeb1df561bb5b70b26ba151"
}
```

Getting a List of Revisions

You can obtain a list of the revisions for a given document by adding the `revs=true` parameter to the request URL:

Request:

```
GET /recipes/SpaghettiWithMeatballs?revs=true  HTTP/1.1
Accept: application/json
Host: localhost:5984
```

Response:

```
HTTP/1.1 200 OK
Cache-Control: must-revalidate
Content-Length: 584
Content-Type: application/json
Date: Wed, 14 Aug 2013 11:38:26 GMT
ETag: "5-fd96acb3256302bf0dd2f32713161f2a"
Server: CouchDB (Erlang/OTP)
```

```
{
    "_id": "SpaghettiWithMeatballs",
    "_rev": "8-6f5ad8db0f34af24a6e0984cd1a6cfb9",
    "_revisions": {
        "ids": [
            "6f5ad8db0f34af24a6e0984cd1a6cfb9",
            "77fba3a059497f51ec99b9b478b569d2",
            "136813b440a00a24834f5cb1ddf5b1f1",
            "fd96acb3256302bf0dd2f32713161f2a",
            "874985bc28906155ba0e2e0538f67b05",
            "0de77a37463bf391d14283e626831f2e",
            "d795d1b924777732fdea76538c558b62",
            "917fa2381192822767f010b95b45325b"
        ],
        "start": 8
    },
    "description": "An Italian-American dish that usually consists of spaghetti, tomato s
    "ingredients": [
        "spaghetti",
        "tomato sauce",
        "meatballs"
    ],
    "name": "Spaghetti with meatballs"
}
```

The returned JSON structure includes the original document, including a _revisions structure that includes the revision information in next form:

- **ids** (*array*): Array of valid revision IDs, in reverse order (latest first)
- **start** (*number*): Prefix number for the latest revision

Obtaining an Extended Revision History

You can get additional information about the revisions for a given document by supplying the revs_info argument to the query:

Request:

```
GET /recipes/SpaghettiWithMeatballs?revs_info=true  HTTP/1.1
Accept: application/json
Host: localhost:5984
```

Response:

```
HTTP/1.1 200 OK
Cache-Control: must-revalidate
Content-Length: 802
Content-Type: application/json
Date: Wed, 14 Aug 2013 11:40:55 GMT
Server: CouchDB (Erlang/OTP)

{
    "_id": "SpaghettiWithMeatballs",
    "_rev": "8-6f5ad8db0f34af24a6e0984cd1a6cfb9",
    "_revs_info": [
        {
            "rev": "8-6f5ad8db0f34af24a6e0984cd1a6cfb9",
            "status": "available"
        },
        {
            "rev": "7-77fba3a059497f51ec99b9b478b569d2",
            "status": "deleted"
```

```
        },
        {
            "rev": "6-136813b440a00a24834f5cb1ddf5b1f1",
            "status": "available"
        },
        {
            "rev": "5-fd96acb3256302bf0dd2f32713161f2a",
            "status": "missing"
        },
        {
            "rev": "4-874985bc28906155ba0e2e0538f67b05",
            "status": "missing"
        },
        {
            "rev": "3-0de77a37463bf391d14283e626831f2e",
            "status": "missing"
        },
        {
            "rev": "2-d795d1b924777732fdea76538c558b62",
            "status": "missing"
        },
        {
            "rev": "1-917fa2381192822767f010b95b45325b",
            "status": "missing"
        }
    ],
    "description": "An Italian-American dish that usually consists of spaghetti, tomato s
    "ingredients": [
        "spaghetti",
        "tomato sauce",
        "meatballs"
    ],
    "name": "Spaghetti with meatballs"
}
```

The returned document contains _revs_info field with extended revision information, including the availability and status of each revision. This array field contains objects with following structure:

- **rev** (*string*): Full revision string

- **status** (*string*): Status of the revision. Maybe one of:

  - available: Revision is available for retrieving with *rev* query parameter

  - missing: Revision is not available

  - deleted: Revision belongs to deleted document

Obtaining a Specific Revision

To get a specific revision, use the rev argument to the request, and specify the full revision number. The specified revision of the document will be returned, including a _rev field specifying the revision that was requested.

Request:

```
GET /recipes/SpaghettiWithMeatballs?rev=6-136813b440a00a24834f5cb1ddf5b1f1  HTTP/1.1
Accept: application/json
Host: localhost:5984
```

Response:

```
HTTP/1.1 200 OK
Cache-Control: must-revalidate
Content-Length: 271
```

```
Content-Type: application/json
Date: Wed, 14 Aug 2013 11:40:55 GMT
Server: CouchDB (Erlang/OTP)

{
    "_id": "SpaghettiWithMeatballs",
    "_rev": "6-136813b440a00a24834f5cb1ddf5b1f1",
    "description": "An Italian-American dish that usually consists of spaghetti, tomato s
    "ingredients": [
        "spaghetti",
        "tomato sauce",
        "meatballs"
    ],
    "name": "Spaghetti with meatballs"
}
```

Retrieving Deleted Documents

CouchDB doesn't actually deletes documents via *DELETE /{db}/{docid}*. Instead of this, it leaves tombstone with very basic information about document. If you just *GET /{db}/{docid}* CouchDB returns 404 Not Found response:

Request:

```
GET /recipes/FishStew  HTTP/1.1
Accept: application/json
Host: localhost:5984
```

Response:

```
HTTP/1.1 404 Object Not Found
Cache-Control: must-revalidate
Content-Length: 41
Content-Type: application/json
Date: Wed, 14 Aug 2013 12:23:27 GMT
Server: CouchDB (Erlang/OTP)

{
    "error": "not_found",
    "reason": "deleted"
}
```

However, you may retrieve document's tombstone by using `rev` query parameter with *GET /{db}/{docid}* request:

Request:

```
GET /recipes/FishStew?rev=2-056f5f44046ecafc08a2bc2b9c229e20  HTTP/1.1
Accept: application/json
Host: localhost:5984
```

Response:

```
HTTP/1.1 200 OK
Cache-Control: must-revalidate
Content-Length: 79
Content-Type: application/json
Date: Wed, 14 Aug 2013 12:30:22 GMT
ETag: "2-056f5f44046ecafc08a2bc2b9c229e20"
Server: CouchDB (Erlang/OTP)

{
    "_deleted": true,
```

```
    "_id": "FishStew",
    "_rev": "2-056f5f44046ecafc08a2bc2b9c229e20"
}
```

Updating an Existing Document

To update an existing document you must specify the current revision number within the `_rev` parameter.

Request:

```
PUT /recipes/SpaghettiWithMeatballs HTTP/1.1
Accept: application/json
Content-Length: 258
Content-Type: application/json
Host: localhost:5984

{
    "_rev": "1-917fa2381192822767f010b95b45325b",
    "description": "An Italian-American dish that usually consists of spaghetti, tomato s
    "ingredients": [
        "spaghetti",
        "tomato sauce",
        "meatballs"
    ],
    "name": "Spaghetti with meatballs",
    "serving": "hot"
}
```

Alternatively, you can supply the current revision number in the `If-Match` HTTP header of the request:

```
PUT /recipes/SpaghettiWithMeatballs HTTP/1.1
Accept: application/json
Content-Length: 258
Content-Type: application/json
If-Match: 1-917fa2381192822767f010b95b45325b
Host: localhost:5984

{
    "description": "An Italian-American dish that usually consists of spaghetti, tomato s
    "ingredients": [
        "spaghetti",
        "tomato sauce",
        "meatballs"
    ],
    "name": "Spaghetti with meatballs",
    "serving": "hot"
}
```

Response:

```
HTTP/1.1 201 Created
Cache-Control: must-revalidate
Content-Length: 85
Content-Type: application/json
Date: Wed, 14 Aug 2013 20:33:56 GMT
ETag: "2-790895a73b63fb91dd863388398483dd"
Location: http://localhost:5984/recipes/SpaghettiWithMeatballs
Server: CouchDB (Erlang/OTP)

{
    "id": "SpaghettiWithMeatballs",
    "ok": true,
```

```
    "rev": "2-790895a73b63fb91dd863388398483dd"
}
```

Copying from a Specific Revision

To copy *from* a specific version, use the `rev` argument to the query string or If-Match:

Request:

```
COPY /recipes/SpaghettiWithMeatballs HTTP/1.1
Accept: application/json
Destination: http://localhost:5984/recipes_old/SpaghettiWithMeatballs_Original
If-Match: 1-917fa2381192822767f010b95b45325b
Host: localhost:5984
```

Response:

```
HTTP/1.1 201 Created
Cache-Control: must-revalidate
Content-Length: 93
Content-Type: application/json
Date: Wed, 14 Aug 2013 14:21:00 GMT
ETag: "1-917fa2381192822767f010b95b45325b"
Location: http://localhost:5984/recipes_old/SpaghettiWithMeatballs_Original
Server: CouchDB (Erlang/OTP)


{
    "id": "SpaghettiWithMeatballs_Original",
    "ok": true,
    "rev": "1-917fa2381192822767f010b95b45325b"
}
```

Copying to an Existing Document

To copy to an existing document, you must specify the current revision string for the target document by appending the `rev` parameter to the Destination header string.

Request:

```
COPY /recipes/SpaghettiWithMeatballs?rev=8-6f5ad8db0f34af24a6e0984cd1a6cfb9 HTTP/1.1
Accept: application/json
Destination: http://localhost:5984/recipes_old/SpaghettiWithMeatballs_Original?rev=1-917f
Host: localhost:5984
```

Response:

```
HTTP/1.1 201 Created
Cache-Control: must-revalidate
Content-Length: 93
Content-Type: application/json
Date: Wed, 14 Aug 2013 14:21:00 GMT
ETag: "2-62e778c9ec09214dd685a981dcc24074""
Location: http://localhost:5984/recipes_old/SpaghettiWithMeatballs_Original
Server: CouchDB (Erlang/OTP)


{
    "id": "SpaghettiWithMeatballs_Original",
    "ok": true,
    "rev": "2-62e778c9ec09214dd685a981dcc24074"
}
```

10.4.2 /db/doc/attachment

HEAD /{db}/{docid}/{attname}

Returns the HTTP headers containing a minimal amount of information about the specified attachment. The method supports the same query arguments as the `GET /{db}/{docid}/{attname}` method, but only the header information (including attachment size, encoding and the MD5 hash as an ETag), is returned.

> **Parameters**
>
> > - **db** – Database name
> > - **docid** – Document ID
> > - **attname** – Attachment name
>
> **Request Headers**
>
> > - If-Match – Document's revision. Alternative to *rev* query parameter
> > - If-None-Match – Attachment's base64 encoded MD5 binary digest. *Optional*
>
> **Query Parameters**
>
> > - **rev** (*string*) – Document's revision. *Optional*
>
> **Response Headers**
>
> > - Accept-Ranges – *Range request aware.* Used for attachments with `application/octet-stream` content type
> > - Content-Encoding – Used compression codec. Available if attachment's `content_type` is in *list of compressible types*
> > - Content-Length – Attachment size. If compression codec was used, this value is about compressed size, not actual
> > - Content-MD5 – Base64 encoded MD5 binary digest
> > - ETag – Double quoted base64 encoded MD5 binary digest
>
> **Status Codes**
>
> > - 200 OK – Attachment exists
> > - 304 Not Modified – Attachment wasn't modified if ETag equals specified If-None-Match header
> > - 401 Unauthorized – Read privilege required
> > - 404 Not Found – Specified database, document or attachment was not found

> **Request**:

```
HEAD /recipes/SpaghettiWithMeatballs/recipe.txt HTTP/1.1
Host: localhost:5984
```

> **Response**:

```
HTTP/1.1 200 OK
Accept-Ranges: none
Cache-Control: must-revalidate
Content-Encoding: gzip
Content-Length: 100
Content-MD5: vVa/YgiE1+Gh0WfoFJAcSg==
Content-Type: text/plain
Date: Thu, 15 Aug 2013 12:42:42 GMT
ETag: "vVa/YgiE1+Gh0WfoFJAcSg=="
Server: CouchDB (Erlang/OTP)
```

`GET /{db}/{docid}/{attname}`

Returns the file attachment associated with the document. The raw data of the associated attachment is returned (just as if you were accessing a static file. The returned Content-Type will be the same as the content type set when the document attachment was submitted into the database.

Parameters

- **db** – Database name

- **docid** – Document ID

- **attname** – Attachment name

Request Headers

- If-Match – Document's revision. Alternative to *rev* query parameter

- If-None-Match – Attachment's base64 encoded MD5 binary digest. *Optional*

Query Parameters

- **rev** (*string*) – Document's revision. *Optional*

Response Headers

- Accept-Ranges – *Range request aware.* Used for attachments with `application/octet-stream`

- Content-Encoding – Used compression codec. Available if attachment's `content_type` is in *list of compressiable types*

- Content-Length – Attachment size. If compression codec is used, this value is about compressed size, not actual

- Content-MD5 – Base64 encoded MD5 binary digest

- ETag – Double quoted base64 encoded MD5 binary digest

Response Stored content

Status Codes

- 200 OK – Attachment exists

- 304 Not Modified – Attachment wasn't modified if ETag equals specified If-None-Match header

- 401 Unauthorized – Read privilege required

- 404 Not Found – Specified database, document or attachment was not found

`PUT /{db}/{docid}/{attname}`

Uploads the supplied content as an attachment to the specified document. The attachment name provided must be a URL encoded string. You must also supply either the `rev` query argument or the If-Match HTTP header for validation, and the HTTP headers (to set the attachment content type).

If case when uploading an attachment using an existing attachment name, CouchDB will update the corresponding stored content of the database. Since you must supply the revision information to add an attachment to the document, this serves as validation to update the existing attachment.

Note: Uploading an attachment updates the corresponding document revision. Revisions are tracked for the parent document, not individual attachments.

Parameters

- **db** – Database name

- **docid** – Document ID

- **attname** – Attachment name

Request Headers

- Content-Type – Attachment MIME type. *Required*
- If-Match – Document revision. Alternative to *rev* query parameter

Query Parameters

- **rev** (*string*) – Document revision. *Required*

Response Headers

- Accept-Ranges – *Range request aware.* Used for attachments with `application/octet-stream`

- Content-Encoding – Used compression codec. Available if attachment's `content_type` is in *list of compressible types*

- Content-Length – Attachment size. If compression codec is used, this value is about compressed size, not actual

- Content-MD5 – Base64 encoded MD5 binary digest

- ETag – Double quoted base64 encoded MD5 binary digest

Response JSON Object

- **id** (*string*) – Document ID

- **ok** (*boolean*) – Operation status

- **rev** (*string*) – Revision MVCC token

Status Codes

- 200 OK – Attachment successfully removed

- 202 Accepted – Request was accepted, but changes are not yet stored on disk

- 400 Bad Request – Invalid request body or parameters

- 401 Unauthorized – Write privileges required

- 404 Not Found – Specified database, document or attachment was not found

- 409 Conflict – Document's revision wasn't specified or it's not the latest

Request:

```
PUT /recipes/SpaghettiWithMeatballs/recipe.txt HTTP/1.1
Accept: application/json
Content-Length: 86
Content-Type: text/plain
Host: localhost:5984
If-Match: 1-917fa2381192822767f010b95b45325b

1. Cook spaghetti
2. Cook meatballs
3. Mix them
4. Add tomato sauce
5. ...
6. PROFIT!
```

Response:

```
HTTP/1.1 201 Created
Cache-Control: must-revalidate
Content-Length: 85
Content-Type: application/json
Date: Thu, 15 Aug 2013 12:38:04 GMT
ETag: "2-ce91aed0129be8f9b0f650a2edcfd0a4"
```

```
Location: http://localhost:5984/recipes/SpaghettiWithMeatballs/recipe.txt
Server: CouchDB (Erlang/OTP)

{
    "id": "SpaghettiWithMeatballs",
    "ok": true,
    "rev": "2-ce91aed0129be8f9b0f650a2edcfd0a4"
}
```

DELETE /{db}/{docid}/{attname}

Deletes the attachment `attachment` of the specified `doc`. You must supply the `rev` query parameter or If-Match with the current revision to delete the attachment.

Note: Deleting an attachment updates the corresponding document revision. Revisions are tracked for the parent document, not individual attachments.

Parameters

- **db** – Database name
- **docid** – Document ID

Request Headers

- Accept –
  - *application/json*
  - *text/plain*
- If-Match – Document revision. Alternative to *rev* query parameter
- **X-Couch-Full-Commit** – Overrides server's *commit policy*. Possible values are: `false` and `true`. *Optional*

Query Parameters

- **rev** (*string*) – Document revision. *Required*
- **batch** (*string*) – Store changes in *batch mode* Possible values: `ok`. *Optional*

Response Headers

- Content-Type –
  - *application/json*
  - *text/plain; charset=utf-8*
- ETag – Double quoted document's new revision

Response JSON Object

- **id** (*string*) – Document ID
- **ok** (*boolean*) – Operation status
- **rev** (*string*) – Revision MVCC token

Status Codes

- 200 OK – Attachment successfully removed
- 202 Accepted – Request was accepted, but changes are not yet stored on disk
- 400 Bad Request – Invalid request body or parameters
- 401 Unauthorized – Write privileges required
- 404 Not Found – Specified database, document or attachment was not found

---

• 409 Conflict – Document's revision wasn't specified or it's not the latest

Request:

```
DELETE /recipes/SpaghettiWithMeatballs?rev=6-440b2dd39c20413045748b42c6aba6e2 HTTP/1.
Accept: application/json
Host: localhost:5984
```

Alternatively, instead of rev query parameter you may use If-Match header:

```
DELETE /recipes/SpaghettiWithMeatballs HTTP/1.1
Accept: application/json
If-Match: 6-440b2dd39c20413045748b42c6aba6e2
Host: localhost:5984
```

Response:

```
HTTP/1.1 200 OK
Cache-Control: must-revalidate
Content-Length: 85
Content-Type: application/json
Date: Wed, 14 Aug 2013 12:23:13 GMT
ETag: "7-05185cf5fcdf4b6da360af939431d466"
Server: CouchDB (Erlang/OTP)

{
    "id": "SpaghettiWithMeatballs",
    "ok": true,
    "rev": "7-05185cf5fcdf4b6da360af939431d466"
}
```

HTTP Range Requests

HTTP allows you to specify byte ranges for requests. This allows the implementation of resumable downloads and skippable audio and video streams alike. This is available for all attachments inside CouchDB.

This is just a real quick run through how this looks under the hood. Usually, you will have larger binary files to serve from CouchDB, like MP3s and videos, but to make things a little more obvious, I use a text file here (Note that I use the *application/octet-stream* :header'Content-Type' instead of *text/plain*).

```
shell> cat file.txt
My hovercraft is full of eels!
```

Now let's store this text file as an attachment in CouchDB. First, we create a database:

```
shell> curl -X PUT http://127.0.0.1:5984/test
{"ok":true}
```

Then we create a new document and the file attachment in one go:

```
shell> curl -X PUT http://127.0.0.1:5984/test/doc/file.txt \
          -H "Content-Type: application/octet-stream" -d@file.txt
{"ok":true,"id":"doc","rev":"1-287a28fa680ae0c7fb4729bf0c6e0cf2"}
```

Now we can request the whole file easily:

```
shell> curl -X GET http://127.0.0.1:5984/test/doc/file.txt
My hovercraft is full of eels!
```

But say we only want the first 13 bytes:

```
shell> curl -X GET http://127.0.0.1:5984/test/doc/file.txt \
          -H "Range: bytes=0-12"
My hovercraft
```

HTTP supports many ways to specify single and even multiple byte ranges. Read all about it in RFC 2616#section-14.27.

Note: Databases that have been created with CouchDB 1.0.2 or earlier will support range requests in 2.0.0, but they are using a less-optimal algorithm. If you plan to make heavy use of this feature, make sure to compact your database with CouchDB 2.0.0 to take advantage of a better algorithm to find byte ranges.

10.5 Design Documents

In CouchDB, design documents provide the main interface for building a CouchDB application. The design document defines the views used to extract information from CouchDB through one or more views. Design documents are created within your CouchDB instance in the same way as you create database documents, but the content and definition of the documents is different. Design Documents are named using an ID defined with the design document URL path, and this URL can then be used to access the database contents.

Views and lists operate together to provide automated (and formatted) output from your database.

10.5.1 `/db/_design/design-doc`

HEAD `/{db}/_design/{ddoc}`

Returns the HTTP Headers containing a minimal amount of information about the specified design document.

See also:

HEAD /{db}/{docid}

GET `/{db}/_design/{ddoc}`

Returns the contents of the design document specified with the name of the design document and from the specified database from the URL. Unless you request a specific revision, the latest revision of the document will always be returned.

See also:

GET /{db}/{docid}

PUT `/{db}/_design/{ddoc}`

The PUT method creates a new named design document, or creates a new revision of the existing design document.

The design documents have some agreement upon their fields and structure. Currently it is the following:

- **language** (*string*): Defines *Query Server key* to process design document functions

- **options** (*object*): View's default options

- **filters** (*object*): *Filter functions* definition

- **lists** (*object*): *List functions* definition

- **rewrites** (*array*): Rewrite rules definition

- **shows** (*object*): *Show functions* definition

- **updates** (*object*): *Update functions* definition

- **validate_doc_update** (*string*): *Validate document update* function source

- **views** (*object*): *View functions* definition.

Note, that for `filters`, `lists`, `shows` and `updates` fields objects are mapping of function name to string function source code. For `views` mapping is the same except that values are objects with `map` and `reduce` (optional) keys which also contains functions source code.

See also:

PUT /{db}/{docid}

DELETE /{db}/_design/{ddoc}
Deletes the specified document from the database. You must supply the current (latest) revision, either by using the `rev` parameter to specify the revision.

See also:

DELETE /{db}/{docid}

COPY /{db}/_design/{ddoc}
The COPY (which is non-standard HTTP) copies an existing design document to a new or existing one.

Note: Copying a design document does automatically reconstruct the view indexes. These will be recreated, as with other views, the first time the new view is accessed.

See also:

COPY /{db}/{docid}

10.5.2 /db/_design/design-doc/attachment

HEAD /{db}/_design/{ddoc}/{attname}
Returns the HTTP headers containing a minimal amount of information about the specified attachment.

See also:

HEAD /{db}/{docid}/{attname}

GET /{db}/_design/{ddoc}/{attname}
Returns the file attachment associated with the design document. The raw data of the associated attachment is returned (just as if you were accessing a static file.

See also:

GET /{db}/{docid}/{attname}

PUT /{db}/_design/{ddoc}/{attname}
Uploads the supplied content as an attachment to the specified design document. The attachment name provided must be a URL encoded string.

See also:

PUT /{db}/{docid}/{attname}

DELETE /{db}/_design/{ddoc}/{attname}
Deletes the attachment of the specified design document.

See also:

DELETE /{db}/{docid}/{attname}

10.5.3 /db/_design/design-doc/_info

GET /{db}/_design/{ddoc}/_info
Obtains information about the specified design document, including the index, index size and current status of the design document and associated index information.

Parameters

- **db** – Database name
- **ddoc** – Design document name

Request Headers

- Accept –
    - *application/json*
    - *text/plain*

Response Headers

- Content-Type –
    - *application/json*
    - *text/plain; charset=utf-8*

Response JSON Object

- **name** (*string*) – Design document name
- **view_index** (*object*) – *View Index Information*

Status Codes

- 200 OK – Request completed successfully

Request:

```
GET /recipes/_design/recipe/_info HTTP/1.1
Accept: application/json
Host: localhost:5984
```

Response:

```
HTTP/1.1 200 OK
Cache-Control: must-revalidate
Content-Length: 263
Content-Type: application/json
Date: Sat, 17 Aug 2013 12:54:17 GMT
Server: CouchDB (Erlang/OTP)

{
    "name": "recipe",
    "view_index": {
        "compact_running": false,
        "data_size": 926691,
        "disk_size": 1982704,
        "language": "python",
        "purge_seq": 0,
        "signature": "a59a1bb13fdf8a8a584bc477919c97ac",
        "update_seq": 12397,
        "updater_running": false,
        "waiting_clients": 0,
        "waiting_commit": false
    }
}
```

View Index Information

The response from *GET /{db}/_design/{ddoc}/_info* contains view_index (*object*) field with the next structure:

- **compact_running** (*boolean*): Indicates whether a compaction routine is currently running on the view
- **data_size** (*number*): Actual size in bytes of the view
- **disk_size** (*number*): Size in bytes of the view as stored on disk
- **language** (*string*): Language for the defined views
- **purge_seq** (*number*): The purge sequence that has been processed

- **signature** (*string*): MD5 signature of the views for the design document

- **update_seq** (*number*): The update sequence of the corresponding database that has been indexed

- **updater_running** (*boolean*): Indicates if the view is currently being updated

- **waiting_clients** (*number*): Number of clients waiting on views from this design document

- **waiting_commit** (*boolean*): Indicates if there are outstanding commits to the underlying database that need to processed

10.5.4 /db/_design/design-doc/_view/view-name

GET /{db}/_design/{ddoc}/_view/{view}
Executes the specified view function from the specified design document.

Parameters

- **db** – Database name
- **ddoc** – Design document name
- **view** – View function name

Request Headers

- Accept –

  - *application/json*

  - *text/plain*

Query Parameters

- **conflicts** (*boolean*) – Includes *conflicts* information in response. Ignored if *include_docs* isn't `true`. Default is `false`

- **descending** (*boolean*) – Return the documents in descending by key order. Default is `false`

- **endkey** (*json*) – Stop returning records when the specified key is reached. *Optional*

- **end_key** (*json*) – Alias for *endkey* param

- **endkey_docid** (*string*) – Stop returning records when the specified document ID is reached. Requires `endkey` to be specified for this to have any effect. *Optional*

- **end_key_doc_id** (*string*) – Alias for *endkey_docid* param

- **group** (*boolean*) – Group the results using the reduce function to a group or single row. Default is `false`

- **group_level** (*number*) – Specify the group level to be used. *Optional*

- **include_docs** (*boolean*) – Include the associated document with each row. Default is `false`.

- **attachments** (*boolean*) – Include the Base64-encoded content of *attachments* in the documents that are included if *include_docs* is `true`. Ignored if *include_docs* isn't `true`. Default is `false`.

- **att_encoding_info** (*boolean*) – Include encoding information in attachment stubs if *include_docs* is `true` and the particular attachment is compressed. Ignored if *include_docs* isn't `true`. Default is `false`.

- **inclusive_end** (*boolean*) – Specifies whether the specified end key should be included in the result. Default is `true`

- **key** (*json*) – Return only documents that match the specified key. *Optional*

- **keys** (*json-array*) – Return only documents where the key matches one of the keys specified in the array. *Optional*

- **limit** (*number*) – Limit the number of the returned documents to the specified number. *Optional*

- **reduce** (*boolean*) – Use the reduction function. Default is `true`

- **skip** (*number*) – Skip this number of records before starting to return the results. Default is `0`

- **stale** (*string*) – Allow the results from a stale view to be used. Supported values: `ok` and `update_after`. *Optional*

- **startkey** (*json*) – Return records starting with the specified key. *Optional*

- **start_key** (*json*) – Alias for *startkey* param

- **startkey_docid** (*string*) – Return records starting with the specified document ID. Requires `startkey` to be specified for this to have any effect. *Optional*

- **start_key_doc_id** (*string*) – Alias for *startkey_docid* param

- **update_seq** (*boolean*) – Response includes an `update_seq` value indicating which sequence id of the database the view reflects. Default is `false`

Response Headers

- Content-Type –
  - *application/json*
  - *text/plain; charset=utf-8*
- ETag – Response signature
- Transfer-Encoding – `chunked`

Response JSON Object

- **offset** (*number*) – Offset where the document list started

- **rows** (*array*) – Array of view row objects. By default the information returned contains only the document ID and revision

- **total_rows** (*number*) – Number of documents in the database/view

- **update_seq** (*number*) – Current update sequence for the database

Status Codes

- 200 OK – Request completed successfully
- 400 Bad Request – Invalid request
- 401 Unauthorized – Read permission required
- 404 Not Found – Specified database, design document or view is missed
- 500 Internal Server Error – View function execution error

Request:

```
GET /recipes/_design/ingredients/_view/by_name HTTP/1.1
Accept: application/json
Host: localhost:5984
```

Response:

```
HTTP/1.1 200 OK
Cache-Control: must-revalidate
Content-Type: application/json
Date: Wed, 21 Aug 2013 09:12:06 GMT
```

```
ETag: "2FOLSBSW4O6WB798XU4AQYA9B"
Server: CouchDB (Erlang/OTP)
Transfer-Encoding: chunked

{
    "offset": 0,
    "rows": [
        {
            "id": "SpaghettiWithMeatballs",
            "key": "meatballs",
            "value": 1
        },
        {
            "id": "SpaghettiWithMeatballs",
            "key": "spaghetti",
            "value": 1
        },
        {
            "id": "SpaghettiWithMeatballs",
            "key": "tomato sauce",
            "value": 1
        }
    ],
    "total_rows": 3
}
```

Changed in version 1.6.0: added `attachments` and `att_encoding_info` parameters

> **Warning:** Using the `attachments` parameter to include attachments in view results is not recommended for large attachment sizes. Also note that the Base64-encoding that is used leads to a 33% overhead (i.e. one third) in transfer size for attachments.

POST /{db}/_design/{ddoc}/_view/{view}
> Executes the specified view function from the specified design document. Unlike *GET /{db}/_design/{ddoc}/_view/{view}* for accessing views, the POST method supports the specification of explicit keys to be retrieved from the view results. The remainder of the POST view functionality is identical to the *GET /{db}/_design/{ddoc}/_view/{view}* API.

Request:

```
POST /recipes/_design/ingredients/_view/by_name HTTP/1.1
Accept: application/json
Content-Length: 37
Host: localhost:5984

{
    "keys": [
        "meatballs",
        "spaghetti"
    ]
}
```

Response:

```
HTTP/1.1 200 OK
Cache-Control: must-revalidate
Content-Type: application/json
Date: Wed, 21 Aug 2013 09:14:13 GMT
ETag: "6R5NM8E872JIJF796VF7WI3FZ"
Server: CouchDB (Erlang/OTP)
Transfer-Encoding: chunked

{
```

```
        "offset": 0,
        "rows": [
            {
                "id": "SpaghettiWithMeatballs",
                "key": "meatballs",
                "value": 1
            },
            {
                "id": "SpaghettiWithMeatballs",
                "key": "spaghetti",
                "value": 1
            }
        ],
        "total_rows": 3
    }
```

View Options

There are two view indexing options that can be defined in a design document as boolean properties of an `options` object. Unlike the others querying options, these aren't URL parameters because they take effect when the view index is generated, not when it's accessed:

- **local_seq** (*boolean*): Makes documents' local sequence numbers available to map functions (as a `_local_seq` document property)

- **include_design** (*boolean*): Allows map functions to be called on design documents as well as regular documents

Querying Views and Indexes

The definition of a view within a design document also creates an index based on the key information defined within each view. The production and use of the index significantly increases the speed of access and searching or selecting documents from the view.

However, the index is not updated when new documents are added or modified in the database. Instead, the index is generated or updated, either when the view is first accessed, or when the view is accessed after a document has been updated. In each case, the index is updated before the view query is executed against the database.

View indexes are updated incrementally in the following situations:

- A new document has been added to the database.

- A document has been deleted from the database.

- A document in the database has been updated.

View indexes are rebuilt entirely when the view definition changes. To achieve this, a 'fingerprint' of the view definition is created when the design document is updated. If the fingerprint changes, then the view indexes are entirely rebuilt. This ensures that changes to the view definitions are reflected in the view indexes.

Note: View index rebuilds occur when one view from the same the view group (i.e. all the views defined within a single a design document) has been determined as needing a rebuild. For example, if if you have a design document with different views, and you update the database, all three view indexes within the design document will be updated.

Because the view is updated when it has been queried, it can result in a delay in returned information when the view is accessed, especially if there are a large number of documents in the database and the view index does not exist. There are a number of ways to mitigate, but not completely eliminate, these issues. These include:

- Create the view definition (and associated design documents) on your database before allowing insertion or updates to the documents. If this is allowed while the view is being accessed, the index can be updated incrementally.

- Manually force a view request from the database. You can do this either before users are allowed to use the view, or you can access the view manually after documents are added or updated.

- Use the *changes feed* to monitor for changes to the database and then access the view to force the corresponding view index to be updated.

- Use a monitor with the *update notification* section of the CouchDB configuration file to monitor for changes to your database, and trigger a view query to force the view to be updated.

None of these can completely eliminate the need for the indexes to be rebuilt or updated when the view is accessed, but they may lessen the effects on end-users of the index update affecting the user experience.

Another alternative is to allow users to access a 'stale' version of the view index, rather than forcing the index to be updated and displaying the updated results. Using a stale view may not return the latest information, but will return the results of the view query using an existing version of the index.

For example, to access the existing stale view by_recipe in the recipes design document:

```
http://localhost:5984/recipes/_design/recipes/_view/by_recipe?stale=ok
```

Accessing a stale view:

- Does not trigger a rebuild of the view indexes, even if there have been changes since the last access.

- Returns the current version of the view index, if a current version exists.

- Returns an empty result set if the given view index does exist.

As an alternative, you use the update_after value to the stale parameter. This causes the view to be returned as a stale view, but for the update process to be triggered after the view information has been returned to the client.

In addition to using stale views, you can also make use of the update_seq query argument. Using this query argument generates the view information including the update sequence of the database from which the view was generated. The returned value can be compared this to the current update sequence exposed in the database information (returned by *GET /{db}*).

Sorting Returned Rows

Each element within the returned array is sorted using native UTF-8 sorting according to the contents of the key portion of the emitted content. The basic order of output is as follows:

- null

- false

- true

- Numbers

- Text (case sensitive, lowercase first)

- Arrays (according to the values of each element, in order)

- Objects (according to the values of keys, in key order)

Request:

```
GET /db/_design/test/_view/sorting HTTP/1.1
Accept: application/json
Host: localhost:5984
```

Response:

```
HTTP/1.1 200 OK
Cache-Control: must-revalidate
Content-Type: application/json
Date: Wed, 21 Aug 2013 10:09:25 GMT
ETag: "8LA1LZPQ37B6R9U8BK9BGQH27"
```

```
Server: CouchDB (Erlang/OTP)
Transfer-Encoding: chunked

{
    "offset": 0,
    "rows": [
        {
            "id": "dummy-doc",
            "key": null,
            "value": null
        },
        {
            "id": "dummy-doc",
            "key": false,
            "value": null
        },
        {
            "id": "dummy-doc",
            "key": true,
            "value": null
        },
        {
            "id": "dummy-doc",
            "key": 0,
            "value": null
        },
        {
            "id": "dummy-doc",
            "key": 1,
            "value": null
        },
        {
            "id": "dummy-doc",
            "key": 10,
            "value": null
        },
        {
            "id": "dummy-doc",
            "key": 42,
            "value": null
        },
        {
            "id": "dummy-doc",
            "key": "10",
            "value": null
        },
        {
            "id": "dummy-doc",
            "key": "hello",
            "value": null
        },
        {
            "id": "dummy-doc",
            "key": "Hello",
            "value": null
        },
        {
            "id": "dummy-doc",
            "key": "\u043f\u0440\u0438\u0432\u0435\u0442",
            "value": null
        },
        {
            "id": "dummy-doc",
```

```
                    "key": [],
                    "value": null
                },
                {

                    "id": "dummy-doc",
                    "key": [
                        1,
                        2,
                        3
                    ],
                    "value": null
                },
                {

                    "id": "dummy-doc",
                    "key": [
                        2,
                        3
                    ],
                    "value": null
                },
                {

                    "id": "dummy-doc",
                    "key": [
                        3
                    ],
                    "value": null
                },
                {

                    "id": "dummy-doc",
                    "key": {},
                    "value": null
                },
                {

                    "id": "dummy-doc",
                    "key": {
                        "foo": "bar"
                    },
                    "value": null
                }
            ],
        "total_rows": 17
}
```

You can reverse the order of the returned view information by using the `descending` query value set to true:

Request:

```
GET /db/_design/test/_view/sorting?descending=true HTTP/1.1
Accept: application/json
Host: localhost:5984
```

Response:

```
HTTP/1.1 200 OK
Cache-Control: must-revalidate
Content-Type: application/json
Date: Wed, 21 Aug 2013 10:09:25 GMT
ETag: "Z4N468R15JBT98OM0AMNSR8U"
Server: CouchDB (Erlang/OTP)
Transfer-Encoding: chunked

{
    "offset": 0,
    "rows": [
```

```
{
    "id": "dummy-doc",
    "key": {
        "foo": "bar"
    },
    "value": null
},
{
    "id": "dummy-doc",
    "key": {},
    "value": null
},
{
    "id": "dummy-doc",
    "key": [
        3
    ],
    "value": null
},
{
    "id": "dummy-doc",
    "key": [
        2,
        3
    ],
    "value": null
},
{
    "id": "dummy-doc",
    "key": [
        1,
        2,
        3
    ],
    "value": null
},
{
    "id": "dummy-doc",
    "key": [],
    "value": null
},
{
    "id": "dummy-doc",
    "key": "\u043f\u0440\u0438\u0432\u0435\u0442",
    "value": null
},
{
    "id": "dummy-doc",
    "key": "Hello",
    "value": null
},
{
    "id": "dummy-doc",
    "key": "hello",
    "value": null
},
{
    "id": "dummy-doc",
    "key": "10",
    "value": null
},
{
    "id": "dummy-doc",
```

```
                "key": 42,
                "value": null
        },
        {
                "id": "dummy-doc",
                "key": 10,
                "value": null
        },
        {
                "id": "dummy-doc",
                "key": 1,
                "value": null
        },
        {
                "id": "dummy-doc",
                "key": 0,
                "value": null
        },
        {
                "id": "dummy-doc",
                "key": true,
                "value": null
        },
        {
                "id": "dummy-doc",
                "key": false,
                "value": null
        },
        {
                "id": "dummy-doc",
                "key": null,
                "value": null
        }
    ],
    "total_rows": 17
}
```

Sorting order and startkey/endkey

The sorting direction is applied before the filtering applied using the startkey and endkey query arguments. For example the following query:

```
GET http://couchdb:5984/recipes/_design/recipes/_view/by_ingredient?startkey=%22carrots%2
Accept: application/json
```

will operate correctly when listing all the matching entries between carrots and egg. If the order of output is reversed with the descending query argument, the view request will return no entries:

```
GET /recipes/_design/recipes/_view/by_ingredient?descending=true&startkey=%22carrots%22&e
Accept: application/json
Host: localhost:5984

{
    "total_rows" : 26453,
    "rows" : [],
    "offset" : 21882
}
```

The results will be empty because the entries in the view are reversed before the key filter is applied, and therefore the endkey of "egg" will be seen before the startkey of "carrots", resulting in an empty list.

Instead, you should reverse the values supplied to the `startkey` and `endkey` parameters to match the descending sorting applied to the keys. Changing the previous example to:

```
GET /recipes/_design/recipes/_view/by_ingredient?descending=true&startkey=%22egg%22&endke
Accept: application/json
Host: localhost:5984
```

Raw collation

By default CouchDB using ICU driver for sorting view results. It's possible use binary collation instead for faster view builds where Unicode collation is not important.

To use raw collation add `"collation": "raw"` key-value pair to the design documents `options` object at the root level. After that, views will be regenerated and new order applied.

See also:

Views Collation

Using Limits and Skipping Rows

By default requestion views result returns all records for it. That's ok when they are small, but this may lead to problems when there are billions of them since the clients might have to read them all and consume all available memory.

But it's possible to reduce output result rows by specifying `limit` query parameter. For example, retrieving the list of recipes using the `by_title` view and limited to 5 returns only 5 records, while there are total 2667 records in view:

Request:

```
GET /recipes/_design/recipes/_view/by_title?limit=5 HTTP/1.1
Accept: application/json
Host: localhost:5984
```

Response:

```
HTTP/1.1 200 OK
Cache-Control: must-revalidate
Content-Type: application/json
Date: Wed, 21 Aug 2013 09:14:13 GMT
ETag: "9Q6Q2GZKPH8D5F8L7PB6DBSS9"
Server: CouchDB (Erlang/OTP)
Transfer-Encoding: chunked

{
    "offset" : 0,
    "rows" : [
        {
            "id" : "3-tiersalmonspinachandavocadoterrine",
            "key" : "3-tier salmon, spinach and avocado terrine",
            "value" : [
                null,
                "3-tier salmon, spinach and avocado terrine"
            ]
        },
        {
            "id" : "Aberffrawcake",
            "key" : "Aberffraw cake",
            "value" : [
                null,
                "Aberffraw cake"
```

```
            ]
        },
        {
            "id" : "Adukiandorangecasserole-microwave",
            "key" : "Aduki and orange casserole - microwave",
            "value" : [
                null,
                "Aduki and orange casserole - microwave"
            ]
        },
        {
            "id" : "Aioli-garlicmayonnaise",
            "key" : "Aioli - garlic mayonnaise",
            "value" : [
                null,
                "Aioli - garlic mayonnaise"
            ]
        },
        {
            "id" : "Alabamapeanutchicken",
            "key" : "Alabama peanut chicken",
            "value" : [
                null,
                "Alabama peanut chicken"
            ]
        }
    ],
    "total_rows" : 2667
}
```

To omit some records you may use `skip` query parameter:

Request:

```
GET /recipes/_design/recipes/_view/by_title?limit=3&skip=2 HTTP/1.1
Accept: application/json
Host: localhost:5984
```

Response:

```
HTTP/1.1 200 OK
Cache-Control: must-revalidate
Content-Type: application/json
Date: Wed, 21 Aug 2013 09:14:13 GMT
ETag: "H3G7YZSNIVRRHO5FXPE16NJHN"
Server: CouchDB (Erlang/OTP)
Transfer-Encoding: chunked

{
    "offset" : 2,
    "rows" : [
        {
            "id" : "Adukiandorangecasserole-microwave",
            "key" : "Aduki and orange casserole - microwave",
            "value" : [
                null,
                "Aduki and orange casserole - microwave"
            ]
        },
        {
            "id" : "Aioli-garlicmayonnaise",
            "key" : "Aioli - garlic mayonnaise",
            "value" : [
                null,
```

```
                "Aioli - garlic mayonnaise"
            ]
        },
        {
            "id" : "Alabamapeanutchicken",
            "key" : "Alabama peanut chicken",
            "value" : [
                null,
                "Alabama peanut chicken"
            ]
        }
    ],
    "total_rows" : 2667
}
```

> **Warning:** Using `limit` and `skip` parameters is not recommended for results pagination. Read *pagination recipe* why it's so and how to make it better.

10.5.5 /db/_design/design-doc/_show/show-name

GET /{db}/_design/{ddoc}/_show/{func}

POST /{db}/_design/{ddoc}/_show/{func}
Applies *show function* for *null* document.

The request and response parameters are depended upon function implementation.

Parameters

- **db** – Database name
- **ddoc** – Design document name
- **func** – Show function name

Response Headers

- ETag – Response signature

Query Parameters

- **format** (*string*) – Format of the returned response. Used by *provides()* function

Status Codes

- 200 OK – Request completed successfully
- 500 Internal Server Error – Query server error

Function:

```
function(doc, req) {
    if (!doc) {
        return {body: "no doc"}
    } else {
        return {body: doc.description}
    }
}
```

Request:

```
GET /recipes/_design/recipe/_show/description HTTP/1.1
Accept: application/json
Host: localhost:5984
```

Response:

```
HTTP/1.1 200 OK
Content-Length: 6
Content-Type: text/html; charset=utf-8
Date: Wed, 21 Aug 2013 12:34:07 GMT
Etag: "7Z2TO7FPEMZ0F4GH0RJCRIOAU"
Server: CouchDB (Erlang/OTP)
Vary: Accept

no doc
```

10.5.6 /db/_design/design-doc/_show/show-name/doc-id

GET /{db}/_design/{ddoc}/_show/{func}/{docid}

POST /{db}/_design/{ddoc}/_show/{func}/{docid}
Applies *show function* for the specified document.

The request and response parameters are depended upon function implementation.

> **Parameters**
>
> > * **db** – Database name
> > * **ddoc** – Design document name
> > * **func** – Show function name
> > * **docid** – Document ID
>
> **Response Headers**
>
> > * ETag – Response signature
>
> **Query Parameters**
>
> > * **format** (*string*) – Format of the returned response. Used by *provides()* function
>
> **Status Codes**
>
> > * 200 OK – Request completed successfully
> > * 500 Internal Server Error – Query server error

Function:

```
function(doc, req) {
    if (!doc) {
        return {body: "no doc"}
    } else {
        return {body: doc.description}
    }
}
```

Request:

```
GET /recipes/_design/recipe/_show/description/SpaghettiWithMeatballs HTTP/1.1
Accept: application/json
Host: localhost:5984
```

Response:

```
HTTP/1.1 200 OK
Content-Length: 88
Content-Type: text/html; charset=utf-8
Date: Wed, 21 Aug 2013 12:38:08 GMT
Etag: "8IEBO8103EI98HDZL5Z4I1T0C"
Server: CouchDB (Erlang/OTP)
```

```
Vary: Accept

An Italian-American dish that usually consists of spaghetti, tomato sauce and meatba
```

10.5.7 /db/_design/design-doc/_list/list-name/view-name

GET /{db}/_design/{ddoc}/_list/{func}/{view}

POST /{db}/_design/{ddoc}/_list/{func}/{view}
Applies *list function* for the *view function* from the same design document.

The request and response parameters are depended upon function implementation.

> **Parameters**
>
> > - **db** – Database name
> > - **ddoc** – Design document name
> > - **func** – List function name
> > - **view** – View function name
>
> **Response Headers**
>
> > - ETag – Response signature
> > - Transfer-Encoding – chunked
>
> **Query Parameters**
>
> > - **format** (*string*) – Format of the returned response. Used by *provides()* function
>
> **Status Codes**
>
> > - 200 OK – Request completed successfully
> > - 500 Internal Server Error – Query server error

Function:

```
function(head, req) {
    var row = getRow();
    if (!row){
        return 'no ingredients'
    }
    send(row.key);
    while(row=getRow()){
        send(', ' + row.key);
    }
}
```

Request:

```
GET /recipes/_design/recipe/_list/ingredients/by_name HTTP/1.1
Accept: text/plain
Host: localhost:5984
```

Response:

```
HTTP/1.1 200 OK
Content-Type: text/plain; charset=utf-8
Date: Wed, 21 Aug 2013 12:49:15 GMT
Etag: "D52L2M1TKQYDD1Y8MEYJR8C84"
Server: CouchDB (Erlang/OTP)
Transfer-Encoding: chunked
Vary: Accept
```

```
meatballs, spaghetti, tomato sauce
```

10.5.8 /db/_design/design-doc/_list/list-name/other-ddoc/view-name

GET /{db}/_design/{ddoc}/_list/{func}/{other-ddoc}/{view}

POST /{db}/_design/{ddoc}/_list/{func}/{other-ddoc}/{view}
Applies *list function* for the *view function* from the other design document.

The request and response parameters are depended upon function implementation.

Parameters

- **db** – Database name
- **ddoc** – Design document name
- **func** – List function name
- **other-ddoc** – Other design document name that holds view function
- **view** – View function name

Response Headers

- ETag – Response signature
- Transfer-Encoding – chunked

Query Parameters

- **format** (*string*) – Format of the returned response. Used by `provides()` function

Status Codes

- 200 OK – Request completed successfully
- 500 Internal Server Error – Query server error

Function:

```
function(head, req) {
    var row = getRow();
    if (!row){
        return 'no ingredients'
    }
    send(row.key);
    while(row=getRow()){
        send(', ' + row.key);
    }
}
```

Request:

```
GET /recipes/_design/ingredient/_list/ingredients/recipe/by_ingredient?key="spaghett
Accept: text/plain
Host: localhost:5984
```

Response:

```
HTTP/1.1 200 OK
Content-Type: text/plain; charset=utf-8
Date: Wed, 21 Aug 2013 12:49:15 GMT
Etag: "5L0975X493R0FB5Z3043POZHD"
Server: CouchDB (Erlang/OTP)
Transfer-Encoding: chunked
Vary: Accept
```

```
spaghetti
```

10.5.9 /db/_design/design-doc/_update/update-name

POST /{db}/_design/{ddoc}/_update/{func}
  Executes *update function* on server side for null document.

  Parameters

  - **db** – Database name
  - **ddoc** – Design document name
  - **func** – Update function name

  Response Headers

  - **X-Couch-Id** – Created/updated document's ID
  - **X-Couch-Update-Newrev** – Created/updated document's revision

  Status Codes

  - 200 OK – No document was created or updated
  - 201 Created – Document was created or updated
  - 500 Internal Server Error – Query server error

Function:

```
function(doc, req) {
    if (!doc){
      return [null, {'code': 400,
                     'json': {'error': 'missed',
                              'reason': 'no document to update'}}]
    } else {
      doc.ingredients.push(req.body);
      return [doc, {'json': {'status': 'ok'}}];
    }
}
```

Request:

```
POST /recipes/_design/recipe/_update/ingredients HTTP/1.1
Accept: application/json
Content-Length: 10
Content-Type: application/json
Host: localhost:5984

something
```

Response:

```
HTTP/1.1 404 Object Not Found
Cache-Control: must-revalidate
Content-Length: 52
Content-Type: application/json
Date: Wed, 21 Aug 2013 14:00:58 GMT
Server: CouchDB (Erlang/OTP)

{
    "error": "missed",
    "reason": "no document to update"
}
```

10.5.10 /db/_design/design-doc/_update/update-name/doc-id

PUT /{db}/_design/{ddoc}/_update/{func}/{docid}
Executes *update function* on server side for the specified document.

> **Parameters**
>
> > • **db** – Database name
> >
> > • **ddoc** – Design document name
> >
> > • **func** – Update function name
> >
> > • **docid** – Document ID
>
> **Response Headers**
>
> > • **X-Couch-Id** – Created/updated document's ID
> >
> > • **X-Couch-Update-Newrev** – Created/updated document's revision
>
> **Status Codes**
>
> > • 200 OK – No document was created or updated
> >
> > • 201 Created – Document was created or updated
> >
> > • 500 Internal Server Error – Query server error

> **Function**:

```
function(doc, req) {
    if (!doc){
        return [null, {'code': 400,
                       'json': {'error': 'missed',
                                'reason': 'no document to update'}}]
    } else {
        doc.ingredients.push(req.body);
        return [doc, {'json': {'status': 'ok'}}];
    }
}
```

> **Request**:

```
POST /recipes/_design/recipe/_update/ingredients/SpaghettiWithMeatballs HTTP/1.1
Accept: application/json
Content-Length: 5
Content-Type: application/json
Host: localhost:5984

love
```

> **Response**:

```
HTTP/1.1 201 Created
Cache-Control: must-revalidate
Content-Length: 16
Content-Type: application/json
Date: Wed, 21 Aug 2013 14:11:34 GMT
Server: CouchDB (Erlang/OTP)
X-Couch-Id: SpaghettiWithMeatballs
X-Couch-Update-NewRev: 12-a5e099df5720988dae90c8b664496baf

{
    "status": "ok"
}
```

10.5.11 /db/_design/design-doc/_rewrite/path

ANY /{db}/_design/{ddoc}/_rewrite/{path}

Rewrites the specified path by rules defined in the specified design document.

The rewrite rules are defined in *array* field of the design document called `rewrites`. Each rule is an *object* with next structure:

- **from** (*string*): The path rule used to bind current uri to the rule. It use pattern matching for that

- **to** (*string*): Rule to rewrite an url. It can contain variables depending on binding variables discovered during pattern matching and query args (url args and from the query member)

- **method** (*string*): HTTP request method to bind the request method to the rule. Default is "`*`"

- **query** (*object*): Query args you want to define they can contain dynamic variable by binding the key

The `to``and ``from` paths may contains string patterns with leading : or * characters.

For example: `/somepath/:var/*`

- This path is converted in Erlang list by splitting /

- Each `var` are converted in atom

- "" are converted to `' '` atom

- The pattern matching is done by splitting / in request url in a list of token

- A string pattern will match equal token

- The star atom (`' * '` in single quotes) will match any number of tokens, but may only be present as the last *pathterm* in a *pathspec*

- If all tokens are matched and all *pathterms* are used, then the *pathspec* matches

The pattern matching is done by first matching the HTTP request method to a rule. `method` is equal to "`*`" by default, and will match any HTTP method. It will then try to match the path to one rule. If no rule matches, then a 404 Not Found response returned.

Once a rule is found we rewrite the request url using the `to` and `query` fields. The identified token are matched to the rule and will replace var. If `' * '` is found in the rule it will contain the remaining part if it exists.

Examples:

Rule	Url	Rewrite to	Tokens
{"**from**": "**/a**", "to": "/some"}	/a	/some	
{"**from**": "**/a/***", "to": "/some/*"}	/a/b/c	/some/b/c	
{"**from**": "**/a/b**", "to": "/some"}	/a/b?k=v	/some?k=v	k=v
{"**from**": "**/a/b**", "to": "/some/:var"}	/a/b	/some/b?var=b	var=b
{"from": "/a/:foo/", "to": "/some/:foo/"}	/a/b/c	/some/b/c?foo=b	foo=b
{"**from**": "**/a/:foo**", "to": "/some", "query": { "k": ":foo" }}	/a/b	/some/?k=b&foo=b	foo=b
{"**from**": "**/a**", "to": "/some/:foo"}	/a?foo=b	/some/?b&foo=b	foo=b

Request method, header, query parameters, request payload and response body are depended on endpoint to which url will be rewritten.

Parameters

- **db** – Database name
- **ddoc** – Design document name
- **path** – URL path to rewrite

10.6 Local (non-replicating) Documents

The Local (non-replicating) document interface allows you to create local documents that are not replicated to other databases. These documents can be used to hold configuration or other information that is required specifically on the local CouchDB instance.

Local documents have the following limitations:

- Local documents are not replicated to other databases.
- The ID of the local document must be known for the document to accessed. You cannot obtain a list of local documents from the database.
- Local documents are not output by views, or the */db/_all_docs* view.

Local documents can be used when you want to store configuration or other information for the current (local) instance of a given database.

A list of the available methods and URL paths are provided below:

Method	Path	Description
GET	/db/_local/id	Returns the latest revision of the non-replicated document
PUT	/db/_local/id	Inserts a new version of the non-replicated document
DELETE	/db/_local/id	Deletes the non-replicated document
COPY	/db/_local/id	Copies the non-replicated document

10.6.1 /db/_local/id

GET /{db}/_local/{docid}

Gets the specified local document. The semantics are identical to accessing a standard document in the specified database, except that the document is not replicated. See *GET /{db}/{docid}*.

PUT /{db}/_local/{docid}

Stores the specified local document. The semantics are identical to storing a standard document in the specified database, except that the document is not replicated. See *PUT /{db}/{docid}*.

DELETE /{db}/_local/{docid}

Deletes the specified local document. The semantics are identical to deleting a standard document in the specified database, except that the document is not replicated. See *DELETE /{db}/{docid}*.

COPY /{db}/_local/{docid}

Copies the specified local document. The semantics are identical to copying a standard document in the specified database, except that the document is not replicated. See *COPY /{db}/{docid}*.

## CHAPTER 11

Cluster Reference

As of 2.0 CouchDB now have two modes of operations:

- Standalone
- Cluster

This part of the documentation is about setting up and maintain a CouchDB cluster.

11.1 Setup

Everything you need to know to prepare the cluster for the installation of CouchDB.

11.1.1 Firewall

If you do not have a firewall between your servers, then you can skip this.

CouchDB in cluster mode uses the port 5984 just as standalone, but is also uses 5986 for the admin interface.

Erlang uses TCP port 4369 (EPMD) to find other nodes, so all servers must be able to speak to each other on this port. In an Erlang Cluster, all nodes are connected to all other nodes. A mesh.

> **Warning:** If you expose the port 4369 to the Internet or any other untrusted network, then the only thing protecting you is the *cookie*.

Every Erlang application then uses other ports for talking to each other. Yes, this means random ports. This will obviously not work with a firewall, but it is possible to force an Erlang application to use a specific port rage.

This documentation will use the range TCP 9100-9200. Open up those ports in your firewalls and it is time to test it.

You need 2 servers with working hostnames. Let us call them server1 and server2.

On server1:

```
erl -sname bus -setcookie 'brumbrum' -kernel inet_dist_listen_min 9100 -kernel inet_dist_
```

Then on server2:

```
erl -sname car -setcookie 'brumbrum' -kernel inet_dist_listen_min 9100 -kernel inet_dist_
```

An explanation to the commands:

- `erl` the Erlang shell.
- `-sname bus` the name of the Erlang node.
- `-setcookie 'brumbrum'` the "password" used when nodes connect to each other.

- `-kernel inet_dist_listen_min 9100` the lowest port in the rage.
- `-kernel inet_dist_listen_max 9200` the highest port in the rage.

This gives us 2 Erlang shells. shell1 on server1, shell2 on server2. Time to connect them. The `.` is to Erlang what `;` is to C.

In shell1:

```
net_kernel:connect_node(car@server2).
```

This will connect to the node called `car` on the server called `server2`.

If that returns true, then you have a Erlang cluster, and the firewalls are open. If you get false or nothing at all, then you have a problem with the firewall.

First time in Erlang? Time to play!

Run in both shells:

```
register(shell, self()).
```

shell1:

```
{shell, car@server2} ! {hello, from, self()}.
```

shell2:

```
flush().
{shell, bus@server1} ! {"It speaks!", from, self()}.
```

shell1:

```
flush().
```

To close the shells, run in both:

```
q().
```

Make CouchDB use the open ports.

Open `sys.config`, on all nodes, and add `inet_dist_listen_min, 9100` and `inet_dist_listen_max, 9200` like below:

```
[
    {lager, [
        {error_logger_hwm, 1000},
        {error_logger_redirect, true},
        {handlers, [
            {lager_console_backend, [debug, {
                lager_default_formatter,
                [
                    date, " ", time,
                    " [", severity, "] ",
                    node, " ", pid, " ",
                    message,
                    "\n"
                ]
            }]}
        ]},
        {inet_dist_listen_min, 9100},
        {inet_dist_listen_max, 9200}
    ]}
].
```

11.1.2 Configuration files

Erlang Cookie

Open up `vm.args` and set the `-setcookie` to something secret. This must be identical on all nodes.

Set `-name` to the name the node will have. All nodes must have a unique name.

Admin

All nodes authenticates users locally, so you must add an admin user to local.ini on all nodes. Otherwise you will not be able to login on the cluster.

11.2 Theory

Before we move on, we need some theory.

As you see in `etc/default.ini` there is a section called [cluster]

```
[cluster]
q=8
r=2
w=2
n=3
```

- `q` - The number of shards.
- `r` - The number of copies of a document with the same revision that have to be read before CouchDB returns with a `200` and the document. If there is only one copy of the document accessible, then that is returned with `200`.
- `w` - The number of nodes that need to save a document before a write is returned with `201`. If the nodes saving the document is $<w$ but >0, `202` is returned.
- `n` - The number of copies there is of every document. Replicas.

When creating a database or doing a read or write you can send your own values with request and thereby overriding the defaults in `default.ini`.

We will focus on the shards and replicas for now.

A shard is a part of a database. The more shards, the more you can scale out. If you have 4 shards, that means that you can have at most 4 nodes. With one shard you can have only one node, just the way CouchDB 1.x is.

Replicas adds fail resistance, as some nodes can be offline without everything comes crashing down.

- `n=1` All nodes must be up.
- `n=2` Any 1 node can be down.
- `n=3` Any 2 nodes can be down.
- etc

Computers goes down and sysadmins pull out network cables in a furious rage from time to time, so using $n<2$ is asking for downtime. Having a to high value of n is adding servers and complexity without any real benefit. The sweetspot is at $n=3$.

Say that we have a database with 3 replicas and 4 shards. That would give us a maximum of 12 nodes. 4*3=12 Every shard have 3 copies.

We can lose any 2 nodes and still read and write all documents.

What happens if we lose more nodes? It depends on how lucky we are. As long as there is at least one copy of every shard online, we can read and write all documents.

So, if we are very lucky then we can lose 8 nodes at maximum.

11.3 Node Management

11.3.1 Adding a node

Go to `http://server1:45984/_membership` to see the name of the node and all the nodes it knows about and are connected too.

```
curl -X GET "http://xxx.xxx.xxx.xxx:5984/_membership" --user admin-user
```

```
{
    "all_nodes":[
        "node1@xxx.xxx.xxx.xxx"],
    "cluster_nodes":[
        "node1@xxx.xxx.xxx.xxx"]
}
```

- `all_nodes` are all the nodes thats this node knows about.

- `cluster_nodes` are the nodes that are connected to this node.

To add a node simply do:

```
curl -X PUT "http://xxx.xxx.xxx.xxx:5986/_nodes/node2@yyy.yyy.yyy.yyy" -d {}
```

Now look at `http://server1:5984/_membership` again.

```
{
    "all_nodes":[
        "node1@xxx.xxx.xxx.xxx",
        "node2@yyy.yyy.yyy.yyy"
    ],
    "cluster_nodes":[
        "node1@xxx.xxx.xxx.xxx",
        "node2@yyy.yyy.yyy.yyy"
    ]
}
```

And you have a 2 node cluster :)

`http://yyy.yyy.yyy.yyy:5984/_membership` will show the same thing, so you only have to add a node once.

11.3.2 Removing a node

Before you remove a node, make sure that you have moved all *shards* away from that node.

To remode `node2` from server `yyy.yyy.yyy.yyy`:

```
curl -X DELETE "http://xxx.xxx.xxx.xxx:5986/_nodes/node2@yyy.yyy.yyy.yyy" -d {}
```

11.4 Database Management

11.4.1 Creating a database

This will create a database with 3 replicas and 8 shards.

```
curl -X PUT "http://xxx.xxx.xxx.xxx:5984/database-name?n=3&q=8" --user admin-user
```

The database is in `data/shards`. Look around on all the nodes and you will find all the parts.

If you do not specify n and q the default will be used. The default is 3 replicas and 8 shards.

11.4.2 Deleteing a database

```
curl -X DELETE "http://xxx.xxx.xxx.xxx:5984/database-name --user admin-user
```

11.5 Sharding

11.5.1 Scaling out

Normally you start small and grow over time. In the beginning you might do just fine with one node, but as your data and number of clients grows, you need to scale out.

For simplicity we will start fresh and small.

Start node1 and add a database to it. To keep it simple we will have 2 shards and no replicas.

```
curl -X PUT "http://xxx.xxx.xxx.xxx:5984/small?n=1&q=2" --user daboss
```

If you look in the directory `data/shards` you will find the 2 shards.

```
data/
+-- shards/
|   +-- 00000000-7fffffff/
|   |    -- small.1425202577.couch
|   +-- 80000000-ffffffff/
|        -- small.1425202577.couch
```

Now, go to the admin panel

```
http://xxx.xxx.xxx.xxx:5986/_utils
```

and look in the database _dbs, it is here that the metadata for each database is stored. As the database is called small, there is a document called small there. Let us look in it. Yes, you can get it with curl too:

```
curl -X GET "http://xxx.xxx.xxx.xxx:5986/_dbs/small"

{
    "_id": "small",
    "_rev": "1-5e2d10c29c70d3869fb7a1fd3a827a64",
    "shard_suffix": [
        46,
        49,
        52,
        50,
        53,
        50,
        48,
        50,
        53,
        55,
        55
    ],
    "changelog": [
        [
            "add",
```

```
            "00000000-7fffffff",
            "node1@xxx.xxx.xxx.xxx"
        ],
        [

            "add",
            "80000000-ffffffff",
            "node1@xxx.xxx.xxx.xxx"
        ]
        ],
        "by_node": {
            "node1@xxx.xxx.xxx.xxx": [
                "00000000-7fffffff",
                "80000000-ffffffff"
            ]
        },
        "by_range": {
            "00000000-7fffffff": [
                "node1@xxx.xxx.xxx.xxx"
            ],
            "80000000-ffffffff": [
                "node1@xxx.xxx.xxx.xxx"
            ]
        }
    }
}
```

- `_id` The name of the database.

- `_rev` The current revision of the metadata.

- `shard_suffix` The numbers after small and before .couch. The number of seconds after UNIX epoch that the database was created. Stored in ASCII.

- `changelog` Self explaining. Only for admins to read.

- `by_node` Which shards each node have.

- `by_rage` On which nodes each shard is.

Nothing here, nothing there, a shard in my sleeve

Start node2 and add it to the cluster. Check in `/_membership` that the nodes are talking with each other.

If you look in the directory `data` on node2, you will see that there is no directory called shards.

Go to Fauxton and edit the metadata for small, so it looks like this:

```
{
    "_id": "small",
    "_rev": "1-5e2d10c29c70d3869fb7a1fd3a827a64",
    "shard_suffix": [
        46,
        49,
        52,
        50,
        53,
        50,
        48,
        50,
        53,
        55,
        55
    ],
    "changelog": [
    [
```

```
                "add",
                "00000000-7fffffff",
                "node1@xxx.xxx.xxx.xxx"
            ],
            [
                "add",
                "80000000-ffffffff",
                "node1@xxx.xxx.xxx.xxx"
            ],
            [
                "add",
                "00000000-7fffffff",
                "node2@yyy.yyy.yyy.yyy"
            ],
            [
                "add",
                "80000000-ffffffff",
                "node2@yyy.yyy.yyy.yyy"
            ]
        ],
        "by_node": {
            "node1@xxx.xxx.xxx.xxx": [
                "00000000-7fffffff",
                "80000000-ffffffff"
            ],
            "node2@yyy.yyy.yyy.yyy": [
                "00000000-7fffffff",
                "80000000-ffffffff"
            ]
        },
        "by_range": {
            "00000000-7fffffff": [
                "node1@xxx.xxx.xxx.xxx",
                "node2@yyy.yyy.yyy.yyy"
            ],
            "80000000-ffffffff": [
                "node1@xxx.xxx.xxx.xxx",
                "node2@yyy.yyy.yyy.yyy"
            ]
        }
    }
}
```

Then press Save and marvel at the magic. The shards are now on node2 too! We now have n=2!

If the shards are large, then you can copy them over manually and only have CouchDB syncing the changes from the last minutes instead.

11.5.2 Moving Shards

Add, then delete

In the world of CouchDB there is no such thing as moving. You can add a new replica to a shard and then remove the old replica, thereby creating the illusion of moving. If you try to uphold this illusion with a database that have n=1, you might find yourself in the following scenario:

1. Copy the shard to a new node.
2. Update the metadata to use the new node.
3. Delete the shard on the old node.
4. Lose all writes made between 1 and 2.

As the realty "I added a new replica of the shard X on node Y and then I waited for them to sync, before I removed the replica of shard X from node Z." is a bit tedious, people and this documentation tend to use the illusion of moving.

Moving

When you get to n=3 you should start moving the shards instead of adding more replicas.

We will stop on n=2 to keep things simple. Start node number 3 and add it to the cluster. Then create the directories for the shard on node3:

```
mkdir -p data/shards/00000000-7fffffff
```

And copy over `data/shards/00000000-7fffffff/small.1425202577.couch` from node1 to node3. Do not move files between the shard directories as that will confuse CouchDB!

Edit the database document in `_dbs` again. Make it so that node3 have a replica of the shard `00000000-7fffffff`. Save the document and let CouchDB sync. If we do not do this, then writes made during the copy of the shard and the updating of the metadata will only have n=1 until CouchDB has synced.

Then update the metadata document so that node2 no longer have the shard `00000000-7fffffff`. You can now safely delete `data/shards/00000000-7fffffff/small.1425202577.couch` on node 2.

The changelog is nothing that CouchDB cares about, it is only for the admins. But for the sake of completeness, we will update it again. Use `delete` for recording the removal of the shard `00000000-7fffffff` from node2.

Start node4, add it to the cluster and do the same as above with shard `80000000-ffffffff`.

All documents added during this operation was saved and all reads responded to without the users noticing anything.

11.5.3 Views

The views needs to be moved together with the shards. If you do not, then CouchDB will rebuild them and this will take time if you have a lot of documents.

The views are stored in `data/.shards`.

It is possible to not move the views and let CouchDB rebuild the view every time you move a shard. As this can take quite some time, it is not recommended.

11.5.4 Reshard? No, Preshard!

Reshard? Nope. It can not be done. So do not create databases with to few shards.

If you can not scale out more because you set the number of shards to low, then you need to create a new cluster and migrate over.

1. Build a cluster with enough nodes to handle one copy of your data.
2. Create a database with the same name, n=1 and with enough shards so you do not have to do this again.
3. Set up 2 way replication between the 2 clusters.
4. Let it sync.
5. Tell clients to use both the clusters.
6. Add some nodes to the new cluster and add them as replicas.
7. Remove some nodes from the old cluster.
8. Repeat 6 and 7 until you have enough nodes in the new cluster to have 3 replicas of every shard.
9. Redirect all clients to the new cluster

10. Turn off the 2 way replication between the clusters.

11. Shut down the old cluster and add the servers as new nodes to the new cluster.

12. Relax!

Creating more shards than you need and then move the shards around is called presharding. The number of shards you need depends on how much data you are going to store. But creating to many shards increases the complexity without any real gain. You might even get lower performance. As an example of this, we can take the author's (15 year) old lab server. It gets noticeably slower with more than one shard and high load, as the hard drive must seek more.

How many shards you should have depends, as always, on your use case and your hardware. If you do not know what to do, use the default of 8 shards.

## CHAPTER 12

JSON Structure Reference

The following appendix provides a quick reference to all the JSON structures that you can supply to CouchDB, or get in return to requests.

12.1 All Database Documents

Field	Description
total_rows	Number of documents in the database/view
offset	Offset where the document list started
update_seq (optional)	Current update sequence for the database
rows [array]	Array of document object

12.2 Bulk Document Response

Field	Description
docs [array]	Bulk Docs Returned Documents
id	Document ID
error	Error type
reason	Error string with extended reason

12.3 Bulk Documents

Field	Description
all_or_nothing (optional)	Sets the database commit mode to use all-or-nothing semantics
docs [array]	Bulk Documents Document
_id (optional)	Document ID
_rev (optional)	Revision ID (when updating an existing document)
_deleted (optional)	Whether the document should be deleted

12.4 Changes information for a database

Field	Description
last_seq	Last change sequence number
results [array]	Changes made to a database
seq	Update sequence number
id	Document ID
changes [array]	List of changes, field-by-field, for this document

12.5 CouchDB Document

Field	Description
_id (optional)	Document ID
_rev (optional)	Revision ID (when updating an existing document)

12.6 CouchDB Error Status

Field	Description
id	Document ID
error	Error type
reason	Error string with extended reason

12.7 CouchDB database information object

Field	Description
db_name	The name of the database.
committed_update_seq	The number of committed updates.
doc_count	The number of documents in the database.
doc_del_count	The number of deleted documents.
compact_running	Set to true if the database compaction routine is operating on this database.
disk_format_version	The version of the physical format used for the data when it is stored on hard disk.
disk_size	Size in bytes of the data as stored on disk. View indexes are not included in the calculation.
instance_start_time	Timestamp indicating when the database was opened, expressed in microseconds since the epoch.
purge_seq	The number of purge operations on the database.
update_seq	The current number of updates made in the database.

12.8 Design Document

Field	Description
_id	Design Document ID
_rev	Design Document Revision
views	View
viewname	View Definition
map	Map Function for View
reduce (optional)	Reduce Function for View

12.9 Design Document Information

Field	Description
name	Name/ID of Design Document
view_index	View Index
compact_running	Indicates whether a compaction routine is currently running on the view
disk_size	Size in bytes of the view as stored on disk
language	Language for the defined views
purge_seq	The purge sequence that has been processed
signature	MD5 signature of the views for the design document
update_seq	The update sequence of the corresponding database that has been indexed
updater_running	Indicates if the view is currently being updated
waiting_clients	Number of clients waiting on views from this design document
waiting_commit	Indicates if there are outstanding commits to the underlying database that need to processed

12.10 Document with Attachments

Field	Description
_id (optional)	Document ID
_rev (optional)	Revision ID (when updating an existing document)
_attachments (optional)	Document Attachment
filename	Attachment information
content_type	MIME Content type string
data	File attachment content, Base64 encoded

12.11 List of Active Tasks

Field	Description
tasks [array]	Active Tasks
pid	Process ID
status	Task status message
task	Task name
type	Operation Type

12.12 Replication Settings

Field	Description
source	Source database name or URL
target	Target database name or URL
create_target (optional)	Creates the target database
continuous (optional)	Configure the replication to be continuous
cancel (optional)	Cancels the replication
doc_ids (optional)	Array of document IDs to be synchronized
proxy (optional)	Address of a proxy server through which replication should occur
since_seq (optional)	Sequence from which the replication should start
filter (optional)	name of the filter function in the form of `ddoc/myfilter`
query_params (optional)	Query parameter that are passed to the filter function; the value should be a document containing parameters as members
use_checkpoints (optional)	Whether to use replication checkpoints or not
checkpoint_interval (optional)	Specifies the checkpoint interval in ms.

12.13 Replication Status

Field	Description
ok	Replication status
session_id	Unique session ID
source_last_seq	Last sequence number read from the source database
history [array]	Replication History
session_id	Session ID for this replication operation
recorded_seq	Last recorded sequence number
docs_read	Number of documents read
docs_written	Number of documents written to target
doc_write_failures	Number of document write failures
start_time	Date/Time replication operation started
start_last_seq	First sequence number in changes stream
end_time	Date/Time replication operation completed
end_last_seq	Last sequence number in changes stream
missing_checked	Number of missing documents checked
missing_found	Number of missing documents found

12.14 Request object

Field	Description
body	Request body data as *string*. If the request method is *GET* this field contains the value `"undefined"`. If the method is *DELETE* or *HEAD* the value is `""` (empty string).
cookie	Cookies *object*.
form	Form data *object*. Contains the decoded body as key-value pairs if the *Content-Type* header was `application/x-www-form-urlencoded`.
headers	Request headers *object*.
id	Requested document id *string* if it was specified or `null` otherwise.
info	*Database information*
method	Request method as *string* or *array*. String value is a method as one of: *HEAD, GET, POST, PUT, DELETE, OPTIONS*, and *TRACE*. Otherwise it will be represented as an array of char codes.
path	List of requested path sections.
peer	Request source IP address.
query	URL query parameters *object*. Note that multiple keys are not supported and the last key value suppresses others.
re-quested_path	List of actual requested path section.
raw_path	Raw requested path *string*.
secObj	*Security Object*.
userCtx	*User Context Object*.
uuid	Generated UUID by a specified algorithm in the config file.

```
{
    "body": "undefined",
    "cookie": {
        "AuthSession": "cm9vdDo1MDZBRjQzRjrfcuikzPRfAn-EA37FmjyfM8G8Lw",
        "m": "3234"
    },
    "form": {},
    "headers": {
        "Accept": "text/html,application/xhtml+xml,application/xml;q=0.9,*/*;q=0.8",
        "Accept-Charset": "ISO-8859-1,utf-8;q=0.7,*;q=0.3",
        "Accept-Encoding": "gzip,deflate,sdch",
        "Accept-Language": "en-US,en;q=0.8",
        "Connection": "keep-alive",
        "Cookie": "m=3234:t|3247:t|6493:t|6967:t|34e2:|18c3:t|2c69:t|5acb:t|ca3:t|c0|:t|5
        "Host": "127.0.0.1:5984",
        "User-Agent": "Mozilla/5.0 (Windows NT 5.2) AppleWebKit/535.7 (KHTML, like Gecko)
    },
    "id": "foo",
    "info": {
        "committed_update_seq": 2701412,
        "compact_running": false,
        "data_size": 7580843252,
        "db_name": "mailbox",
        "disk_format_version": 6,
        "disk_size": 14325313673,
        "doc_count": 2262757,
        "doc_del_count": 560,
        "instance_start_time": "1347601025628957",
        "purge_seq": 0,
        "update_seq": 2701412
    },
    "method": "GET",
    "path": [
        "mailbox",
        "_design",
        "request",
```

```
            "_show",
            "dump",
            "foo"
    ],
    "peer": "127.0.0.1",
    "query": {},
    "raw_path": "/mailbox/_design/request/_show/dump/foo",
    "requested_path": [
        "mailbox",
        "_design",
        "request",
        "_show",
        "dump",
        "foo"
    ],
    "secObj": {
        "admins": {
            "names": [
                "Bob"
            ],
            "roles": []
        },
        "members": {
            "names": [
                "Mike",
                "Alice"
            ],
            "roles": []
        }
    },
    "userCtx": {
        "db": "mailbox",
        "name": "Mike",
        "roles": [
            "user"
        ]
    },
    "uuid": "3184f9d1ea934e1f81a24c71bde5c168"
}
```

12.15 Response object

Field	Description
code	HTTP status code *number*.
json	JSON encodable *object*. Implicitly sets *Content-Type* header as `application/json`.
body	Raw response text *string*. Implicitly sets *Content-Type* header as `text/html; charset=utf-8`.
base64	Base64 encoded *string*. Implicitly sets *Content-Type* header as `application/binary`.
headers	Response headers *object*. *Content-Type* header from this object overrides any implicitly assigned one.
stop	*boolean* signal to stop iteration over view result rows (for list functions only)

Warning: The `body`, `base64` and `json` object keys are overlapping each other where the last one wins. Since most realizations of key-value objects do not preserve the key order or if they are mixed, confusing situations can occure. Try to use only one of them.

Note: Any custom property makes CouchDB raise an internal exception. Furthermore, the *Response object* could be a simple string value which would be implicitly wrapped into a `{ "body": ... }` object.

12.16 Returned CouchDB Document with Detailed Revision Info

Field	Description
_id (optional)	Document ID
_rev (optional)	Revision ID (when updating an existing document)
_revs_info [array]	CouchDB document extended revision info
rev	Full revision string
status	Status of the revision

12.17 Returned CouchDB Document with Revision Info

Field	Description
_id (optional)	Document ID
_rev (optional)	Revision ID (when updating an existing document)
_revisions	CouchDB document revisions
ids [array]	Array of valid revision IDs, in reverse order (latest first)
start	Prefix number for the latest revision

12.18 Returned Document with Attachments

Field	Description
_id (optional)	Document ID
_rev (optional)	Revision ID (when updating an existing document)
_attachments (optional)	Document attachment
filename	Attachment
stub	Indicates whether the attachment is a stub
content_type	MIME Content type string
length	Length (bytes) of the attachment data
revpos	Revision where this attachment exists

12.19 Security Object

Field	Description
admins	Roles/Users with admin privileges
roles [array]	List of roles with parent privilege
names [array]	List of users with parent privilege
members	Roles/Users with non-admin privileges
roles [array]	List of roles with parent privilege
names [array]	List of users with parent privilege

```
{
    "admins": {
        "names": [
            "Bob"
        ],
        "roles": []
    },
    "members": {
        "names": [
```

```
            "Mike",
            "Alice"
        ],
        "roles": []
    }
}
```

12.20 User Context Object

Field	Description
db	Database name in the context of the provided operation.
name	User name.
roles	List of user roles.

```
{
    "db": "mailbox",
    "name": null,
    "roles": [
        "_admin"
    ]
}
```

12.21 View Head Information

Field	Description
total_rows	Number of documents in the view
offset	Offset where the document list started

```
{
    "total_rows": 42,
    "offset": 3
}
```

## CHAPTER 13

Experimental Features

This is a list of experimental features in CouchDB. They are included in a release because the development team is requesting feedback from the larger developer community. As such, please play around with these features and send us feedback, thanks!

Use at your own risk! Do not rely on these features for critical applications.

13.1 NodeJS Query Server

The NodeJS Query Server is an alternative runtime environment for the default JavaScript Query Server that runs on top of Node.JS and not SpiderMonkey like the default Query Server.

13.1.1 Setup

You will need to install Node.JS version 0.10.0 or later. See Node.JS Downloads for options.

1. Install the *couchjs-node* binary. Either from the CouchDB sources:

```
cd src/couchjs-node
npm link
```

Or via NPM:

```
npm install -g couchjs
```

Note: NPM in non-standard locations If your Node.JS installation doesn't store binaries in */usr/local/bin* you will need to adjust CouchDB's configuration. Add this to your *local.ini* file:

```
[query_servers]
nodejs = /path/to/couchjs-node /path/to/couchdb/share/server/main.js
```

And then restart your CouchDB instance.

2. Done. Now you can create design documents with the *language* parameter set to *nodejs* and all JavaScript functions in this design document will be processed by the Node.JS query server.

Enjoy!

13.1.2 Differences from the SpiderMonkey Query Server

V8 and SpiderMonkey roughly behave similar, but there might be engine- specific differences that make or break a JavaScript function in one or the other server.

13.2 Plugins

See *src/couch_plugins/README.md*.

13.3 Content-Security-Policy (CSP) Header Support for /_utils (Fauxton)

This will just work with Fauxton, and not Futon. You can enable it in your config: you can enable the feature in general and change the default header that is sent for everything in /_utils.

```
[csp]
enable = true
```

Then restart CouchDB.

Have fun!

## CHAPTER 14

Contributing to this Documentation

The documentation lives in the CouchDB source tree. We'll start by forking and closing the CouchDB GitHub mirror. That will allow us to send the contribution to CouchDB with a pull request.

If you don't have a GitHub account yet, it is a good time to get one, they are free. If you don't want to use GitHub, there are alternate ways to contributing back, that we'll cover next time.

Go to https://github.com/apache/couchdb and click the "fork" button in the top right. This will create a fork of CouchDB in your GitHub account. Mine is *janl*, so my fork lives at https://github.com/janl/couchdb. In the header, it tells me me my "GitHub Clone URL". We need to copy that and start a terminal:

```
$ git clone https://github.com/janl/couchdb.git
$ cd couchdb
$ subl .
```

I'm opening the whole CouchDB source tree in my favourite editor. It gives me the usual directory listing:

```
.git/
.gitignore
.mailmap
.travis.yml
AUTHORS
BUGS
CHANGES
DEVELOPERS
INSTALL
INSTALL.Unix
INSTALL.Windows
LICENSE
Makefile.am
NEWS
NOTICE
README
THANKS.in
acinclude.m4.in
bin/
bootstrap
build-aux/
configure.ac
etc/
license.skip
share/
src/
test/
utils/
var/
```

The documentation sources live in *share/doc/src*, you can safely ignore all the other files and directories.

First we should determine where we want to document this inside the documentation. We can look through http://docs.couchdb.org/en/latest/ for inspiration. The JSON Structure Reference looks like a fine place to write this up.

The current state includes mostly tables describing the JSON structure (after all, that's the title of this chapter), but some prose about the number representation can't hurt. For future reference, since the topic in the thread includes views and different encoding in views (as opposed to the storage engine), we should remember to make a note in the views documentation as well, but we'll leave this for later.

Let's try and find the source file that builds the file http://docs.couchdb.org/en/latest/json-structure.html – we are in luck, under *share/doc/src* we find the file *json-structure.rst*. That looks promising. *.rst* stands for ReStructured Text (see http://thomas-cokelaer.info/tutorials/sphinx/rest_syntax.html for a markup reference), which is an ascii format for writing documents, documentation in this case. Let's have a look and open it.

We see ascii tables with some additional formatting, all looking like the final HTML. So far so easy. For now, let's just add to the bottom of this. We can worry about organising this better later.

We start by adding a new headline:

```
Number Handling
===============
```

Now we paste in the rest of the main email of the thread. It is mostly text, but it includes some code listings. Let's mark them up. We'll turn:

```
ejson:encode(ejson:decode(<<"1.1">>)).
<<"1.1000000000000000888">>
```

Into:

```
.. code-block:: erlang

    ejson:encode(ejson:decode(<<"1.1">>)).
    <<"1.1000000000000000888">>
```

And we follow along with the other code samples. We turn:

```
Spidermonkey

$ js -h 2>&1 | head -n 1
JavaScript-C 1.8.5 2011-03-31
$ js
js> JSON.stringify(JSON.parse("1.0123456789012345678901234567890123456789"))
"1.0123456789012346"
js> var f = JSON.stringify(JSON.parse("1.0123456789012345678901234567890123456789")
js> JSON.stringify(JSON.parse(f))
"1.0123456789012346"
```

into:

```
Spidermonkey::

    $ js -h 2>&1 | head -n 1
    JavaScript-C 1.8.5 2011-03-31
    $ js
    js> JSON.stringify(JSON.parse("1.0123456789012345678901234567890123456789"))
    "1.0123456789012346"
    js> var f = JSON.stringify(JSON.parse("1.0123456789012345678901234567890123456789"))
    js> JSON.stringify(JSON.parse(f))
    "1.0123456789012346"
```

And then follow all the other ones.

I cleaned up the text a little but to make it sound more like a documentation entry as opposed to a post on a mailing list.

The next step would be to validate that we got all the markup right. I'll leave this for later. For now we'll contribute our change back to CouchDB.

First, we commit our changes:

```
$ > git commit -am 'document number encoding'
[master a84b2cf] document number encoding
1 file changed, 199 insertions(+)
```

Then we push the commit to our CouchDB fork:

```
$ git push origin master
```

Next, we go back to our GitHub page https://github.com/janl/couchdb and click the "Pull Request" button. Fill in the description with something useful and hit the "Send Pull Request" button.

And we're done!

14.1 Style Guidelines for this Documentation

When you make a change to the documentation, you should make sure that you follow the style. Look through some files and you will see that the style is quite straightforward. If you do not know if your formating is in compliance with the style, ask yourself the following question:

```
Is it needed for correct syntax?
```

If the answer is `No.` then it is probably not.

These guidelines strive be simple, without contradictions and exceptions. The best style is the one that is followed because it seems to be the natural way of doing it.

14.1.1 The guidelines

The guidelines are in descending priority.

1. Syntax

    • Correct syntax is always more important than style. This includes configuration files, HTML responses, etc.

2. Encoding

    • All files are `UTF-8`.

3. Line ending

    • All lines end with `\n`.

    • No trailing whitespaces.

4. Line length

    • The maximum line length is `80` characters.

5. Links

    • All internal links are relative.

6. Indentation

    • 4 spaces.

7. Titles

    • The highest level titles in a file is over and underlined with =.

    • Lower level titles are underlined with the following characters in descending order:

```
  =  -  ^  *   + #  `  :  .  "  ~  _
```

- Over and underline match the title length.

8. Empty lines

    - No empty line at the end of the file.

    - Lists may separated each item with an empty line.

```
  =  -  ^  *   + #  `  :  .  "  ~  _
```

## CHAPTER 15

Release History

15.1 2.0.x Branch

- *Upgrade Notes*
- *Version 2.0.0*

15.1.1 Upgrade Notes

Note: TBD

15.1.2 Version 2.0.0

Note: TBD

15.2 1.6.x Branch

- *Upgrade Notes*
- *Version 1.6.0*

15.2.1 Upgrade Notes

The *Proxy Authentication* handler was renamed to proxy_authentication_handler to follow the *_authentication_handler form of all other handlers. The old proxy_authentification_handler name is marked as deprecated and will be removed in future releases. It's strongly recommended to update *httpd/authentication_handlers* option with new value in case if you had used such handler.

15.2.2 Version 1.6.0

- COUCHDB-2200: support Erlang/OTP 17.0 #35e16032

- Fauxton: many improvements in our experimental new user interface, including switching the code editor from CodeMirror to Ace as well as better support for various browsers.

- Add the `max_count` option (*UUIDs Configuration*) to allow rate-limiting the amount of UUIDs that can be requested from the */_uuids* handler in a single request (*CVE 2014-2668*).

- COUCHDB-1986: increase socket buffer size to improve replication speed for large documents and attachments, and fix tests on BSD-like systems. #9a0e561b

- COUCHDB-1953: improve performance of multipart/related requests. #ce3e89dc

- COUCHDB-2221: verify that authentication-related configuration settings are well-formed. #dbe769c6

- COUCHDB-1922: fix CORS exposed headers. #4f619833

- Rename `proxy_authentification_handler` to `proxy_authentication_handler`. #c66ac4a8

- COUCHDB-1795: ensure the startup script clears the pid file on termination. #818ef4f9

- COUCHDB-1962: replication can now be performed without having write access to the source database (#1d5fe2aa), the replication checkpoint interval is now configurable (#0693f98e).

- COUCHDB-2025: add support for SOCKS5 proxies for replication. #fcd76c9

- COUCHDB-1930: redirect to the correct page after submitting a new document with a different ID than the one suggested by Futon. #4906b591

- COUCHDB-1923: add support for *attachments* and *att_encoding_info* options (formerly only available on the documents API) to the view API. #ca41964b

- COUCHDB-1647: for failed replications originating from a document in the *_replicator* database, store the failure reason in the document. #08cac68b

- A number of improvements for the documentation.

15.3 1.5.x Branch

- *Version 1.5.1*
- *Version 1.5.0*

> **Warning:** *Version 1.5.1* contains important security fixes. Previous *1.5.x* releases are not recommended for regular usage.

15.3.1 Version 1.5.1

- Add the `max_count` option (*UUIDs Configuration*) to allow rate-limiting the amount of UUIDs that can be requested from the */_uuids* handler in a single request (*CVE 2014-2668*).

15.3.2 Version 1.5.0

- COUCHDB-1781: The official documentation has been overhauled. A lot of content from other sources have been merged, and the index page has been rebuilt to make the docs much more accessible. #54813a7

- A new administration UI, codenamed Fauxton, has been included as an experimental preview. It can be accessed at `/_utils/fauxton/`. There are too many improvements here to list them all. We are looking for feedback from the community on this preview release.

- COUCHDB-1888: Fixed an issue where admin users would be restricted by the `public_fields` feature.

- Fixed an issue with the JavaScript CLI test runner. #be76882, #54813a7

- COUCHDB-1867: An experimental plugin feature has been added. See src/couch_plugin/README.md for details. We invite the community to test and report any findings.

- COUCHDB-1894: An experimental Node.js-based query server runtime has been added. See *Experimental Features* for details. We invite the community to test and report any findings.

- COUCHDB-1901: Better retry mechanism for transferring attachments during replication. #4ca2cec

15.4 1.4.x Branch

- *Upgrade Notes*
- *Version 1.4.0*

Warning: *1.4.x Branch* is affected by the issue described in *CVE-2014-2668: DoS (CPU and memory consumption) via the count parameter to /_uuids.* Upgrading to a more recent release is strongly recommended.

15.4.1 Upgrade Notes

We now support Erlang/OTP R16B and R16B01; the minimum required version is R14B.

User document role values must now be strings. Other types of values will be refused when saving the user document.

15.4.2 Version 1.4.0

- COUCHDB-1139: it's possible to apply *list* functions to _all_docs view. #54fd258e

- COUCHDB-1632: Ignore epilogues in multipart/related MIME attachments. #2b4ab67a

- COUCHDB-1634: Reduce PBKDF2 work factor. #f726bc4d

- COUCHDB-1684: Support for server-wide changes feed reporting on creation, updates and deletion of databases. #917d8988

- COUCHDB-1772: Prevent invalid JSON output when using *all_or_nothing* *of bulk API*. #dfd39d57

- Add a configurable whitelist of user document properties. #8d7ab8b1

- COUCHDB-1852: Support Last-Event-ID header in EventSource changes feeds. #dfd2199a

- Allow storing pre-hashed admin passwords via *config API*. #c98ba561

- Automatic loading of CouchDB plugins. #3fab6bb5

- Much improved documentation, including an *expanded description* of *validate_doc_update* functions (commit:*ef9ac469*) and a description of how CouchDB handles JSON *number values* (#bbd93f77).

- Split up *replicator_db* tests into multiple independent tests.

15.5 1.3.x Branch

- *Upgrade Notes*
- *Version 1.3.1*
- *Version 1.3.0*

> **Warning:** *1.3.x Branch* is affected by the issue described in *CVE-2014-2668: DoS (CPU and memory consumption) via the count parameter to /_uuids*. Upgrading to a more recent release is strongly recommended.

15.5.1 Upgrade Notes

You can upgrade your existing CouchDB 1.0.x installation to 1.3.0 without any specific steps or migration. When you run CouchDB, the existing data and index files will be opened and used as normal.

The first time you run a compaction routine on your database within 1.3.0, the data structure and indexes will be updated to the new version of the CouchDB database format that can only be read by CouchDB 1.3.0 and later. This step is not reversible. Once the data files have been updated and migrated to the new version the data files will no longer work with a CouchDB 1.0.x release.

> **Warning:** If you want to retain support for opening the data files in CouchDB 1.0.x you must back up your data files before performing the upgrade and compaction process.

15.5.2 Version 1.3.1

Replicator

- COUCHDB-1788: Tolerate missing source and target fields in _replicator docs. #869f42e2

Log System

- COUCHDB-1794: Fix bug in WARN level logging from 1.3.0.
- Don't log about missing .compact files. #06f1a8dc

View Server

- COUCHDB-1792: Fix the -S option to couchjs to increase memory limits. #cfaa66cd

Miscellaneous

- COUCHDB-1784: Improvements to test suite and VPATH build system. #01afaa4f
- Improve documentation: better structure, improve language, less duplication.

15.5.3 Version 1.3.0

Database core

- COUCHDB-1512: Validate bind address before assignment. #09ead8a0
- Restore `max_document_size` protection. #bf1eb135

Documentation

- COUCHDB-1523: Import CouchBase documentation and convert them into Sphinx docs

Futon

- COUCHDB-509: Added view request duration to Futon. #2d2c7d1c

- COUCHDB-627: Support all timezones. #b1a049bb

- COUCHDB-1383: Futon view editor won't allow you to save original view after saving a revision. #cc48342

- COUCHDB-1470: Futon raises popup on attempt to navigate to missed/deleted document. #5da40eef

- COUCHDB-1473, COUCHDB-1472: Disable buttons for actions that the user doesn't have permissions to. #7156254d

HTTP Interface

- COUCHDB-431: Introduce experimental *CORS support*. #b90e4021

- COUCHDB-764, COUCHDB-514, COUCHDB-430: Fix sending HTTP headers from `_list` function, #2a74f88375

- COUCHDB-887: Fix `bytes` and `offset` parameters semantic for *_log* resource (explanation) #ad700014

- COUCHDB-986: Added Server-Sent Events protocol to db changes API. See http://www.w3.org/TR/eventsource/ for details. #093d2aa6

- COUCHDB-1026: Database names are encoded with respect of special characters in the rewriter now. #272d6415

- COUCHDB-1097: Allow *OPTIONS* request to shows and lists functions. #9f53704a

- COUCHDB-1210: Files starting with underscore can be attached and updated now. #05858792

- COUCHDB-1277: Better query parameter support and code clarity: #7e3c69ba

    - Responses to documents created/modified via form data *POST* to /db/doc or copied with *COPY* should now include *Location* header.

    - Form data POST to /db/doc now includes an *ETag* response header.

    - `?batch=ok` is now supported for *COPY* and *POST* /db/doc updates.

    - `?new_edits=false` is now supported for more operations.

- COUCHDB-1285: Allow configuration of vendor and modules version in CouchDB welcome message. #3c24a94d

- COUCHDB-1321: Variables in rewrite rules breaks OAuth authentication. #c307ba95

- COUCHDB-1337: Use MD5 for attachment ETag header value. #6d912c9f

- COUCHDB-1381: Add jquery.couch support for Windows 8 Metro apps. #dfc5d37c

- COUCHDB-1441: Limit recursion depth in the URL rewriter. Defaults to a maximum of 100 invocations but is configurable. #d076976c

- COUCHDB-1442: No longer rewrites the *X-CouchDB-Requested-Path* during recursive calls to the rewriter. #56744f2f

- COUCHDB-1501: *Changes feed* now can take special parameter `since=now` to emit changes since current point of time. #3bbb2612

- COUCHDB-1502: Allow users to delete own _users doc. #f0d6f19bc8

- COUCHDB-1511: CouchDB checks *roles* field for *_users* database documents with more care. #41205000

- COUCHDB-1537: Include user name in show/list *ETags*. #ac320479

- Send a 202 response for *_restart*. #b213e16f

- Make password hashing synchronous when using the /_config/admins API. #08071a80

- Add support to serve single file with CouchDB, #2774531ff2

- Allow any 2xx code to indicate success, #0d50103cfd

- Fix _session_ for IE7.

- Restore 400 error for empty PUT, #2057b895

- Return X-Couch-Id header if doc is created, #98515bf0b9

- Support auth cookies with : characters, #d9566c831d

Log System

- COUCHDB-1380: Minor fixes for logrotate support.

- Improve file I/O error logging and handling, #4b6475da

- Module Level Logging, #b58f069167

- Log 5xx responses at error level, #e896b0b7

- Log problems opening database at ERROR level except for auto-created system dbs, #41667642f7

Replicator

- COUCHDB-1248: *HTTP 500* error now doesn't occurs when replicating with ?doc_ids=null. #bea76dbf

- COUCHDB-1259: Stabilize replication id, #c6252d6d7f

- COUCHDB-1323: Replicator now acts as standalone application. #f913ca6e

- COUCHDB-1363: Fix rarely occurred, but still race condition in changes feed if a quick burst of changes happens while replication is starting the replication can go stale. #573a7bb9

- COUCHDB-1557: Upgrade some code to use BIFs bring good improvements for replication.

Security

- COUCHDB-1060: Passwords are now hashed using the PBKDF2 algorithm with a configurable work factor. #7d418134

Source Repository

- The source repository was migrated from SVN to Git.

Storage System

- Fixed unnecessary conflict when deleting and creating a document in the same batch.

Test Suite

- COUCHDB-1321: Moved the JS test suite to the CLI.

- COUCHDB-1338: Start CouchDB with port=0. While CouchDB might be already running on the default port 5984, port number 0 let the TCP stack figure out a free port to run. #127cbe3

- COUCHDB-1339: Use shell trap to catch dying beam processes during test runs. #2921c78

- COUCHDB-1389: Improved tracebacks printed by the JS CLI tests.

- COUCHDB-1563: Ensures urlPrefix is set in all ajax requests. #07a6af222
- Fix race condition for test running on faster hardware.
- Improved the reliability of a number of tests.

URL Rewriter & Vhosts

- COUCHDB-1026: Database name is encoded during rewriting (allowing embedded /'s, etc). #272d6415

UUID Algorithms

- COUCHDB-1373: Added the utc_id algorithm #5ab712a2

Query and View Server

- COUCHDB-111: Improve the errors reported by the javascript view server to provide a more friendly error report when something goes wrong. #0c619ed
- COUCHDB-410: More graceful error handling for JavaScript validate_doc_update functions.
- COUCHDB-1372: _stats builtin reduce function no longer produces error for empty view result.
- COUCHDB-1444: Fix missed_named_view error that occurs on existed design documents and views. #b59ac98b
- COUCHDB-1445: CouchDB tries no more to delete view file if it couldn't open it, even if the error is *emfile*.
- COUCHDB-1483: Update handlers requires valid doc ids. #72ea7e38
- COUCHDB-1491: Clenaup view tables. #c37204b7
- Deprecate E4X support, #cdfdda2314

Windows

- COUCHDB-1482: Use correct linker flag to build *snappy_nif.dll* on Windows. #a6eaf9f1
- Allows building cleanly on Windows without cURL, #fb670f5712

15.6 1.2.x Branch

- *Upgrade Notes*
- *Version 1.2.2*
- *Version 1.2.1*
- *Version 1.2.0*

15.6.1 Upgrade Notes

Warning: This version drops support for the database format that was introduced in version 0.9.0. Compact your older databases (that have not been compacted for a long time) before upgrading, or they will become inaccessible.

> **Warning:** *Version 1.2.1* contains important security fixes. Previous *1.2.x* releases are not recommended for regular usage.

Security changes

The interface to the _users and _replicator databases have been changed so that non-administrator users can see less information:

- In the _users database:
    - User documents can now only be read by the respective users, as well as administrators. Other users cannot read these documents.
    - Views can only be defined and queried by administrator users.
    - The _changes feed can only be queried by administrator users.
- In the _replicator database:
    - Documents now have a forced owner field that corresponds to the authenticated user that created them.
    - Non-owner users will not see confidential information like passwords or OAuth tokens in replication documents; they can still see the other contents of those documents. Administrators can see everything.
    - Views can only be defined and queried by administrators.

Database Compression

The new optional (but enabled by default) compression of disk files requires an upgrade of the on-disk format (5 -> 6) which occurs on creation for new databases and views, and on compaction for existing files. This format is not supported in previous releases, so rollback would require replication to the previous CouchDB release or restoring from backup.

Compression can be disabled by setting compression = none in your local.ini [couchdb] section, but the on-disk format will still be upgraded.

15.6.2 Version 1.2.2

Build System

- Fixed issue in *couchdb* script where stopped status returns before process exits.

HTTP Interface

- Reset rewrite counter on new request, avoiding unnecessary request failures due to bogus rewrite limit reports.

15.6.3 Version 1.2.1

Build System

- Fix couchdb start script.
- Win: fix linker invocations.

Futon

- Disable buttons that aren't available for the logged-in user.

HTTP Interface

- No longer rewrites the `X-CouchDB-Requested-Path` during recursive calls to the rewriter.
- Limit recursion depth in the URL rewriter. Defaults to a maximum of 100 invocations but is configurable.

Security

- Fixed *CVE-2012-5641: Information disclosure via unescaped backslashes in URLs on Windows*
- Fixed *CVE-2012-5649: JSONP arbitrary code execution with Adobe Flash*
- Fixed *CVE-2012-5650: DOM based Cross-Site Scripting via Futon UI*

Replication

- Fix potential timeouts.

View Server

- Change use of signals to avoid broken view groups.

15.6.4 Version 1.2.0

Authentication

- Fix use of OAuth with VHosts and URL rewriting.
- OAuth secrets can now be stored in the users system database as an alternative to key value pairs in the .ini configuration. By default this is disabled (secrets are stored in the .ini) but can be enabled via the .ini configuration key *use_users_db* in the *couch_httpd_oauth* section.
- Documents in the _users database are no longer publicly readable.
- Confidential information in the _replication database is no longer publicly readable.
- Password hashes are now calculated by CouchDB. Clients are no longer required to do this manually.
- Cookies used for authentication can be made persistent by enabling the .ini configuration key *allow_persistent_cookies* in the *couch_httpd_auth* section.

Build System

- cURL is no longer required to build CouchDB as it is only used by the command line JS test runner. If cURL is available when building CouchJS you can enable the HTTP bindings by passing -H on the command line.
- Temporarily made *make check* pass with R15B. A more thorough fix is in the works (COUCHDB-1424).
- Fixed –with-js-include and –with-js-lib options.
- Added –with-js-lib-name option.

Futon

- The *Status* screen (active tasks) now displays two new task status fields: *Started on* and *Updated on*.

- Futon remembers view code every time it is saved, allowing to save an edit that amounts to a revert.

HTTP Interface

- Added a native JSON parser.

- The _active_tasks API now offers more granular fields. Each task type is now able to expose different properties.

- Added built-in changes feed filter *_view*.

- Fixes to the *_changes* feed heartbeat option which caused heartbeats to be missed when used with a filter. This caused timeouts of continuous pull replications with a filter.

- Properly restart the SSL socket on configuration changes.

OAuth

- Updated bundled *erlang_oauth* library to the latest version.

Replicator

- A new replicator implementation. It offers more performance and configuration options.

- Passing non-string values to query_params is now a 400 bad request. This is to reduce the surprise that all parameters are converted to strings internally.

- Added optional field *since_seq* to replication objects/documents. It allows to bootstrap a replication from a specific source sequence number.

- Simpler replication cancellation. In addition to the current method, replications can now be canceled by specifying the replication ID instead of the original replication object/document.

Storage System

- Added optional database and view index file compression (using Google's snappy or zlib's deflate). This feature is enabled by default, but it can be disabled by adapting local.ini accordingly. The on-disk format is upgraded on compaction and new DB/view creation to support this.

- Several performance improvements, most notably regarding database writes and view indexing.

- Computation of the size of the latest MVCC snapshot data and all its supporting metadata, both for database and view index files. This information is exposed as the *data_size* attribute in the database and view group information URIs.

- The size of the buffers used for database and view compaction is now configurable.

- Added support for automatic database and view compaction. This feature is disabled by default, but it can be enabled via the .ini configuration.

- Performance improvements for the built-in changes feed filters *_doc_ids* and *_design*.

View Server

- Add CoffeeScript (http://coffeescript.org/) as a first class view server language.

- Fixed old index file descriptor leaks after a view cleanup.

- The requested_path property keeps the pre-rewrite path even when no VHost configuration is matched.

- Fixed incorrect reduce query results when using pagination parameters.

- Made icu_driver work with Erlang R15B and later.

15.7 1.1.x Branch

- *Upgrade Notes*
- *Version 1.1.2*
- *Version 1.1.1*
- *Version 1.1.0*

15.7.1 Upgrade Notes

> **Warning:** *Version 1.1.2* contains important security fixes. Previous *1.1.x* releases are not recommended for regular usage.

15.7.2 Version 1.1.2

Build System

- Don't *ln* the *couchjs* install target on Windows

- Remove ICU version dependency on Windows.

- Improve SpiderMonkey version detection.

HTTP Interface

- ETag of attachment changes only when the attachment changes, not the document.

- Fix retrieval of headers larger than 4k.

- Allow OPTIONS HTTP method for list requests.

- Don't attempt to encode invalid json.

Log System

- Improvements to log messages for file-related errors.

Replicator

- Fix pull replication of documents with many revisions.

- Fix replication from an HTTP source to an HTTP target.

Security

- Fixed *CVE-2012-5641: Information disclosure via unescaped backslashes in URLs on Windows*
- Fixed *CVE-2012-5649: JSONP arbitrary code execution with Adobe Flash*
- Fixed *CVE-2012-5650: DOM based Cross-Site Scripting via Futon UI*

View Server

- Avoid invalidating view indexes when running out of file descriptors.

15.7.3 Version 1.1.1

- Support SpiderMonkey 1.8.5
- Add configurable maximum to the number of bytes returned by _log.
- Allow CommonJS modules to be an empty string.
- Bump minimum Erlang version to R13B02.
- Do not run deleted validate_doc_update functions.
- ETags for views include current sequence if include_docs=true.
- Fix bug where duplicates can appear in _changes feed.
- Fix bug where update handlers break after conflict resolution.
- Fix bug with _replicator where include "filter" could crash couch.
- Fix crashes when compacting large views.
- Fix file descriptor leak in _log
- Fix missing revisions in _changes?style=all_docs.
- Improve handling of compaction at max_dbs_open limit.
- JSONP responses now send "text/javascript" for Content-Type.
- Link to ICU 4.2 on Windows.
- Permit forward slashes in path to update functions.
- Reap couchjs processes that hit reduce_overflow error.
- Status code can be specified in update handlers.
- Support provides() in show functions.
- _view_cleanup when ddoc has no views now removes all index files.
- max_replication_retry_count now supports "infinity".
- Fix replication crash when source database has a document with empty ID.
- Fix deadlock when assigning couchjs processes to serve requests.
- Fixes to the document multipart PUT API.
- Fixes regarding file descriptor leaks for databases with views.

15.7.4 Version 1.1.0

Note: All CHANGES for 1.0.2 and 1.0.3 also apply to 1.1.0.

Externals

- Added OS Process module to manage daemons outside of CouchDB.
- Added HTTP Proxy handler for more scalable externals.

Futon

- Added a "change password"-feature to Futon.

HTTP Interface

- Native SSL support.
- Added support for HTTP range requests for attachments.
- Added built-in filters for _changes_: _doc_ids_ and _design_.
- Added configuration option for TCP_NODELAY aka "Nagle".
- Allow POSTing arguments to _changes_.
- Allow _keys_ parameter for GET requests to views.
- Allow wildcards in vhosts definitions.
- More granular ETag support for views.
- More flexible URL rewriter.
- Added support for recognizing "Q values" and media parameters in HTTP Accept headers.
- Validate doc ids that come from a PUT to a URL.

Replicator

- Added _replicator_ database to manage replications.
- Fixed issues when an endpoint is a remote database accessible via SSL.
- Added support for continuous by-doc-IDs replication.
- Fix issue where revision info was omitted when replicating attachments.
- Integrity of attachment replication is now verified by MD5.

Storage System

- Multiple micro-optimizations when reading data.

URL Rewriter & Vhosts

- Fix for variable substituion

View Server

- Added CommonJS support to map functions.
- Added _stale=update_after_ query option that triggers a view update after returning a _stale=ok_ response.
- Warn about empty result caused by _startkey_ and _endkey_ limiting.
- Built-in reduce function _sum_ now accepts lists of integers as input.

• Added view query aliases start_key, end_key, start_key_doc_id and end_key_doc_id.

15.8 1.0.x Branch

• *Upgrade Notes*
• *Version 1.0.4*
• *Version 1.0.3*
• *Version 1.0.2*
• *Version 1.0.1*
• *Version 1.0.0*

15.8.1 Upgrade Notes

Note, to replicate with a 1.0 CouchDB instance you must first upgrade in-place your current CouchDB to 1.0 or 0.11.1 – backporting so that 0.10.x can replicate to 1.0 wouldn't be that hard. All that is required is patching the replicator to use the application/json content type.

• _log and _temp_views are now admin-only resources.

• _bulk_docs now requires a valid *Content-Type* header of application/json.

• *JSONP* is disabled by default. An .ini option was added to selectively enable it.

• The key, startkey and endkey properties of the request object passed to *list* and *show* functions now contain JSON objects representing the URL encoded string values in the query string. Previously, these properties contained strings which needed to be converted to JSON before using.

> **Warning:** *Version 1.0.4* contains important security fixes. Previous *1.0.x* releases are not recommended for regular usage.

15.8.2 Version 1.0.4

HTTP Interface

• Fix missing revisions in _changes?style=all_docs.

• Fix validation of attachment names.

Log System

• Fix file descriptor leak in _log.

Replicator

• Fix a race condition where replications can go stale

Security

• Fixed *CVE-2012-5641: Information disclosure via unescaped backslashes in URLs on Windows*

• Fixed *CVE-2012-5649: JSONP arbitrary code execution with Adobe Flash*

• Fixed *CVE-2012-5650: DOM based Cross-Site Scripting via Futon UI*

View System

- Avoid invalidating view indexes when running out of file descriptors.

15.8.3 Version 1.0.3

General

- Fixed compatibility issues with Erlang R14B02.

Etap Test Suite

- Etap tests no longer require use of port 5984. They now use a randomly selected port so they won't clash with a running CouchDB.

Futon

- Made compatible with jQuery 1.5.x.

HTTP Interface

- Fix bug that allows invalid UTF-8 after valid escapes.
- The query parameter *include_docs* now honors the parameter *conflicts*. This applies to queries against map views, _all_docs and _changes.
- Added support for inclusive_end with reduce views.

Replicator

- Enabled replication over IPv6.
- Fixed for crashes in continuous and filtered changes feeds.
- Fixed error when restarting replications in OTP R14B02.
- Upgrade ibrowse to version 2.2.0.
- Fixed bug when using a filter and a limit of 1.

Security

- Fixed OAuth signature computation in OTP R14B02.
- Handle passwords with : in them.

Storage System

- More performant queries against _changes and _all_docs when using the *include_docs* parameter.

Windows

- Windows builds now require ICU >= 4.4.0 and Erlang >= R14B03. See COUCHDB-1152, and COUCHDB-963 + OTP-9139 for more information.

15.8.4 Version 1.0.2

Futon

- Make test suite work with Safari and Chrome.
- Fixed animated progress spinner.
- Fix raw view document link due to overzealous URI encoding.
- Spell javascript correctly in loadScript(uri).

HTTP Interface

- Allow reduce=false parameter in map-only views.
- Fix parsing of Accept headers.
- Fix for multipart GET APIs when an attachment was created during a local-local replication. See COUCHDB-1022 for details.

Log System

- Reduce lengthy stack traces.
- Allow logging of native <xml> types.

Replicator

- Updated ibrowse library to 2.1.2 fixing numerous replication issues.
- Make sure that the replicator respects HTTP settings defined in the config.
- Fix error when the ibrowse connection closes unexpectedly.
- Fix authenticated replication (with HTTP basic auth) of design documents with attachments.
- Various fixes to make replication more resilient for edge-cases.

Storage System

- Fix leaking file handles after compacting databases and views.
- Fix databases forgetting their validation function after compaction.
- Fix occasional timeout errors after successfully compacting large databases.
- Fix ocassional error when writing to a database that has just been compacted.
- Fix occasional timeout errors on systems with slow or heavily loaded IO.
- Fix for OOME when compactions include documents with many conflicts.
- Fix for missing attachment compression when MIME types included parameters.
- Preserve purge metadata during compaction to avoid spurious view rebuilds.
- Fix spurious conflicts introduced when uploading an attachment after a doc has been in a conflict. See COUCHDB-902 for details.
- Fix for frequently edited documents in multi-master deployments being duplicated in _changes and _all_docs. See COUCHDB-968 for details on how to repair.
- Significantly higher read and write throughput against database and view index files.

View Server

- Don't trigger view updates when requesting *_design/doc/_info*.

- Fix for circular references in CommonJS requires.

- Made isArray() function available to functions executed in the query server.

- Documents are now sealed before being passed to map functions.

- Force view compaction failure when duplicated document data exists. When this error is seen in the logs users should rebuild their views from scratch to fix the issue. See COUCHDB-999 for details.

15.8.5 Version 1.0.1

Authentication

- **Enable basic-auth popup when required to access the server, to prevent** people from getting locked out.

Build and System Integration

- Included additional source files for distribution.

Futon

- User interface element for querying stale (cached) views.

HTTP Interface

- Expose *committed_update_seq* for monitoring purposes.

- Show fields saved along with _deleted=true. Allows for auditing of deletes.

- More robust Accept-header detection.

Replicator

- Added support for replication via an HTTP/HTTPS proxy.

- Fix pull replication of attachments from 0.11 to 1.0.x.

- Make the _changes feed work with non-integer seqnums.

Storage System

- Fix data corruption bug COUCHDB-844. Please see http://couchdb.apache.org/notice/1.0.1.html for details.

15.8.6 Version 1.0.0

Security

- Added authentication caching, to avoid repeated opening and closing of the users database for each request requiring authentication.

Storage System

- Small optimization for reordering result lists.

- More efficient header commits.

- Use O_APPEND to save lseeks.

- Faster implementation of pread_iolist(). Further improves performance on concurrent reads.

View Server

- Faster default view collation.

- Added option to include update_seq in view responses.

15.9 0.11.x Branch

- *Upgrade Notes*
- *Version 0.11.2*
- *Version 0.11.1*
- *Version 0.11.0*

15.9.1 Upgrade Notes

> **Warning:** *Version 0.11.2* contains important security fixes. Previous *0.11.x* releases are not recommended for regular usage.

Changes Between 0.11.0 and 0.11.1

- `_log` and `_temp_views` are now admin-only resources.

- `_bulk_docs` now requires a valid *Content-Type* header of `application/json`.

- *JSONP* is disabled by default. An .ini option was added to selectively enable it.

- The `key`, `startkey` and `endkey` properties of the request object passed to *list* and *show* functions now contain JSON objects representing the URL encoded string values in the query string. Previously, these properties contained strings which needed to be converted to JSON before using.

Changes Between 0.10.x and 0.11.0

show, list, update and validation functions

The `req` argument to show, list, update and validation functions now contains the member method with the specified HTTP method of the current request. Previously, this member was called `verb`. `method` is following RFC 2616 (HTTP 1.1) closer.

_admins -> _security

The */db/_admins* handler has been removed and replaced with a */db/_security* object. Any existing *_admins* will be dropped and need to be added to the security object again. The reason for this is that the old system made no distinction between names and roles, while the new one does, so there is no way to automatically upgrade the old admins list.

The security object has 2 special fields, `admins` and `readers`, which contain lists of names and roles which are admins or readers on that database. Anything else may be stored in other fields on the security object. The entire object is made available to validation functions.

json2.js

JSON handling in the query server has been upgraded to use json2.js. This allows us to use faster native JSON serialization when it is available.

In previous versions, attempts to serialize undefined would throw an exception, causing the doc that emitted undefined to be dropped from the view index. The new behavior is to serialize undefined as null. Applications depending on the old behavior will need to explicitly check for undefined.

Another change is that E4X's XML objects will not automatically be stringified. XML users will need to call `my_xml_object.toXMLString()` to return a string value. #8d3b7ab3

WWW-Authenticate

The default configuration has been changed to avoid causing basic-auth popups which result from sending the WWW-Authenticate header. To enable basic-auth popups, uncomment the `httpd/WWW-Authenticate` line in *local.ini*.

Query server line protocol

The query server line protocol has changed for all functions except *map*, *reduce*, and *rereduce*. This allows us to cache the entire design document in the query server process, which results in faster performance for common operations. It also gives more flexibility to query server implementators and shouldn't require major changes in the future when adding new query server features.

UTF8 JSON

JSON request bodies are validated for proper UTF-8 before saving, instead of waiting to fail on subsequent read requests.

_changes line format

Continuous changes are now newline delimited, instead of having each line followed by a comma.

15.9.2 Version 0.11.2

Authentication

- User documents can now be deleted by admins or the user.

Futon

- Add some Futon files that were missing from the Makefile.

HTTP Interface

- Better error messages on invalid URL requests.

Replicator

- Fix bug when pushing design docs by non-admins, which was hanging the replicator for no good reason.
- Fix bug when pulling design documents from a source that requires basic-auth.

Security

- Avoid potential DOS attack by guarding all creation of atoms.
- Fixed *CVE-2010-2234: Apache CouchDB Cross Site Request Forgery Attack*

15.9.3 Version 0.11.1

Build and System Integration

- Output of *couchdb –help* has been improved.
- Fixed compatibility with the Erlang R14 series.
- Fixed warnings on Linux builds.
- Fixed build error when aclocal needs to be called during the build.
- Require ICU 4.3.1.
- Fixed compatibility with Solaris.

Configuration System

- Fixed timeout with large .ini files.

Futon

- Use "expando links" for over-long document values in Futon.
- Added continuous replication option.
- Added option to replicating test results anonymously to a community CouchDB instance.
- Allow creation and deletion of config entries.
- Fixed display issues with doc ids that have escaped characters.
- Fixed various UI issues.

HTTP Interface

- Mask passwords in active tasks and logging.
- Update mochijson2 to allow output of BigNums not in float form.
- Added support for X-HTTP-METHOD-OVERRIDE.
- Better error message for database names.
- Disable jsonp by default.
- Accept gzip encoded standalone attachments.
- Made max_concurrent_connections configurable.
- Made changes API more robust.
- Send newly generated document rev to callers of an update function.

JavaScript Clients

- Added tests for couch.js and jquery.couch.js
- Added changes handler to jquery.couch.js.
- Added cache busting to jquery.couch.js if the user agent is msie.
- Added support for multi-document-fetch (via _all_docs) to jquery.couch.js.
- Added attachment versioning to jquery.couch.js.
- Added option to control ensure_full_commit to jquery.couch.js.
- Added list functionality to jquery.couch.js.
- Fixed issues where bulkSave() wasn't sending a POST body.

Log System

- Log HEAD requests as HEAD, not GET.
- Keep massive JSON blobs out of the error log.
- Fixed a timeout issue.

Replication System

- Refactored various internal APIs related to attachment streaming.
- Fixed hanging replication.
- Fixed keepalive issue.

Security

- Added authentication redirect URL to log in clients.
- Fixed query parameter encoding issue in oauth.js.
- Made authentication timeout configurable.
- Temporary views are now admin-only resources.

Storage System

- Don't require a revpos for attachment stubs.

- Added checking to ensure when a revpos is sent with an attachment stub, it's correct.

- Make file deletions async to avoid pauses during compaction and db deletion.

- Fixed for wrong offset when writing headers and converting them to blocks, only triggered when header is larger than 4k.

- Preserve _revs_limit and instance_start_time after compaction.

Test Suite

- Made the test suite overall more reliable.

View Server

- Provide a UUID to update functions (and all other functions) that they can use to create new docs.

- Upgrade CommonJS modules support to 1.1.1.

- Fixed erlang filter funs and normalize filter fun API.

- Fixed hang in view shutdown.

URL Rewriter & Vhosts

- Allow more complex keys in rewriter.

- Allow global rewrites so system defaults are available in vhosts.

- Allow isolation of databases with vhosts.

- Fix issue with passing variables to query parameters.

15.9.4 Version 0.11.0

Build and System Integration

- Updated and improved source documentation.

- Fixed distribution preparation for building on Mac OS X.

- Added support for building a Windows installer as part of 'make dist'.

- Bug fix for building couch.app's module list.

- ETap tests are now run during make distcheck. This included a number of updates to the build system to properly support VPATH builds.

- Gavin McDonald set up a build-bot instance. More info can be found at http://ci.apache.org/buildbot.html

Futon

- Added a button for view compaction.

- JSON strings are now displayed as-is in the document view, without the escaping of new-lines and quotes. That dramatically improves readability of multi-line strings.

- Same goes for editing of JSON string values. When a change to a field value is submitted, and the value is not valid JSON it is assumed to be a string. This improves editing of multi-line strings a lot.

- Hitting tab in textareas no longer moves focus to the next form field, but simply inserts a tab character at the current caret position.

- Fixed some font declarations.

HTTP Interface

- Provide Content-MD5 header support for attachments.

- Added URL Rewriter handler.

- Added virtual host handling.

Replication

- Added option to implicitly create replication target databases.

- Avoid leaking file descriptors on automatic replication restarts.

- Added option to replicate a list of documents by id.

- Allow continuous replication to be cancelled.

Runtime Statistics

- Statistics are now calculated for a moving window instead of non-overlapping timeframes.

- Fixed a problem with statistics timers and system sleep.

- Moved statistic names to a term file in the priv directory.

Security

- Fixed CVE-2010-0009: Apache CouchDB Timing Attack Vulnerability.

- Added default cookie-authentication and users database.

- Added Futon user interface for user signup and login.

- Added per-database reader access control lists.

- Added per-database security object for configuration data in validation functions.

- Added proxy authentication handler

Storage System

- Adds batching of multiple updating requests, to improve throughput with many writers. Removed the now redundant couch_batch_save module.

- Adds configurable compression of attachments.

View Server

- Added optional 'raw' binary collation for faster view builds where Unicode collation is not important.

- Improved view index build time by reducing ICU collation callouts.

- Improved view information objects.

- Bug fix for partial updates during view builds.

- Move query server to a design-doc based protocol.

- Use json2.js for JSON serialization for compatiblity with native JSON.

- Major refactoring of couchjs to lay the groundwork for disabling cURL support. The new HTTP interaction acts like a synchronous XHR. Example usage of the new system is in the JavaScript CLI test runner.

15.10 0.10.x Branch

- *Upgrade Notes*
- *Version 0.10.2*
- *Version 0.10.1*
- *Version 0.10.0*

15.10.1 Upgrade Notes

> **Warning:** *Version 0.10.2* contains important security fixes. Previous *0.10.x* releases are not recommended for regular usage.

Modular Configuration Directories

CouchDB now loads configuration from the following places (glob(7) syntax) in order:

- PREFIX/default.ini

- PREFIX/default.d/*

- PREFIX/local.ini

- PREFIX/local.d/*

The configuration options for *couchdb* script have changed to:

```
-a FILE      add configuration FILE to chain
-A DIR       add configuration DIR to chain
-n           reset configuration file chain (including system default)
-c           print configuration file chain and exit
```

Show and List API change

Show and List functions must have a new structure in 0.10. See Formatting_with_Show_and_List for details.

Stricter enforcing of reduciness in reduce-functions

Reduce functions are now required to reduce the number of values for a key.

View query reduce parameter strictness

CouchDB now considers the parameter `reduce=false` to be an error for queries of map-only views, and responds with status code 400.

15.10.2 Version 0.10.2

Build and System Integration

- Fixed distribution preparation for building on Mac OS X.

Security

- Fixed *CVE-2010-0009: Apache CouchDB Timing Attack Vulnerability*

Replicator

- Avoid leaking file descriptors on automatic replication restarts.

15.10.3 Version 0.10.1

Build and System Integration

- Test suite now works with the distcheck target.

Replicator

- Stability enhancements regarding redirects, timeouts, OAuth.

Query Server

- Avoid process leaks
- Allow list and view to span languages

Stats

- Eliminate new process flood on system wake

15.10.4 Version 0.10.0

Build and System Integration

- Changed *couchdb* script configuration options.
- Added default.d and local.d configuration directories to load sequence.

HTTP Interface

- Added optional cookie-based authentication handler.
- Added optional two-legged OAuth authentication handler.

Storage Format

- Add move headers with checksums to the end of database files for extra robust storage and faster storage.

View Server

- Added native Erlang views for high-performance applications.

15.11 0.9.x Branch

- *Upgrade Notes*
- *Version 0.9.2*
- *Version 0.9.1*
- *Version 0.9.0*

15.11.1 Upgrade Notes

Response to Bulk Creation/Updates

The response to a bulk creation / update now looks like this

```
[
    {"id": "0", "rev": "3682408536"},
    {"id": "1", "rev": "3206753266"},
    {"id": "2", "error": "conflict", "reason": "Document update conflict."}
]
```

Database File Format

The database file format has changed. CouchDB itself does yet not provide any tools for migrating your data. In the meantime, you can use third-party scripts to deal with the migration, such as the dump/load tools that come with the development version (trunk) of couchdb-python.

Renamed "count" to "limit"

The view query API has been changed: count has become limit. This is a better description of what the parameter does, and should be a simple update in any client code.

Moved View URLs

The view URLs have been moved to design document resources. This means that paths that used to be like:

```
http://hostname:5984/mydb/_view/designname/viewname?limit=10
```

will now look like:

```
http://hostname:5984/mydb/_design/designname/_view/viewname?limit=10.
```

See the REST, Hypermedia, and CouchApps thread on dev for details.

Attachments

Names of attachments are no longer allowed to start with an underscore.

Error Codes

Some refinements have been made to error handling. CouchDB will send 400 instead of 500 on invalid query parameters. Most notably, document update conflicts now respond with *409 Conflict* instead of *412 Precondition Failed*. The error code for when attempting to create a database that already exists is now 412 instead of 409.

ini file format

CouchDB 0.9 changes sections and configuration variable names in configuration files. Old .ini files won't work. Also note that CouchDB now ships with two .ini files where 0.8 used couch.ini there are now *default.ini* and *local.ini*. *default.ini* contains CouchDB's standard configuration values. local.ini is meant for local changes. *local.ini* is not overwritten on CouchDB updates, so your edits are safe. In addition, the new runtime configuration system persists changes to the configuration in *local.ini*.

15.11.2 Version 0.9.2

Build and System Integration

- Remove branch callbacks to allow building couchjs against newer versions of Spidermonkey.

Replication

- Fix replication with 0.10 servers initiated by an 0.9 server (COUCHDB-559).

15.11.3 Version 0.9.1

Build and System Integration

- PID file directory is now created by the SysV/BSD daemon scripts.
- Fixed the environment variables shown by the configure script.
- Fixed the build instructions shown by the configure script.
- Updated ownership and permission advice in *README* for better security.

Configuration and stats system

- Corrected missing configuration file error message.
- Fixed incorrect recording of request time.

Database Core

- Document validation for underscore prefixed variables.
- Made attachment storage less sparse.
- Fixed problems when a database with delayed commits pending is considered idle, and subject to losing changes when shutdown. (COUCHDB-334)

External Handlers

- Fix POST requests.

Futon

- Redirect when loading a deleted view URI from the cookie.

HTTP Interface

- Attachment requests respect the "rev" query-string parameter.

JavaScript View Server

- Useful JavaScript Error messages.

Replication

- Added support for Unicode characters transmitted as UTF-16 surrogate pairs.
- URL-encode attachment names when necessary.
- Pull specific revisions of an attachment, instead of just the latest one.
- Work around a rare chunk-merging problem in ibrowse.
- Work with documents containing Unicode characters outside the Basic Multilingual Plane.

15.11.4 Version 0.9.0

Build and System Integration

- The *couchdb* script now supports system chainable configuration files.
- The Mac OS X daemon script now redirects STDOUT and STDERR like SysV/BSD.
- The build and system integration have been improved for portability.
- Added COUCHDB_OPTIONS to etc/default/couchdb file.
- Remove COUCHDB_INI_FILE and COUCHDB_PID_FILE from etc/default/couchdb file.
- Updated *configure.ac* to manually link *libm* for portability.
- Updated *configure.ac* to extended default library paths.
- Removed inets configuration files.
- Added command line test runner.
- Created dev target for make.

Configuration and stats system

- Separate default and local configuration files.
- HTTP interface for configuration changes.
- Statistics framework with HTTP query API.

Database Core

- Faster B-tree implementation.
- Changed internal JSON term format.
- Improvements to Erlang VM interactions under heavy load.
- User context and administrator role.
- Update validations with design document validation functions.
- Document purge functionality.
- Ref-counting for database file handles.

Design Document Resource Paths

- Added httpd_design_handlers config section.
- Moved _view to httpd_design_handlers.
- Added ability to render documents as non-JSON content-types with _show and _list functions, which are also httpd_design_handlers.

Futon Utility Client

- Added pagination to the database listing page.
- Implemented attachment uploading from the document page.
- Added page that shows the current configuration, and allows modification of option values.
- Added a JSON "source view" for document display.
- JSON data in view rows is now syntax highlighted.
- Removed the use of an iframe for better integration with browser history and bookmarking.
- Full database listing in the sidebar has been replaced by a short list of recent databases.
- The view editor now allows selection of the view language if there is more than one configured.
- Added links to go to the raw view or document URI.
- Added status page to display currently running tasks in CouchDB.
- JavaScript test suite split into multiple files.
- Pagination for reduce views.

HTTP Interface

- Added client side UUIDs for idempotent document creation
- HTTP COPY for documents
- Streaming of chunked attachment PUTs to disk
- Remove negative count feature
- Add include_docs option for view queries
- Add multi-key view post for views
- Query parameter validation
- Use stale=ok to request potentially cached view index

- External query handler module for full-text or other indexers.

- Etags for attachments, views, shows and lists

- Show and list functions for rendering documents and views as developer controlled content-types.

- Attachment names may use slashes to allow uploading of nested directories (useful for static web hosting).

- Option for a view to run over design documents.

- Added newline to JSON responses. Closes bike-shed.

Replication

- Using ibrowse.

- Checkpoint replications so failures are less expensive.

- Automatically retry of failed replications.

- Stream attachments in pull-replication.

15.12 0.8.x Branch

- *Version 0.8.1-incubating*
- *Version 0.8.0-incubating*

15.12.1 Version 0.8.1-incubating

Build and System Integration

- The *couchdb* script no longer uses *awk* for configuration checks as this was causing portability problems.

- Updated *sudo* example in *README* to use the *-i* option, this fixes problems when invoking from a directory the *couchdb* user cannot access.

Database Core

- Fix for replication problems where the write queues can get backed up if the writes aren't happening fast enough to keep up with the reads. For a large replication, this can exhaust memory and crash, or slow down the machine dramatically. The fix keeps only one document in the write queue at a time.

- Fix for databases sometimes incorrectly reporting that they contain 0 documents after compaction.

- CouchDB now uses ibrowse instead of inets for its internal HTTP client implementation. This means better replication stability.

Futon

- The view selector dropdown should now work in Opera and Internet Explorer even when it includes opt-groups for design documents. (COUCHDB-81)

JavaScript View Server

- Sealing of documents has been disabled due to an incompatibility with SpiderMonkey 1.9.

- Improve error handling for undefined values emitted by map functions. (COUCHDB-83)

HTTP Interface

- Fix for chunked responses where chunks were always being split into multiple TCP packets, which caused problems with the test suite under Safari, and in some other cases.

- Fix for an invalid JSON response body being returned for some kinds of views. (COUCHDB-84)

- Fix for connections not getting closed after rejecting a chunked request. (COUCHDB-55)

- CouchDB can now be bound to IPv6 addresses.

- The HTTP *Server* header now contains the versions of CouchDB and Erlang.

15.12.2 Version 0.8.0-incubating

Build and System Integration

- CouchDB can automatically respawn following a server crash.

- Database server no longer refuses to start with a stale PID file.

- System logrotate configuration provided.

- Improved handling of ICU shared libraries.

- The *couchdb* script now automatically enables SMP support in Erlang.

- The *couchdb* and *couchjs* scripts have been improved for portability.

- The build and system integration have been improved for portability.

Database Core

- The view engine has been completely decoupled from the storage engine. Index data is now stored in separate files, and the format of the main database file has changed.

- Databases can now be compacted to reclaim space used for deleted documents and old document revisions.

- Support for incremental map/reduce views has been added.

- To support map/reduce, the structure of design documents has changed. View values are now JSON objects containing at least a *map* member, and optionally a *reduce* member.

- View servers are now identified by name (for example *javascript*) instead of by media type.

- Automatically generated document IDs are now based on proper UUID generation using the crypto module.

- The field *content-type* in the JSON representation of attachments has been renamed to *content_type* (underscore).

Futon

- When adding a field to a document, Futon now just adds a field with an autogenerated name instead of prompting for the name with a dialog. The name is automatically put into edit mode so that it can be changed immediately.

- Fields are now sorted alphabetically by name when a document is displayed.

- Futon can be used to create and update permanent views.

- The maximum number of rows to display per page on the database page can now be adjusted.

- Futon now uses the XMLHTTPRequest API asynchronously to communicate with the CouchDB HTTP server, so that most operations no longer block the browser.

- View results sorting can now be switched between ascending and descending by clicking on the *Key* column header.

- Fixed a bug where documents that contained a @ character could not be viewed. (COUCHDB-12)

- The database page now provides a *Compact* button to trigger database compaction. (COUCHDB-38)

- Fixed portential double encoding of document IDs and other URI segments in many instances. (COUCHDB-39)

- Improved display of attachments.

- The JavaScript Shell has been removed due to unresolved licensing issues.

JavaScript View Server

- SpiderMonkey is no longer included with CouchDB, but rather treated as a normal external dependency. A simple C program (*_couchjs*) is provided that links against an existing SpiderMonkey installation and uses the interpreter embedding API.

- View functions using the default JavaScript view server can now do logging using the global *log(message)* function. Log messages are directed into the CouchDB log at *INFO* level. (COUCHDB-59)

- The global *map(key, value)* function made available to view code has been renamed to *emit(key, value)*.

- Fixed handling of exceptions raised by view functions.

HTTP Interface

- CouchDB now uses MochiWeb instead of inets for the HTTP server implementation. Among other things, this means that the extra configuration files needed for inets (such as *couch_httpd.conf*) are no longer used.

- The HTTP interface now completely supports the *HEAD* method. (COUCHDB-3)

- Improved compliance of *Etag* handling with the HTTP specification. (COUCHDB-13)

- Etags are no longer included in responses to document *GET* requests that include query string parameters causing the JSON response to change without the revision or the URI having changed.

- The bulk document update API has changed slightly on both the request and the response side. In addition, bulk updates are now atomic.

- CouchDB now uses *TCP_NODELAY* to fix performance problems with persistent connections on some platforms due to nagling.

- Including a *?descending=false* query string parameter in requests to views no longer raises an error.

- Requests to unknown top-level reserved URLs (anything with a leading underscore) now return a *unknown_private_path* error instead of the confusing *illegal_database_name*.

- The Temporary view handling now expects a JSON request body, where the JSON is an object with at least a *map* member, and optional *reduce* and *language* members.

- Temporary views no longer determine the view server based on the Content-Type header of the *POST* request, but rather by looking for a *language* member in the JSON body of the request.

- The status code of responses to *DELETE* requests is now 200 to reflect that that the deletion is performed synchronously.

## CHAPTER 16

Security Issues Information

16.1 CVE-2010-0009: Apache CouchDB Timing Attack Vulnerability

Date 31.03.2010

Affected Apache CouchDB 0.8.0 to 0.10.1

Severity Important

Vendor The Apache Software Foundation

16.1.1 Description

Apache CouchDB versions prior to version *0.11.0* are vulnerable to timing attacks, also known as side-channel information leakage, due to using simple break-on-inequality string comparisons when verifying hashes and passwords.

16.1.2 Mitigation

All users should upgrade to CouchDB *0.11.0*. Upgrades from the *0.10.x* series should be seamless. Users on earlier versions should consult with *upgrade notes*.

16.1.3 Example

A canonical description of the attack can be found in http://codahale.com/a-lesson-in-timing-attacks/

16.1.4 Credit

This issue was discovered by *Jason Davies* of the Apache CouchDB development team.

16.2 CVE-2010-2234: Apache CouchDB Cross Site Request Forgery Attack

Date 21.02.2010

Affected Apache CouchDB 0.8.0 to 0.11.1

Severity Important

Vendor The Apache Software Foundation

16.2.1 Description

Apache CouchDB versions prior to version *0.11.1* are vulnerable to Cross Site Request Forgery (CSRF) attacks.

16.2.2 Mitigation

All users should upgrade to CouchDB *0.11.2* or *1.0.1*.

Upgrades from the *0.11.x* and *0.10.x* series should be seamless.

Users on earlier versions should consult with upgrade notes.

16.2.3 Example

A malicious website can *POST* arbitrary JavaScript code to well known CouchDB installation URLs (like http://localhost:5984/) and make the browser execute the injected JavaScript in the security context of CouchDB's admin interface Futon.

Unrelated, but in addition the JSONP API has been turned off by default to avoid potential information leakage.

16.2.4 Credit

This CSRF issue was discovered by a source that wishes to stay anonymous.

16.3 CVE-2010-3854: Apache CouchDB Cross Site Scripting Issue

Date 28.01.2011

Affected Apache CouchDB 0.8.0 to 1.0.1

Severity Important

Vendor The Apache Software Foundation

16.3.1 Description

Apache CouchDB versions prior to version *1.0.2* are vulnerable to Cross Site Scripting (XSS) attacks.

16.3.2 Mitigation

All users should upgrade to CouchDB *1.0.2*.

Upgrades from the *0.11.x* and *0.10.x* series should be seamless.

Users on earlier versions should consult with upgrade notes.

16.3.3 Example

Due to inadequate validation of request parameters and cookie data in Futon, CouchDB's web-based administration UI, a malicious site can execute arbitrary code in the context of a user's browsing session.

16.3.4 Credit

This XSS issue was discovered by a source that wishes to stay anonymous.

16.4 CVE-2012-5641: Information disclosure via unescaped backslashes in URLs on Windows

Date 14.01.2013

Affected All Windows-based releases of Apache CouchDB, up to and including 1.0.3, 1.1.1, and 1.2.0 are vulnerable.

Severity Moderate

Vendor The Apache Software Foundation

16.4.1 Description

A specially crafted request could be used to access content directly that would otherwise be protected by inbuilt CouchDB security mechanisms. This request could retrieve in binary form any CouchDB database, including the _users_ or _replication_ databases, or any other file that the user account used to run CouchDB might have read access to on the local filesystem. This exploit is due to a vulnerability in the included MochiWeb HTTP library.

16.4.2 Mitigation

Upgrade to a supported CouchDB release that includes this fix, such as:

- *1.0.4*
- *1.1.2*
- *1.2.1*
- *1.3.x*

All listed releases have included a specific fix for the MochiWeb component.

16.4.3 Work-Around

Users may simply exclude any file-based web serving components directly within their configuration file, typically in *local.ini*. On a default CouchDB installation, this requires amending the `httpd_global_handlers/favicon.ico` and `httpd_global_handlers/_utils` lines within `httpd_global_handlers`:

```
[httpd_global_handlers]
favicon.ico = {couch_httpd_misc_handlers, handle_welcome_req, <<"Forbidden">>}
_utils = {couch_httpd_misc_handlers, handle_welcome_req, <<"Forbidden">>}
```

If additional handlers have been added, such as to support Adobe's Flash *crossdomain.xml* files, these would also need to be excluded.

16.4.4 Acknowledgement

The issue was found and reported by Sriram Melkote to the upstream MochiWeb project.

16.4.5 References

- https://github.com/melkote/mochiweb/commit/ac2bf

16.5 CVE-2012-5649: JSONP arbitrary code execution with Adobe Flash

Date 14.01.2013

Affected Releases up to and including 1.0.3, 1.1.1, and 1.2.0 are vulnerable, if administrators have enabled JSONP.

Severity Moderate

Vendor The Apache Software Foundation

16.5.1 Description

A hand-crafted JSONP callback and response can be used to run arbitrary code inside client-side browsers via Adobe Flash.

16.5.2 Mitigation

Upgrade to a supported CouchDB release that includes this fix, such as:

- *1.0.4*
- *1.1.2*
- *1.2.1*
- *1.3.x*

All listed releases have included a specific fix.

16.5.3 Work-Around

Disable JSONP or don't enable it since it's disabled by default.

16.6 CVE-2012-5650: DOM based Cross-Site Scripting via Futon UI

Date 14.01.2013

Affected Apache CouchDB releases up to and including 1.0.3, 1.1.1, and 1.2.0 are vulnerable.

Severity Moderate

Vendor The Apache Software Foundation

16.6.1 Description

Query parameters passed into the browser-based test suite are not sanitised, and can be used to load external resources. An attacker may execute JavaScript code in the browser, using the context of the remote user.

16.6.2 Mitigation

Upgrade to a supported CouchDB release that includes this fix, such as:

- *1.0.4*
- *1.1.2*

- *1.2.1*

- *1.3.x*

All listed releases have included a specific fix.

16.6.3 Work-Around

Disable the Futon user interface completely, by adapting *local.ini* and restarting CouchDB:

```
[httpd_global_handlers]
_utils = {couch_httpd_misc_handlers, handle_welcome_req, <<"Forbidden">>}
```

Or by removing the UI test suite components:

- share/www/verify_install.html

- share/www/couch_tests.html

- share/www/custom_test.html

16.6.4 Acknowledgement

This vulnerability was discovered & reported to the Apache Software Foundation by Frederik Braun.

16.7 CVE-2014-2668: DoS (CPU and memory consumption) via the count parameter to /_uuids

Date 26.03.2014

Affected Apache CouchDB releases up to and including 1.3.1, 1.4.0, and 1.5.0 are vulnerable.

Severity Moderate

Vendor The Apache Software Foundation

16.7.1 Description

The */_uuids* resource's *count* query parameter is able to take unreasonable huge numeric value which leads to exhaustion of server resources (CPU and memory) and to DoS as the result.

16.7.2 Mitigation

Upgrade to a supported CouchDB release that includes this fix, such as:

- *1.5.1*

- *1.6.0*

All listed releases have included a specific fix to

16.7.3 Work-Around

Disable the */_uuids* handler completely, by adapting *local.ini* and restarting CouchDB:

```
[httpd_global_handlers]
_uuids =
```

Reporting New Security Problems with Apache CouchDB

The Apache Software Foundation takes a very active stance in eliminating security problems and denial of service attacks against Apache CouchDB.

We strongly encourage folks to report such problems to our private security mailing list first, before disclosing them in a public forum.

Please note that the security mailing list should only be used for reporting undisclosed security vulnerabilities in Apache CouchDB and managing the process of fixing such vulnerabilities. We cannot accept regular bug reports or other queries at this address. All mail sent to this address that does not relate to an undisclosed security problem in the Apache CouchDB source code will be ignored.

If you need to report a bug that isn't an undisclosed security vulnerability, please use the bug reporting page.

Questions about:

- How to configure CouchDB securely

- If a vulnerability applies to your particular application

- Obtaining further information on a published vulnerability

- Availability of patches and/or new releases

should be address to the users mailing list. Please see the mailing lists page for details of how to subscribe.

The private security mailing address is: security@couchdb.apache.org

Please read how the Apache Software Foundation handles security reports to know what to expect.

Note that all networked servers are subject to denial of service attacks, and we cannot promise magic workarounds to generic problems (such as a client streaming lots of data to your server, or re-requesting the same URL repeatedly). In general our philosophy is to avoid any attacks which can cause the server to consume resources in a non-linear relationship to the size of inputs.

Chapter 17. Reporting New Security Problems with Apache CouchDB

## CHAPTER 18

About CouchDB Documentation

18.1 License

```
                        Apache License
                  Version 2.0, January 2004
                http://www.apache.org/licenses/

TERMS AND CONDITIONS FOR USE, REPRODUCTION, AND DISTRIBUTION

1. Definitions.

    "License" shall mean the terms and conditions for use, reproduction,
    and distribution as defined by Sections 1 through 9 of this document.

    "Licensor" shall mean the copyright owner or entity authorized by
    the copyright owner that is granting the License.

    "Legal Entity" shall mean the union of the acting entity and all
    other entities that control, are controlled by, or are under common
    control with that entity. For the purposes of this definition,
    "control" means (i) the power, direct or indirect, to cause the
    direction or management of such entity, whether by contract or
    otherwise, or (ii) ownership of fifty percent (50%) or more of the
    outstanding shares, or (iii) beneficial ownership of such entity.

    "You" (or "Your") shall mean an individual or Legal Entity
    exercising permissions granted by this License.

    "Source" form shall mean the preferred form for making modifications,
    including but not limited to software source code, documentation
    source, and configuration files.

    "Object" form shall mean any form resulting from mechanical
    transformation or translation of a Source form, including but
    not limited to compiled object code, generated documentation,
    and conversions to other media types.

    "Work" shall mean the work of authorship, whether in Source or
    Object form, made available under the License, as indicated by a
    copyright notice that is included in or attached to the work
    (an example is provided in the Appendix below).

    "Derivative Works" shall mean any work, whether in Source or Object
    form, that is based on (or derived from) the Work and for which the
    editorial revisions, annotations, elaborations, or other modifications
    represent, as a whole, an original work of authorship. For the purposes
    of this License, Derivative Works shall not include works that remain
```

separable from, or merely link (or bind by name) to the interfaces of,
the Work and Derivative Works thereof.

"Contribution" shall mean any work of authorship, including
the original version of the Work and any modifications or additions
to that Work or Derivative Works thereof, that is intentionally
submitted to Licensor for inclusion in the Work by the copyright owner
or by an individual or Legal Entity authorized to submit on behalf of
the copyright owner. For the purposes of this definition, "submitted"
means any form of electronic, verbal, or written communication sent
to the Licensor or its representatives, including but not limited to
communication on electronic mailing lists, source code control systems,
and issue tracking systems that are managed by, or on behalf of, the
Licensor for the purpose of discussing and improving the Work, but
excluding communication that is conspicuously marked or otherwise
designated in writing by the copyright owner as "Not a Contribution."

"Contributor" shall mean Licensor and any individual or Legal Entity
on behalf of whom a Contribution has been received by Licensor and
subsequently incorporated within the Work.

2. Grant of Copyright License. Subject to the terms and conditions of
   this License, each Contributor hereby grants to You a perpetual,
   worldwide, non-exclusive, no-charge, royalty-free, irrevocable
   copyright license to reproduce, prepare Derivative Works of,
   publicly display, publicly perform, sublicense, and distribute the
   Work and such Derivative Works in Source or Object form.

3. Grant of Patent License. Subject to the terms and conditions of
   this License, each Contributor hereby grants to You a perpetual,
   worldwide, non-exclusive, no-charge, royalty-free, irrevocable
   (except as stated in this section) patent license to make, have made,
   use, offer to sell, sell, import, and otherwise transfer the Work,
   where such license applies only to those patent claims licensable
   by such Contributor that are necessarily infringed by their
   Contribution(s) alone or by combination of their Contribution(s)
   with the Work to which such Contribution(s) was submitted. If You
   institute patent litigation against any entity (including a
   cross-claim or counterclaim in a lawsuit) alleging that the Work
   or a Contribution incorporated within the Work constitutes direct
   or contributory patent infringement, then any patent licenses
   granted to You under this License for that Work shall terminate
   as of the date such litigation is filed.

4. Redistribution. You may reproduce and distribute copies of the
   Work or Derivative Works thereof in any medium, with or without
   modifications, and in Source or Object form, provided that You
   meet the following conditions:

   (a) You must give any other recipients of the Work or
       Derivative Works a copy of this License; and

   (b) You must cause any modified files to carry prominent notices
       stating that You changed the files; and

   (c) You must retain, in the Source form of any Derivative Works
       that You distribute, all copyright, patent, trademark, and
       attribution notices from the Source form of the Work,
       excluding those notices that do not pertain to any part of
       the Derivative Works; and

   (d) If the Work includes a "NOTICE" text file as part of its
       distribution, then any Derivative Works that You distribute must

include a readable copy of the attribution notices contained
within such NOTICE file, excluding those notices that do not
pertain to any part of the Derivative Works, in at least one
of the following places: within a NOTICE text file distributed
as part of the Derivative Works; within the Source form or
documentation, if provided along with the Derivative Works; or,
within a display generated by the Derivative Works, if and
wherever such third-party notices normally appear. The contents
of the NOTICE file are for informational purposes only and
do not modify the License. You may add Your own attribution
notices within Derivative Works that You distribute, alongside
or as an addendum to the NOTICE text from the Work, provided
that such additional attribution notices cannot be construed
as modifying the License.

You may add Your own copyright statement to Your modifications and
may provide additional or different license terms and conditions
for use, reproduction, or distribution of Your modifications, or
for any such Derivative Works as a whole, provided Your use,
reproduction, and distribution of the Work otherwise complies with
the conditions stated in this License.

5. Submission of Contributions. Unless You explicitly state otherwise,
   any Contribution intentionally submitted for inclusion in the Work
   by You to the Licensor shall be under the terms and conditions of
   this License, without any additional terms or conditions.
   Notwithstanding the above, nothing herein shall supersede or modify
   the terms of any separate license agreement you may have executed
   with Licensor regarding such Contributions.

6. Trademarks. This License does not grant permission to use the trade
   names, trademarks, service marks, or product names of the Licensor,
   except as required for reasonable and customary use in describing the
   origin of the Work and reproducing the content of the NOTICE file.

7. Disclaimer of Warranty. Unless required by applicable law or
   agreed to in writing, Licensor provides the Work (and each
   Contributor provides its Contributions) on an "AS IS" BASIS,
   WITHOUT WARRANTIES OR CONDITIONS OF ANY KIND, either express or
   implied, including, without limitation, any warranties or conditions
   of TITLE, NON-INFRINGEMENT, MERCHANTABILITY, or FITNESS FOR A
   PARTICULAR PURPOSE. You are solely responsible for determining the
   appropriateness of using or redistributing the Work and assume any
   risks associated with Your exercise of permissions under this License.

8. Limitation of Liability. In no event and under no legal theory,
   whether in tort (including negligence), contract, or otherwise,
   unless required by applicable law (such as deliberate and grossly
   negligent acts) or agreed to in writing, shall any Contributor be
   liable to You for damages, including any direct, indirect, special,
   incidental, or consequential damages of any character arising as a
   result of this License or out of the use or inability to use the
   Work (including but not limited to damages for loss of goodwill,
   work stoppage, computer failure or malfunction, or any and all
   other commercial damages or losses), even if such Contributor
   has been advised of the possibility of such damages.

9. Accepting Warranty or Additional Liability. While redistributing
   the Work or Derivative Works thereof, You may choose to offer,
   and charge a fee for, acceptance of support, warranty, indemnity,
   or other liability obligations and/or rights consistent with this
   License. However, in accepting such obligations, You may act only
   on Your own behalf and on Your sole responsibility, not on behalf

```
        of any other Contributor, and only if You agree to indemnify,
        defend, and hold each Contributor harmless for any liability
        incurred by, or claims asserted against, such Contributor by reason
        of your accepting any such warranty or additional liability.

END OF TERMS AND CONDITIONS

APPENDIX: How to apply the Apache License to your work.

    To apply the Apache License to your work, attach the following
    boilerplate notice, with the fields enclosed by brackets "[]"
    replaced with your own identifying information. (Don't include
    the brackets!)  The text should be enclosed in the appropriate
    comment syntax for the file format. We also recommend that a
    file or class name and description of purpose be included on the
    same "printed page" as the copyright notice for easier
    identification within third-party archives.

Copyright [yyyy] [name of copyright owner]

Licensed under the Apache License, Version 2.0 (the "License");
you may not use this file except in compliance with the License.
You may obtain a copy of the License at

    http://www.apache.org/licenses/LICENSE-2.0

Unless required by applicable law or agreed to in writing, software
distributed under the License is distributed on an "AS IS" BASIS,
WITHOUT WARRANTIES OR CONDITIONS OF ANY KIND, either express or implied.
See the License for the specific language governing permissions and
limitations under the License.
```

stats

update_notification

uuids

vendor

vhosts

view_compaction

www.ingramcontent.com/pod-product-compliance
Lightning Source LLC
LaVergne TN
LVHW060133070326
832902LV00018B/2780